)int

D0521208

PHP & MYSQL:
NOVICE TO NINJA

C.1

BY KEVIN YANK
5TH EDITION

PHP & MySQL: Novice to Ninja

by Kevin Yank

Copyright © 2012 SitePoint Pty. Ltd.

Product Manager: Simon Mackie   **Editor:** Kelly Steele

Technical Editor: Diana MacDonald   **Cover Designer:** Alex Walker

Indexer: Fred Brown

Printing History: **Latest Update:** May 2012

   1st Ed. Aug. 2001, 2nd Ed. Feb. 2003,
   3rd Ed. Oct. 2004, 4th Ed. Jul. 2009
   5th Ed. May 2012

Published by SitePoint Pty. Ltd.

48 Cambridge Street Collingwood
VIC Australia 3066
Web: www.sitepoint.com
Email: business@sitepoint.com

ISBN 978-0-9871530-8-1 (print)

ISBN 978-0-9872478-1-0 (ebook)
Printed and bound in the United States of America

About the Author

Kevin Yank has been building websites for over 15 years, and has produced numerous books, articles, courses, newsletters, and podcasts on the subject.

Hired as SitePoint's first staff writer in 2001, Kevin wrote the then new company's first book, *Build Your Own Database Driven Website Using PHP & MySQL*. Five editions later and you are reading the latest incarnation of that very book. He went on to co-author two more books (*Simply JavaScript* and *Everything You Know About CSS Is Wrong!*), and has written for the *SitePoint Tech Times* email newsletter and co-hosted the *SitePoint Podcast*.

As learnable.com's Chief Instructor, Kevin produced popular online courses on topics including JavaScript, PHP and MySQL, and HTML and CSS. He also provided help and advice for instructors building other new additions to the Learnable library of online courses.

These days, Kevin is CTO at Avalanche Technology Group, a creator and distributor of digital products and services in the Australian and worldwide markets. He lives in Melbourne, Australia with his partner Jessica and their dog, cat, and two guinea pigs.

Kevin has a passion for making web technology easy to understand for anyone.

About SitePoint

SitePoint specializes in publishing fun, practical, and easy-to-understand content for Web professionals. Visit http://www.sitepoint.com/ to access our blogs, books, newsletters, articles, and community forums.

Summary of Contents

To my parents, Cheryl and Richard, for making all this possible

Table of Contents

Chapter 3   Introducing PHP 49

Chapter 4   Publishing MySQL Data on the
Web 91

Chapter 5   Relational Database Design 141

Chapter 6   Structured PHP Programming 161

Chapter 7   A Content Management System 187

Chapter 8 Content Formatting with Regular Expressions

Chapter 9 Cookies, Sessions, and Access Control

Appendix A Manual Installation Instructions

Appendix B MySQL Syntax Reference

Preface

PHP and MySQL have changed.

Back in 2001, when I wrote the first edition of this book (it was called *Build Your Own Database Driven Web Site with PHP & MySQL* back then), readers were astonished to discover that you could create a site full of web pages without having to write a separate HTML file for each page. **PHP** stood out from the crowd of programming languages, mainly because it was easy enough for almost anyone to learn and free to download and install. The **MySQL** database, likewise, provided a simple and free solution to a problem that, up until that point, had been solvable only by expert programmers with corporate budgets.

Back then, PHP and MySQL were special—heck, they were downright miraculous! But over the years, they have gained plenty of fast-moving competition. In an age when anyone with a free WordPress[1] account can set up a full-featured blog in 30 seconds flat, it's no longer enough for a programming language like PHP to be easy to learn; nor is it enough for a database like MySQL to be free.

Indeed, as you sit down to read this book, you probably have ambitions that extend beyond what you can throw together using the free point-and-click tools of the Web. You might even be thinking of building an exciting new point-and-click tool of your own. WordPress, after all, is built using PHP and MySQL, so why limit your vision to anything less?

To keep up with the competition, and with the needs of more demanding projects, PHP and MySQL have had to evolve. PHP is now a far more intricate and powerful language than it was back in 2001, and MySQL is a vastly more complex and capable database. Learning PHP and MySQL today opens up a lot of doors that would have remained closed to the PHP and MySQL experts of 2001.

That's the good news. The bad news is that, in the same way that a butter knife is easier to figure out than a Swiss Army knife (and less likely to cause self-injury!), all these dazzling new features and improvements have indisputably made PHP and MySQL more difficult for beginners to learn.

---

[1] http://wordpress.com/

Worse yet, PHP has completely abandoned several of the beginner-friendly features that gave it a competitive advantage in 2001, because they turned out to be oversimplifications, or could lead inexperienced programmers into building websites with gaping security holes. This is a problem if you're the author of a beginner's book about PHP and MySQL.

PHP and MySQL have changed, and those changes have made writing this book a lot more difficult. But they have also made this book a lot more important. The more twisty the path, the more valuable the map, right?

In this book, I'll provide you with a practical look at what's involved in building a database driven website using PHP and MySQL. If your web host provides PHP and MySQL support, you're in great shape. If not, I'll show you how to install them on Windows, Mac OS X, and Linux computers, so don't sweat it.

This book is your map to the twisty path that every beginner must navigate to learn PHP and MySQL today. Grab your favorite walking stick; let's go hiking!

Who Should Read This Book

This book is aimed at intermediate and advanced web designers looking to make the leap into server-side programming. You'll be expected to be comfortable with simple HTML, as I'll make use of it without much in the way of explanation. No knowledge of Cascading Style Sheets (CSS) or JavaScript is assumed or required, but if you *do* know JavaScript, you'll find it will make learning PHP a breeze, since these languages are quite similar.

By the end of this book, you can expect to have a grasp of what's involved in building a database driven website. If you follow the examples, you'll also learn the basics of PHP (a server-side scripting language that gives you easy access to a database, and a lot more) and **Structured Query Language (SQL**—the standard language for interacting with relational databases) as supported by MySQL, the most popular free database engine available today. Most importantly, you'll come away with everything you need to start on your very own database driven site!

What's in This Book

This book comprises the following 12 chapters. Read them in order from beginning to end to gain a complete understanding of the subject, or skip around if you only need a refresher on a particular topic.

Chapter 1: *Installation*

Before you can start building your database driven website, you must first ensure that you have the right tools for the job. In this first chapter, I'll tell you where to obtain the two essential components you'll need: the PHP scripting language and the MySQL database management system. I'll step you through the setup procedures on Windows, Linux, and Mac OS X, and show you how to test that PHP is operational on your web server.

Chapter 2: *Introducing MySQL*

Although I'm sure you'll be anxious to start building dynamic web pages, I'll begin with an introduction to databases in general, and the MySQL relational database management system in particular. If you have never worked with a relational database before, this should definitely be an enlightening chapter that will whet your appetite for what's to come! In the process, you'll build up a simple database to be used in later chapters.

Chapter 3: *Introducing PHP*

Here's where the fun really starts. In this chapter, I'll introduce you to the PHP scripting language, which you can use to build dynamic web pages that present up-to-the-moment information to your visitors. Readers with previous programming experience will probably only need a quick skim of this chapter, as I explain the essentials of the language from the ground up. This is a must-read chapter for beginners, however, as the rest of this book relies heavily on the basic concepts presented here.

Chapter 4: *Publishing MySQL Data on the Web*

In this chapter you'll bring together PHP and MySQL, which you'll have seen separately in the previous chapters, to create some of your first database driven web pages. You'll explore the basic techniques of using PHP to retrieve information from a database and display it on the Web in real time. I'll also show you how to use PHP to create web-based forms for adding new entries to, and modifying existing information in, a MySQL database on the fly.

Chapter 5: *Relational Database Design*

Although you'll have worked with a very simple sample database in the previous chapters, most database driven websites require the storage of more complex forms of data than you'll have dealt with at this point. Far too many database driven website designs are abandoned midstream or are forced to start again from the beginning, because of mistakes made early on during the design of the database structure. In this critical chapter you'll learn the essential principles of good database design, emphasizing the importance of data normalization. If you're unsure what that means, then this is definitely an important chapter for you to read!

Chapter 6: *Structured PHP Programming*

Techniques to better structure your code are useful in all but the simplest of PHP projects. The PHP language offers many facilities to help you do this, and in this chapter, I'll cover some of the simple techniques that exist to keep your code manageable and maintainable. You'll learn to use include files to avoid having to write the same code more than once when it's needed by many pages of your site, and I'll show you how to write your own functions to extend the built-in capabilities of PHP and to streamline the code that appears within your scripts.

Chapter 7: *A Content Management System*

In many ways the climax of the book, this chapter is the big payoff for all you frustrated site builders who are tired of updating hundreds of pages whenever you need to make a change to a site's design. I'll walk you through the code for a basic content management system that allows you to manage a database of jokes, their categories, and their authors. A system like this can be used to manage simple content on your website; just a few modifications, and you'll have a site administration system that will have your content providers submitting content for publication on your site in no time—all without having to know a shred of HTML!

Chapter 8: *Content Formatting with Regular Expressions*

Just because you're implementing a nice, easy tool to allow site administrators to add content to your site without their knowing HTML, that content can still be jazzed up, instead of settling for just plain, unformatted text. In this chapter, I'll show you some neat tweaks you can make to the page that displays the contents of your database—tweaks that allow it to incorporate simple formatting such as bold or italicized text, among other options.

Chapter 9: *Cookies, Sessions, and Access Control*

What are sessions, and how are they related to cookies, a long-suffering technology for preserving stored data on the Web? What makes persistent data so important in current ecommerce systems and other web applications? This chapter answers all those questions by explaining how PHP supports both cookies and sessions, and explores the link between the two. You'll then put these pieces together to build a simple shopping cart system, as well as an access control system for your website.

Chapter 10: *MySQL Administration*

While MySQL is a good, simple database solution for those without the need for many frills, it does have some complexities of its own that you'll need to understand if you're going to rely on a MySQL database to store your content. In this section, I'll teach you how to perform backups of, and manage access to, your MySQL database. In addition to a couple of inside tricks (like what to do if you forget your MySQL password), I'll explain how to speed up your database when it gets slow, and how to link together the data in your database in useful ways.

Chapter 11: *Advanced SQL Queries*

In Chapter 5 we saw what was involved in modeling complex relationships between pieces of information in a relational database like MySQL. Although the theory was quite sound, putting these concepts into practice requires that you learn a few more tricks of Structured Query Language. In this chapter, I'll cover some of the more advanced features of this language to help you juggle complex data like a pro.

Chapter 12: *Binary Data*

Some of the most interesting applications of database driven web design include some juggling of binary files. Online file storage services are prime examples, but even a system as simple as a personal photo gallery can benefit from storing binary files (that is, pictures) in a database for retrieval and management on the fly. In this chapter, I'll demonstrate how to speed up your website by creating static copies of dynamic pages at regular intervals—using PHP, of course! With these basic file-juggling skills in hand, you'll go on to develop a simple online file storage and viewing system, and learn the ins and outs of working with binary data in MySQL.

Where to Find Help

PHP and MySQL are moving targets, so chances are good that, by the time you read this, some minor detail or other of these technologies has changed from what's described in this book. Thankfully, SitePoint has a thriving community of PHP developers ready and waiting to help you out if you run into trouble, and we also maintain a list of known errata for this book you can consult for the latest updates.

The SitePoint Forums

The SitePoint Forums[2] are discussion forums where you can ask questions about anything related to web development. You may, of course, answer questions, too. That's how a discussion forum site works—some people ask, some people answer and most people do a bit of both. Sharing your knowledge benefits others and strengthens the community. A lot of fun and experienced web designers and developers hang out there. It's a good way to learn new stuff, have questions answered in a hurry, and just have fun.

The SitePoint Forums include separate forums for PHP and MySQL:

- PHP: http://www.sitepoint.com/forums/forumdisplay.php?34-PHP
- Databases & MySQL:
  http://www.sitepoint.com/forums/forumdisplay.php?88-Databases-amp-MySQL

The Book's Website

Located at http://www.sitepoint.com/books/phpmysql5/, the website that supports this book will give you access to the following facilities:

The Code Archive

As you progress through this book, you'll note a number of references to the code archive. This is a downloadable ZIP archive that contains each and every line of

---

[2] http://www.sitepoint.com/forums/

example source code that's printed in this book. If you want to cheat (or save yourself from carpal tunnel syndrome), go ahead and download the archive.[3]

Updates and Errata

No book is perfect, and we expect that watchful readers will be able to spot at least one or two mistakes before the end of this one. The Errata page on the book's website will always have the latest information about known typographical and code errors.

The SitePoint Newsletters

In addition to books like this one, SitePoint publishes free email newsletters such as the *SitePoint* newsletter, *PHPMaster*, *CloudSpring*, *RubySource*, *DesignFestival*, and *BuildMobile*. In them you'll read about the latest news, product releases, trends, tips, and techniques for all aspects of web development. Sign up to one or more of these newsletters at http://www.sitepoint.com/newsletter/.

Your Feedback

If you're unable to find an answer through the forums, or if you wish to contact us for any other reason, the best place to write is books@sitepoint.com. We have a well-staffed email support system set up to track your inquiries, and if our support team members are unable to answer your question, they'll send it straight to us. Suggestions for improvements, as well as notices of any mistakes you may find, are especially welcome.

---

[3] http://www.sitepoint.com/books/phpmysql5/code.php

Conventions Used in This Book

You'll notice that we've used certain typographic and layout styles throughout this book to signify different types of information. Look out for the following items.

Code Samples

Code in this book will be displayed using a fixed-width font, like so:

```
<h1>A Perfect Summer's Day</h1>
<p>It was a lovely day for a walk in the park. The birds
were singing and the kids were all back at school.</p>
```

If the code is to be found in the book's code archive, the name of the file will appear at the top of the program listing, like this:

```
                                                      example.css
.footer {
  background-color: #CCC;
  border-top: 1px solid #333;
}
```

If only part of the file is displayed, this is indicated by the word *excerpt*:

```
                                             example.css (excerpt)
  border-top: 1px solid #333;
```

If additional code is to be inserted into an existing example, the new code will be displayed in bold:

```
function animate() {
  new_variable = "Hello";
}
```

Also, where existing code is required for context, rather than repeat all the code, a ⋮ will be displayed:

```
function animate() {
  ⋮
  return new_variable;
}
```

Some lines of code are intended to be entered on one line, but we've had to wrap them because of page constraints. A ➥ indicates a line break that exists for formatting purposes only, and should be ignored.

```
URL.open("http://www.sitepoint.com/blogs/2007/05/28/user-style-she
➥ets-come-of-age/");
```

Tips, Notes, and Warnings

Hey, You!

Tips will give you helpful little pointers.

Ahem, Excuse Me ...

Notes are useful asides that are related—but not critical—to the topic at hand. Think of them as extra tidbits of information.

Make Sure You Always ...

... pay attention to these important points.

Watch Out!

Warnings will highlight any gotchas that are likely to trip you up along the way.

Installation

In this book, I will guide you as you take your first steps beyond the static world of building web pages with the purely client-side technologies of HTML, CSS, and JavaScript. Together, we'll explore the world of database driven websites and discover the dizzying array of dynamic tools, concepts, and possibilities that they open up. Whatever you do, don't look down!

Okay, maybe you *should* look down. After all, that's where the rest of this book is. But remember, you were warned!

Before you build your first dynamic website, you must gather together the tools you'll need for the job. In this chapter, I'll show you how to download and set up the two software packages required. Can you guess what they are? I'll give you a hint: their names feature prominently on the cover of this book! They are, of course, PHP and MySQL.

If you're used to building websites with HTML, CSS, and perhaps even a smattering of JavaScript, you're probably familiar with uploading the files that make up your site to a certain location. It might be a web hosting service you've paid for, web space provided by your Internet Service Provider (ISP), or maybe a web server set up by the IT department of the company that you work for. In any case, once you copy your files to any of these destinations, a software program called a **web server** is able to find and serve up copies of those files whenever they're requested by a web browser like Internet Explorer, Google Chrome, Safari, or Firefox. Common web server software programs you may have heard of include Apache HTTP Server (Apache) and Internet Information Services (IIS).

PHP is a **server-side scripting language**. You can think of it as a plugin for your web server that enables it to do more than just send exact copies of the files that web browsers ask for. With PHP installed, your web server will be able to run little programs (called **PHP scripts**) that can do tasks like retrieve up-to-the-minute information from a database and use it to generate a web page on the fly before sending it to the browser that requested it. Much of this book will focus on writing PHP scripts to do exactly that. PHP is completely free to download and use.

For your PHP scripts to retrieve information from a database, you must first *have* a database. That's where **MySQL** comes in. MySQL is a **relational database management system**, or **RDBMS**. We'll discuss the exact role it plays and how it works later, but briefly it's a software program that's able to organize and manage many pieces of information efficiently while keeping track of how all those pieces of information are related to each other. MySQL also makes that information really easy to access with server-side scripting languages such as PHP, and, like PHP, is completely free for most uses.

The goal of this first chapter is to set you up with a web server equipped with PHP and MySQL. I'll provide step-by-step instructions that work on recent Windows and Mac OS X, so no matter what flavor of computer you're using, the instructions you need should be right here.[1]

Your Own Web Server

If you're lucky, your current web host's web server already has PHP and MySQL installed. Most do—that's one of the reasons why PHP and MySQL are so popular. If your web host is so equipped, the good news is that you'll be able to publish your

---

[1] Linux users, you'll find instructions in Appendix A, because I suspect that most of you will probably want to install it your own way, regardless of what I write here.

first database driven website without having to shop for a web host that supports the right technologies.

However, you're still going to need to install PHP and MySQL yourself. That's because you need your own PHP-and-MySQL-equipped web server on which to test your database driven website before you publish it for all the world to see.

When developing static websites, you can simply load your HTML files directly from your hard disk into your browser to see how they look. There's no web server software involved when you do this, which is fine, because web browsers can read and understand HTML code all by themselves.

When it comes to dynamic websites built using PHP and MySQL, though, your web browser needs some help! Web browsers are unable to understand PHP scripts; rather, PHP scripts contain instructions for a PHP-savvy web server to execute in order to *generate* the HTML code that browsers can understand. So, in addition to the web server that will host your site publicly, you also require your own private web server to use in the development of your site.

If you work for a company with an especially helpful IT department, you may find there's already a development web server provided for you. The typical setup is that you must work on your site's files on a network drive hosted by an internal web server that can be safely used for development. When you're ready to deploy the site to the public, your files are copied from the network drive to the public web server.

If you're lucky enough to work in this kind of environment, you can skip most of this chapter; however, you'll want to ask the IT boffins responsible for the development server the same questions I've covered in the section called "What to Ask Your Web Host". That's because you'll need to have that critical information handy when you start using the PHP and MySQL support they've so helpfully provided.

Windows Installation

In this section, I'll show you how to start running a PHP-and-MySQL-equipped web server on a Windows XP, Windows Vista, or Windows 7 computer. If you're using an operating system other than Windows, you can safely skip this section.

The easiest way to get a web server up and running on Windows is to use a free software package called XAMPP for Windows. This all-in-one program includes built-in copies of Apache, PHP, and MySQL. Let me take you through the process of installing it.

The Do-it-yourself Option

In past editions of this book, I recommended that you set up Apache, PHP, and MySQL individually, using the official installation packages for each. This is a good practice for beginners, I argued, because it gives you a strong sense of how these pieces all fit together.

Unfortunately, this meant that many readers spent their first few hours in "PHP Land" wrestling their way through a protracted sequence of detailed installation instructions. Worse still, sometimes the finer points of these became outdated due to some subtle change to one of the software packages.

Nowadays, I strongly believe that the best way to learn PHP and MySQL is to start *using* them right away. The quicker and more hassle-free the installation process, the better. That's why I ask you to use XAMPP in this edition. In addition, there's every chance you're just dabbling in this stuff, so why junk up your computer with a bunch of separate but interdependent pieces of software that will be tricky to remove?

Nevertheless, if you're a die-hard do-it-yourselfer, a tech-savvy power user, or if you simply reach the end of this book and wonder how the pros do it, I've included a detailed set of installation instructions for individual packages in Appendix A. Feel free to follow them instead of the instructions in this section if you're that way inclined.

1. Download the latest version of XAMPP for Windows from the Apache Friends website[2] (you'll need to scroll down to find the download links). Grab the Installer version that is recommended (as of this writing, XAMPP for Windows 1.7.7 is 81MB in size), then double-click the file to launch the installer, as shown in Figure 1.1.

---

[2] http://www.apachefriends.org/en/xampp-windows.html

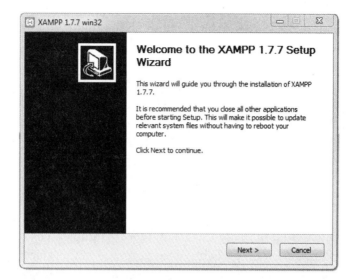

Figure 1.1. The XAMPP Installer

User Account Control (UAC) warning

Depending on the version of Windows you're using and your exact system configuration, the XAMPP installer may display the warning message shown in Figure 1.2.

Although this message is a little alarming at first, be assured it's no big deal. It simply recommends not to install XAMPP in **C:\Program Files** as you do most programs due to problems this will cause with file permissions. The installer defaults to installing in **C:\xampp** anyway.

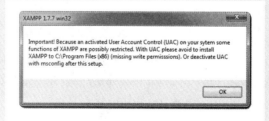

Figure 1.2. XAMPP may warn you about "User Account Control (UAC)"

2.   The installer will prompt you for a location to install XAMPP. The default of **c:\xampp** shown in Figure 1.3 is an ideal choice, but if you have feel strongly about installing it elsewhere (such as on a different drive), go ahead and specify your preferred location. Just avoid the usual **C:\Program Files** (or similar) location, since XAMPP requires permissions that Windows restricts for files in that folder.

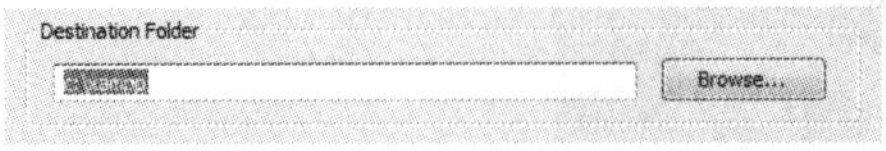

Figure 1.3. The default destination folder is a good choice

3.   The installer will prompt you with a number of options. The default selections shown in Figure 1.4 are probably what you want at this stage. If you like to keep a clean desktop, you might want to uncheck the **Create a XAMPP desktop icon** checkbox. If you want your Apache and MySQL servers running at all times (rather than having to start them manually whenever you sit down to do some development), you can check the **Install Apache as service** and **Install MySQL as service** checkboxes. In the following instructions, though, I'll assume you haven't.

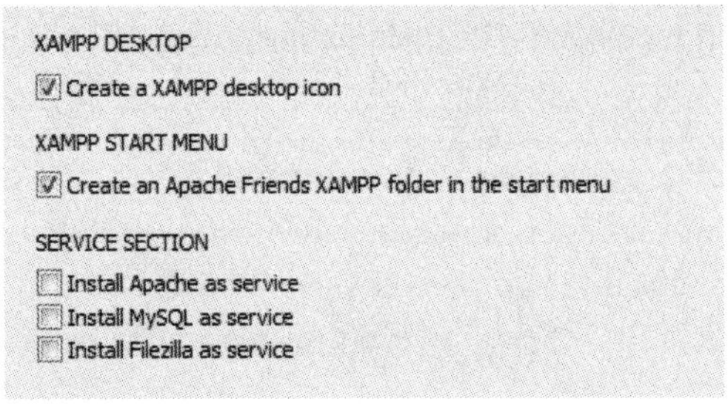

Figure 1.4. The default options are fine

4.   Once the installer has completed, you'll be prompted to start the XAMPP Control Panel. Click **No** so that I can show you how to start it the conventional way. Once its work is done, the installer will quit.

5.   At this point, I recommend shutting down and restarting your computer (even though the XAMPP installer won't ask you to). In my testing, the next steps failed to work until I restarted my system, and posts on the XAMPP support forum support this.[3]

[3] http://www.apachefriends.org/f/viewtopic.php?f=16&t=48484

Once the installation is complete and your system has restarted, you can fire up the XAMPP Control Panel. You'll find it on the **Start** menu under **All Programs** > **Apache Friends** > **XAMPP** > **XAMPP Control Panel**. An orange XAMPP icon will appear in your Windows System Tray (although by default it will disappear after a few seconds), and the XAMPP Control Panel Application shown in Figure 1.5 will open.

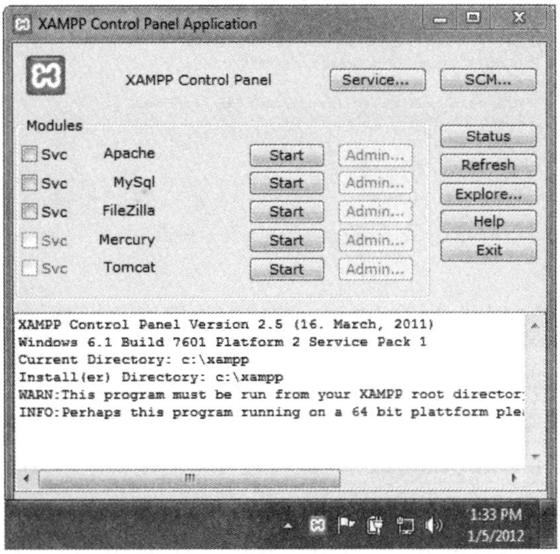

Figure 1.5. The XAMPP Control Panel

Click the **Start** buttons next to **Apache** and **MySql** (sic) in the **Modules** list to launch the Apache and MySQL servers built into XAMPP. A green **Running** status indicator should appear next to each server in the list.

Depending on your Windows version and configuration, you'll probably receive a Windows Firewall alert for each server, like the one in Figure 1.6. This will happen when the servers attempt to start listening for browser requests from the outside world.

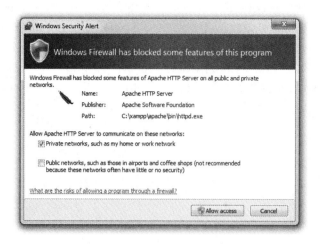

Figure 1.6. This security alert tells you Apache is doing its job

If you want to make absolutely sure that only you can access your development servers, click **Cancel**. You'll still be able to connect to the web server using a browser running on your own computer. In some cases, however, it can be handy to access your server from another computer on your network (such as from a co-worker's machine, to demonstrate the amazing website you have built); for this reason, I recommend selecting the **Private networks, such as my home or work network** option and clicking **Allow access**.

Why doesn't my server start?

If your Apache or MySQL server fails to start, there are a number of possible causes. By far the most common reason is that you already have a web server (be it another copy of Apache or Microsoft's Internet Information Services) or MySQL server running on your computer.

Look around your Start menu and the **Uninstall a program** section of your Windows Control Panel to see if you can spot another installation of Apache HTTP Server or MySQL in order to shut off or uninstall. There's another program similar to XAMPP called WampServer, which, if installed, could be the cause of the problem.

If you think you might have Microsoft's own web server—Internet Information Services (IIS)—running on your system, you can try following Microsoft's instructions for shutting it down.[4]

---

[4] http://technet.microsoft.com/en-us/library/cc732317(WS.10).aspx

Still stuck? The advice in the XAMPP for Windows FAQ[5] might help, especially if you're running Skype (as it can interfere with web servers in some network configurations).

Once both servers appear to be running smoothly, click the **Admin…** button next to **Apache**. Launch your web browser and load http://localhost/xampp/, the XAMPP for Windows admin page shown in Figure 1.7.

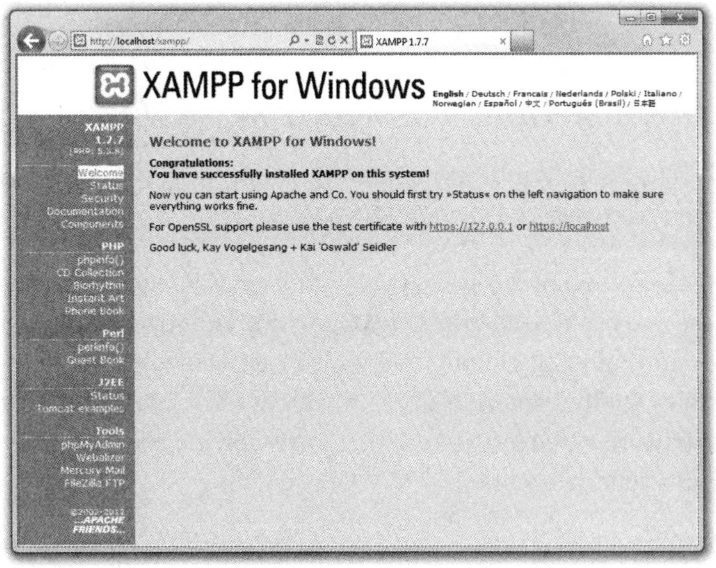

Figure 1.7. The admin page provided by XAMPP confirms your Apache web server is running

If you see this page it means your web server is up and running, because the page you're looking at was loaded from it! Notice that the URL in your browser's address bar starts with http://localhost/ (some modern browsers will hide the protocol, "http://"); **localhost** is a special hostname that always points to your own computer. Throughout this book, whenever you want to load a web page from your own web server, you'll use a URL that starts with http://localhost/.

When you're done working with the XAMPP Control Panel, shut it down by clicking the **Exit** button. Alternatively, you can just close the window, which will leave the XAMPP icon in the Windows System Tray (if you have configured it to remain

---

[5] http://www.apachefriends.org/en/faq-xampp-windows.html#nostart

visible). Clicking the icon will promptly launch the XAMPP Control Panel again when you need it.

XAMPP Control Panel Leaves the Lights On

When you exit the XAMPP Control Panel, the Apache and MySQL servers will keep running on your system. If you've finished coding for the day, I'd advise you to click the **Stop** button for each of these servers to shut them down before you quit the XAMPP Control Panel. There's no sense slowing down those Facebook games you play in the evening by running unnecessary servers!

Set the MySQL Root Password in XAMPP

Once you've set up your Windows computer with the proper servers, you now need to assign a **root password** for MySQL in XAMPP.

MySQL only allows authorized users to view and manipulate the information stored in its databases, so you'll need to tell MySQL who's authorized and who isn't. When MySQL is first installed, it's configured with a user named "root" that has access to do most tasks without entering a password. Therefore, your first task should be to assign a password to the root user so that unauthorized users are prohibited from tampering with your databases.

Why bother?

It's important to realize that MySQL, just like a web server, can be accessed from any computer on the same network. If you're working on a computer connected to the Internet, then, depending on the security measures you've taken, anyone in the world could connect to your MySQL server. The need to pick a difficult-to-guess password should be immediately obvious!

XAMPP makes it easy to resolve this and other configuration security issues with your new servers. With the Apache and MySQL servers running, open this address in your web browser: http://localhost/security/. Alternatively, you can click the **Security** link in the menu on the XAMPP administration page.

This page will list any security issues that XAMPP can identify with your current server configuration. Among them, you should see "The MySQL admin user root has NO password." Scroll down past the table and click the link that will fix the problems listed.

The very first section of the resulting form will prompt you to set a MySQL root user password. Go ahead and set one you'll remember. Leave the **PhpMyAdmin authentification** (sic) set to **cookie**, and use the option to save the password to a file if you think you might forget it (but beware that the password will be saved where a person using your computer could find it). Click the **Password changing** button to change your password, then stop and start your MySQL server using the XAMPP Control Panel.

Seriously, don't forget this password. It's a pain to change it if you do, but I'll show you how in Chapter 10. Here's a spot for you to record your MySQL root password in case you need to:

My MySQL Root Password (Windows)

root user password: _____

XAMPP Directory Protection

XAMPP's security page will also warn you that your web pages are accessible to anyone on your network. While this is technically true, I'm not too worried if a co-worker or family member could stumble on my work-in-progress website; furthermore, most home and office network configurations will prevent people outside your network from accessing the web server running on your computer.

That said, if you want to follow XAMPP's advice to set a username and password that will be required to view pages on your web server, feel free to set one.

Mac OS X Installation

In this section, I'll show you how to start running a PHP-and-MySQL-equipped web server on a Mac computer running Mac OS X version 10.5 (Leopard). If you're not using a Mac, you can safely skip this section.

Mac OS X distinguishes itself by being the only consumer OS to install both Apache and PHP as components of every standard installation. (For that matter, it also comes with Ruby, Python, and Perl—all of which are popular web programming languages.) That said, they take a few tweaks to switch on, and you will need a MySQL database server as well. The simplest way to handle it is to ignore the built-in software and install everything you need in a convenient, all-in-one package.

MAMP (which stands for Mac, Apache, MySQL, and PHP) is a free all-in-one program that includes built-in copies of recent versions of the Apache web server, PHP, and MySQL. Let me take you through the process of installing it.

The Do-it-yourself Option

In past editions of this book, I recommended that you set up the built-in versions of Apache and PHP that come with Mac OS X, and install MySQL using its official installation package. This is a good practice for beginners, I argued, because it gives you a strong sense of how these pieces all fit together.

Unfortunately, this meant that many readers spent their first few hours in "PHP Land" wrestling their way through a protracted sequence of detailed installation instructions. Worse still, sometimes the finer points of these became outdated due to some subtle change to one of the software packages.

Nowadays, I strongly believe that the best way to learn PHP and MySQL is to start *using* them right away. The quicker and more hassle-free the installation process, the better. That's why I ask you to use MAMP in this edition. There's also every chance you're just dabbling in this stuff, so why spend time tweaking the innards of your operating system when you can leave them safely set to the factory defaults?

Nevertheless, if you're a die-hard do-it-yourselfer, a tech-savvy power user, or if you simply reach the end of this book and wonder how the pros do it, I've included a detailed set of installation instructions for the individual packages in Appendix A. Feel free to follow them instead of the instructions in this section if you're that way inclined.

1. Download the latest version from the MAMP website[6] (you want the free MAMP, not the commercial MAMP PRO). After downloading the file (as of this writing, MAMP 2.0.5 is about 116MB in size), double-click it to unzip the installer (**MAMP.pkg**). Then double-click it to launch the MAMP Installer, which is shown in Figure 1.8.

---

[6] http://www.mamp.info

Figure 1.8. The MAMP package

 Look Out Below!

The next step is a tricky one. Make sure you read on first before clicking blindly through the installer!

2.   During the installation, you'll be prompted to choose whether or not to perform a standard installation. At this step, instead of clicking the **Install** button, click **Customize**. This will give you the opportunity to deselect **MAMP PRO** (which the installer will otherwise sneakily install in the hopes that you'll decide to buy it after all). This is especially important because the free MAMP will display a worrying warning message at startup if MAMP PRO is installed.

Miss this step?

If you missed this step and allowed the installer to put MAMP PRO on your system, it's easy enough to remove.

Open your **Applications** folder, double-click on the new **MAMP PRO** folder, and double-click to run the **MAMP PRO Uninstaller**. Click each checkbox in the **Uninstaller** window. Once they're all checked, click **Uninstall**. Quit the Uninstaller.

Browse to your **Applications** folder and find the new **MAMP** folder there. Open it, and double-click the **MAMP** icon inside to launch MAMP. As MAMP starts up, the following will happen. First, the MAMP window shown in Figure 1.9 will appear. The two status indicators will switch from red to green as the built-in Apache and MySQL servers start up. Next, MAMP will open your default web browser and load the MAMP welcome page, shown in Figure 1.10.

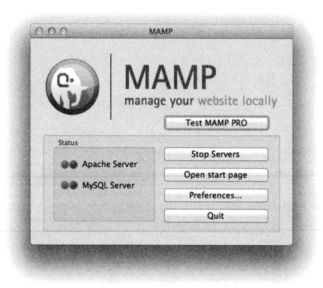

Figure 1.9. The MAMP window

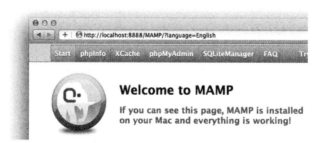

Figure 1.10. The MAMP welcome page confirms Apache, PHP, and MySQL are up and running

If you see this page it means your web server is up and running, because the page you're looking at was loaded from it! Notice that the URL in your browser's address bar starts with http://localhost:8888/ (some modern browsers will hide the protocol, "http://"); **localhost** is a special hostname that always points to your own computer. The "8888" is the **port number** that the browser is using to connect to your computer.

Every server running on a computer listens on a unique port number. Usually, websites are hosted on port 80, and browsers use that to connect when no port number is specified by the URL. By default, MAMP comes configured so that Apache will listen on port 8888 and MySQL will listen on port 8889. This ensures that MAMP will work even if your Mac already has a web server installed and listening on port 80, or a MySQL server listening on port 3306 (the standard MySQL server port).[7]

The code and instructions in the rest of this book will assume your web server is running on port 80 and your MySQL server is on port 3306. Now would be a good time to see if MAMP will run happily using these standard port numbers. Here's how:

1. In the MAMP window, click **Stop Servers**. Wait for the indicators to turn red.

2. Click the **Preferences...** button and navigate to the **Ports** tab.

3. Click the **Set to default Apache and MySQL ports** button so that Apache will use port 80 and MySQL will use port 3306. Click **OK**.

4. Click **Start Servers**. MAMP will prompt you to enter your password, because running a server on an "official" Internet port number like 80 requires administrator privileges.

If both indicators turn green, click the **Open start page** button again, and verify that the MAMP welcome page shows up this time with a URL starting with http://localhost/ (no port number). If so, you're in good shape!

If one or both indicators don't turn red in step 1, or if the welcome page fails to load correctly, in all likelihood you have yourself a port conflict. Somewhere on your Mac is another web or MySQL server that's already using one or both of those ports. One place to check is the **Sharing** icon in System Preferences. If **Web Sharing** is en-

---

[7] Of course, there are no guarantees that another application won't be using port 8888 or 8889 on your system! I've had trouble with Playback by Yazsoft (an application for streaming media to game consoles like the Xbox 360 and PlayStation 3), which uses port 8888 when it is running. If in doubt, try a different port number!

abled, Mac OS X's built-in Apache server is running (normally on port 80). Another option is to try shutting down various applications. Under some conditions, Skype for Mac has prevented MAMP's MySQL server from launching for me, for example.

If, in the end, you're only able to make MAMP run happily on its default port numbers (8888 and 8889), go ahead and use them. Whenever this book mentions a URL starting with http://localhost/, you'll have to add the port number (http://localhost:8888/), and when the time comes to connect to MySQL, I'll tell you how to specify a nonstandard port number.

One last change to make to the default MAMP configuration is to switch on PHP error display. By default, when you make a serious mistake in your PHP code (and believe me, we all make plenty!), MAMP's Apache server will produce a blank web page. As a developer needing to figure out what you typed wrong, that's rather unhelpful; I'd much prefer to see a detailed error message in my browser window.

The reason why MAMP comes with the error display switched off is so that if you decide to host a publicly accessible website using it, visitors to the site won't see embarrassing error messages when you make a mistake. What's embarrassing on a public website, however, is practically *essential* in the development stage.

To switch on PHP error display, open the **MAMP** folder in your Mac's **Applications** folder. From there, drill down into **bin/php/**. This **php** folder will contain a subfolder for each version of PHP that comes with MAMP. You can double-check in MAMP's Preferences to be sure, but it's probably configured to run the most recent version, so open that folder (it's **php5.3.6** in my copy of MAMP 2.0.5), and then open the **conf** subfolder. Open the **php.ini** file in your favorite text editor (TextEdit will work fine), and look for these lines:

```
; Print out errors (as a part of the output).  For production web
➥ sites,
; you're strongly encouraged to turn this feature off, and use
➥ error logging
; instead (see below).  Keeping display_errors enabled on a
➥ production web site
; may reveal security information to end users, such as file paths
➥ on your Web
; server, your database schema or other information.
display_errors = Off
```

Change the Off in that last line to On and save the file. Now click **Stop Servers**, then **Start Servers** in MAMP to restart Apache with the new configuration. That's it—PHP will now display helpful (if a little soul-crushing) error messages.

When you're done working with MAMP, shut it down (along with its built-in servers) by clicking the **Quit** button in the MAMP window. And when you're next ready to do some work on a database driven website, just fire it up again!

Set the MySQL Root Password in MAMP

Once MAMP is up and running on your Mac with the relevant servers, your very next action should be to assign a **root password** for MySQL.

MySQL only allows authorized users to view and manipulate the information stored in its databases, so you'll need to tell MySQL who's authorized and who's not. When MAMP first installs MySQL, it's configured with a user named "root" that has access to perform most tasks. The password for this user is "root"—not exactly Fort Knox! Hence why your first task should be to assign a new password to the root user, preventing any tampering with your databases.

Why bother?

It's important to realize that MySQL, just like a web server, can be accessed from any computer on the same network. So if you're working on a computer connected to the Internet, depending on the security measures you've taken, anyone in the world could connect to your MySQL server. The need to pick a password that's difficult for anyone to guess should be immediately obvious!

To set your MySQL root password, first make sure MAMP and its servers are running. Then open the Mac OS X **Terminal** application (found in the **Utilities** folder in the **Applications** folder) and type these commands (hitting **Enter** after each one):

1.
```
cd /Applications/MAMP/Library/bin/
```

This navigates to the **Library/bin/** subfolder of your MAMP installation, which is where the Terminal utility programs are kept.

2.
```
./mysqladmin -u root -p password "newpassword"
```

Replace *newpassword* with the new password you want to assign to your MySQL root user.

When you hit **Enter** you'll be prompted to enter the current password: **root**.

3.   Quit Terminal.

Your password is now set, but this creates a new problem: MAMP itself needs unrestricted access to your MySQL server so that it can control it. If you click the **Open start page** button in MAMP at this point, you'll receive an error message: "Error: Could not connect to MySQL server!" Obviously, we need to tell MAMP what our new MySQL root password is.

You must edit several files in the MAMP folder to make it work again. You can open each of these files in TextEdit, or whichever text editor you prefer to use.

Editing PHP Scripts in Mac OS X with TextEdit

TextEdit has a nasty habit of mistaking **.php** files for HTML documents when opening them, and attempting to display them as formatted text. To avoid this, you must select the **Ignore rich text commands** checkbox in the **Open** dialog box.

/Applications/MAMP/bin/mamp/index.php

Find the line that looks like this:

```
$link = @mysql_connect(':/Applications/MAMP/tmp/mysql/mysql.sock',
    'root', 'root');
```

Replace the second 'root' with your new MySQL root password (that is, 'newpassword').

/Applications/MAMP/bin/phpMyAdmin/config.inc.php

This is a large file, so you may need to use your text editor's Find feature to locate these lines:

```
$cfg['Servers'][$i]['user']     = 'root';
➡ // MySQL user
$cfg['Servers'][$i]['password'] = 'root';
```

```
➡              // MySQL password (only needed

➡ // with 'config' auth_type)
```

Again, replace the second `'root'` with your new MySQL root password (that's `'newpassword'`).

/Applications/MAMP/bin/checkMysql.sh
/Applications/MAMP/bin/quickCheckMysqlUpgrade.sh
/Applications/MAMP/bin/repairMysql.sh
/Applications/MAMP/bin/stopMysql.sh
/Applications/MAMP/bin/upgradeMysql.sh

The contents of each of these little files starts out looking a little like this (this is **checkMysql.sh**):

```
# /bin/sh
/Applications/MAMP/Library/bin/mysqlcheck --all-databases --check
➡ --check-upgrade -u root -proot
➡ --socket=/Applications/MAMP/tmp/mysql/mysql.sock
```

See that `-proot`? The p stands for "password" and the rest *is* the password. Change it to your new password (`-pnewpassword`).

Make the same change to each of these five files.

With all those changes made and saved, MAMP should work normally again, with your MySQL server nice and secure from outside intrusion!

Oh, and don't forget this password. It's kind of a pain to change it if you do (I'll show you how in Chapter 10). Here's a spot for you to record your MySQL root password in case you need to.

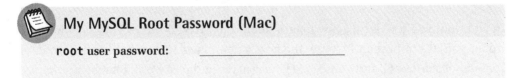

My MySQL Root Password (Mac)

root user password: _____

Linux Installation

These days, most people who run Linux as their operating system of choice are tech-savvy enough to know how to install software like Apache, PHP, and MySQL. Indeed, they probably feel strongly about *how* they should be installed, which would doubtlessly clash with any instructions I'd provide here.

If this describes you, go ahead and install the most recent versions of Apache, PHP, and MySQL that you're comfortable installing, using whichever package manager or build process pushes your buttons. Nothing in this book is going to be so advanced that the minutiae of how you configure these packages will matter.

That said, just in case you're one of the rare Linux users who could use some guidance on installing, I've included a detailed set of instructions for Linux users in Appendix A.

What to Ask Your Web Host

While you tinker with PHP and MySQL on your own computer, it's a good idea to start collecting the information you'll need when it comes time to deploy your first database driven website to the public. Here's a rundown of the details you should ask of your web host.

First, you'll need to know how to transfer files to your web host. You'll be uploading PHP scripts to your host the same way you normally send the HTML files, CSS files, and images that make up a static website; so if you already know how to do that, there's no need to bother your host. If you're just starting with a new host, however, you'll have to be aware of what file transfer protocol it supports (FTP or SFTP), as well as knowing what username and password to use when connecting with your (S)FTP program. You also must know what directory to put files into so that they're accessible to web browsers.

In addition, you'll require a few details about the MySQL server your host has set up for you. It's important to know the host name to use in order to connect to it (possibly localhost), and your MySQL username and password, which may or may not be the same as your (S)FTP credentials. Your web host will probably have provided an empty database for you to use, which prevents you from interfering with other users' databases who may share the same MySQL server with you. If they have provided this, you should establish the name of that database.

Have you taken all that in? Here's a spot to record the information you'll need about your web host.

My Hosting Details

File transfer protocol (circle one):

- ◼ FTP
- ◼ SFTP

(S)FTP host name: _____

(S)FTP username: _____

(S)FTP password: _____

MySQL host name: _____

MySQL username: _____

MySQL password: _____

MySQL database name: _____

Your First PHP Script

It would be unfair of me to help you install everything, but then stop short of giving you a taste of what a PHP script looks like until Chapter 3. So here's a morsel to whet your appetite.

Open your favorite text or HTML editor and create a new file called **today.php**. Type this into the file:

chapter1/today.php

```
<!DOCTYPE html>
<html lang="en">
  <head>
    <meta charset="utf-8">
    <title>Today&rsquo;s Date</title>
  </head>
```

```
<body>
  <p>Today&rsquo;s date (according to this web server) is
    <?php

    echo date('l, F jS Y.');

    ?>
  </p>
</body>
</html>
```

It's a Letter, Not a Number

The most important line of the code is this one:

```
echo date('l, F jS Y.');
```

Unfortunately, it's also the one most people type wrong when reading this book. See the character before the comma? It's not the number one (1), it's a lowercase L (l).

Editing PHP Scripts in Windows with Notepad

To save a file with a .php extension in Notepad, you'll need to either select *All Files* as the file type, or surround the filename with quotes in the **Save As** dialog box. Otherwise, Notepad will unhelpfully save the file as **today.php.txt**, which will fail to work.

Editing PHP Scripts in Mac OS X with TextEdit

Be careful when using TextEdit to edit .php files, as it will save them in Rich Text Format with an invisible **.rtf** filename extension by default. To save a new **.php** file, you must first remember to convert the file to plain text by selecting **Format > Make Plain Text** (⇧+⌘+T) from the TextEdit menu.

TextEdit also has a nasty habit of mistaking existing **.php** files for HTML documents when opening them, and attempting to display them as formatted text. To avoid this, you must select the **Ignore rich text commands** checkbox in the **Open** dialog box.

Try a Free IDE!

As you can tell from the preceding warnings, the text editors provided with current operating systems are a touch unsuitable for editing PHP scripts. However, there are a number of solid text editors and Integrated Development Environments (IDEs) with rich support for editing PHP scripts that you can download for free. Here are a few that work on Windows, Mac OS X, and Linux:

NetBeans   http://www.netbeans.org/features/php/
Aptana   http://www.aptana.com/php
Komodo Edit   http://www.activestate.com/komodo_edit/

If you'd prefer not to type out all the code, you can download this file—along with the rest of the code in this book—from the code archive. See the Preface for details on how to download the code archive.

Save the file, and move it to the **web root** directory of your local web server.

Where's my server's web root directory?

If you're using an Apache server that you installed manually, the web root directory is the **htdocs** directory within your Apache installation (that's **C:\Program Files\Apache Software Foundation\Apache2.2\htdocs** on Windows and **/usr/local/apache2/htdocs** on Linux).

For the Apache server built into XAMPP, the web root directory is the **htdocs** directory within your XAMPP installation directory. You can reach it simply by choosing from the Start menu: **All Programs > Apache Friends > XAMPP > XAMPP htdocs folder**.

If the Apache server you're using is built into Mac OS X, the web root directory is **/Library/WebServer/Documents**. It can be easily accessed by clicking the **Open Computer Website Folder…** button under **Web Sharing** in the **Sharing** preference panel in System Preferences.

The Apache server built into MAMP has a web root directory in the **htdocs** folder inside the MAMP folder (**/Applications/MAMP/htdocs**). If you prefer using another folder as your web root, you can change it on the **Apache** tab of the MAMP application's Preferences. This facility makes it especially easy to switch between multiple web development projects by pointing MAMP at different folders.

Open your web browser of choice, and type http://localhost/today.php (or
http://localhost:*port*/today.php if Apache is configured to run on a port other than
the default of 80) into the address bar to view the file you just created.[8]

You Must Type the URL

You might be used to previewing your web pages by double-clicking on them, or
by using the **File > Open...** feature of your browser. These methods tell your browser
to load the file directly from your computer's hard drive, so they won't work with
PHP files.

As previously mentioned, PHP scripts require your web server to read and execute
the PHP code they contain before sending the HTML code that's generated to the
browser. Only by typing the URL (http://localhost/today.php) will your browser
request the file from your web server for this to happen.

Figure 1.11 shows what the web page generated by your first PHP script should
look like.

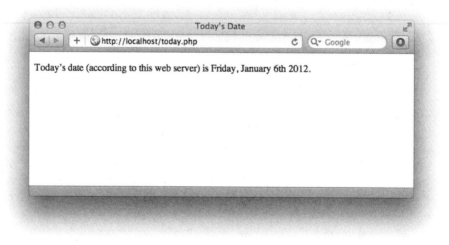

Figure 1.11. See your first PHP script in action!

Neat, huh? If you use the **View Source** feature in your browser, all you'll see is a
regular HTML file with the date in it. The PHP code (everything between <?php and

---

[8] If you installed Apache on Windows, you may have selected the option to run it on port 8080. If you're
using MAMP, it's configured by default to run Apache on port 8888.

?> in the code above) was interpreted by the web server and converted to normal text before it was sent to your browser. The beauty of PHP, and other server-side scripting languages, is that the web browser can remain ignorant—the web server does all the work!

If you're worried that the code you typed made little sense to you, rest assured that you'll be up to speed on exactly how it works by the end of Chapter 3.

If the date is missing, or if your browser prompts you to download the PHP file instead of displaying it, something is amiss with your web server's PHP support. If you can, use **View Source** in your browser to look at the code of the page. You'll probably see the PHP code right there in the page. Since the browser fails to understand PHP, it just sees <?php … ?> as one long invalid HTML tag, which it ignores. Double-check that you've requested the file from your web server rather than your hard disk (that is, the location bar in your browser shows a URL beginning with http://localhost/), and make sure that your web server supports PHP. You should be fine as long as you followed the installation instructions earlier in this chapter.

Full Toolbox, Dirty Hands

You should now be fully equipped with a web server that supports PHP scripts, a MySQL database server, and a basic understanding of how to use each of these. You should even have gotten your hands dirty by writing and successfully testing your first PHP script!

If the **today.php** script didn't work for you, drop by the SitePoint Forums[9] and we'll be glad to help you figure out the problem.

In Chapter 2, you'll learn the basics of relational databases and start working with MySQL. I'll also introduce you to the language of database: Structured Query Language. If you've never worked with a database before, it'll be a real eye-opener!

---

[9] http://www.sitepoint.com/forums/

Chapter

Introducing MySQL

In Chapter 1, we installed and set up two software programs: the Apache web server with PHP, and the MySQL database server. If you followed my recommendation, you would have set them up using an all-in-one package like XAMPP or MAMP, but don't let that diminish your sense of accomplishment!

As I explained in that chapter, PHP is a server-side scripting language that lets you insert instructions into your web pages that your web server software (in most cases, Apache) will execute before it sends those pages to browsers that request them. In a brief example, I showed how it was possible to insert the current date into a web page every time it was requested.

Now, that's all well and good, but it *really* gets interesting when a database is added to the mix. In this chapter, we'll learn what a database is, and how to work with your own MySQL databases using Structured Query Language.

An Introduction to Databases

A database server (in our case, MySQL) is a program that can store large amounts of information in an organized format that's easily accessible through programming languages like PHP. For example, you could tell PHP to look in the database for a list of jokes that you'd like to appear on your website.

In this example, the jokes would be stored entirely in the database. The advantage of this approach is twofold: First, instead of writing an HTML page for each joke, you could write a single PHP script that was designed to fetch any joke from the database and display it by generating an HTML page for it on the fly. Second, adding a joke to your website would be a simple matter of inserting the joke into the database. The PHP code would take care of the rest, automatically displaying the new joke along with the others when it fetched the list from the database.

Let's run with this example as we look at how data is stored in a database. A database is composed of one or more **tables**, each of which contains a list of **items**, or *things*. For our joke database, we'd probably start with a table called joke that would contain a list of jokes. Each table in a database has one or more **columns**, or **fields**. Each column holds a certain piece of information about each item in the table. In our example, our joke table might have one column for the text of the jokes, and another for the dates on which the jokes were added to the database. Each joke stored in this way would be said to be a **row** or **entry** in the table. These rows and columns form a table that looks like Figure 2.1.

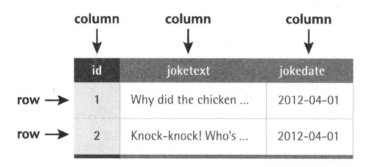

Figure 2.1. A typical database table containing a list of jokes

Notice that, in addition to columns for the joke text (joketext) and the date of the joke (jokedate), I've included a column named id. As a matter of good design, a database table should always provide a means by which we can identify each of its rows uniquely. Since it's possible that two identical jokes could be entered on the same date, we can't rely upon the joketext and jokedate columns to tell all the jokes apart. The function of the id column, therefore, is to assign a unique number to each joke so that we have an easy way to refer to them and to keep track of which joke is which. We'll take a closer look at database design issues like this in Chapter 5.

To review, the table in Figure 2.1 is a three-column table with two rows, or entries. Each row in the table contains three fields, one for each column in the table: the joke's ID, its text, and the date of the joke. With this basic terminology under your belt, you're ready to dive into using MySQL.

Using phpMyAdmin to Run SQL Queries

Just as a web server is designed to respond to requests from a client (a web browser), the MySQL database server responds to requests from **client programs**. Later in this book, we'll write our own MySQL client programs in the form of PHP scripts, but for now we can use a client program that comes bundled with both XAMPP and MAMP: phpMyAdmin.

phpMyAdmin is itself a sophisticated web application written in PHP. Besides being included in XAMPP and MAMP, phpMyAdmin is provided by most commercial web hosts who offer PHP and MySQL as a tool for developers to manage their websites' MySQL databases. Much like PHP and MySQL, phpMyAdmin's ubiquity makes it an attractive tool for beginners to learn and use.

Don't have phpMyAdmin?

If you opted to follow the manual setup instructions in Appendix A rather than use the all-in-one package offered by XAMPP or MAMP to set up your web server, you probably don't have phpMyAdmin installed on your server. The good news is that you can download and install it from the phpMyAdmin website,[1] where instructions are provided.

If you're using XAMPP on Windows, you can access phpMyAdmin by clicking the **Admin...** button next to **MySql** (sic) in the XAMPP Control Panel window, as shown in Figure 2.2.

---

[1] http://www.phpmyadmin.net/

Figure 2.2. Click the **Admin...** button to open phpMyAdmin

To access phpMyAdmin using MAMP on Mac OS X, click the **Open start page** button in the MAMP window. Then click the **phpMyAdmin** tab at the top of the screen, as shown in Figure 2.3.

Figure 2.3. You can access phpMyAdmin from MAMP's start page

Either way, you should now have phpMyAdmin open in your default web browser, which should look like Figure 2.4. As of this writing, XAMPP includes the more recent (and better-looking) version 3.4 of phpMyAdmin, so I'll be showing screenshots of that. If you're using the older version 3.3, it won't look quite as nice, but it should work just the same.

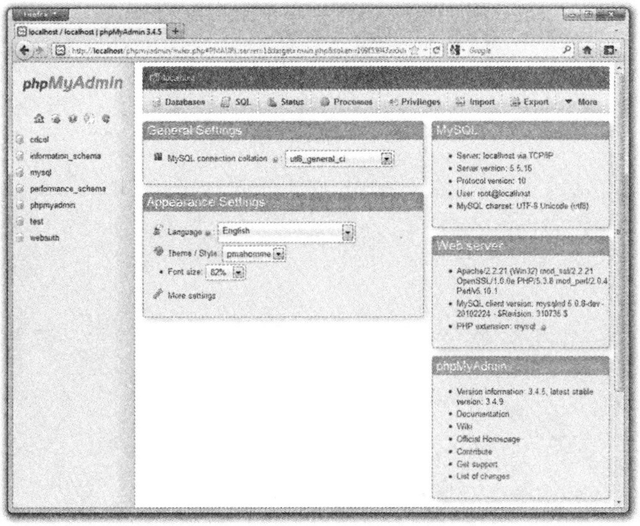

Figure 2.4. If you can see this, you have phpMyAdmin

If you go clicking around phpMyAdmin, you'll discover all the tools you need to manage every aspect of your MySQL server and the data it contains. For now, I'm going to ignore all of those features and focus on a particular one: the SQL query window.

See the row of buttons just beneath the phpMyAdmin logo? Clicking the second icon, indicated in Figure 2.5, opens the SQL query window shown in Figure 2.6.

Figure 2.5. Click the second button ...

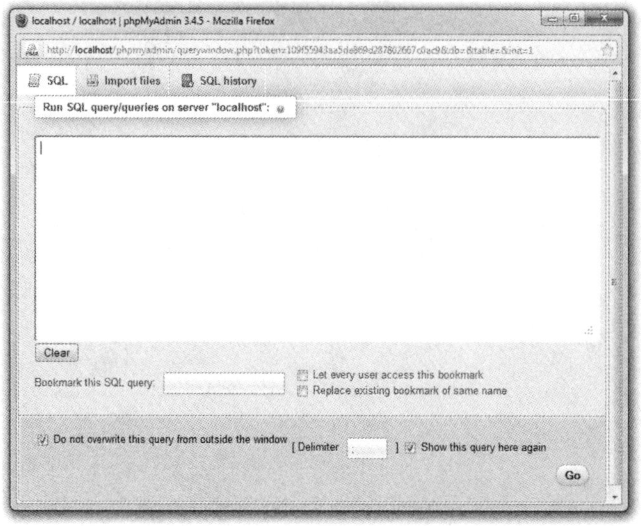

Figure 2.6. ... to open the SQL query window

Into that big, empty text box you can type commands to ask your database server questions or make it perform tasks. Let's try a few simple commands to take a look around your MySQL server.

The MySQL server can actually keep track of more than one database. This allows a web host to set up a single MySQL server for use by several of its subscribers, for example. So, your first step after connecting to the server should be to choose a database with which to work. First, let's retrieve a list of databases on the current server.

Type this command into the SQL query window, then click **Go**:

```
SHOW DATABASES
```

You might think at first that nothing has happened, but you should now see the results in the main phpMyAdmin window, as shown in Figure 2.7.

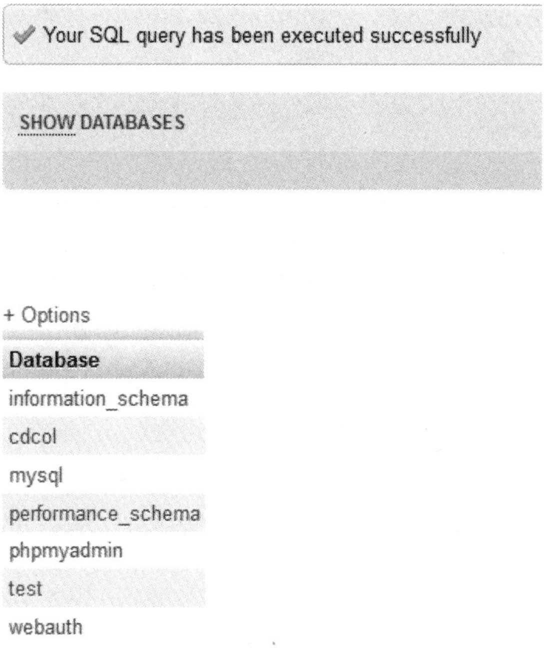

Figure 2.7. The query results are displayed in the main phpMyAdmin window

Your list of databases might be as long as the one shown in Figure 2.7, or if you're running MAMP it may only contain two critical databases. XAMPP uses additional databases to store configuration of its own, whereas MAMP is designed to avoid cluttering up your MySQL server with its own data. Either way, you will have databases named `information_schema` and `mysql`.

The MySQL server uses the first database, named `information_schema`, to keep track of all the other databases on the server. Unless you're doing some very advanced stuff, you'll probably leave this database alone.

The second database, `mysql`, is special too. MySQL uses it to keep track of users, their passwords, and what they're allowed to do. We'll steer clear of this for now, but we'll revisit it in Chapter 10 when we discuss MySQL administration.

A third database, named `test`, is a sample database that's included with MySQL out of the box (again, MAMP does away with this database so you can start clean). If you see it in the list, you can delete the `test` database because you'll be creating your own database in a moment.

Deleting stuff in MySQL is called "dropping" it, and the command for doing so is appropriately named:

```
DROP DATABASE test
```

If you type this command into the SQL query window and click **Go**, phpMyAdmin will probably display an error message: **"DROP DATABASE" statements are disabled**. This message indicates that a safety feature built into phpMyAdmin is preventing you from running dangerous-looking queries like this one.

If you want to be able to drop databases (and this is probably a good ability to have, given the amount of experimentation I'm going to encourage you to do in this book), there is a way to do so tucked away in phpMyAdmin. In the main phpMyAdmin window, click the **Databases** tab (the leftmost tab at the top of the main window area). You'll be presented with a list of databases on the server, with a checkbox next to each. Check the one you want to delete (test in this case); then click the **Drop** button at the bottom-right of the list as shown in Figure 2.8.

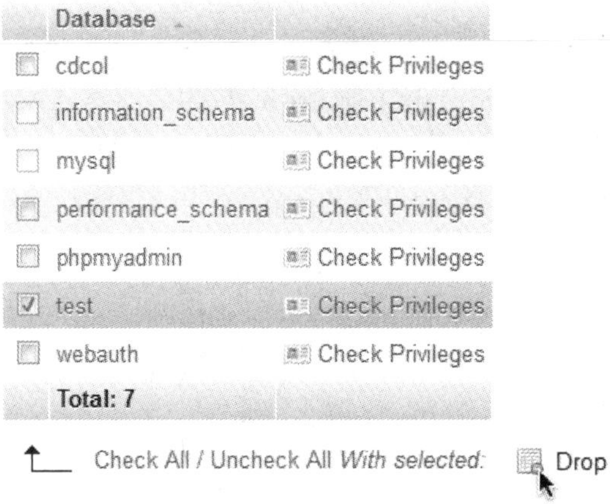

Figure 2.8. The ability to drop a database in phpMyAdmin is well hidden

phpMyAdmin presents one last prompt to make sure you mean to obliterate the database. If you confirm this, MySQL will obediently delete the database, and phpMyAdmin will display a message to verify it was successful.

Note that there are *other* potentially hazardous commands you can send to MySQL in addition to DROP DATABASE, but phpMyAdmin won't always protect you if you make a mistake. You have to be very careful to type your commands correctly in the SQL query window, otherwise you can destroy your entire database—along with all the information it contains—with a single command!

Structured Query Language

The commands we'll use to direct MySQL throughout the rest of this book are part of a standard called **Structured Query Language**, or **SQL** (pronounced as either "sequel" or "ess-cue-ell"—take your pick). Commands in SQL are also referred to as **queries**; I'll use these two terms interchangeably.

SQL is the standard language for interacting with most databases, so, even if you move from MySQL to a database like Microsoft SQL Server in the future, you'll find that the majority of commands are identical. It's important that you understand the distinction between SQL and MySQL. MySQL is the database server software that you're using. SQL is the language that you use to interact with that database.

 Learn SQL in Depth

In this book, I'll teach you the essentials of SQL that every PHP developer needs to know. If you decide to make a career out of building database driven websites, it pays to know some of the more advanced details of SQL, especially when it comes to making your sites run as quickly and smoothly as possible. To dive deeper into SQL, I highly recommend the book *Simply SQL*[2] by Rudy Limeback.

Creating a Database

When the time comes to deploy your first database driven website on the Web, you're likely to find that your web host or IT department has already created a MySQL database to use. Since you're in charge of your own MySQL server, however, you'll need to create your own database to use in developing your site.

It's just as easy to create a database as it is to delete one. Open the SQL query window again, and type this command:

```
CREATE DATABASE ijdb
```

[2] http://www.sitepoint.com/books/sql1/

I chose to name the database ijdb, for Internet Joke Database,[3] because that fits with the example I gave at the beginning of this chapter: a website that displays a database of jokes. Feel free to give the database any name you like, though.

Case Sensitivity in SQL Queries

Most MySQL commands are not case-sensitive, which means you can type CREATE DATABASE, create database, or even CrEaTe DaTaBaSe, and it will know what you mean. Database names and table names, however, are case-sensitive when the MySQL server is running on an operating system with a case-sensitive file system (such as Linux or Mac OS X, depending on your system configuration).

Additionally, table, column, and other names must be spelled exactly the same when they're used more than once in the same query.

For consistency, this book will respect the accepted convention of typing database commands in all capitals, and database entities (databases, tables, columns, and so on) in all lowercase.

Now that you have a database, you need to tell phpMyAdmin that you want to use it. You've probably noticed by now that the left-hand sidebar in the main phpMy-Admin window contains a list of all the databases on your MySQL server. When you clicked **Go** to run your CREATE DATABASE command (you *did* click **Go**, didn't you?), this sidebar updated to show your new database's name in a drop-down menu, as shown in Figure 2.9.

Figure 2.9. phpMyAdmin autoselects your new database for you

---

[3] With a tip of the hat to the Internet Movie Database [http://www.imdb.com].

It's nice of phpMyAdmin to autoselect your new database for you, but you'll need to know how to select it yourself. Click the home button (the first in the row of icons beneath the phpMyAdmin logo) to go back to the home page of phpMyAdmin. The sidebar will once again display a list of all databases on your server.

To select a database to work with, just click its name in the sidebar. With your database selected, click the **Query window** button again to open a new SQL query window. This query window is slightly different from the last one: the caption for the text box now says **Run SQL query/queries on database ijdb**. Commands typed into this query window will run on your new database, instead of your MySQL server as a whole.

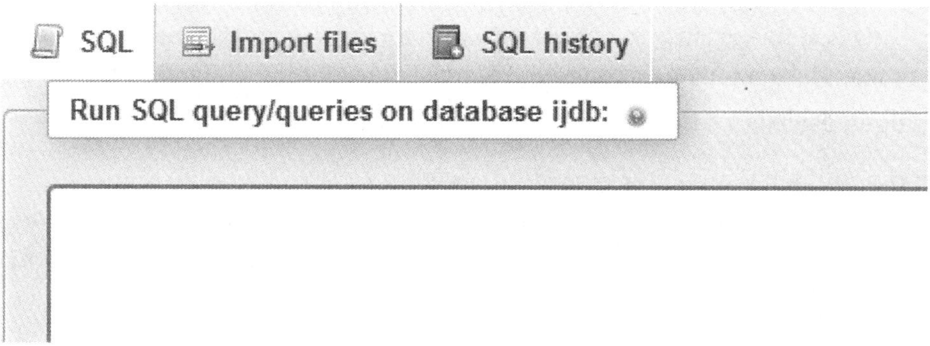

Figure 2.10. You must open a new query window to work with this database

You're now ready to use your database. Since a database is empty until you add tables to it, our first order of business is to create a table that will hold your jokes (now might be a good time to think of some!).

Creating a Table

The SQL commands we've encountered so far have been reasonably simple, but as tables are so flexible, it takes a more complicated command to create them. The basic form of the command is as follows:

```
CREATE TABLE table_name (
  column1Name column1Type column1Details,
  column2Name column2Type column2Details,
  ⋮
) DEFAULT CHARACTER SET charset ENGINE=InnoDB
```

Let's continue with the `joke` table I showed you in Figure 2.1. You'll recall that it had three columns: `id` (a number), `joketext` (the text of the joke), and `jokedate` (the date on which the joke was entered). This is the command to create that table:

```
CREATE TABLE joke (
    id INT NOT NULL AUTO_INCREMENT PRIMARY KEY,
    joketext TEXT,
    jokedate DATE NOT NULL
) DEFAULT CHARACTER SET utf8 ENGINE=InnoDB
```

Looks scary, huh? Let's break it down:

CREATE TABLE joke (

This first line is fairly simple; it says that we want to create a new table named `joke`. The opening parenthesis (`(`) marks the beginning of the list of columns in the table.

id INT NOT NULL AUTO_INCREMENT PRIMARY KEY,

This second line says that we want a column called `id` that contains an integer (INT); that is, a whole number. The rest of this line deals with special details for the column:

1. First, when creating a row in this table, this column cannot be left blank (NOT NULL).

2. Next, if we don't specify a value for this column when we add a new entry to the table, we want MySQL to automatically pick a value that's one more than the highest value in the table so far (AUTO_INCREMENT).

3. Finally, this column is to act as a unique identifier for the entries in the table, so all values in this column must be unique (PRIMARY KEY).

joketext TEXT,

This third line is super simple; it says that we want a column called `joketext`, which will contain text (TEXT).

jokedate DATE NOT NULL

This fourth line defines our last column, called `jokedate`; this will contain a date (DATE) that cannot be left blank (NOT NULL).

) DEFAULT CHARACTER SET utf8

The closing parenthesis ()) marks the end of the list of columns in the table.

DEFAULT CHARACTER SET utf8 tells MySQL that you'll be storing UTF-8 encoded text in this table. UTF-8 is the most common encoding used for web content, so you should employ it in all your database tables that you intend to use on the Web.

ENGINE=InnoDB

This tells MySQL which **storage engine** to use to create this table.

Think of a storage engine as a file format. When building a website, you'll typically choose to use the JPEG format for the photos on your site, but stick with the PNG format for the images that make up your site design. Both formats are supported by browsers, but they each have strengths and weaknesses. Likewise, MySQL supports multiple formats for database tables.

The InnoDB format is by far the best choice for website databases like the one we'll build in this book. The older MyISAM format is the default, however, so we must tell MySQL that we want it to create an InnoDB table.

Note that we assigned a specific data type to each column we created. id will contain integers, joketext will contain text, and jokedate will contain dates. MySQL requires you to specify in advance a data type for each column. This helps to keep your data organized, and allows you to compare the values within a column in powerful ways, as we'll see later. For a list of MySQL data types, see Appendix D.

Now, if you type the above command correctly and click **Go**, the main phpMyAdmin window will confirm that the query executed successfully, and your first table will be created. If you made a typing mistake, phpMyAdmin will tell you there was a problem with the query you typed, and will try to indicate where it had trouble understanding what you meant.

Let's have a look at your new table to make sure it was created properly. Type the following command into the SQL query window, and click **Go**:

```
SHOW TABLES
```

phpMyAdmin should display the output shown in Figure 2.11.

+ Options

Tables_in_ijdb

joke

Figure 2.11. phpMyAdmin lists the tables in the currently selected database

This is a list of all the tables in your database (which we named ijdb). The list contains only one table: the joke table you just created. So far, everything seems fine. Let's take a closer look at the joke table itself using a DESCRIBE query:

```
DESCRIBE joke
```

As you can see in Figure 2.12, there are three columns (or fields) in this table, which appear as the three rows in this table of results. The details are a little cryptic, but if you look at them closely, you should be able to figure out what they mean. It's nothing to be worried about, though. You have better things to do, like adding some jokes to your table!

Field	Type	Null	Key	Default	Extra
id	int(11)	NO	PRI	NULL	auto_increment
joketext	text	YES		NULL	
jokedate	date	NO		NULL	

Figure 2.12. phpMyAdmin lists the columns in the joke table as rows

We need to look at just one more task before we do that, though: deleting a table. This task is as frighteningly easy as deleting a database with a DROP DATABASE command—except that phpMyAdmin won't protect you here. *Don't* run this command with your joke table, unless you actually do want to be rid of it! If you really want to try it, be prepared to re-create your joke table from scratch:

```
DROP TABLE tableName
```

Inserting Data into a Table

Your database is created and your table is built; all that's left is to put some jokes into the database. The command that inserts data into a database is called, appropriately enough, INSERT. This command can take two basic forms:

```
INSERT INTO tableName SET
  column1Name = column1Value,
  column2Name = column2Value,
  ⋮
```

```
INSERT INTO tableName
  (column1Name, column2Name, …)
  VALUES (column1Value, column2Value, …)
```

So, to add a joke to our table, we can use either of these commands:

```
INSERT INTO joke SET
joketext = "Why did the chicken cross the road? To get to the other
↪ side!",
jokedate = "2012-04-01"
```

```
INSERT INTO joke
(joketext, jokedate) VALUES (
"Why did the chicken cross the road? To get to the other side!",
"2012-04-01")
```

Note that in both forms of the INSERT command, the order in which you list the columns must match the order in which you list the values. Otherwise, the order of the columns isn't important. Go ahead and swap the order of the column and value pairs and try the query.

As you typed the query, you'll have noticed that we used double quotes (") to mark where the text of the joke started and ended. A piece of text enclosed in quotes this way is called a **text string**, and this is how you represent most data values in SQL. For instance, the dates are typed as text strings, too, in the form "YYYY-MM-DD".

If you prefer, you can type text strings surrounded with single quotes (') instead of double quotes:

```
INSERT INTO joke SET
joketext = 'Why did the chicken cross the road? To get to the other
➥ side!',
jokedate = '2012-04-01'
```

You might be wondering what happens when there are quotes used within the joke's text. Well, if the text contains single quotes, you would surround it with double quotes. Conversely, if the text contains double quotes, surround it with single quotes.

If the text you want to include in your query contains both single *and* double quotes, you'll have to **escape** the conflicting characters within your text string. You escape a character in SQL by adding a backslash (\) immediately before it. This tells MySQL to ignore any "special meaning" this character might have. In the case of single or double quotes, it tells MySQL not to interpret the character as the end of the text string.

To make this as clear as possible, here's an example of an INSERT command for a joke containing both single and double quotes:

```
INSERT INTO joke
(joketext, jokedate) VALUES (
'Knock-knock! Who\'s there? Boo! "Boo" who? Don\'t cry; it\'s only a
➥ joke!',
"2012-04-01")
```

As you can see, I've marked the start and end of the text string for the joke text using single quotes. I've therefore had to escape the three single quotes (the apostrophes) within the string by putting backslashes before them. MySQL would see these backslashes and know to treat the single quotes as characters within the string, rather than end-of-string markers.

If you're especially clever, you might now be wondering how to include actual backslashes in SQL text strings. The answer is to type a double-backslash (\\), which MySQL will treat as a single backslash in the string of text.

Now that you know how to add entries to a table, let's see how we can view those entries.

Viewing Stored Data

The command that we use to view data stored in database tables, SELECT, is the most complicated command in the SQL language. The reason for this complexity is that the chief strength of a database is its flexibility in data retrieval. At this early point in our experience with databases, we need only focus on fairly simple lists of results, so let's consider the simpler forms of the SELECT command here.

This command will list everything that's stored in the joke table:

```
SELECT * FROM joke
```

Read aloud, this command says "select everything from joke." If you try this command, your results will resemble Figure 2.13.

id	joketext	jokedate
1	Why did the chicken cross the road? To get to the ...	2012-04-01

Figure 2.13. phpMyAdmin lists the full contents of the joke table

If you were doing serious work on such a database, you might be tempted to stop and read all the hilarious jokes in the database at this point. To save yourself the distraction, you might want to tell MySQL to omit the joketext column. The command for doing this is as follows:

```
SELECT id, jokedate FROM joke
```

This time, instead of telling it to "select everything," we told it precisely which columns we wanted to see. The result should look like Figure 2.14.

id	jokedate
1	2012-04-01

Figure 2.14. You can select only what you need

What if we'd like to see *some* of the joke text? As well as being able to name specific columns that we want the SELECT command to show us, we can use functions to modify each column's display. One function, called LEFT, enables us to tell MySQL to display a column's contents up to a specified number of characters. For example, let's say we wanted to see only the first 20 characters of the joketext column. Here's the command we'd use:

```
SELECT id, LEFT(joketext, 20), jokedate FROM joke
```

The results are shown in Figure 2.15.

id	LEFT(joketext, 20)	jokedate
1	Why did the chicken	2012-04-01

Figure 2.15. The LEFT function trims the text to a specified length

See how that worked? Another useful function is COUNT, which lets us count the number of results returned. If, for example, you wanted to find out how many jokes were stored in your table, you could use the following command:

```
SELECT COUNT(*) FROM joke
```

As you can see in Figure 2.16, you have just one joke in your table.

COUNT(*)
1

Figure 2.16. The COUNT function counts the rows

So far, the examples we've looked at have fetched all the entries in the table; however, you can limit your results to only those database entries that have the specific attributes you want. You set these restrictions by adding what's called a **WHERE clause** to the SELECT command. Consider this example:

```
SELECT COUNT(*) FROM joke WHERE jokedate >= "2012-01-01"
```

This query will count the number of jokes that have dates greater than or equal to January 1, 2012. In the case of dates, "greater than or equal to" means "on or after." Another variation on this theme lets you search for entries that contain a certain piece of text. Check out this query:

```
SELECT joketext FROM joke WHERE joketext LIKE "%chicken%"
```

This query displays the full text of all jokes containing the text "chicken" in their joketext column. The LIKE keyword tells MySQL that the named column must match the given pattern.[4] In this case, the pattern we've used is "%chicken%". The % signs indicate that the text "chicken" may be preceded and/or followed by any string of text.

Conditions may also be combined in the WHERE clause to further restrict results. For example, to display knock-knock jokes from April 2012 only, you could use the following query:

```
SELECT joketext FROM joke WHERE
joketext LIKE "%knock%" AND
jokedate >= "2012-04-01" AND
jokedate < "2012-05-01"
```

Enter a few more jokes into the table (for example, the "Knock-Knock" joke mentioned earlier) and experiment with SELECT queries (for ideas, see Chapter 4).

You can do a lot with the SELECT command, so I'd encourage you to become quite familiar with it. We'll look at some of its more advanced features later, when we need them.

Modifying Stored Data

Having entered data into a database table, you might find that you'd like to change it. Whether you're correcting a spelling mistake, or changing the date attached to a joke, such alterations are made using the UPDATE command. This command contains elements of the SELECT and INSERT commands, since the command both picks out entries for modification and sets column values. The general form of the UPDATE command is as follows:

```
UPDATE tableName SET
  colName = newValue, …
WHERE conditions
```

---

[4] In case you were curious, LIKE is case-insensitive, so this pattern will also match a joke that contains "Chicken," or even "FuNkYcHiCkEn."

So, for example, if we wanted to change the date on the joke we entered earlier, we'd use the following command:

```
UPDATE joke SET jokedate = "2013-04-01" WHERE id = "1"
```

Here's where that id column comes in handy, enabling you to easily single out a joke for changes. The WHERE clause used here works just as it did in the SELECT command. This next command, for example, changes the date of all entries that contain the word "chicken":

```
UPDATE joke SET jokedate = "2010-04-01"
WHERE joketext LIKE "%chicken%"
```

Deleting Stored Data

Deleting entries in SQL is dangerously easy, which you've probably noticed is a recurring theme. Here's the command syntax:

```
DELETE FROM tableName WHERE conditions
```

To delete all chicken jokes from your table, you'd use the following query:

```
DELETE FROM joke WHERE joketext LIKE "%chicken%"
```

 Careful with That Enter Key!

Believe it or not, the WHERE clause in the DELETE command is optional. Consequently, you should be very careful when typing this command! If you leave the WHERE clause out, the DELETE command will then apply to *all entries in the table*.

The following command will empty the joke table in one fell swoop:

```
DELETE FROM joke
```

Scary, huh?

Let PHP Do the Typing

There's a lot more to the MySQL database server software and SQL than the handful of basic commands I've presented here, but these commands are by far the most commonly used.

At this stage, you might be thinking that databases seem a little cumbersome. SQL can be tricky to type, as its commands tend to be long and verbose compared to other computer languages. You're probably dreading the thought of typing in a complete library of jokes in the form of INSERT commands.

Don't sweat it! As we proceed through this book, you'll be surprised at how few SQL queries you actually type by hand. Generally, you'll be writing PHP scripts that type your SQL for you. For example, if you want to be able to insert a bunch of jokes into your database, you'll typically create a PHP script for adding jokes that includes the necessary INSERT query, with a placeholder for the joke text. You can then run that PHP script whenever you have jokes to add. The PHP script prompts you to enter your joke, then issues the appropriate INSERT query to your MySQL server.

For now, however, it's important to gain a good feel for typing SQL by hand. It will give you a strong sense of the inner workings of MySQL databases, and will make you appreciate all the more the work that PHP will save you!

To date, we've only worked with a single table, but to realize the true power of a relational database, you'll need to learn how to use multiple tables together to represent potentially complex relationships between the items stored in your database. I'll cover all this and more in Chapter 5, in which I'll discuss database design principles and show off some more advanced examples.

In the meantime, we've accomplished our objective, and you can comfortably interact with MySQL using the phpMyAdmin query window. In Chapter 3, the fun continues as we delve into the PHP language, and use it to create several dynamically generated web pages.

If you like, you can practice with MySQL a little before you move on by creating a decent-sized joke table (for our purposes, five should be enough). This library of jokes will come in handy when you reach Chapter 4.

Introducing PHP

PHP is a **server-side language**. This concept may be a little difficult to grasp, especially if you've only ever designed websites using client-side languages like HTML, CSS, and JavaScript.

A server-side language is similar to JavaScript in that it allows you to embed little programs (scripts) into the HTML code of a web page. When executed, these programs give you greater control over what appears in the browser window than HTML alone can provide. The key difference between JavaScript and PHP is the stage of loading the web page at which these embedded programs are executed.

Client-side languages like JavaScript are read and executed by the web browser after downloading the web page (embedded programs and all) from the web server. In contrast, server-side languages like PHP are run by the web *server*, before sending the web page to the browser. Whereas client-side languages give you control over how a page behaves once it's displayed by the browser, server-side languages let you generate customized pages on the fly before they're even sent to the browser.

Once the web server has executed the PHP code embedded in a web page, the result takes the place of the PHP code in the page. All the browser sees is standard HTML code when it receives the page, hence the name "server-side language." Let's look back at the **today.php** example presented in Chapter 1:

chapter3/today.php

```
<!DOCTYPE html>
<html lang="en">
  <head>
    <meta charset="utf-8">
    <title>Today&rsquo;s Date</title>
  </head>
  <body>
    <p>Today&rsquo;s date (according to this web server) is
      <?php

      echo date('l, F jS Y.');

      ?>
    </p>
  </body>
</html>
```

Most of this is plain HTML except the line between <?php and ?> is PHP code. <?php marks the start of an embedded PHP script and ?> marks its end. The web server is asked to interpret everything between these two delimiters and convert it to regular HTML code before it sends the web page to the requesting browser. The browser is presented with the following:

```
<!DOCTYPE html>
<html lang="en">
  <head>
    <meta charset="utf-8">
    <title>Today&rsquo;s Date</title>
  </head>
  <body>
    <p>Today&rsquo;s date (according to this web server) is
      Sunday, April 1st 2012.
    </p>
  </body>
</html>
```

Notice that all signs of the PHP code have disappeared. In its place the output of the script has appeared, and it looks just like standard HTML. This example demonstrates several advantages of server-side scripting:

No browser compatibility issues

PHP scripts are interpreted by the web server alone, so there's no need to worry about whether the language features you're using are supported by the visitor's browser.

Access to server-side resources

In the above example, we placed the date according to the web server into the web page. If we had inserted the date using JavaScript, we'd only be able to display the date according to the computer on which the web browser was running. Granted, there are more impressive examples of the exploitation of server-side resources, such as inserting content pulled out of a MySQL database (*hint, hint …*).

Reduced load on the client

JavaScript can delay the display of a web page significantly (especially on mobile devices!), as the browser must run the script before it can display the web page. With server-side code this burden is passed to the web server, which you can make as beefy as your application requires (and your wallet can afford).

Basic Syntax and Statements

PHP syntax will be very familiar to anyone with an understanding of JavaScript, C, C++, C#, Objective-C, Java, Perl, or any other C-derived language. But if these languages are unfamiliar to you, or if you're new to programming in general, there's no need to worry about it.

A PHP script consists of a series of commands, or **statements**. Each statement is an instruction that must be followed by the web server before it can proceed to the next instruction. PHP statements, like those in the aforementioned languages, are always terminated by a semicolon (;).

This is a typical PHP statement:

```
echo 'This is a <strong>test</strong>!';
```

This is an echo statement, which is used to generate content (usually HTML code) to send to the browser. An echo statement simply takes the text it's given and inserts it into the page's HTML code at the position of the PHP script where it was contained.

In this case, we've supplied a string of text to be output: 'This is a <strong>test</strong>!'. Notice that the string of text contains HTML tags (<strong> and </strong>), which is perfectly acceptable. So, if we take this statement and put it into a complete web page, here's the resulting code:

chapter3/echo.php

```
<!DOCTYPE html>
<html lang="en">
  <head>
    <meta charset="utf-8">
    <title>Today&rsquo;s Date</title>
  </head>
  <body>
    <p><?php echo 'This is a <strong>test</strong>!'; ?></p>
  </body>
</html>
```

If you place this file on your web server and then request it using a web browser, your browser will receive this HTML code:

```
<!DOCTYPE html>
<html lang="en">
  <head>
    <meta charset="utf-8">
    <title>Today&rsquo;s Date</title>
  </head>
  <body>
    <p>This is a <strong>test</strong>!</p>
  </body>
</html>
```

The **today.php** example we looked at earlier contained a slightly more complex echo statement:

chapter3/today.php *(excerpt)*

```
echo date('l, F jS Y.');
```

Instead of giving echo a simple string of text to output, this statement invokes a **built-in function** called date and passes *it* a string of text: '1, F jS Y.'. You can think of built-in functions as tasks that PHP knows how to do without you needing to spell out the details. PHP has many built-in functions that let you do everything, from sending email to working with information stored in various types of databases.

When you invoke a function in PHP—that is, ask it to do its job—you're said to be **calling** that function. Most functions **return** a value when they're called; PHP then behaves as if you'd actually just typed that returned value instead in your code. In this case, our echo statement contains a call to the date function, which returns the current date as a string of text (the format of which is specified by the text string in the function call). The echo statement therefore outputs the value returned by the function call.

You may wonder why we need to surround the string of text with both parentheses ((…)) and single quotes ('…'). As in SQL, quotes are used in PHP to mark the beginning and end of strings of text, so it makes sense for them to be there. The parentheses serve two purposes. First, they indicate that date is a function that you want to call. Second, they mark the beginning and end of a list of **arguments** that you wish to provide, in order to tell the function what you want it to do.[1] In the case of the date function, you need to provide a string of text that describes the format in which you want the date to appear.[2] Later on, we'll look at functions that take more than one argument, and we'll separate those arguments with commas. We'll also consider functions that take no arguments at all. These functions will still need the parentheses, even though there will be nothing to type between them.

Variables, Operators, and Comments

Variables in PHP are identical to variables in most other programming languages. For the uninitiated, a **variable** can be thought of as a name given to an imaginary box into which any **literal value** may be placed. The following statement creates a variable called $testVariable (all variable names in PHP begin with a dollar sign) and assigns it a literal value of 3:

---

[1] I'm fairly sure they're called arguments because that's what often happens when you try to tell someone what to do.

[2] A full reference is available in the online documentation for the date function [http://www.php.net/date/].

```
$testVariable = 3;
```

PHP is a **loosely typed** language. This means that a single variable may contain any type of data, be it a number, a string of text, or some other kind of value, and may store different types of values over its lifetime. The following statement, if you were to type it after the aforementioned statement, assigns a new value to the existing $testVariable. Where it used to contain a number, it now contains a string of text:

```
$testVariable = 'Three';
```

The equals sign we used in the last two statements is called the **assignment operator**, as it's used to assign values to variables. Other operators may be used to perform various mathematical operations on values:

```
$testVariable = 1 + 1;  // assigns a value of 2
$testVariable = 1 - 1;  // assigns a value of 0
$testVariable = 2 * 2;  // assigns a value of 4
$testVariable = 2 / 2;  // assigns a value of 1
```

From these examples, you can probably tell that + is the **addition operator**, - is the **subtraction operator**, * is the **multiplication operator**, and / is the **division operator**. These are all called **arithmetic operators**, because they perform arithmetic on numbers.

Each arithmetic line ends with a **comment**. Comments enable you to describe what your code is doing. They insert explanatory text into your code—text that the PHP interpreter will ignore. Comments begin with // and they finish at the end of the same line. If you want a comment to span several lines, start it with /*, and end it with */. The PHP interpreter will ignore everything between these two delimiters. I'll be using comments throughout the rest of this book to help explain some of the code I present.

Returning to the operators, one that sticks strings of text together is called the **string concatenation operator**:

```
$testVariable = 'Hi ' . 'there!';  // assigns a value of 'Hi there!'
```

Variables may be used almost anywhere that you use a literal value. Consider this series of statements:

```php
$var1 = 'PHP';            // assigns a value of 'PHP' to $var1
$var2 = 5;                // assigns a value of 5 to $var2
$var3 = $var2 + 1;        // assigns a value of 6 to $var3
$var2 = $var1;            // assigns a value of 'PHP' to $var2
echo $var1;               // outputs 'PHP'
echo $var2;               // outputs 'PHP'
echo $var3;               // outputs '6'
echo $var1 . ' rules!';   // outputs 'PHP rules!'
echo "$var1 rules!";      // outputs 'PHP rules!'
echo '$var1 rules!';      // outputs '$var1 rules!'
```

Note the last two lines in particular. You can include the name of a variable right inside a text string and have the value inserted in its place if you surround the string with double quotes instead of single quotes. This process of converting variable names to their values is known as **variable interpolation**; however, as the last line demonstrates, a string surrounded with single quotes will not interpolate the variable names it contains.

Arrays

An **array** is a special kind of variable that contains multiple values. If you think of a variable as a box that contains a value, an array can be thought of as a box with compartments where each compartment is able to store an individual value.

The simplest way to create an array in PHP is to use the `array` command:

```php
$myArray = array('one', 2, '3');
```

This code creates an array called `$myArray` that contains three values: `'one'`, 2, and `'3'`. Just like an ordinary variable, each space in an array can contain any type of value. In this case, the first and third spaces contain strings, while the second contains a number.

To access a value stored in an array, you need to know its **index**. Typically, arrays use numbers as indices to point to the values they contain, starting with zero. That is, the first value (or element) of an array has index 0, the second has index 1, the third has index 2, and so on. Therefore, the index of the nth element of an array is

n–1. Once you know the index of the value you're interested in, you can retrieve that value by placing that index in square brackets after the array variable name:

```
echo $myArray[0];        // outputs 'one'
echo $myArray[1];        // outputs '2'
echo $myArray[2];        // outputs '3'
```

Each value stored in an array is called an **element** of that array. You can use an index in square brackets to add new elements, or assign new values to existing array elements:

```
$myArray[1] = 'two';     // assign a new value
$myArray[3] = 'four';    // create a new element
```

You can also add elements to the end of an array using the assignment operator as usual, but leaving empty the square brackets that follow the variable name:

```
$myArray[] = 'the fifth element';
echo $myArray[4];        // outputs 'the fifth element'
```

While numbers are the most common choice for array indices, there's another possibility. You can also use strings as indices to create what's called an **associative array**. It's called this because it *associates* values with meaningful indices. In this example, we associate a date (in the form of a string) with each of three names:

```
$birthdays['Kevin'] = '1978-04-12';
$birthdays['Stephanie'] = '1980-05-16';
$birthdays['David'] = '1983-09-09';
```

The array command also lets you create associative arrays, if you prefer that method. Here's how we'd use it to create the $birthdays array:

```
$birthdays = array('Kevin' => '1978-04-12', 'Stephanie' =>
  '1980-05-16', 'David' => '1983-09-09');
```

Now, if we want to know Kevin's birthday, we look it up using the name as the index:

```
echo 'My birthday is: ' . $birthdays['Kevin'];
```

This type of array is especially important when it comes to user interaction in PHP, as we'll see in the next section. I'll demonstrate other uses of arrays throughout this book.

User Interaction and Forms

For most database driven websites these days, you need to do more than dynamically generate pages based on database data; you must also provide some degree of interactivity, even if it's just a search box.

Veterans of JavaScript tend to think of interactivity in terms of event listeners, which let you react directly to the actions of the user; for example, the movement of the cursor over a link on the page. Server-side scripting languages such as PHP have a more limited scope when it comes to support for user interaction. As PHP code is only activated when a request is made to the server, user interaction occurs solely in a back-and-forth fashion: the user sends requests to the server, and the server replies with dynamically generated pages.[3]

The key to creating interactivity with PHP is to understand the techniques we can employ to send information about a user's interaction, along with a request for a new web page. As it turns out, PHP makes this quite easy.

Passing Variables in Links

The simplest way to send information along with a page request is to use the **URL query string**. If you've ever seen a URL containing a question mark that follows the filename, you've witnessed this technique in use. For example, if you search for "SitePoint" on Google, it will take you to a URL that looks like this one to see the search results:

```
http://www.google.com/search?hl=en&q=SitePoint
```

---

[3] To some extent, the rise of Ajax techniques in the JavaScript world in recent years has changed this. It's now possible for JavaScript code—responding to a user action such as mouse movement—to send a request to the web server, invoking a PHP script. For the purposes of this book, however, we'll stick to non-Ajax applications. If you'd like to learn all about Ajax, check out *jQuery: Novice to Ninja* [http://www.sitepoint.com/books/ajax1/] by Earle Castledine and Craig Sharkie.

See the question mark in the URL? See how the text that follows the question mark contains your search query (`SitePoint`)? That information is being sent along with the request for http://www.google.com/search.

Let's code up an easy example of our own. Create a regular HTML file called **name.html** (no **.php** filename extension is required, since there will be no PHP code in this file) and insert this link:

chapter3/links1/name.html *(excerpt)*

```
<a href="name.php?name=Kevin">Hi, I&rsquo;m Kevin!</a>
```

This is a link to a file called **name.php**, but as well as linking to the file, you're also passing a variable along with the page request. The variable is passed as part of the query string, which is the portion of the URL that follows the question mark. The variable is called `name` and its value is `Kevin`. To restate, you have created a link that loads **name.php**, and informs the PHP code contained in that file that `name` equals `Kevin`.

To really understand the effect of this link, we need to look at **name.php**. Create it as a new HTML file, but, this time, note the **.php** filename extension: this tells the web server that it can expect to interpret some PHP code in the file. In the `<body>` of this new web page, type the following:

chapter3/links1/name.php *(excerpt)*

```php
<?php
$name = $_GET['name'];
echo 'Welcome to our website, ' . $name . '!';
?>
```

Now, put these two files (**name.html** and **name.php**) onto your web server, and load the first file in your browser (the URL should be like http://localhost/name.html, or http://localhost:8888/name.html if your web server is running on a port other than 80). Click the link in that first page to request the PHP script. The resulting page should say "Welcome to our website, Kevin!", as shown in Figure 3.1.

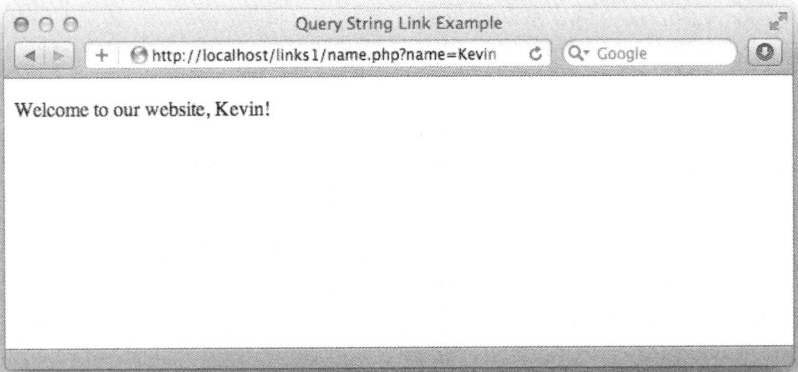

Figure 3.1. Greet users with a personalized welcome message

Let's take a closer look at the code that made this possible. This is the most important line:

chapter3/links1/name.php *(excerpt)*

```
$name = $_GET['name'];
```

If you were paying close attention in the section called "Arrays", you'll recognize what this line does. It assigns the value stored in the 'name' element of the array called $_GET to a new variable called $name. But where does the $_GET array come from?

It turns out that $_GET is one of a number of variables that PHP automatically creates when it receives a request from a browser. PHP creates $_GET as an array variable that contains any values passed in the URL query string. $_GET is an associative array, so the value of the name variable passed in the query string can be accessed as $_GET['name']. Your **name.php** script assigns this value to an ordinary PHP variable ($name), then displays it as part of a text string using an echo statement:

chapter3/links1/name.php *(excerpt)*

```
echo 'Welcome to our website, ' . $name . '!';
```

The value of the $name variable is inserted into the output string using the string concatenation operator (.) that we looked at in the section called "Variables, Operators, and Comments".

But look out: there is a **security hole** lurking in this code! Although PHP is an easy programming language to learn, it turns out it's also especially easy to introduce security issues into websites using PHP if you're unaware of what precautions to take. Before we go any further with the language, I want to make sure you're able to spot and fix this particular security issue, since it's probably the most common on the Web today.

The security issue here stems from the fact that the **name.php** script is generating a page containing content that is under the control of the user—in this case, the $name variable. Although the $name variable will normally receive its value from the URL query string in the link on the **name.html** page, a malicious user could edit the URL to send a different value for the name variable.

To see how this would work, click the link in **name.html** again. When you see the resulting page (with the welcome message containing the name "Kevin"), take a look at the URL in the address bar of your browser. It should look similar to this:

```
http://localhost/name.php?name=Kevin
```

Edit the URL to insert a <b> tag before the name, and a </b> tag following the name:

```
http://localhost/name.php?name=<b>Kevin</b>
```

Hit **Enter** to load this new URL, and note that the name in the page is now bold, as shown in Figure 3.2.[4]

---

[4] You might notice that some browsers will automatically convert the < and > characters into URL escape sequences (%3C and %3E, respectively), but either way PHP will receive the same value.

Figure 3.2. Easy exploitation will only embolden attackers!

See what's happening here? The user can type any HTML code into the URL, and your PHP script includes it in the code of the generated page without question. If the code is as innocuous as a <b> tag there's no problem, but a malicious user could include sophisticated JavaScript code that performed some low action like stealing the user's password. All the attacker would have to do is publish the modified link on some other site under the attacker's control, and then entice one of your users to click it. The attacker could even embed the link in an email and send it to your users. If one of your users clicked the link, the attacker's code would be included in your page and the trap would be sprung!

I hate to scare you with this talk of malicious hackers attacking your users by turning your own PHP code against you, particularly when you're only just learning the language. The fact is that PHP's biggest weakness as a language is how easy it is to introduce security issues like this. Some might say that much of the energy you spend learning to write PHP to a professional standard is spent on avoiding security issues. The sooner you're exposed to these issues, however, the sooner you become accustomed to avoiding them, and the less of a stumbling block they'll be for you in future.

So, how can we generate a page containing the user's name without opening it up to abuse by attackers? The solution is to treat the value supplied for the $name variable as plain text to be displayed on your page, rather than as HTML to be included in the page's code. This is a subtle distinction, so let me show you what I mean.

Open up your **name.php** file again and edit the PHP code it contains so that it looks like this:[5]

```
                                    chapter3/links2/name.php (excerpt)
<?php
$name = $_GET['name'];
echo 'Welcome to our website, ' .
    htmlspecialchars($name, ENT_QUOTES, 'UTF-8') . '!';
?>
```

There's a lot going on in this code, so let me break it down for you. The first line is the same as it was previously, assigning to $name the value of the 'name' element from the $_GET array. The echo statement that follows it is drastically different, though. Whereas previously, we simply dumped the $name variable, naked, into the echo statement, this version of the code uses the built-in PHP function htmlspecialchars to perform a critical conversion.

Remember, the security hole occurs because in **name.html**, HTML code in the $name variable is dumped directly into the code of the generated page, and can therefore do anything that HTML code can do. What htmlspecialchars does is convert "special HTML characters" like < and > into HTML character entities like < and >, which prevents them from being interpreted as HTML code by the browser. I'll demonstrate this for you in a moment.

First, let's take a closer look at this new code. The call to the htmlspecialchars function is the first example in this book of a PHP function that takes more than one argument. Here's the function call all by itself:

```
htmlspecialchars($name, ENT_QUOTES, 'UTF-8')
```

---

[5] In the code archive for this book, you'll find the updated files in the **links2** subfolder.

The first argument is the $name variable (the text to be converted). The second argument is the PHP constant[6] ENT_QUOTES, which tells htmlspecialchars to convert single and double quotes in addition to other special characters. The third parameter is the string 'UTF-8', which tells PHP what character encoding to use to interpret the text you give it.

The Perks and Pitfalls of UTF-8 with PHP

You may have discerned that all the example HTML pages in this book contain the following <meta> tag near the top:

```
<meta charset="utf-8">
```

This tag tells the browser receiving this page that the HTML code of the page is encoded as UTF-8 text.[7]

In a few pages, we'll reach the section called "Passing Variables in Forms" on building HTML forms. By encoding your pages as UTF-8, your users can submit text containing thousands of foreign characters that your site would otherwise be unable to handle.

Unfortunately, many of PHP's built-in functions, such as htmlspecialchars, assume you're using the much simpler ISO-8859-1 (or Latin-1) character encoding by default. Therefore, you need to let them know you're using UTF-8 when utilizing these functions.

If you can, you should also tell your text editor to save your HTML and PHP files as UTF-8 encoded text; this is only required if you want to type advanced characters (such as curly quotes or dashes) or foreign characters (like "é") into your HTML or PHP code. The code in this book plays it safe and uses HTML character entities (for example, ’ for a curly right quote), which will work regardless.

---

[6] A PHP constant is like a variable whose value you're unable to change. Unlike variables, constants don't start with a dollar sign. PHP comes with a number of built-in constants like ENT_QUOTES that are used to control built-in functions like htmlspecialchars.

[7] UTF-8 is one of many standards for representing text as a series of ones and zeros in computer memory, called character encodings. If you're curious to learn all about character encodings, check out *The Definitive Guide to Web Character Encoding* [http://www.sitepoint.com/article/guide-web-character-encoding/].

Open up **name.html** in your browser and click the link that now points to your updated **name.php**. Once again, you'll see the welcome message "Welcome to our website, Kevin!" As you did before, modify the URL to include <b> and </b> tags surrounding the name:

```
http://localhost/name.php?name=<b>Kevin</b>
```

This time when you hit **Enter**, instead of the name turning bold in the page, you should see the actual text that you typed as shown in Figure 3.3.

Figure 3.3. It sure is ugly, but it's secure!

If you view the source of the page, you can confirm that the htmlspecialchars function did its job and converted the < and > characters present in the provided name into the < and > HTML character entities, respectively. This prevents malicious users from injecting unwanted code into your site. If they try anything like that, the code is harmlessly displayed as plain text on the page.

We'll make extensive use of the htmlspecialchars function throughout this book to guard against this sort of security hole. No need to worry too much if you're having trouble grasping the details of how to use it just at the minute. Before long, you'll find its use becomes second nature. For now, let's look at some more advanced ways of passing values to PHP scripts when we request them.

Passing a single variable in the query string was nice, but it turns out you can pass *more* than one value if you want to! Let's look at a slightly more complex version of the previous example. Open up your **name.html** file again, and change the link to point to **name.php** with this more complicated query string:[8]

chapter3/links3/name.html *(excerpt)*

```
<a href="name.php?firstname=Kevin&amp;lastname=Yank">Hi,
   I&rsquo;m Kevin Yank!</a>
```

This time, our link passes two variables: `firstname` and `lastname`. The variables are separated in the query string by an ampersand (`&`, which must be written as `&amp;` in HTML—yes, even in a link URL!). You can pass even more variables by separating each *name=value* pair from the next with an ampersand.

As before, we can use the two variable values in our **name.php** file:

chapter3/links3/name.php *(excerpt)*

```
<?php
$firstName = $_GET['firstname'];
$lastName = $_GET['lastname'];
echo 'Welcome to our website, ' .
    htmlspecialchars($firstName, ENT_QUOTES, 'UTF-8') . ' ' .
    htmlspecialchars($lastName, ENT_QUOTES, 'UTF-8') . '!';
?>
```

The `echo` statement is becoming quite sizable now, but it should still make sense to you. Using a series of string concatenations (`.`), it outputs "Welcome to our website," followed by the value of `$firstName` (made safe for display using `htmlspecialchars`), a space, the value of `$lastName` (again, treated with `htmlspecialchars`), and finally an exclamation mark.

The result is shown in Figure 3.4.

---

[8] The updated version of the files may be found in the code archive in the **links3** subfolder.

Figure 3.4. Create an even more personalized welcome message

This is all well and good, but we still have yet to achieve our goal of true user inter-action, where the user can enter arbitrary information and have it processed by PHP. To continue with our example of a personalized welcome message, we'd like to invite the user to type their name and have it appear in the resulting page. To enable the user to type in a value, we'll need to use an HTML form.

Passing Variables in Forms

Rip the link out of **name.html** and replace it with this HTML code to create the form:[9]

chapter3/forms1/name.html *(excerpt)*

```
<form action="name.php" method="get">
  <div><label for="firstname">First name:
    <input type="text" name="firstname" id="firstname"></label>
  </div>
  <div><label for="lastname">Last name:
    <input type="text" name="lastname" id="lastname"></label>
  </div>
  <div><input type="submit" value="GO"></div>
</form>
```

The form this code produces is shown in Figure 3.5.

---

[9] The updated version of the files are in the `forms1` subfolder in the code archive.

Figure 3.5. Make your own welcome message

Function Over Form

This form is quite plain looking, I'll grant you. Some judicious application of CSS would make this and all other examples in this book more attractive. Since this is a book about PHP and MySQL, however, I'm sticking with the plain look. Check out SitePoint's *The CSS3 Anthology*[10] for advice on styling your forms with CSS.

This form has the exact same effect as the second link we looked at in the section called "Passing Variables in Links" (with `firstname=Kevin&amp;lastname=Yank` in the query string), except that you can now enter whichever names you like. When you click the submit button (labeled **GO**), the browser will load **name.php**, and add the variables and their values to the query string for you automatically. It retrieves the names of the variables from the `name` attributes of the `<input type="text">` tags, and obtains the values from the text the user types into the text fields.

Apostrophes in Form Fields

If you're burdened with the swollen ego of most programmers (myself included), you probably took this opportunity to type your *own* name into this form. Who can blame you?

---

[10] http://www.sitepoint.com/books/cssant4/

> If your last name happens to include an apostrophe (for example, Molly O'Reilly), the welcome message you saw may have included a stray backslash before the apostrophe (that is, "Welcome to our website, Molly O\'Reilly!").
>
> This bothersome backslash is due to a PHP security feature called **magic quotes**, which we'll learn about in Chapter 4. Until then, please bear with me.

The `method` attribute of the `<form>` tag is used to tell the browser how to send the variables and their values along with the request. A value of `get` (as used in **name.html** above) causes them to be passed via the query string (and appear in PHP's `$_GET` array), but there is an alternative. It can be undesirable—or even technically unfeasible—to have the values appear in the query string. What if we included a `<textarea>` tag in the form, to let the user enter a large amount of text? A URL whose query string contained several paragraphs of text would be ridiculously long, and would possibly exceed the maximum length for a URL in today's browsers. The alternative is for the browser to pass the information invisibly, behind the scenes.

Edit your **name.html** file once more. Modify the form `method` by setting it to `post`:[11]

chapter3/forms2/name.html *(excerpt)*

```
<form action="name.php" method="post">
  <div><label for="firstname">First name:
    <input type="text" name="firstname" id="firstname"></label>
  </div>
  <div><label for="lastname">Last name:
    <input type="text" name="lastname" id="lastname"></label>
  </div>
  <div><input type="submit" value="GO"></div>
</form>
```

This new value for the `method` attribute instructs the browser to send the form variables invisibly as part of the page request, rather than embedding them in the query string of the URL.

As we are no longer sending the variables as part of the query string, they stop appearing in PHP's `$_GET` array. Instead, they are placed in another array reserved especially for "posted" form variables: `$_POST`. We must therefore modify **name.php** to retrieve the values from this new array:

---

[11] The updated files are in **forms2** in the code archive.

chapter3/forms2/name.php *(excerpt)*

```php
<?php
$firstname = $_POST['firstname'];
$lastname = $_POST['lastname'];
echo 'Welcome to our website, ' .
    htmlspecialchars($firstname, ENT_QUOTES, 'UTF-8') . ' ' .
    htmlspecialchars($lastname, ENT_QUOTES, 'UTF-8') . '!';
?>
```

Figure 3.6 shows what the resulting page looks like once this new form is submitted.

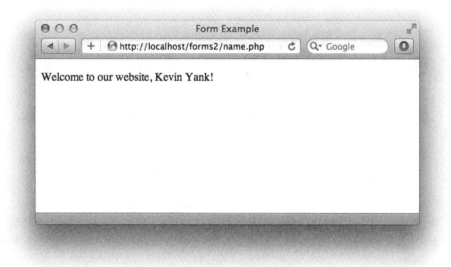

Figure 3.6. This personalized welcome is achieved without a query string

The form is functionally identical to the previous one; the only difference is that the URL of the page that's loaded when the user clicks the **GO** button will be without a query string. On the one hand, this lets you include large values (or sensitive values such as passwords) in the data that's submitted by the form without their appearing in the query string. On the other hand, if the user bookmarks the page that results from the form's submission, that bookmark will be useless, as it lacks the submitted values. This, incidentally, is the main reason why search engines use the query string to submit search terms. If you bookmark a search results page on Google, you can use that bookmark to perform the same search again later, because the search terms are contained in the URL.

Sometimes, you want access to a variable without having to worry about whether it was sent as part of the query string or a form post. In cases like these, the special $_REQUEST array comes in handy. It contains all the variables that appear in both $_GET and $_POST. With this variable, we can modify our form processing script one more time so that it can receive the first and last names of the user from either source:[12]

chapter3/forms3/name.php *(excerpt)*

```php
<?php
$firstname = $_REQUEST['firstname'];
$lastname = $_REQUEST['lastname'];
echo 'Welcome to our website, ' .
    htmlspecialchars($firstname, ENT_QUOTES, 'UTF-8') . ' ' .
    htmlspecialchars($lastname, ENT_QUOTES, 'UTF-8') . '!';
?>
```

That covers the basics of using forms to produce rudimentary user interaction with PHP. We'll look at more advanced issues and techniques in later examples.

Control Structures

All the examples of PHP code we've seen so far have been either one-statement scripts that output a string of text to the web page, or a series of statements that were to be executed one after the other in order. If you've ever written programs in other languages (JavaScript, Objective-C, Ruby, or Python), you already know that practical programs are rarely so simple.

PHP, just like any other programming language, provides facilities that enable you to affect the **flow of control**. That is, the language contains special statements that you can use to deviate from the one-after-another execution order that has dominated our examples so far. Such statements are called **control structures**. Don't understand? Don't worry! A few examples will illustrate it perfectly.

The most basic, and most often used, control structure is the **if statement**. The flow of a program through an if statement can be visualized as in Figure 3.7.

---

[12] The files in the code archive are located in the **forms3** subfolder.

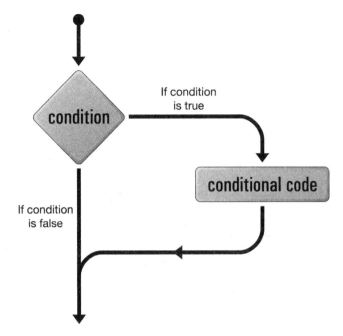

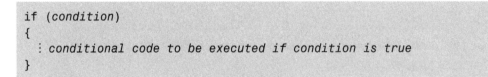

Figure 3.7. The logical flow of an if statement[13]

Here's what an if statement looks like in PHP code:

```
if (condition)
{
  ⋮ conditional code to be executed if condition is true
}
```

This control structure lets us tell PHP to execute a set of statements only if some condition is met.

If you'll indulge my vanity for a moment, here's an example that shows a twist on the personalized welcome page example we created earlier. Start by opening up **name.html** for editing again. For simplicity, let's alter the form it contains so that it submits a single name variable to **name.php**:[14]

---

[13] This diagram and several similar ones in this book were originally designed by Cameron Adams for the book, *Simply JavaScript* (Melbourne: SitePoint, 2006), which we wrote together. I have reused them here with his permission, and my thanks.

[14] I've placed the updated versions of the files in the **if** subfolder in the code archive.

chapter3/if/name.html *(excerpt)*

```
<form action="name.php" method="post">
  <div><label for="name">Name:
    <input type="text" name="name" id="name"></label>
  </div>
  <div><input type="submit" value="GO"/></div>
</form>
```

Now edit **name.php**. Replace the PHP code it contains with the following:

chapter3/if/name.php *(excerpt)*

```
$name = $_REQUEST['name'];
if ($name == 'Kevin')
{
  echo 'Welcome, oh glorious leader!';
}
```

Now, if the name variable passed to the page has a value of 'Kevin', a special message will be displayed as shown in Figure 3.8.

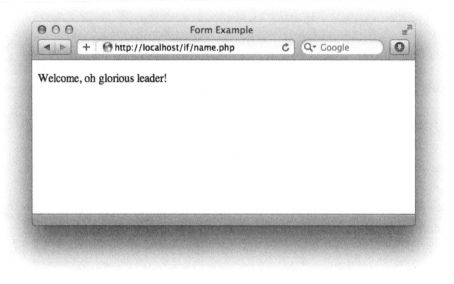

Figure 3.8. It's good to be the king

If a name other than Kevin is entered, this example becomes inhospitable: the conditional code within the `if` statement fails to execute, and the resulting page will be blank!

To offer a warmer welcome to all the plebs with names other than Kevin, we can use an **if-else statement** instead. The flow of an if-else statement is shown in Figure 3.9.

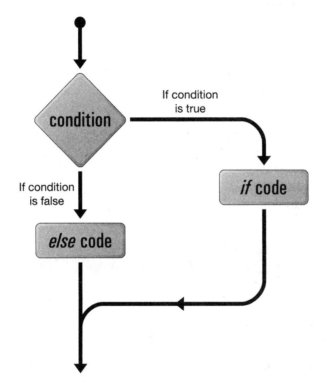

Figure 3.9. The logical flow of an `if-else` statement

The `else` portion of an `if-else` statement is tacked onto the end of the `if` portion:[15]

chapter3/ifelse1/name.php *(excerpt)*

```
$name = $_REQUEST['name'];
if ($name == 'Kevin')
{
  echo 'Welcome, oh glorious leader!';
}
```

---

[15] This updated version of the example is located in the **ifelse1** subfolder in the code archive.

```
else
{
  echo 'Welcome to our website, ' .
     htmlspecialchars($name, ENT_QUOTES, 'UTF-8') . '!';
}
```

Now if you submit a name other than Kevin, you should see the usual welcome message shown in Figure 3.10.

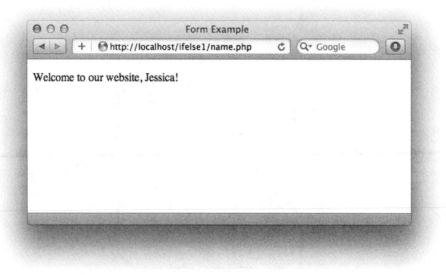

Figure 3.10. You gotta remember your peeps

The == used in the condition above is the **equal operator**, which is used to compare two values to see whether they're equal.

Double Trouble

Remember to type the double-equals (==). A common mistake among beginning PHP programmers is to type a condition like this with a single equals sign:

```
if ($name = 'Kevin')        // Missing equals sign!
```

This condition is using the assignment operator (=) that I introduced back in the section called "Variables, Operators, and Comments", instead of the equal operator

(==). Consequently, instead of comparing the value of $name to the string 'Kevin', it will actually *set* the value of $name to 'Kevin'. Oops!

To make matters worse, the if statement will use this assignment operation as a condition, which it will consider to be true, so the conditional code within the if statement will always be executed, regardless of what the original value of $name happened to be.

Conditions can be more complex than a single check for equality. Recall that our form examples would receive a first and last name. If we wanted to display a special message only for a particular person, we'd have to check the values of *both* names.

To do this, edit **name.html** back to the two-field version of the form:[16]

chapter3/ifelse2/name.html (excerpt)

```
<form action="name.php" method="post">
  <div><label for="firstname">First name:
    <input type="text" name="firstname" id="firstname"></label>
  </div>
  <div><label for="lastname">Last name:
    <input type="text" name="lastname" id="lastname"></label>
  </div>
  <div><input type="submit" value="GO"></div>
</form>
```

Next, open up **name.php** and update the PHP code to match the following (I've highlighted the changes in bold):

chapter3/ifelse2/name.php (excerpt)

```
$firstName = $_REQUEST['firstname'];
$lastName = $_REQUEST['lastname'];
if ($firstName == 'Kevin' and $lastName == 'Yank')
{
  echo 'Welcome, oh glorious leader!';
}
else
{
  echo 'Welcome to our website, ' .
```

---

[16] The updated files for this version of the example are in the **ifelse2** subfolder in the code archive.

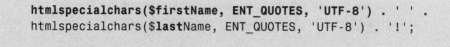

```
       htmlspecialchars($firstName, ENT_QUOTES, 'UTF-8') . ' ' .
       htmlspecialchars($lastName, ENT_QUOTES, 'UTF-8') . '!';
  }
```

This updated condition will be true if and only if $firstName has a value of 'Kevin' and $lastName has a value of 'Yank'. The **and operator** in the condition makes the whole condition true only if both comparisons are true. A similar operator is the **or operator**, which makes the whole condition true if one or both of two simple conditions are true. If you're more familiar with the JavaScript or C forms of these operators (&& and || for and and or, respectively), that's fine—they work in PHP as well.

Figure 3.11 shows that having just one of the names right in this example fails to cut the mustard.

We'll look at more complicated conditions as the need arises. For the time being, a general familiarity with if-else statements is sufficient.

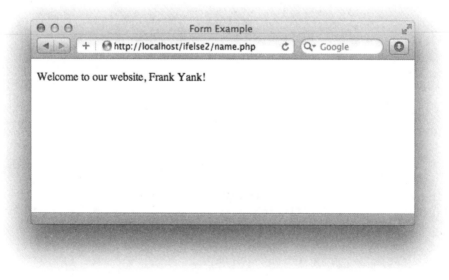

Figure 3.11. Frankly, my dear …

Another often-used PHP control structure is the **while loop**. Where the if-else statement allowed us to choose whether or not to execute a set of statements depending on some condition, the while loop allows us to use a condition to determine how many *times* we'll execute a set of statements repeatedly.

Figure 3.12 shows how a while loop operates.

Here's what a while loop looks like in code:

```
while (condition)
{
    : statement(s) to execute repeatedly as long as condition is true
}
```

The while loop works very similarly to an if statement. The difference arises when the condition is true and the statement(s) are executed. Instead of continuing the execution with the statement that follows the closing brace (}), the condition is checked again. If the condition is still true, the statement(s) are executed a second time, and a third, and will continue to be executed as long as the condition remains true. The first time the condition evaluates false (whether it's the first time it's checked, or the 101st), the execution jumps immediately to the statement that follows the while loop, after the closing brace.

Loops like these come in handy whenever you're working with long lists of items (such as jokes stored in a database … *hint, hint*), but for now I'll illustrate with a trivial example, counting to ten:

chapter3/count10.php (excerpt)

```
$count = 1;
while ($count <= 10)
{
   echo "$count ";
   ++$count;
}
```

This code may look a bit frightening, I know, but let me talk you through it line by line:

$count = 1;
    The first line creates a variable called $count and assigns it a value of 1.

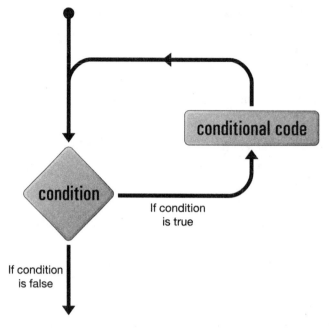

Figure 3.12. The logical flow of a `while` loop

`while ($count <= 10)`

> The second line is the start of a `while` loop, the condition being that the value of $count is less than or equal (<=) to 10.

`{`

> The opening brace marks the beginning of the block of conditional code for the `while` loop. This conditional code is often called the **body** of the loop, and is executed over and over again, as long as the condition holds true.

`echo "$count ";`

> This line simply outputs the value of $count, followed by a space. To make the code as readable as possible, I've used a double-quoted string to take advantage of variable interpolation (as explained in the section called "Variables, Operators, and Comments"), rather than use the string concatenation operator.

`++$count;`

> The fourth line adds one to the value of $count (++$count is a shortcut for $count = $count + 1—either one would work).

```
}
```
The closing brace marks the end of the while loop's body.

So here's what happens when this code is executed. The first time the condition is checked, the value of $count is 1, so the condition is definitely true. The value of $count (1) is output, and $count is given a new value of 2. The condition is still true the second time it's checked, so the value (2) is output and a new value (3) is assigned. This process continues, outputting the values 3, 4, 5, 6, 7, 8, 9, and 10. Finally, $count is given a value of 11, and the condition is found to be false, which ends the loop.

The net result of the code is shown in Figure 3.13.

Figure 3.13. PHP demonstrates kindergarten-level math skills

The condition in this example used a new operator: <= (**less than or equal**). Other numerical comparison operators of this type include >= (**greater than or equal**), < (**less than**), > (**greater than**), and != (**not equal**). That last one also works when comparing text strings, by the way.

Another type of loop that's designed specifically to handle examples like the previous one—in which we're counting through a series of values until some condition is met—is called a **for loop**. Figure 3.14 shows the flow of a for loop.

Here's what it looks like in code:

```
for (declare counter; condition; increment counter)
{
    statement(s) to execute repeatedly as long as condition is true
}
```

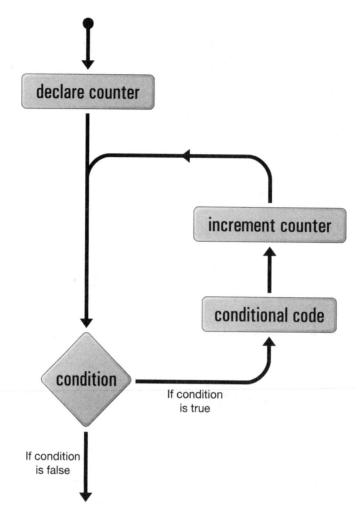

Figure 3.14. The logical flow of a for loop

The *declare counter* statement is executed once at the start of the loop; the *condition* statement is checked each time through the loop before the statements in the body are executed; the *increment counter* statement is executed each time through the loop after the statements in the body.

Here's what the "counting to 10" example looks like when implemented with a for loop:

```php
for ($count = 1; $count <= 10; ++$count)
{
  echo "$count ";
}
```

As you can see, the statements that initialize and increment the $count variable join the condition on the first line of the for loop. Although, at first glance, the code seems a little more difficult to read, putting all the code that deals with controlling the loop in the same place actually makes it easier to understand once you're used to the syntax. Many of the examples in this book will use for loops, so you'll have plenty of opportunity to practice reading them.

Hiding the Seams

You're now armed with a working knowledge of the basic syntax of the PHP programming language. You understand that you can take any HTML web page, rename it with a **.php** file name extension, and inject PHP code into it to generate page content on the fly. Not bad for a day's work!

Before we go any further, however, I want to stop and cast a critical eye over the examples we've discussed so far. Assuming your objective is to create database driven websites that hold up to professional standards, there are a few unsightly blemishes we need to clean up.

The techniques in the rest of this chapter will add a coat of professional polish that can set your work apart from the crowd of amateur PHP developers out there. I'll rely on these techniques throughout the rest of this book to ensure that, no matter how simple the example, you can feel confident in the quality of the product you're delivering.

Avoid Advertising Your Technology Choices

The examples we've seen so far have contained a mixture of plain HTML files (with names ending in **.html**) and files that contain a mixture of HTML and PHP (with names ending in **.php**). Although this distinction between file types may be useful to you, the developer, there's no reason for your users to know which site pages rely on PHP code to generate them.

Furthermore, although PHP is a very strong choice of technology to build almost any database driven website, the day may come when you want to switch from PHP to some new technology. When it does, do you really want all the URLs for dynamic pages on your site to become invalid as you change the file names to reflect your new language of choice?

These days, professional developers place a lot of importance on the URLs they put out into the world. In general, URLs should be as permanent as possible, so it makes no sense to embrittle them with little "advertisements" for the programming language you used to build each individual page.

An easy way to eliminate filename extensions in your URLs is to take advantage of directory indexes. When a URL points at a directory on your web server, instead of a particular file, the web server will look for a file named **index.html** or **index.php** inside that directory, and display that file in response to the request.

For example, take the **today.php** page that I introduced at the end of Chapter 1. Rename it from **today.php** to **index.php**. Then, instead of dropping it in the root of your web server, create a subdirectory named **today** and drop the **index.php** file in there. Now, load http://localhost/today/ in your browser (or http://localhost:8888/today/ or similar if you need to specify a port number for your server).

Figure 3.15 shows the example with its new URL. This URL omits the unnecessary **.php** extension, and is shorter and more memorable—desirable qualities when it comes to URLs today.

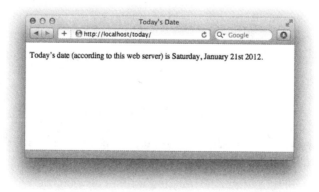

Figure 3.15. A more fashionable URL

Use PHP Templates

In the simple examples we've seen so far, inserting PHP code directly into your HTML pages has been a reasonable approach. As the amount of PHP code that goes into generating your average page grows, however, maintaining this mixture of HTML and PHP code can become unmanageable.

Particularly if you work in a team of not-so-savvy web designers, PHP-wise, having large blocks of cryptic PHP code intermingled with the HTML is a recipe for disaster. It's far too easy for designers to accidentally modify the PHP code, causing errors they'll be unable to fix.

A much more robust approach is to separate out the bulk of your PHP code so that it resides in its own file, leaving the HTML largely unpolluted by PHP code.

The key to doing this is the PHP **include statement**. With an include statement, you can insert the contents of another file into your PHP code at the point of the statement. To show you how this works, let's rebuild the "count to ten" for loop example we looked at earlier.

Start by creating a new directory called **count10**, and create a file named **index.php** in this directory. Open the file for editing and type in this code:

```
                                              chapter3/count10/index.php
<?php
$output = '';  ❶
for ($count = 1; $count <= 10; ++$count)
{
  $output .= "$count ";  ❷
}

include 'count.html.php';  ❸
```

Yes, that's the *complete* code for this file. It contains no HTML code whatsoever. The for loop should be familiar to you by now, but let me point out the interesting parts of this code:

  Instead of echoing out the numbers 1 to 10, this script will add these numbers to a variable named $output. At the start of this script, therefore, we set this variable to contain an empty string.

This line adds each number (followed by a space) to the end of the $output variable. The .= operator you see here is a shorthand way to add a value to the end of an existing string variable, by combining the assignment and string concatenation operators into one. The longhand version of this line is $output = $output . "$count ";, but the .= operator saves you some typing.

❸ This is an include statement, which instructs PHP to execute the contents of the **count.html.php** file at this location.[17]

Finally, you might have noticed that the file doesn't end with a ?> to match the opening <?php. You can put it in if you really want to, but it's unnecessary. If a PHP file ends with PHP code, there's no need to indicate where that code ends—the end of the file does it for you. The big brains of the PHP world generally prefer to leave it off the end of files like this one that contain only PHP code.

Since the final line of this file includes the **count.html.php** file, you should create this next:

```
                                              chapter3/count10/count.html.php
<!DOCTYPE html>
<html lang="en">
  <head>
    <meta charset="utf-8">
    <title>Counting to Ten</title>
  </head>
  <body>
    <p>
      <?php echo $output; ?>
    </p>
  </body>
</html>
```

---

[17] Outside of this book, you'll often see includes coded with parentheses surrounding the filename, as if include were a function like date or htmlspecialchars, which is far from the case. These parentheses, when used, only serve to complicate the filename expression, and are therefore avoided in this book. The same goes for echo, another popular one-liner.

This file is almost entirely plain HTML, except for the one line that outputs the value of the $output variable. This is the same $output variable that was created by the **index.php** file.

What we've created here is a **PHP template**: an HTML page with only very small snippets of PHP code that insert dynamically generated values into an otherwise static HTML page. Rather than embedding the complex PHP code that generates those values in the page, we put the code to generate the values in a separate PHP script—**index.php** in this case.

Using PHP templates like this enables you to hand over your templates to HTML-savvy designers without worrying about what they might do to your PHP code. It also lets you focus on your PHP code without being distracted by the surrounding HTML code.

I like to name my PHP template files so that they end with **.html.php**. As far as your web server is concerned, though, these are still **.php** files; the **.html.php** suffix serves as a useful reminder that these files contain both HTML and PHP code.

Many Templates, One Controller

What's nice about using include statements to load your PHP template files is that you can have *multiple* include statements in a single PHP script, as well as have it display different templates under various circumstances!

A PHP script that responds to a browser request by selecting one of several PHP templates to fill in and send back is commonly called a **controller**. A controller contains the logic that controls which template is sent to the browser.

Let's revisit one more example from earlier in this chapter: the welcome form that prompts a visitor for a first and last name.

We'll start with the PHP template for the form. For this, we can just reuse the **name.html** file we created earlier. Create a directory named **welcome** and save a copy of **name.html** called **form.html.php** into this directory. The only code you need to change in this file is the action attribute of the <form> tag:

```
                                          chapter3/welcome/form.html.php
<!DOCTYPE html>
<html lang="en">
  <head>
    <meta charset="utf-8">
    <title>Form Example</title>
  </head>
  <body>
    <form action="" method="post">
      <div><label for="firstname">First name:
        <input type="text" name="firstname" id="firstname"></label>
      </div>
      <div><label for="lastname">Last name:
        <input type="text" name="lastname" id="lastname"></label>
      </div>
      <div><input type="submit" value="GO"></div>
    </form>
  </body>
</html>
```

As you can see, we're leaving the action attribute blank. This tells the browser to
submit the form back to the same URL it received it from: in this case, the URL of
the controller that included this template file.

Let's take a look at the controller for this example. Create an **index.php** script in the
welcome directory alongside your form template. Type the following code into this
file:

```
                                           chapter3/welcome/index.php
<?php
if (!isset($_REQUEST['firstname'])) ❶
{
  include 'form.html.php'; ❷
}
else ❸
{
  $firstName = $_REQUEST['firstname'];
  $lastName = $_REQUEST['lastname'];
  if ($firstName == 'Kevin' and $lastName == 'Yank')
  {
    $output = 'Welcome, oh glorious leader!'; ❹
  }
```

```
  else
  {
    $output = 'Welcome to our website, ' .
        htmlspecialchars($firstName, ENT_QUOTES, 'UTF-8') . ' ' .
        htmlspecialchars($lastName, ENT_QUOTES, 'UTF-8') . '!';
  }

  include 'welcome.html.php'; ⑤
}
```

This code should look quite familiar at first glance; it's a lot like the **name.php** script we wrote earlier. Let me explain the differences:

① The controller's first task is to decide whether the current request is a submission of the form in **form.html.php** or not. You can do this by checking if the request contains a firstname variable. If it does, PHP will have stored the value in $_REQUEST['firstname'].

isset is a built-in PHP function that will tell you if a particular variable (or array element) has been assigned a value or not. If $_REQUEST['firstname'] has a value, isset($_REQUEST['firstname']) will be true. If $_REQUEST['firstname'] is unset, isset($_REQUEST['firstname']) will be false.

For the sake of readability, I like to put the code that sends the form in my controller first. We need this if statement to check if $_REQUEST['firstname'] is *not* set. To do this, we use the **not operator** (!). By putting this operator before the name of a function, you reverse the value that function returns—from true to false, or from false to true.

Thus, if the request does *not* contain a firstname variable, then !isset($_REQUEST['firstname']) will return true, and the body of the if statement will be executed.

② If the request is not a form submission, the controller includes the **form.html.php** file to display the form.

③ If the request *is* a form submission, the body of the else statement is executed instead.

This code pulls the `firstname` and `lastname` variables out of the `$_REQUEST` array, and then generates the appropriate welcome message for the name submitted.

 Instead of `echo`ing the welcome message, the controller stores the welcome message in a variable named $output.

 After generating the appropriate welcome message, the controller includes the **welcome.html.php** template, which will display that welcome message.

All that's left is to write the **welcome.html.php** template. Here it is:

chapter3/welcome/welcome.html.php

```
<!DOCTYPE html>
<html lang="en">
  <head>
    <meta charset="utf-8">
    <title>Form Example</title>
  </head>
  <body>
    <p>
      <?php echo $output; ?>
    </p>
  </body>
</html>
```

That's it! Fire up your browser and point it at http://localhost/welcome/ (or http://localhost:8888/welcome/ or similar if you need to specify a port number for your web server). You'll be prompted for your name, and when you submit the form, you'll see the appropriate welcome message. The URL should stay the same throughout this process.

One of the benefits of maintaining the same URL throughout this process of prompting the user for a name and displaying the welcome message is that the user can bookmark the page at any time during this process and gain a sensible result; whether it's the form page or the welcome message that's bookmarked, when the user returns, the form will be present once again. In the previous version of this example, where the welcome message had its own URL, returning to that URL without submitting the form would have generated a broken welcome message

("Welcome to our website, !"), or a PHP error message, depending on your server configuration.

Why so forgetful?

In Chapter 9, I'll show you how to remember the user's name between visits.

Bring on the Database

In this chapter, we've seen the PHP server-side scripting language in action as we've explored all the basic language features: statements, variables, operators, comments, and control structures. The sample applications we've seen have been reasonably simple, but we've still taken the time to ensure they have attractive URLs, and that the HTML templates for the pages they generate are uncluttered by the PHP code that controls them.

As you may have begun to suspect, the real power of PHP is in its hundreds (even thousands) of built-in functions that let you access data in a MySQL database, send email, dynamically generate images, and even create Adobe Acrobat PDF files on the fly.

In Chapter 4, we'll delve into the MySQL functions built into PHP, and see how to publish the joke database we created in Chapter 2 to the Web. This chapter will set the scene for the ultimate goal of this book: creating a complete content management system for your website in PHP and MySQL.

Publishing MySQL Data on the Web

This is it—the stuff you signed up for! In this chapter, you'll learn how to take information stored in a MySQL database and display it on a web page for all to see.

So far, you've installed and learned the basics of MySQL, a relational database engine, and PHP, a server-side scripting language. Now you're ready to learn how to use these tools together to create a true database driven website!

The Big Picture

Before we leap forward, it's worth taking a step back for a clear picture of our ultimate goal. We have two powerful tools at our disposal: the PHP scripting language and the MySQL database engine. It's important to understand how these will fit together.

The whole idea of a database driven website is to allow the content of the site to reside in a database, so that content may be pulled dynamically from the database to create web pages for viewing on a regular browser. So, at one end of the system you have a visitor to your site using a web browser to request a page. That browser expects to receive a standard HTML document in return. At the other end you have the content of your site, which sits in one or more tables in a MySQL database that only understands how to respond to SQL queries (commands).

As shown in Figure 4.1, the PHP scripting language is the go-between that speaks both languages. It processes the page request and fetches the data from the MySQL database (using SQL queries just like those you used to create a table of jokes in Chapter 2). It then spits it out dynamically as the nicely formatted HTML page that the browser expects.

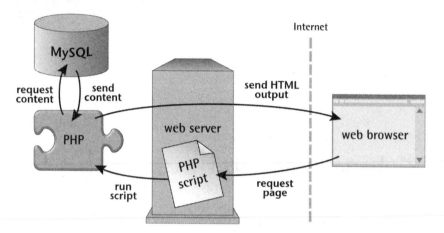

Figure 4.1. PHP retrieves MySQL data to produce web pages

Just so it's clear and fresh in your mind, this is what happens when there's a visitor to a page on your database driven website:

1. The visitor's web browser requests the web page from your web server.

2. The web server software (typically Apache) recognizes that the requested file is a PHP script, so the server fires up the PHP interpreter to execute the code contained in the file.

3. Certain PHP commands (which will be the focus of this chapter) connect to the MySQL database and request the content that belongs in the web page.

4. The MySQL database responds by sending the requested content to the PHP script.

5. The PHP script stores the content into one or more PHP variables, then uses echo statements to output the content as part of the web page.

6.   The PHP interpreter finishes up by handing a copy of the HTML it has created to the web server.

7.   The web server sends the HTML to the web browser as it would a plain HTML file, except that instead of coming directly from an HTML file, the page is the output provided by the PHP interpreter. The browser has no way of knowing this, however. From its perspective, it's requesting and receiving a web page like any other.

Creating a MySQL User Account

In order for PHP to connect to your MySQL database server, it will need to use a username and password. So far, all that your joke database contains is a number of pithy *bon mots*, but before long it may contain sensitive information like email addresses and other private details about the users of your website. For this reason, MySQL is designed to be very secure, giving you tight control over what connections it will accept and what those connections are allowed to do.

In Chapter 1, we set the password for the root user of your MySQL database server. Now, you *could* use that username and password to connect your PHP scripts to your MySQL server, but you really shouldn't. The root user is an all-powerful administration account; if the password for that account fell into the wrong hands, a malicious user could wreak serious havoc. In most cases, there will be other layers of security preventing this from happening (for example, a firewall that prevents connections to your database from outside your web host's network), but it's better to be safe than sorry.

Instead, you should create a new user account with only the specific privileges it needs to work on the `ijdb` database that your website depends upon. Let's do that now:

1.   Open up phpMyAdmin as you did in Chapter 2:

      ▧ On Windows, open the XAMPP Control Panel and click the **Admin...** button next to **MySql** (sic) to launch phpMyAdmin in your browser.

      ▧ On Mac OS X, launch MAMP and click the **Open start page** button if the start page fails to open automatically. Click the **phpMyAdmin** tab at the top of the start page to load phpMyAdmin.

2.   Click the `ijdb` database in the list on the left-hand side of the phpMyAdmin interface, as shown in Figure 4.2.

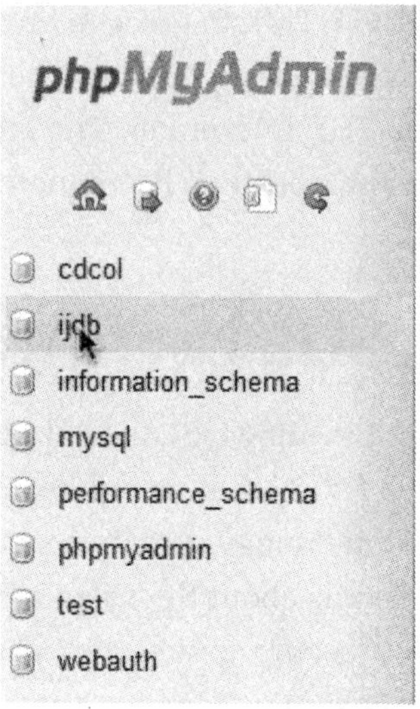

Figure 4.2. Select the `ijdb` database

3.   In the main part of the interface, above the list of tables in your database (of which there should be only one—`joke`), click the **Privileges** tab.

Figure 4.3. Click the **Privileges** tab

4.   You should now be looking at the list of **Users having access to "ijdb"** shown in Figure 4.4.

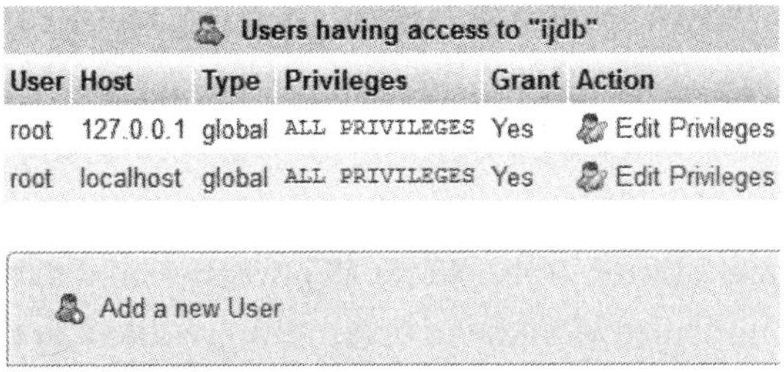

Figure 4.4. Just who has access to 'ijdb'?

As you can see, only the root user has access to the ijdb database at this point.[1]

5. Click the **Add a new User** link at the bottom of the list, and fill in the new user details as follows:

User name   (Use text field) **ijdbuser**

If you prefer, you can just name the user ijdb. It's common to give an account restricted to accessing a single database the name of that database. I've chosen to name it ijdbuser in this book to help clarify the distinction between the name of the database (ijdb) and the user account that is allowed to access it (ijdbuser).

Host   (Local) **localhost**

Because your MySQL database server is running on the same computer as your web server, we can restrict this account to only accept connections from localhost. If you needed to accept connections from other computers too, you would leave the default option of **Any host** alone.[2]

Password   (Use text field) **mypassword**

---

[1] If you're wondering why the root user is listed twice, it's because MySQL actually comes configured with *two* root user accounts: one for accepting connections from the IP address 127.0.0.1, and another for accepting connections from the hostname localhost. Normally 127.0.0.1 and localhost both refer to your own computer, but, depending on how you connect, it may see the connection coming from one or the other. We'll explore this issue in greater detail in Chapter 10.

[2] For now, I strongly recommend you stick with a **Local** account. **Any host** accounts can cause problems that we'll explore in Chapter 10.

This is just the password I'm going to use in this book. You should probably have your own unique password, and remember it for later use in the PHP scripts you're going to write.

6. Under **Database for user**, select **Grant all privileges on database "ijdb"**. This will give the account *carte blanche* to do anything it likes to the ijdb database, but only that database.

7. Under **Global privileges**, leave everything unchecked. The options here would enable the account to execute specific query types on *any* database. We want to keep this account restricted to our single database.

8. At the bottom of the form, click **Go**.

As shown in Figure 4.5, phpMyAdmin should confirm that you've added a new user, even showing you the SQL queries it sent to the database server to do it. Don't worry about learning these queries; they're documented in the MySQL manual if you ever need to look them up, but it's usually much easier just to use phpMyAdmin to manage access to your MySQL server.

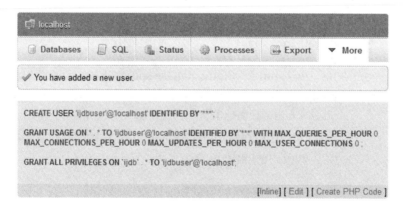

Figure 4.5. phpMyAdmin shows you what you've done

Connecting to MySQL with PHP

Before you can retrieve content from your MySQL database for inclusion in a web page, you must know how to establish a connection to MySQL from inside a PHP script. So far, you've used a PHP web application called phpMyAdmin to connect to your database. Just as the PHP scripts in phpMyAdmin can connect directly to a running MySQL server, so too can your own PHP scripts; support for connecting to databases like MySQL is provided by the PHP Data Objects (PDO) extension that is built into PHP.

Here's how you use PDO to establish a connection to a MySQL server:

```
new PDO('mysql:host=hostname;dbname=database', 'username',
  'password')
```

For now, think of new PDO as a built-in function, just like the date function we used in Chapter 3. If you're thinking "Hey, functions can't have *spaces* in their names!", you are smarter than the average bear, and I'll explain exactly what's going on here in a moment. In any case, it takes three arguments:

1. A string specifying the type of database (mysql:), the hostname of the server (host=hostname;), and the name of the database (dbname=database).

2. The MySQL username you want PHP to use.

3. The MySQL password for that username.

You may remember from Chapter 3 that PHP functions usually return a value when they're called. This new PDO "function" returns a value called a **PDO object** that identifies the connection that's been established. Since we intend to make use of the connection, we should hold onto this value by storing it in a variable. Here's how that looks, with the necessary values filled in to connect to your database:

```
                                    chapter4/connect/index.php (excerpt)

$pdo = new PDO('mysql:host=localhost;dbname=ijdb', 'ijdbuser',
  'mypassword');
```

As described, the exact values of the three function parameters may differ for your MySQL server; at the very least, you'll need to substitute in the password you set for your ijdbuser user (assuming you used a different password to mypassword, the one I chose). What's important to see here is that the value returned by new PDO is stored in a variable named $pdo.

The MySQL server is a completely separate piece of software from the web server; therefore, we must consider the possibility that the server may be unavailable or inaccessible due to a network outage, or because the username/password combination you provided is rejected by the server, or because you just forgot to start your MySQL server! In such cases, `new PDO` won't run, and throw a PHP exception.

If you're wondering what it means to "throw a PHP exception," brace yourself—you're about to discover some more features of the PHP language!

A **PHP exception** is what happens when you tell PHP to perform a task, and it's unable to do it. PHP will **try** to do what it's told but will fail, and in order to tell you about the failure, it will **throw** an exception at you. As a responsible developer, it's your job to **catch** that exception and do something about it.

Catch!

If you don't catch an exception, PHP will stop running your PHP script and display a spectacularly ugly error message. That error message will even reveal the code of your script that threw the error. In this case, that code contains your MySQL username and password, so it's especially important to avoid the error message being seen by users!

To catch an exception, you should surround the code that might throw an exception with a **try-catch statement**:

```
try
{
    ⋮ do something risky
}
catch (ExceptionType $e)
{
    ⋮ handle the exception
}
```

You can think of a `try-catch` statement like an `if-else` statement, except that the second block of code is what happens if the first block of code fails to run.

Confused yet? I know I'm throwing (no pun intended) a lot of new concepts at you, but let me put it all together and show you what we have; I think it will make more sense that way:

```
try
{
  $pdo = new PDO('mysql:host=localhost;dbname=ijdb', 'idjbuser',
    'mypassword');
}
catch (PDOException $e)
{
  $output = 'Unable to connect to the database server.';
  include 'output.html.php';
  exit();
}
```

As you can see, this code is a **try-catch** statement. In the **try** block at the top, we attempt to connect to the database using **new PDO**. If this succeeds, we store the resulting PDO object in **$pdo** so that we can work with our new database connection.

But if our database connection attempt fails, PHP will throw a **PDOException**, which is the type of exception that **new PDO** throws. Our **catch** block, therefore, says that it will catch a **PDOException** (and store it in a variable named **$e**). Inside that block, we set the variable **$output** to contain a message about what went wrong. We then include the template **output.html.php**. This is a generic template that simply outputs the value of the **$output** variable:

chapter4/connect/output.html.php

```
<!DOCTYPE html>
<html lang="en">
  <head>
    <meta charset="utf-8">
    <title>Script Output</title>
  </head>
  <body>
    <p>
      <?php echo $output; ?>
    </p>
  </body>
</html>
```

Finally, after outputting the message, the last statement in the **catch** block calls the built-in **exit** function.

exit is the first example in this book of a function that can be called with no parameters. When called this way, all this function does is cause PHP to stop executing the script at this point. This ensures that the rest of the code in our controller (which in most cases will depend on a successful database connection) will not be executed if the connection has failed.

I hope that the aforementioned code is now making some sense to you. Feel free to go back to the start of this section and read it all again if you're lost—there were a number of tricky concepts in there. Once you have a firm grip on the code, however, you'll probably realize that I've still left one mystery unexplained: PDOs. Just what exactly is new PDO, and when I said it returns a "PDO object," just what exactly is an object?

A Crash Course in Object Oriented Programming

You may have noticed the word "object" beginning to creep into my vocabulary in the previous section. PDO is the PHP Data *Objects* extension, and new PDO returns a PDO *object*. In this section, I'd like to explain what objects are all about.

Perhaps you've come across the term **object oriented programming (OOP)** in your own explorations of PHP or of programming in general. OOP is an advanced style of programming that's especially suited to building really complex programs with a lot of moving parts. Most programming languages in active use today support OOP; some of them even *require* you to work in an OOP style. PHP is a little more easygoing about it, and leaves it up to the developer to decide whether or not to write their scripts in the OOP style.

So far, we've written our PHP code in a simpler style called **procedural programming**, and we'll continue to do so for most of this book. Procedural style is well suited to the relatively simple projects we'll tackle here. Some very complex and successful PHP projects are written in the procedural programming style (you've heard of WordPress,[3] right?).

That said, the PDO extension that we'll use to connect to and work with a MySQL database is designed in the object oriented programming style. What this means is that rather than simply calling a function to connect to MySQL and then calling other functions that use that connection, we must first create a PDO *object* that will

---

[3] http://wordpress.org/

represent our database connection, and then use the features of that object to work with the database.

Creating an object is a lot like calling a function. In fact, you've already seen how to do it:

```
$pdo = new PDO('mysql:host=localhost;dbname=ijdb', 'ijdbuser',
  'mypassword');
```

The new keyword tells PHP that you want to create a new object. You then leave a space and specify a **class name**, which tells PHP what type of object you want to create. Just as PHP comes with a bunch of built-in functions that you can call, PHP comes with a library of classes that you can create objects from. new PDO, therefore, tells PHP to create a new PDO object; that is, a new object of the built-in PDO class.

In PHP an object is a value, just like a string, number, or array. You can store an object in a variable or pass it to a function as an argument—all the same stuff you can do with other PHP values. Objects, however, have some additional useful features.

First of all, an object behaves a lot like an array in that it acts as a container for other values. As we saw in Chapter 3, you can access a value inside an array by specifying its index (for example, birthdays['Kevin']). When it comes to objects, the concepts are similar but the names and code are different. Rather than accessing the value stored in an array index, we say that we're accessing a **property** of the object. Instead of using square brackets to specify the name of the property we want to access, we use **arrow notation**; for instance, $myObject->someProperty:

```
$myObject = new SomeClass();    // create an object
$myObject->someProperty = 123;  // set a property's value
echo $myObject->someProperty;   // get a property's value
```

Whereas arrays are normally used to store a list of *similar* values (such as an array of birthdays), objects are used to store a list of *related* values (for example, the properties of a database connection). Still, if that's all objects did, there wouldn't be much point to them: we might just as well use an array to store these values, right? Of course, objects do more.

In addition to storing a collection of properties and their values, objects can contain a group of PHP functions designed to bring us more useful features. A function stored in an object is called a **method** (one of the more confusing names in the programming world, if you ask me). To call a method, we again use arrow notation—$myObject->someMethod():

```
$myObject = new SomeClass();     // create an object
$myObject->someMethod();         // call a method
```

Just like standalone functions, methods can take arguments and return values.

At this stage, this is probably all sounding a little complicated and pointless, but trust me: pulling together collections of variables (properties) and functions (methods) into little bundles called objects results in much tidier and easier-to-read code for certain tasks—working with a database being just one of them. One day, you may even want to develop custom classes that you can use to create objects of your own devising.

For now, however, we'll stick with the classes that come included with PHP. Let's keep working with the PDO object we've created, and see what we can do by calling one of its methods.

Configuring the Connection

So far, I've shown you how to create a PDO object to establish a connection with your MySQL database, and how to display a meaningful error message when something goes wrong:

```php
<?php
try
{
  $pdo = new PDO('mysql:host=localhost;dbname=ijdb', 'ijdbuser',
    'mypassword');
}
catch (PDOException $e)
{
  $output = 'Unable to connect to the database server.';
  include 'output.html.php';
  exit();
}
```

Assuming the connection succeeds, though, you need to configure it before use. You can configure your connection by calling some methods of your new PDO object.

Our first task is to configure how our PDO object handles errors. You've already learned how to use a try-catch statement to handle any problems PHP might run into when connecting to your database; however, by default, PDO switches to a "silent failure" mode after establishing a successful connection,[4] which makes it more difficult for us to find out when something goes wrong and handle it gracefully. We'd like our PDO object to throw a PDOException any time it fails to do what we ask. We can configure it do to so by calling the PDO object's setAttribute method:

chapter4/connect/index.php *(excerpt)*

```
$pdo->setAttribute(PDO::ATTR_ERRMODE, PDO::ERRMODE_EXCEPTION);
```

The two values we're passing as arguments are constants, just like the ENT_QUOTES constant that you learned to pass to the htmlspecialchars function in Chapter 3. Don't be thrown by the PDO:: at the start of their names; that just indicates that these constants are part of the PDO class that we're using, rather than constants built into the PHP language itself. Essentially, what we're saying with this line is that we want to set the PDO attribute that controls the error mode (PDO::ATTR_ERRMODE) to the mode that throws exceptions (PDO::ERRMODE_EXCEPTION).[4]

Next, we need to configure the character encoding of our database connection. As I mentioned briefly in Chapter 3, you should use UTF-8 encoded text in your websites to maximize the range of characters users have at their disposal when filling in forms on your site. By default, when PHP connects to MySQL, it uses the simpler ISO-8859-1 (or Latin-1) encoding instead of UTF-8. Therefore, we now need to set our new PDO object to use the UTF-8 encoding.

If you go searching, you'll find several ways to set the character encoding of a MySQL connection, but the most reliable way is to run this SQL query: SET NAMES "utf8". The PDO object we have stored in $pdo has a method called exec that we can use to send SQL queries to the database to be executed. Here's what that looks like:

---

[4] You can read about the details of PDO's error-handling modes in the PHP Manual [http://php.net/manual/en/pdo.error-handling.php].

chapter4/connect/index.php *(excerpt)*

```php
$pdo->exec('SET NAMES "utf8"');
```

Although I fully expect the exec method to run just fine, if it *did* fail to execute the query for some reason (let's say our MySQL server fell over immediately after we connected to it), we should be prepared to catch the PDOException that it would throw. The easiest way to do so is to tuck our configuration statements into the same try block where we first create our PDO object. The complete code that we use to connect to MySQL and then configure that connection, therefore, is this:

chapter4/connect/index.php *(excerpt)*

```php
<?php
try
{
  $pdo = new PDO('mysql:host=localhost;dbname=ijdb', 'ijdbuser',
    'mypassword');
  $pdo->setAttribute(PDO::ATTR_ERRMODE, PDO::ERRMODE_EXCEPTION);
  $pdo->exec('SET NAMES "utf8"');
}
catch (PDOException $e)
{
  $output = 'Unable to connect to the database server.';
  include 'output.html.php';
  exit();
}
```

To polish off this example, let's display a status message that indicates when everything has gone right. Here's the complete code of our controller:

chapter4/connect/index.php

```php
<?php
try
{
  $pdo = new PDO('mysql:host=localhost;dbname=ijdb', 'ijdbuser',
    'mypassword');
  $pdo->setAttribute(PDO::ATTR_ERRMODE, PDO::ERRMODE_EXCEPTION);
  $pdo->exec('SET NAMES "utf8"');
}
catch (PDOException $e)
{
```

```
  $output = 'Unable to connect to the database server.';
  include 'output.html.php';
  exit();
}

$output = 'Database connection established.';
include 'output.html.php';
```

Fire up this example in your browser (if you put the **index.php** and **output.html.php** files in a directory named **connect** on your web server, the URL will be along the lines of http://localhost/connect/). If your MySQL server is up and running, and everything is working properly, you should see the message indicating success in Figure 4.6.

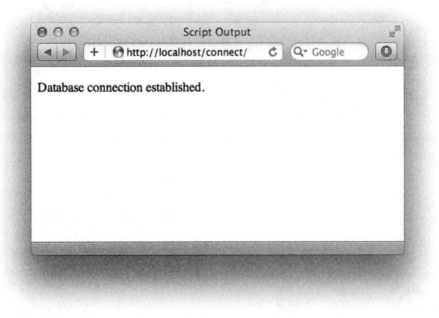

Figure 4.6. A successful connection

If PHP is unable to connect to your MySQL server, or if the username and password you provided are incorrect, you'll instead see a similar screen to that in Figure 4.7. To make sure your error-handling code is working properly, you might want to misspell your password intentionally to test it out.

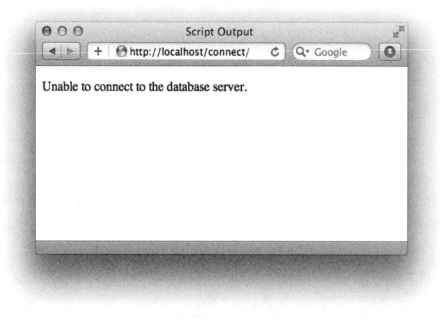

Figure 4.7. A connection failure

This error message might be fine for visitors to your site, but what if you see this message unexpectedly while working on your site? How are you supposed to fix it? Well, the first step should be to find out exactly what's gone wrong. You can do that by tweaking the `catch` block that displays the error message:

```
                                    chapter4/connect/index.php (excerpt)

catch (PDOException $e)
{
  $output = 'Unable to connect to the database server.';
  include 'output.html.php';
  exit();
}
```

In order to diagnose and fix this error, we'd like to see some more detail about the problem by including it in the error message that's displayed. We can do that using the exception we've just caught.

If you look closely at the first line of the `catch` block, you can see that in addition to telling PHP that we're willing to catch a `PDOException`, we're asking it to store the exception in a variable called $e. When an exception is caught, the value stored in that variable is actually another PHP object; in fact, *all* exceptions are represented by PHP objects! Like the PDO object we have stored in $pdo, the PDOException object has properties we can access and methods we can call.

In order to find out what caused the exception, we can ask for the error message stored in the exception:

```
catch (PDOException $e)
{
  $output = 'Unable to connect to the database server: ' .
➥ $e->getMessage();
  include 'output.html.php';
  exit();
}
```

As you can see, we're calling the getMessage method on the object stored in $e, and tacking the value it returns onto the end of our error message using the string concatenation operator (.). With that change in place, Figure 4.8 shows what the error message will look like if you have the wrong password in your PHP code.

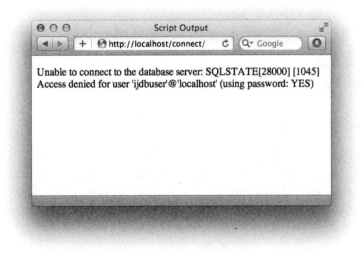

Figure 4.8. The detailed error message resulting from an incorrect password

If you instead made a typing mistake when you specified the character set for the connection to use, you'll receive the detailed error message seen in Figure 4.9.

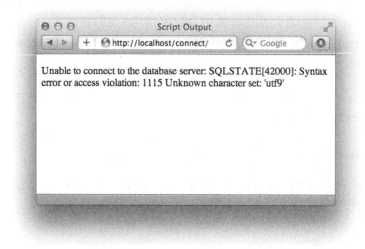

Figure 4.9. The detailed error message resulting from an invalid character set

If you're curious, try inserting some other mistakes in your database connection code (for example, a misspelled database name) and observe the detailed error messages that result. When you're done, and your database connection is working correctly, go back to the simple error message. This way your visitors won't be bombarded with technical gobbledygook if a genuine problem emerges with your database server.

With a connection established and a database selected, you're ready to begin using the data stored in the database.

PHP Automatically Disconnects

You might be wondering what happens to the connection with the MySQL server after the script has finished executing. If you really want to, you can force PHP to disconnect from the server by discarding the PDO object that represents your connection. You do this by setting the variable containing the object to null:

```
$pdo = null;  // disconnect from the database server
```

That said, PHP will automatically close any open database connections when it finishes running your script, so you can usually just let PHP clean up after you.

Sending SQL Queries with PHP

In Chapter 2, we connected to the MySQL database server using phpMyAdmin, which allowed us to type SQL queries (commands) and view the results of those queries immediately. The PDO object offers a similar mechanism—the exec method:

```
$pdo->exec(query)
```

Here, *query* is a string containing whatever SQL query you want to execute. Indeed, we used exec in the section called "Configuring the Connection" to send the SET NAMES "utf8" query that establishes the character set to be used by the database connection.

As you know, if there's a problem executing the query (for instance, if you made a typing mistake in your SQL query), this method will throw a PDOException for you to catch.

Consider the following example, which attempts to produce the joke table we created in Chapter 2:

chapter4/createtable/index.php (excerpt)

```
try
{
  $sql = 'CREATE TABLE joke (
        id INT NOT NULL AUTO_INCREMENT PRIMARY KEY,
        joketext TEXT,
        jokedate DATE NOT NULL
      ) DEFAULT CHARACTER SET utf8 ENGINE=InnoDB';
  $pdo->exec($sql);
}
catch (PDOException $e)
{
  $output = 'Error creating joke table: ' . $e->getMessage();
  include 'output.html.php';
  exit();
}

$output = 'Joke table successfully created.';
include 'output.html.php';
```

Note once again that we use the same `try-catch` statement technique to handle possible errors produced by the query. This example also uses the `getMessage` method to retrieve a detailed error message from the MySQL server. Figure 4.10 shows the error that's displayed when, for example, the `joke` table already exists.

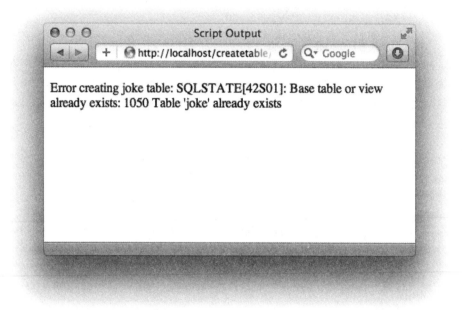

Figure 4.10. The CREATE TABLE query fails because the table already exists

For `DELETE`, `INSERT`, and `UPDATE` queries (which serve to modify stored data), the `exec` method returns the number of table rows (entries) that were affected by the query. Consider the SQL command following, which we used in Chapter 2 to set the dates of all jokes that contained the word "chicken":

```
                                    chapter4/updatechicken/index.php (excerpt)
try
{
  $sql = 'UPDATE joke SET jokedate="2012-04-01"
      WHERE joketext LIKE "%chicken%"';
  $affectedRows = $pdo->exec($sql);
}
catch (PDOException $e)
{
```

```
    $output = 'Error performing update: ' . $e->getMessage();
    include 'output.html.php';
    exit();
}
```

By storing the value returned from the `exec` method in `$affectedRows`, we can display the number of rows affected by this update:

chapter4/updatechicken/index.php *(excerpt)*

```
$output = "Updated $affectedRows rows.";
include 'output.html.php';
```

Figure 4.11 shows the output of this example, assuming there's only one "chicken" joke in your database.

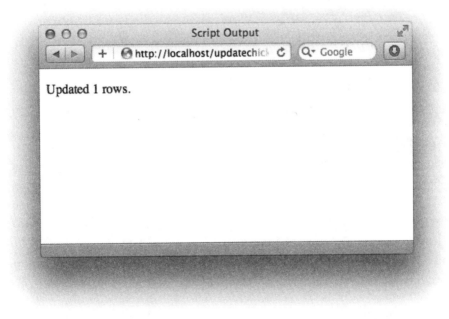

Figure 4.11. The number of database records updated is displayed

If you refresh the page to run the same query again, you should see the message change as per Figure 4.12. It indicates that no rows were updated, since the new date being applied to the jokes is the same as the existing date.

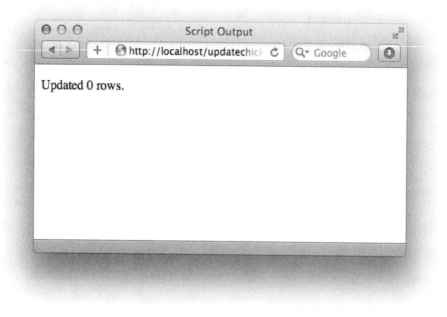

Figure 4.12. MySQL lets you know when you're wasting its time

SELECT queries are treated a little differently, as they can retrieve a lot of data and PHP provides ways to handle that information.

Handling SELECT Result Sets

For most SQL queries, the exec method works just fine. The query does something to your database, and you get the number of affected rows (if any) from the method's return value. SELECT queries, however, require something a little fancier than exec. You'll recall that SELECT queries are used to view stored data in the database. Instead of only affecting the database, SELECT queries have results—we need a method to return them.

The query method looks just like exec in that it accepts an SQL query as an argument to be sent to the database server; what it returns, however, is a PDOStatement object, which represents a **result set** containing a list of all the rows (entries) returned from the query.

chapter4/listjokes/index.php *(excerpt)*

```php
try
{
  $sql = 'SELECT joketext FROM joke';
  $result = $pdo->query($sql);
}
catch (PDOException $e)
{
  $error = 'Error fetching jokes: ' . $e->getMessage();
  include 'error.html.php';
  exit();
}
```

Just as before, errors are displayed using a very simple PHP template:

chapter4/listjokes/error.html.php

```php
<!DOCTYPE html>
<html lang="en">
  <head>
    <meta charset="utf-8">
    <title>Script Error</title>
  </head>
  <body>
    <p>
      <?php echo $error; ?>
    </p>
  </body>
</html>
```

Provided that no error was encountered in processing the query, this code will store a result set (in the form of a PDOStatement object) into the variable $result. This result set contains the text of all the jokes stored in the joke table. As there's no practical limit on the number of jokes in the database, the result set can be quite big.

I mentioned back in Chapter 3 that the while loop is a useful control structure for dealing with large amounts of data. Indeed, you could use a while loop here to process the rows in the result set one at a time:

```
while ($row = $result->fetch())
{
    ⋮ process the row
}
```

The condition for the `while` loop is probably different to the conditions you're used to, so let me explain how it works. Consider the condition as a statement all by itself:

```
$row = $result->fetch();
```

The `fetch` method of the `PDOStatement` object returns the next row in the result set as an array (we discussed arrays in Chapter 3). When there are no more rows in the result set, `fetch` returns `false` instead.[5]

Now, the above statement assigns a value to the `$row` variable, but, at the same time, the statement as a whole takes on that same value. This is what lets you use the statement as a condition in the `while` loop. Since a `while` loop will keep looping until its condition evaluates to `false`, this loop will occur as many times as there are rows in the result set, with `$row` taking on the value of the next row each time the loop executes. All that's left to figure out is how to retrieve the values out of the `$row` variable each time the loop runs.

Rows of a result set returned by `fetch` are represented as associative arrays, with the indices named after the table columns in the result set. If `$row` is a row in our result set, `$row['joketext']` is the value in the `joketext` column of that row.

Our goal in this code is to store away the text of all the jokes so that we can display them in a PHP template. The best way to do this is to store each joke as a new item in an array, `$jokes`:

chapter4/listjokes/index.php *(excerpt)*

```
while ($row = $result->fetch())
{
    $jokes[] = $row['joketext'];
}
```

---

[5] This is one case where asking a PDO object to do something it cannot do (as `fetch` cannot return the next row when there are no rows left in the result set) will *not* throw a `PDOException`. If it did, we'd be unable to use the `fetch` method in a `while` loop condition the way we do here.

With the jokes pulled out of the database, we can now pass them along to a PHP template (**jokes.html.php**) for display.

To summarize, here's the complete code of the controller for this example:

```php
<?php
try
{
  $pdo = new PDO('mysql:host=localhost;dbname=ijdb', 'ijdbuser',
    'mypassword');
  $pdo->setAttribute(PDO::ATTR_ERRMODE, PDO::ERRMODE_EXCEPTION);
  $pdo->exec('SET NAMES "utf8"');
}
catch (PDOException $e)
{
  $error = 'Unable to connect to the database server.';
  include 'error.html.php';
  exit();
}

try
{
  $sql = 'SELECT joketext FROM joke';
  $result = $pdo->query($sql);
}
catch (PDOException $e)
{
  $error = 'Error fetching jokes: ' . $e->getMessage();
  include 'error.html.php';
  exit();
}

while ($row = $result->fetch())
{
  $jokes[] = $row['joketext'];
}

include 'jokes.html.php';
```

All that's left to complete this example is to write the **jokes.html.php** template.

In this template, we need to display the contents of an array for the first time, rather than just a simple variable. The most common way to process an array in PHP is to use a loop. We've already seen `while` loops and `for` loops; the `foreach` loop is particularly helpful for processing arrays:

```
foreach (array as $item)
{
  : process each $item
}
```

Instead of a condition, the parentheses at the top of a `foreach` loop contain an array, followed by the keyword `as`, and then the name of a new variable that will be used to store each item of the array in turn. The body of the loop is then executed once for each item in the array; each time that item is stored in the specified variable so that the code can access it directly.

It's common to use a `foreach` loop in a PHP template to display in turn each item of an array. Here's how this might look for our `$jokes` array:

```
<?php
foreach ($jokes as $joke)
{
?>
  : HTML code to output each $joke
<?php
}
?>
```

With this blend of PHP code to describe the loop and HTML code to display it, the code looks rather untidy. Because of this, it's common to use an alternative way of writing the `foreach` loop when it's used in a template:

```
foreach (array as $item):
  : process each $item
endforeach;
```

Here's how this form of the code looks in a template:

```
<?php foreach ($jokes as $joke): ?>
  : HTML code to output each $joke
<?php endforeach; ?>
```

With this new tool in hand, we can write our template to display the list of jokes:

chapter4/listjokes/jokes.html.php

```php
<!DOCTYPE html>
<html lang="en">
  <head>
    <meta charset="utf-8">
    <title>List of Jokes</title>
  </head>
  <body>
    <p>Here are all the jokes in the database:</p>
    <?php foreach ($jokes as $joke): ?>
      <blockquote>
        <p><?php echo htmlspecialchars($joke, ENT_QUOTES, 'UTF-8');
            ?>
        </p>
      </blockquote>
    <?php endforeach; ?>
  </body>
</html>
```

Each joke is displayed in a paragraph (<p>) contained within a block quote (<blockquote>), since we're effectively quoting the author of each joke in this page.

Because jokes might conceivably contain characters that could be interpreted as HTML code (for example, <, >, or &), we must use htmlspecialchars to ensure that these are translated into HTML character entities (that is, <, >, and &) so that they're displayed correctly.

Figure 4.13 shows what this page looks like once you've added a couple of jokes to the database.

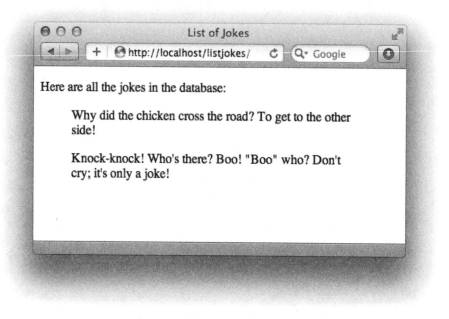

Figure 4.13. All my best material—in one place!

You Can Use `foreach` to Loop through a Result Set, Too!

Remember how we used a `while` loop in our controller to fetch the rows out of the `PDOStatement` result set one at a time?

chapter4/listjokes/index.php (excerpt)

```
while ($row = $result->fetch())
{
  $jokes[] = $row['joketext'];
}
```

It turns out `PDOStatement` objects are designed to behave just like arrays when you pass them to a `foreach` loop. You can therefore slightly simplify your database processing code using a `foreach` loop instead of a `while` loop:

```
foreach ($result as $row)
{
  $jokes[] = $row['joketext'];
}
```

I'll be using this tidier `foreach` form in the rest of this book.

Inserting Data into the Database

In this section, I'll demonstrate how to use the tools at your disposal to enable site visitors to add their own jokes to the database.

If you want to let visitors to your site enter new jokes, you'll obviously need a form. Here's a template for a form that will fit the bill:

chapter4/addjoke/form.html.php

```
<!DOCTYPE html>
<html lang="en">
  <head>
    <meta charset="utf-8">
    <title>Add Joke</title>
    <style type="text/css">
    textarea {
      display: block;
      width: 100%;
    }
    </style>
  </head>
  <body>
    <form action="?" method="post">
      <div>
        <label for="joketext">Type your joke here:</label>
        <textarea id="joketext" name="joketext" rows="3" cols="40">
        </textarea>
      </div>
      <div><input type="submit" value="Add"></div>
    </form>
  </body>
</html>
```

Once submitted, this form will request the same PHP script that generated the form—the controller script (**index.php**)—as we've seen before. You'll notice, however, that instead of leaving the `action` attribute empty (`""`), we set its value to ?. As we'll see in a moment, the URL used to display the form in this example will feature a query string, and setting the `action` to ? strips that query string off the URL when submitting the form.

Figure 4.14 shows what this form looks like in a browser.

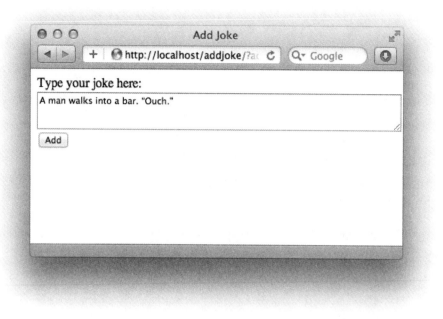

Figure 4.14. Another nugget of comic genius is added to the database

When this form is submitted, the request will include a variable, `joketext`, that contains the text of the joke as typed into the text area. This variable will then appear in the `$_POST` and `$_REQUEST` arrays created by PHP.

Let's tie this form into the preceding example, which displayed the list of jokes in the database. Add a link to the top of the list that invites the user to add a joke:

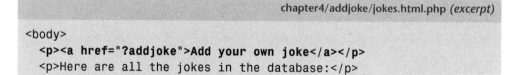

chapter4/addjoke/jokes.html.php *(excerpt)*

```
<body>
  <p><a href="?addjoke">Add your own joke</a></p>
  <p>Here are all the jokes in the database:</p>
```

Like the form, this link points back to the very same PHP script used to generate this page, but this time it adds a query string (`?addjoke`), indicating the user's intention to add a new joke. Our controller can detect this query string and use it as a signal to display the "Add Joke" form instead of the list of jokes.

Let's make the necessary changes to the controller now:

chapter4/addjoke/index.php *(excerpt)*

```
if (isset($_GET['addjoke']))
{
  include 'form.html.php';
  exit();
}
```

This opening if statement checks if the query string contains a variable named addjoke. This is how we detect that the user clicked the new link. Even though there is no value specified by the query string (?addjoke) for the addjoke variable, it does create it, which we can detect with isset($_GET['addjoke']).

When we detect this variable, we display the form by including **form.html.php**, and then exit.

Once the user fills out the form and submits it, that form submission results in another request to this controller. This we detect by checking if $_POST['joketext'] is set:

chapter4/addjoke/index.php *(excerpt)*

```
if (isset($_POST['joketext']))
{
```

To insert the submitted joke into the database, we must execute an INSERT query using the value stored in $_POST['joketext'] to fill in the joketext column of the joke table. This might lead you to write some code like this:

```
$sql = 'INSERT INTO joke SET
    joketext="' . $_POST['joketext'] . '",
    jokedate="today's date"';
$pdo->exec($sql);
```

There is a serious problem with this code, however: the contents of $_POST['joketext'] are entirely under the control of the user who submitted the form. If a malicious user were to type some nasty SQL code into the form, this script would feed it to your MySQL server without question. This type of attack is called an **SQL injection attack**, and in the early days of PHP it was one of the most common security holes that hackers found and exploited in PHP-based websites.[6]

These attacks were so feared, in fact, that the team behind PHP added some built-in protection against SQL injections to the language; it still remains enabled by default in many PHP installations today. Called **magic quotes**, this protective feature of PHP automatically analyzes all values submitted by the browser and inserts backslashes (\) in front of any "dangerous" characters like apostrophes—which can cause problems if they're included in an SQL query inadvertently.

The problem with the magic quotes feature is that it causes as many problems as it prevents. First of all, the characters that it detects and the method it uses to sanitize them (prefixing them with a backslash) are only valid in some circumstances. Depending on the character encoding of your site and the database server you're using, these measures may be completely ineffective.

Second, when a submitted value is used for some purpose *other* than creating an SQL query, those backslashes can be really bothersome. I mentioned this briefly in Chapter 3 when, in the welcome message example, the magic quotes feature would insert a spurious backslash into the user's last name if it contained an apostrophe.

In short, magic quotes was a bad idea, so much so that it's scheduled to be removed from PHP in version 6. In the meantime, however, you have to deal with the problems it creates in your code. The easiest way to do this is to detect if magic quotes is enabled on your web server and, if so, to *undo* the modifications it has made to the submitted values.[7] Thankfully, the PHP Manual[8] provides a snippet of code that will do this:

---

[6] In many programming niches, SQL injection attacks are still surprisingly effective, as developers don't expect them. Consider this remarkable attempt to cause traffic cameras to drop their databases: "SQL Injection Licence (sic) Plate Hopes to Foil Euro Traffic Cameras."
[http://www.gizmodo.com.au/2010/03/sql-injection-license-plate-hopes-to-foil-euro-traffic-cameras/]

[7] You can disable magic quotes—and save your web server a lot of work—by setting the `magic_quotes_gpc` option in your **php.ini** file to `Off`. To make sure your code still functions if this setting is changed, however, you should still deal with magic quotes in your code when it's enabled.

[8] http://www.php.net/manual/en/security.magicquotes.disabling.php

```
                                   chapter4/addjoke/index.php (excerpt)
if (get_magic_quotes_gpc())
{
  $process = array(&$_GET, &$_POST, &$_COOKIE, &$_REQUEST);
  while (list($key, $val) = each($process))
  {
    foreach ($val as $k => $v)
    {
      unset($process[$key][$k]);
      if (is_array($v))
      {
        $process[$key][stripslashes($k)] = $v;
        $process[] = &$process[$key][stripslashes($k)];
      }
      else
      {
        $process[$key][stripslashes($k)] = stripslashes($v);
      }
    }
  }
  unset($process);
}
```

Don't try to understand the inner workings of this code. To keep it short, I've used several advanced PHP features that we're yet to cover—and one or two others that are beyond the scope of this book. Just drop this code into the top of your controller—and indeed any other PHP script that will receive user input in the form of query variables or a form submission (or, as we'll learn in Chapter 9, browser cookies). And be assured that from this point forward, I'll remind you whenever this code is required by an example.[9]

With the damage done by magic quotes reversed, you're now free to use submitted values in your SQL queries the *right* way: using prepared statements.

A **prepared statement** is an SQL query that you've sent to your database server ahead of time, giving the server a chance to prepare it for execution—but not actually execute it. The SQL code in prepared statements can contain **placeholders** that you'll supply the values for later, when the query *is* to be executed. When filling

---

[9] In Chapter 6, I'll show you how to reduce the burden of repeatedly including this code snippet in your controller code.

in these placeholders, PDO is smart enough to guard against "dangerous" characters automatically.

Here's how to prepare an INSERT query and then execute it safely with $_POST['joketext'] as the text of the joke:

```
$sql = 'INSERT INTO joke SET
    joketext = :joketext,
    jokedate = "today's date"';
$s = $pdo->prepare($sql);
$s->bindValue(':joketext', $_POST['joketext']);
$s->execute();
```

Let's break this down one statement at a time. First, we write out our SQL query as a PHP string and store it in a variable ($sql) as usual. What's unusual about this INSERT query, however, is that no value is specified for the joketext column; instead, it contains a placeholder for this value (:joketext). Don't worry about the jokedate field just now—we'll circle back to it in a moment.

Next, we call the prepare method of our PDO object ($pdo), passing it our SQL query as an argument. This sends the query to the MySQL server, asking it to *prepare* to run the query. MySQL can't run it yet—there's no value for the joketext column. The prepare method returns a PDOStatement object (yes, the same kind of object that gives us the results from a SELECT query), which we store in $s.

Now that MySQL has prepared our statement for execution, we can send it the missing value(s) by calling the bindValue method of our PDOStatement object ($s). We call this method once for each value to be supplied (in this case, we only need to supply one value: the joke text), passing as arguments the placeholder that we want to fill in (':joketext') and the value we want to fill it with ($_POST['joketext']). Because MySQL knows we're sending it a discrete value, rather than SQL code that needs to be parsed, there's no risk of characters in the value being interpreted as SQL code. Using prepared statements, SQL injection vulnerabilities simply aren't possible!

Finally, we call the PDOStatement object's execute method to tell MySQL to execute the query with the value(s) we've supplied.[10]

The lingering question in this code is how to assign today's date to the jokedate field. We *could* write some fancy PHP code to generate today's date in the YYYY-MM-DD format that MySQL requires, but it turns out that MySQL itself has a function to do this: CURDATE:

```
$sql = 'INSERT INTO joke SET
    joketext = :joketext,
    jokedate = CURDATE()';
$s = $pdo->prepare($sql);
$s->bindValue(':joketext', $_POST['joketext']);
$s->execute();
```

The MySQL function CURDATE is used here to assign the current date as the value of the jokedate column. MySQL actually has dozens of these functions, but I'll introduce them only as required. Appendix C provides a reference describing all commonly used MySQL functions.

Now that we have our query, we can complete the if statement we started earlier to handle submissions of the "Add Joke" form:

chapter4/addjoke/index.php *(excerpt)*

```
if (isset($_POST['joketext']))
{
  try
  {
    $sql = 'INSERT INTO joke SET
        joketext = :joketext,
        jokedate = CURDATE()';
    $s = $pdo->prepare($sql);
    $s->bindValue(':joketext', $_POST['joketext']);
    $s->execute();
  }
  catch (PDOException $e)
  {
    $error = 'Error adding submitted joke: ' . $e->getMessage();
```

---

[10] Yes, this PDOStatement method is called execute, unlike the similar method of PDO objects, which is called exec. PHP has many strengths, but consistency isn't one of them.

```
    include 'error.html.php';
    exit();
  }
```

```
  header('Location: .');
  exit();
}
```

But wait! This `if` statement has one more trick up its sleeve. Once we've added the new joke to the database, instead of displaying the PHP template as previously, we want to redirect the user's browser back to the list of jokes. That way they are able to see the newly added joke among them. That's what the two lines highlighted in bold at the end of the `if` statement above do.

In order to achieve the desired result, your first instinct might be to allow the controller to simply fetch the list of jokes from the database after adding the new joke, and displaying the list using the **jokes.html.php** template as usual. The problem with doing this is that the list of jokes, from the browser's perspective, would be the result of having submitted the "Add Joke" form. If the user were then to refresh the page, the browser would resubmit that form, causing another copy of the new joke to be added to the database! This is rarely the desired behavior.

Instead, we want the browser to treat the updated list of jokes as a normal web page that's able to be reloaded without resubmitting the form. The way to do this is to answer the browser's form submission with an **HTTP redirect**[11]—a special response that tells the browser "the page you're looking for is over *here*."

The PHP `header` function provides the means of sending special server responses like this one, by letting you insert specific **headers** into the response sent to the browser. In order to signal a redirect, you must send a `Location` header with the URL of the page to which you wish to direct the browser:

```
header('Location: URL');
```

In this case, we want to send the browser back to the very same page: our controller. We're asking the browser to submit another request, this time without a form sub-

---

[11] HTTP stands for HyperText Transfer Protocol, and is the language that describes the request/response communications that are exchanged between the visitor's web browser and your web server.

mission attached to it, rather than sending the browser to another location. Since we want to point the browser at our controller (**index.php**) using the URL of the parent directory, we can simply tell the browser to reload the current directory, which is expressed as a period (.).

Here are the two lines that redirect the browser back to our controller after adding the new joke to the database:

chapter4/addjoke/index.php (excerpt)

```
  header('Location: .');
  exit();
}
```

> 💡 **$_SERVER['PHP_SELF'] is the URL of the Current Page**
>
> Another common means of obtaining the URL of the current page in PHP is with $_SERVER['PHP_SELF'].
>
> Like $_GET, $_POST, and $_REQUEST, $_SERVER is an array variable that's automatically created by PHP. It contains a whole bunch of information supplied by your web server. In particular, $_SERVER['PHP_SELF'] will always be set to the URL of the PHP script that your web server used to generate the current page.
>
> Unfortunately, because the web server automatically translates a request for http://localhost/addjoke/ to a request for http://localhost/addjoke/index.php, $_SERVER['PHP_SELF'] will contain the latter URL. Redirecting the browser to . lets us preserve the shorter, more memorable form of the URL.
>
> For this reason, I've avoided using $_SERVER['PHP_SELF'] in this book; however, I thought you might like to know what it does, since it's so commonly used in basic PHP examples around the Web.

The rest of the controller is responsible for displaying the list of jokes as before. Here's the complete code of the controller:

chapter4/addjoke/index.php

```php
<?php
if (get_magic_quotes_gpc())
{
  $process = array(&$_GET, &$_POST, &$_COOKIE, &$_REQUEST);
```

```php
  while (list($key, $val) = each($process))
  {
    foreach ($val as $k => $v)
    {
      unset($process[$key][$k]);
      if (is_array($v))
      {
        $process[$key][stripslashes($k)] = $v;
        $process[] = &$process[$key][stripslashes($k)];
      }
      else
      {
        $process[$key][stripslashes($k)] = stripslashes($v);
      }
    }
  }
  unset($process);
}

if (isset($_GET['addjoke']))
{
  include 'form.html.php';
  exit();
}

try
{
  $pdo = new PDO('mysql:host=localhost;dbname=ijdb', 'ijdbuser',
    'mypassword');
  $pdo->setAttribute(PDO::ATTR_ERRMODE, PDO::ERRMODE_EXCEPTION);
  $pdo->exec('SET NAMES "utf8"');
}
catch (PDOException $e)
{
  $error = 'Unable to connect to the database server.';
  include 'error.html.php';
  exit();
}

if (isset($_POST['joketext']))
{
  try
  {
    $sql = 'INSERT INTO joke SET
        joketext = :joketext,
```

```
      jokedate = CURDATE()';
    $s = $pdo->prepare($sql);
    $s->bindValue(':joketext', $_POST['joketext']);
    $s->execute();
  }
  catch (PDOException $e)
  {
    $error = 'Error adding submitted joke: ' . $e->getMessage();
    include 'error.html.php';
    exit();
  }

  header('Location: .');
  exit();
}

try
{
  $sql = 'SELECT joketext FROM joke';
  $result = $pdo->query($sql);
}
catch (PDOException $e)
{
  $error = 'Error fetching jokes: ' . $e->getMessage();
  include 'error.html.php';
  exit();
}

while ($row = $result->fetch())
{
  $jokes[] = $row['joketext'];
}

include 'jokes.html.php';
```

As you review this to ensure it all makes sense to you, note that the code that connects to the database by creating a new PDO object must come before any of the code that runs database queries. A database connection is unnecessary to display the "Add Joke" form, though, so that code can come at the very top of the controller script.

Load this up and add a new joke or two as per Figure 4.15 to the database via your browser.

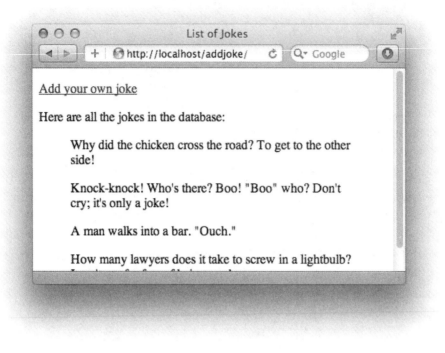

Figure 4.15. Look, Ma—no SQL!

There you have it. With a single controller (**index.php**) pulling the strings, you're able to view existing jokes in—and add new jokes to—your MySQL database.

Deleting Data from the Database

In this section, we'll make one final enhancement to our joke database site. Next to each joke on the page, we'll place a button labeled **Delete**; when clicked, it will remove that joke from the database and display the updated joke list.

If you like a challenge, you might want to take a stab at writing this feature yourself before you read on to see my solution. Although we're implementing a brand new feature, we'll mainly be using the same tools as employed in the previous examples in this chapter. Here are a few hints to start you off:

■ You'll still be able to do it all with a single controller script (**index.php**).

■ The SQL DELETE command will be required, which I introduced in Chapter 2.

To delete a particular joke in your controller, you'll need to identify it uniquely. The id column in the joke table was created to serve this purpose. You're going to have to pass the ID of the joke to be deleted with the request to delete a joke. The easiest way to do this is to use a hidden form field.

At the very least, take a few moments to think about how you'd approach this. When you're ready to see the solution, read on!

To begin with, we need to modify the SELECT query that fetches the list of jokes from the database. In addition to the joketext column, we must also fetch the id column so that we can identify each joke uniquely:

chapter4/deletejoke/index.php (excerpt)

```
try
{
  $sql = 'SELECT id, joketext FROM joke';
  $result = $pdo->query($sql);
}
catch (PDOException $e)
{
  $error = 'Error fetching jokes: ' . $e->getMessage();
  include 'error.html.php';
  exit();
}
```

We also have to modify the while loop that stores the database results into the $jokes array. Instead of simply storing the text of each joke as an item in the array, we store both the ID and text of each joke. One way to do this is to make each item in the $jokes array an array in its own right:

chapter4/deletejoke/index.php (excerpt)

```
while ($row = $result->fetch())
{
  $jokes[] = array('id' => $row['id'], 'text' => $row['joketext']);
}
```

The foreach version

If you've already switched to using a `foreach` loop to process your database result rows, that will work just fine too:

```
foreach ($result as $row)
{
  $jokes[] = array('id' => $row['id'], 'text' =>
    $row['joketext']);
}
```

Once this `while` loop runs its course, we'll have the `$jokes` array, each item of which is an associative array with two items: the ID of the joke and its text. For each joke (`$jokes[n]`), we can therefore retrieve its ID (`$jokes[n]['id']`) and its text (`$jokes[n]['text']`).

Our next step is to update the **jokes.html.php** template to retrieve each joke's text from this new array structure, as well as provide a **Delete** button for each joke:

chapter4/deletejoke/jokes.html.php (excerpt)

```
<?php foreach ($jokes as $joke): ?>
  <form action="?deletejoke" method="post"> ❶
    <blockquote>
      <p>
        <?php echo htmlspecialchars($joke['text'], ENT_QUOTES, ❷
          'UTF-8'); ?>
        <input type="hidden" name="id" value="<?php
          echo $joke['id']; ?>"> ❸
        <input type="submit" value="Delete"> ❹
      </p>
    </blockquote>
  </form> ❺
<?php endforeach; ?>
```

Here are the highlights of this updated code:

❶   Each joke will be displayed in a form, which, if submitted, will delete that joke. We signal this to our controller using the `?deletejoke` query string in the `action` attribute.

❷ Since each joke in the $jokes array is now represented by a two-item array instead of a simple string, we must update this line to retrieve the text of the joke. We do this using $joke['text'] instead of just $joke.

❸ When we submit the form to delete this joke, we send along the ID of the joke to be deleted. To do this, we need a form field containing the joke's ID, but we'd prefer to keep this field hidden from the user; that's why we use a hidden form field (`<input type="hidden">`). The name of this field is id, and its value is the ID of the joke to be deleted ($joke['id']).

Unlike the text of the joke, the ID is not a user-submitted value, so there's no need to worry about making it HTML-safe with htmlspecialchars. We can rest assured it will be a number, since it's automatically generated by MySQL for the id column when the joke is added to the database.

❹ This submit button (`<input type="submit">`) submits the form when clicked. Its value attribute gives it a label of Delete.

❺ Finally, we close the form for this joke.

 This Markup Could Be Better

If you know your HTML, you're probably thinking that those `<input>` tags belong outside of the blockquote element, since they aren't a part of the quoted text (the joke).

Strictly speaking, that's true: the form and its inputs should really be either before or after the blockquote. Unfortunately, making that tag structure display clearly requires a little Cascading Style Sheets (CSS) code that's really beyond the scope of this book.

Rather than teach you CSS layout techniques in a book about PHP and MySQL, I've decided to go with this imperfect markup. If you plan to use this code in the real world, you should invest some time into learning CSS (or at least secure the services of a CSS guru); that way you can take complete control of your HTML markup without worrying about the CSS required to make it look nice.

Figure 4.16 shows what the joke list looks like with the **Delete** buttons added.

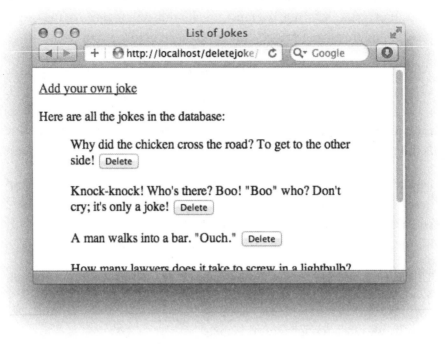

Figure 4.16. Each button can delete its respective joke

All that remains to make this new feature work is to update the controller. It can then process the form submission that results from clicking one of our new **Delete** buttons:

```
                                    chapter4/deletejoke/index.php (excerpt)
if (isset($_GET['deletejoke']))
{
  try
  {
    $sql = 'DELETE FROM joke WHERE id = :id';
    $s = $pdo->prepare($sql);
    $s->bindValue(':id', $_POST['id']);
    $s->execute();
  }
  catch (PDOException $e)
  {
    $error = 'Error deleting joke: ' . $e->getMessage();
    include 'error.html.php';
    exit();
```

```
  }

  header('Location: .');
  exit();
}
```

This chunk of code works exactly like the one we added to process the "Add Joke" code earlier in the chapter. We start by preparing a DELETE query with a placeholder for the joke ID that we wish to delete.[12] We then bind the submitted value of $_POST['id'] to that placeholder and execute the query. Once that query is achieved, we use the PHP header function to ask the browser to send a new request to view the updated list of jokes.

Why Not a Link?

If you tackled this example yourself, your first instinct might have been to provide a **Delete** hyperlink for each joke, instead of going to the trouble of writing an entire HTML form containing a **Delete** button for each joke on the page. Indeed, the code for such a link would be much simpler:

```
<?php foreach ($jokes as $joke): ?>
  <blockquote>
    <p>
      <?php echo htmlspecialchars($joke['text'], ENT_QUOTES,
          'UTF-8'); ?>
      <a href="?deletejoke&amp;id=<?php echo $joke['id'];
          ?>">Delete</a>
    </p>
  </blockquote>
<?php endforeach; ?>
```

In short, hyperlinks should never be used to perform *actions* (such as deleting a joke); they must only be used to provide a link to some related content. The same goes for forms with method="get", which should only be used to perform queries

---

[12] You might think that a prepared statement is unnecessary in this instance to protect our database from SQL injection attacks, since the joke ID is provided by a hidden form field invisible to the user. In fact, *all* form fields—even hidden ones—are ultimately under the user's control. There are widely distributed browser add-ons, for example, that will make hidden form fields visible and available for editing by the user. Remember: any value submitted by the browser is ultimately suspect when it comes to protecting your site's security.

of existing data. Actions must only ever be performed as a result of a form with `method="post"` being submitted.

The reason why is that forms with `method="post"` are treated differently by browsers and related software. If you were to submit a form with `method="post"` and then click the **Refresh** button in your browser, for example, the browser would ask if you're certain you wish to resubmit the form. Browsers have no similar protection against resubmission when it comes to links and forms with `method="get"`.

Similarly, web accelerator software (and some modern browsers) will automatically follow hyperlinks present on a page in the background, so that the target pages will be available for immediate display if the user clicks one of those links. If your site deleted a joke as a result of a hyperlink being followed, you could find your jokes being deleted automatically by your users' browsers!

Here's the complete code of the finished controller. If you have any questions, make sure to post them in the SitePoint Forums![13]

chapter4/deletejoke/index.php

```php
<?php
if (get_magic_quotes_gpc())
{
  $process = array(&$_GET, &$_POST, &$_COOKIE, &$_REQUEST);
  while (list($key, $val) = each($process))
  {
    foreach ($val as $k => $v)
    {
      unset($process[$key][$k]);
      if (is_array($v))
      {
        $process[$key][stripslashes($k)] = $v;
        $process[] = &$process[$key][stripslashes($k)];
      }
      else
      {
        $process[$key][stripslashes($k)] = stripslashes($v);
      }
    }
  }
```

---

[13] http://www.sitepoint.com/forums/

```php
    unset($process);
}

if (isset($_GET['addjoke']))
{
  include 'form.html.php';
  exit();
}

try
{
  $pdo = new PDO('mysql:host=localhost;dbname=ijdb', 'ijdbuser',
    'mypassword');
  $pdo->setAttribute(PDO::ATTR_ERRMODE, PDO::ERRMODE_EXCEPTION);
  $pdo->exec('SET NAMES "utf8"');
}
catch (PDOException $e)
{
  $error = 'Unable to connect to the database server.';
  include 'error.html.php';
  exit();
}

if (isset($_POST['joketext']))
{
  try
  {
    $sql = 'INSERT INTO joke SET
        joketext = :joketext,
        jokedate = CURDATE()';
    $s = $pdo->prepare($sql);
    $s->bindValue(':joketext', $_POST['joketext']);
    $s->execute();
  }
  catch (PDOException $e)
  {
    $error = 'Error adding submitted joke: ' . $e->getMessage();
    include 'error.html.php';
    exit();
  }

  header('Location: .');
  exit();
}
```

```php
if (isset($_GET['deletejoke']))
{
  try
  {
    $sql = 'DELETE FROM joke WHERE id = :id';
    $s = $pdo->prepare($sql);
    $s->bindValue(':id', $_POST['id']);
    $s->execute();
  }
  catch (PDOException $e)
  {
    $error = 'Error deleting joke: ' . $e->getMessage();
    include 'error.html.php';
    exit();
  }

  header('Location: .');
  exit();
}

try
{
  $sql = 'SELECT id, joketext FROM joke';
  $result = $pdo->query($sql);
}
catch (PDOException $e)
{
  $error = 'Error fetching jokes: ' . $e->getMessage();
  include 'error.html.php';
  exit();
}

while ($row = $result->fetch())
{
  $jokes[] = array('id' => $row['id'], 'text' => $row['joketext']);
}

include 'jokes.html.php';
```

Mission Accomplished

In this chapter, you learned all about PHP Data Objects (PDO), a collection of built-in PHP classes (PDO, PDOException, and PDOStatement) that allow you to interface with a MySQL database server by creating objects and then calling the methods they provide. While you were at it, you also picked up the basics of object oriented programming (OOP), no mean feat for a PHP beginner!

Using PDO objects, you built your first database driven website, which published the `ijdb` database online and allowed visitors to add and delete jokes.

In a way, you could say this chapter achieved the stated mission of this book: to teach you how to build a database driven website. Of course, the example in this chapter contained only the bare essentials. In the rest of the book, I'll show you how to flesh out the skeleton you learned to build in this chapter.

In Chapter 5, we return to the SQL Query window in phpMyAdmin. We'll learn how to use relational database principles and advanced SQL queries to represent more complex types of information, and give our visitors credit for the jokes they add!

Relational Database Design

Since Chapter 2, we've worked with a very simple database of jokes, composed of a single table named, appropriately enough, joke. While this database has served us well as an introduction to MySQL databases, there's more to relational database design than can be understood from this simple example. In this chapter, we'll expand on this database and learn a few new features of MySQL, in an effort to realize and appreciate the real power that relational databases have to offer.

Be forewarned that I will cover several topics only in an informal, nonrigorous sort of way. As any computer science major will tell you, database design is a serious area of research, with tested and mathematically provable principles that, while useful, are beyond the scope of this text.

For more complete coverage of database design concepts and SQL in general, pick up a copy of *Simply SQL*.[1] If you're *really* into learning the hard principles behind relational databases, *Database in Depth*[2] (Sebastopol: O'Reilly, 2005) is a worthwhile read.

---

[1] http://www.sitepoint.com/books/sql1/
[2] http://oreilly.com/catalog/9780596100124/

Giving Credit Where Credit Is Due

To start off, let's recall the structure of our `joke` table. It contains three columns: `id`, `joketext`, and `jokedate`. Together, these columns allow us to identify jokes (`id`), and keep track of their text (`joketext`) and the date they were entered (`jokedate`). For your reference, here's the SQL code that creates this table and inserts a couple of entries:[3]

```
chapter5/sql/jokes1.sql

# Code to create a simple joke table

CREATE TABLE joke (
  id INT NOT NULL AUTO_INCREMENT PRIMARY KEY,
  joketext TEXT,
  jokedate DATE NOT NULL
) DEFAULT CHARACTER SET utf8 ENGINE=InnoDB;


# Adding jokes to the table

INSERT INTO joke SET
joketext = 'Why did the chicken cross the road? To get to the other
➥ side!',
jokedate = '2009-04-01';

INSERT INTO joke
(joketext, jokedate) VALUES (
'Knock-knock! Who\'s there? Boo! "Boo" who? Don\'t cry; it\'s only a
➥ joke!',
"2009-04-01"
);
```

Now, let's say we wanted to track another piece of information about our jokes: the names of the people who submitted them. It would be natural to add a new column to our `joke` table for this. The SQL `ALTER TABLE` command (which we've yet to see) lets us do exactly that.

---

[3] If you ever need to re-create your database from scratch, you can use phpMyAdmin to drop all the tables and then go to the **Import** tab of the now-empty `ijdb` database and feed it this SQL file. phpMyAdmin will run all the commands it contains, thereby restoring the database. In this way, you can use the **.sql** files in the code archive for this book as database snapshots to load up whenever you need them.

Open up phpMyAdmin as you did in Chapter 2, select your database (`ijdb` if you used the name I suggested), and type this command:

```
ALTER TABLE joke ADD COLUMN authorname VARCHAR(255)
```

This code adds a column called `authorname` to your table. The type declared is a **variable-length character string** of up to 255 characters, VARCHAR(255)—plenty of space for even very esoteric names. Let's also add a column for the authors' email addresses:

```
ALTER TABLE joke ADD COLUMN authoremail VARCHAR(255)
```

For more information about the `ALTER TABLE` command, see Appendix B. Just to make sure the two columns were added properly, we'll ask MySQL to describe the table to us:[4]

```
DESCRIBE joke
```

This should give you a table of results like the one in Figure 5.1.

Field	Type	Null	Key	Default	Extra
id	int(11)	NO	PRI	NULL	auto_increment
joketext	text	YES		NULL	
jokedate	date	NO		NULL	
authorname	varchar(255)	YES		NULL	
authoremail	varchar(255)	YES		NULL	

Figure 5.1. Our `joke` table now contains five columns

Looks good, right? Obviously, to accommodate this expanded table structure, we'd need to make changes to the HTML and PHP form code we wrote in Chapter 4 that allowed us to add new jokes to the database. Using `UPDATE` queries, we could now add author details to all the jokes in the table. But before we spend too much time on such changes, we should stop and consider whether this new table design was the right choice here. In this case, it turns out it wasn't.

---

[4] Instead of typing the `DESCRIBE` query yourself, you could just select the `joke` table in phpMyAdmin and click the **Structure** tab. At this point in your database administration career, though, it's advisable to take every opportunity you can to become familiar with SQL queries like `DESCRIBE`.

Rule of Thumb: Keep Entities Separate

As your knowledge of database driven websites continues to grow, you may decide that a personal joke list is too limited. In fact, you might receive more submitted jokes than you have original jokes of your own. Let's say you decide to launch a website where people from all over the world can share jokes with each other. Adding the author's name and email address to each joke certainly makes a lot of sense, but the method we used above leads to potential problems:

- What if a frequent contributor to your site named Joan Smith changed her email address? She might begin to submit new jokes using the new address, but her old address would still be attached to the jokes she'd submitted in the past. Looking at your database, you might simply think there were two people named Joan Smith who had submitted jokes. She might inform you of the change of address, and you may try to update all the old jokes with the new address, but if you missed just one joke, your database would still contain incorrect information. Database design experts refer to this sort of problem as an **update anomaly**.

- It would be natural for you to rely on your database to provide a list of all the people who've ever submitted jokes to your site. In fact, you could easily obtain a mailing list using the following query:

```
SELECT DISTINCT authorname, authoremail
FROM joke
```

The word DISTINCT in the above query stops MySQL from outputting duplicate result rows. For example, if Joan Smith submits 20 jokes to your site, using the DISTINCT option would cause her name to only appear once in the list instead of 20 times.

Then, if for some reason, you decided to remove all the jokes that a particular author had submitted to your site, you'd remove any record of this person from the database in the process, and you'd no longer be able to email him or her with information about your site! Database design experts call this a **delete anomaly**. As your mailing list might be a major source of income for your site, it's unwise to go throwing away an author's email address just because you disliked the jokes that person submitted.

You have no guarantee that Joan Smith will enter her name the same way each time; consider the variations: Joan Smith, J. Smith, Smith, Joan—you catch my drift. This makes keeping track of a particular author exceedingly difficult, especially if Joan Smith also has several email addresses she likes to use.

These problems—and more—can be dealt with very easily using established database design principles. Instead of storing the information for the authors in the joke table, let's create an entirely new table for our list of authors. Just as we have an id column in our joke table to identify each joke with a unique number, we'll use an identically named column in our new table to identify our authors. We can then use those author IDs in our joke table to associate authors with their jokes. The complete database layout is shown in Figure 5.2.

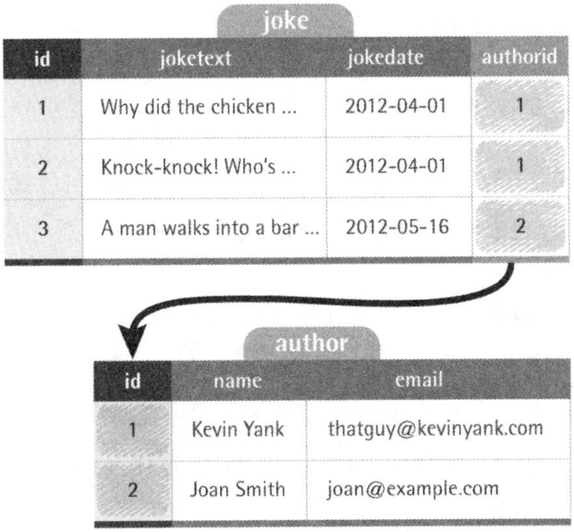

Figure 5.2. The authorid field associates each row in joke with a row in author

These tables show that there are three jokes and two authors. The authorid column of the joke table establishes a **relationship** between the two tables, indicating that Kevin Yank submitted jokes 1 and 2 and Joan Smith submitted joke 3. Notice that since each author now only appears once in the database, and independently of the jokes submitted, we've avoided all the potential problems just outlined.

What's really important to note about this database design is that we're storing information about two types of *things* (jokes and authors), so it's most appropriate to have two tables. This is a rule of thumb that you should always keep in mind when designing a database: *each type of entity (or "thing") about which you want to be able to store information should be given its own table.*

To set up the aforementioned database from scratch is fairly simple (involving just two CREATE TABLE queries), but since we'd like to make these changes in a nondestructive manner (that is, without losing any of our precious knock-knock jokes), we will use the ALTER TABLE command again. First, we remove the author-related columns in the joke table:

```
ALTER TABLE joke DROP COLUMN authorname
```

```
ALTER TABLE joke DROP COLUMN authoremail
```

Now, we create our new table:

```
CREATE TABLE author (
  id INT NOT NULL AUTO_INCREMENT PRIMARY KEY,
  name VARCHAR(255),
  email VARCHAR(255)
) DEFAULT CHARACTER SET utf8 ENGINE=InnoDB
```

Finally, we add the authorid column to our joke table:

```
ALTER TABLE joke ADD COLUMN authorid INT
```

If you prefer, here are the CREATE TABLE commands that will create the two tables from scratch:

chapter5/sql/2tables.sql (excerpt)

```
# Code to create a simple joke table that stores an author ID

CREATE TABLE joke (
  id INT NOT NULL AUTO_INCREMENT PRIMARY KEY,
  joketext TEXT,
  jokedate DATE NOT NULL,
  authorid INT
) DEFAULT CHARACTER SET utf8 ENGINE=InnoDB;

# Code to create a simple author table
```

```
CREATE TABLE author (
  id INT NOT NULL AUTO_INCREMENT PRIMARY KEY,
  name VARCHAR(255),
  email VARCHAR(255)
) DEFAULT CHARACTER SET utf8 ENGINE=InnoDB;
```

All that's left to do is add some authors to the new table, and assign authors to all the existing jokes in the database by filling in the authorid column.[5] Go ahead and do this now if you like—it should give you some practice with INSERT and UPDATE queries. If you're rebuilding the database from scratch, however, here's a series of INSERT queries that will do the trick:

chapter5/sql/2tables.sql *(excerpt)*

```
# Adding authors to the database
# We specify the IDs so they are known when we add the jokes below.

INSERT INTO author SET
  id = 1,
  name = 'Kevin Yank',
  email = 'thatguy@kevinyank.com';

INSERT INTO author (id, name, email)
VALUES (2, 'Joan Smith', 'joan@example.com');

# Adding jokes to the database

INSERT INTO joke SET
  joketext = 'Why did the chicken cross the road? To get to the
➥ other side!',
  jokedate = '2012-04-01',
  authorid = 1;

INSERT INTO joke (joketext, jokedate, authorid)
VALUES (
  'Knock-knock! Who\'s there? Boo! "Boo" who? Don\'t cry; it\'s only
➥ a joke!',
  '2012-04-01',
  1
);
```

---

[5] For now, you'll have to do this manually. But rest assured, in Chapter 7 we'll see how PHP can insert entries with the correct IDs automatically, reflecting the relationships between them.

```
INSERT INTO joke (joketext, jokedate, authorid)
VALUES (
  'A man walks into a bar. "Ouch."',
  '2012-04-01',
  2
);
```

SELECT with Multiple Tables

With your data now separated into two tables, it may seem that you're complicating the process of data retrieval. Consider, for example, our original goal: to display a list of jokes with the name and email address of the author next to each joke. In the single-table solution, you could gain all the information needed to produce such a list using a single SELECT query in your PHP code:

```
try
{
  $sql = 'SELECT joketext, authorname, authoremail FROM joke';
  $result = $pdo->query($sql);
}
catch (PDOException $e)
{
  $error = 'Error fetching jokes ' . $e->getMessage();
  include 'error.html.php';
  exit();
}

foreach ($result as $row)
{
  $jokes[] = array(
    'id' => $row['id'],
    'text' => $row['joketext'],
    'name' => $row['authorname'],
    'email' => $row['authoremail']
  );
}
```

With our new database layout, this would, at first, no longer seem possible. As the author details of each joke are no longer stored in the joke table, you might think that you'd have to fetch those details separately for each joke you wanted to display. The code required would involve a call to the PDO query method for each and every joke to be displayed. This would be messy and slow. As your database of jokes increased in size, the overhead of all those queries would drag down your site's performance in a big way.

Taking all this into account, it would seem that the "old way" was the better solution, despite its weaknesses. Fortunately, relational databases like MySQL are designed to make it easy to work with data stored in multiple tables! Using a new form of the SELECT statement, called a **join**, you can have the best of both worlds. Joins allow you to treat related data in multiple tables as if they were stored in a single table. Here's what the syntax of a simple join looks like:

```
SELECT columns
FROM table1 INNER JOIN table2
  ON condition(s) for data to be related
```

In your case, the columns we're interested in are id and joketext in the joke table, and name and email in the author table. The condition for an entry in the joke table to be related to an entry in the author table is that the value of the authorid column in the joke table is equal to the value of the id column in the author table.

Let's look at an example of a join. The first two queries show you what's contained in the two tables—they're unnecessary to perform the join. The third query is where the action's at:

```
SELECT id, LEFT(joketext, 20), authorid FROM joke
```

The results of this query are shown in Figure 5.3.

id	LEFT(joketext, 20)	authorid
1	Why did the chicken	1
2	Knock-knock! Who's t	1
3	A man walks into a b	2

Figure 5.3. A peek at the contents of the joke table

```
SELECT * FROM author
```

The results of this query are shown in Figure 5.4.

id	name	email
1	Kevin Yank	thatguy@kevinyank.com
2	Joan Smith	joan@example.com

Figure 5.4. A peek at the contents of the `author` table

```
SELECT joke.id, LEFT(joketext, 20), name, email
FROM joke INNER JOIN author
  ON authorid = author.id
```

Finally, Figure 5.5 shows the results of this query.

id	LEFT(joketext, 20)	name	email
1	Why did the chicken	Kevin Yank	thatguy@kevinyank.com
2	Knock-knock! Who's t	Kevin Yank	thatguy@kevinyank.com
3	A man walks into a b	Joan Smith	joan@example.com

Figure 5.5. The results of your first join

See? The results of the third `SELECT`—a join—group the values stored in the two tables into a single table of results, with related data correctly appearing together. Even though the data is stored in two tables, you can still access all the information you need to produce the joke list on your web page with a single database query. Note in the query that, since there are columns named `id` in both tables, you must specify the name of the table when you refer to either `id` column. The `joke` table's id is referred to as `joke.id`, while the `author` table's `id` column is `author.id`. If the table name is unspecified, MySQL won't know which `id` you're referring to, and will produce the error shown in Figure 5.6:

```
SELECT id, LEFT(joketext, 20), name, email
FROM joke INNER JOIN author
  ON authorid = id
```

#1052 - Column 'id' in field list is ambiguous

Figure 5.6. MySQL has a low tolerance for ambiguity

Now that you know how to access the data stored in your two tables efficiently, you can rewrite the code for your joke list to take advantage of joins:

```php
try
{
  $sql = 'SELECT joke.id, joketext, name, email
      FROM joke INNER JOIN author
        ON authorid = author.id';
  $result = $pdo->query($sql);
}
catch (PDOException $e)
{
  $error = 'Error fetching jokes: ' . $e->getMessage();
  include 'error.html.php';
  exit();
}

foreach ($result as $row)
{
  $jokes[] = array(
    'id' => $row['id'],
    'text' => $row['joketext'],
    'name' => $row['name'],
    'email' => $row['email']
  );
}

include 'jokes.html.php';
```

You can then update your template to display the author information for each joke:

```php
<?php foreach ($jokes as $joke): ?>
  <form action="?deletejoke" method="post">
    <blockquote>
      <p>
        <?php echo htmlspecialchars($joke['text'], ENT_QUOTES,
 'UTF-8'); ?>
        <input type="hidden" name="id" value="<?php echo
 $joke['id']; ?>">
        <input type="submit" value="Delete">
        (by <a href="mailto:<?php
```

```
        echo htmlspecialchars($joke['email'], ENT_QUOTES,
            'UTF-8'); ?>"><?php
        echo htmlspecialchars($joke['name'], ENT_QUOTES,
            'UTF-8'); ?></a>)
    </p>
  </blockquote>
  </form>
<?php endforeach; ?>
```

The resulting display is shown in Figure 5.7.

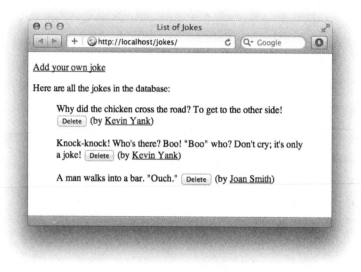

Figure 5.7. I wrote all the best ones myself

The more you work with databases, the more you'll come to realize the power of combining data from separate tables into a single table of results. Consider, for example, the following query, which displays a list of all jokes written by Joan Smith:

```
SELECT joketext
FROM joke INNER JOIN author
  ON authorid = author.id
WHERE name = "Joan Smith"
```

The results that are output from this query, shown in Figure 5.8, come only from the joke table, but the query uses a join to let it search for jokes based on a value stored in the author table. There will be plenty more examples of clever queries like this throughout the book, but this example alone illustrates that the practical applications of joins are many and varied, and, in almost all cases, can save you a lot of work!

joketext

A man walks into a bar. "Ouch."

Figure 5.8. Joan's joke

Simple Relationships

The type of database layout for a given situation is usually dictated by the form of relationship that exists between the data that it needs to store. In this section, I'll examine the typical relationship types, and explain how best to represent them in a relational database.

In the case of a simple **one-to-one relationship**, a single table is all you'll need. An example of a one-to-one relationship is the email address of each author in our joke database. Since there will be one email address for each author, and one author for each email address, there's no reason to split the addresses into a separate table.[6]

A **many-to-one relationship** is a little more complicated, but you've already seen one of these as well. Each joke in our database is associated with just one author, but many jokes may have been written by that one author. This joke–author relationship is many-to-one. I've already covered the problems that result from storing the information associated with a joke's author in the same table as the joke itself. In brief, it can result in many copies of the same data, which are difficult to keep synchronized and waste space. If we split the data into two tables and use an ID column to link them together (making joins possible as shown before), all these problems disappear.

A **one-to-many relationship** is simply a many-to-one relationship seen from the opposite direction. As the joke–author relationship is many-to-one, the author–joke relationship is one-to-many (there is one author for, potentially, many jokes). This is easy to see in theory, but when you're coming at a problem from the opposite

---

[6] There are exceptions to this rule. For example, if a single table grows very large with lots of columns, some of which are rarely used in SELECT queries, it can make sense to split those columns out into their own table. This can improve the performance of queries on the now-smaller table.

direction, it's less obvious. In the case of jokes and authors, we started with a library of jokes (the many) and then wanted to assign an author to each of them (the one). Let's now look at a hypothetical design problem where we start with the one and want to add the many.

Say we wanted to allow each of the authors in our database (the one) to have multiple email addresses (the many). When an inexperienced person in database design approaches a one-to-many relationship like this one, often the first thought is to try to store multiple values in a single database field, as shown in Figure 5.9.

author		
id	name	email
1	Kevin Yank	thatguy@kevinyank.com, kyank@example.com
2	Joan Smith	joan@example.com, jsmith@example.com

Figure 5.9. Never overload a table field to store multiple values as is done here

This would work, but to retrieve a single email address from the database, we'd need to break up the string by searching for commas (or whatever special character you chose to use as a separator); it's a not-so-simple, potentially time-consuming operation. Try to imagine the PHP code necessary to remove one particular email address from a specific author! In addition, you'd need to allow for much longer values in the email column, which could result in wasted disk space because the majority of authors would have just one email address.

Now take a step back, and realize that this one-to-many relationship is just the same as the many-to-one relationship we faced between jokes and authors. The solution, therefore, is also the same: split the new entities (in this case, email addresses) into their own table. The resulting database structure is shown in Figure 5.10.

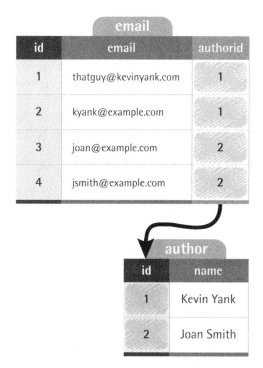

Figure 5.10. The authorid field associates each row of email with one row of author

Using a join with this structure, we can easily list the email addresses associated with a particular author:

```
SELECT email
FROM author INNER JOIN email
  ON authorid = author.id
WHERE name = "Kevin Yank"
```

Many-to-many Relationships

Okay, you now have a steadily growing database of jokes published on your website. It's growing so quickly, in fact, that the number of jokes has become unmanageable! Your site visitors are faced with a mammoth page that contains hundreds of jokes without any structure whatsoever. We need to make a change.

You decide to place your jokes into the following categories: Knock-knock jokes, "Crossing the road" jokes, Lawyer jokes, Light bulb jokes, and Political jokes. Remembering our rule of thumb from earlier, you identify joke categories as a new entity, and create a table for them:

```
CREATE TABLE category (
  id INT NOT NULL AUTO_INCREMENT PRIMARY KEY,
  name VARCHAR(255)
) DEFAULT CHARACTER SET utf8 ENGINE=InnoDB
```

Now you come to the daunting task of assigning categories to your jokes. It occurs to you that a "political" joke might also be a "crossing the road" joke, and a "knock-knock" joke might also be a "lawyer" joke. A single joke might belong to many categories, and each category will contain many jokes. This is a **many-to-many** relationship.

Once again, many inexperienced developers begin to think of ways to store several values in a single column, because the obvious solution is to add a `category` column to the `joke` table and use it to list the IDs of those categories to which each joke belongs. A second rule of thumb would be useful here: *if you need to store multiple values in a single field, your design is probably flawed.*

The correct way to represent a many-to-many relationship is by using a **lookup table**. This is a table that contains no actual data, but lists pairs of entries that are related. Figure 5.11 shows what the database design would look like for our joke categories.

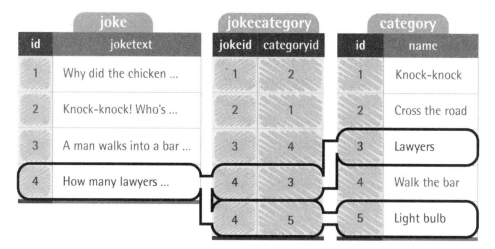

Figure 5.11. The `jokecategory` table associates pairs of rows from the `joke` and `category` tables

The jokecategory table associates joke IDs (jokeid) with category IDs (categoryid). In this example, we can see that the joke that starts with "How many lawyers …" belongs to both the Lawyers and Light bulb categories.

A lookup table is created in much the same way as is any other table. The difference lies in the choice of the primary key. Every table we've created so far has had a column named id that was designated to be the PRIMARY KEY when the table was created. Designating a column as a primary key tells MySQL to forbid two entries in that column from having the same value. It also speeds up join operations based on that column.

In the case of a lookup table, there is no single column that we want to force to have unique values. Each joke ID may appear more than once, as a joke may belong to more than one category, and each category ID may appear more than once, as a category may contain many jokes. What we want to prevent is the same *pair* of values appearing in the table twice. And, since the sole purpose of this table is to facilitate joins, the speed benefits offered by a primary key would come in very handy. For this reason, we usually create lookup tables with a multicolumn primary key as follows:

```
CREATE TABLE jokecategory (
  jokeid INT NOT NULL,
  categoryid INT NOT NULL,
  PRIMARY KEY (jokeid, categoryid)
) DEFAULT CHARACTER SET utf8 ENGINE=InnoDB
```

This creates a table in which the jokeid and categoryid columns together form the primary key. This enforces the uniqueness that's appropriate to a lookup table, preventing a particular joke from being assigned to a specific category more than once, and speeds up joins that make use of this table.[7]

Now that your lookup table is in place and contains category assignments, you can use joins to create several interesting and practical queries. This query lists all jokes in the Knock-knock category:

---

[7] If you like, you can use the CREATE TABLE and INSERT commands in Example 7.1 to create the jokecategory table from scratch (and others, including the jokes within the tables) to follow along.

```
SELECT joketext
FROM joke INNER JOIN jokecategory
  ON joke.id = jokeid
INNER JOIN category
  ON categoryid = category.id
WHERE name = "Knock-knock"
```

As you can see, this query uses *two* joins. First, it takes the `joke` table and joins it to the `jokecategory` table; then it takes that joined data and joins it to the `category` table. As your database structure becomes more complex, multijoin queries like this one become common.

The following query lists the categories that contain jokes beginning with "How many lawyers …":

```
SELECT name
FROM joke INNER JOIN jokecategory
  ON joke.id = jokeid
INNER JOIN category
  ON categoryid = category.id
WHERE joketext LIKE "How many lawyers%"
```

And this query—which also makes use of our `author` table to join together the contents of *four tables*—lists the names of all authors who have written knock-knock jokes:

```
SELECT author.name
FROM joke INNER JOIN author
  ON authorid = author.id
INNER JOIN jokecategory
  ON joke.id = jokeid
INNER JOIN category
  ON categoryid = category.id
WHERE category.name = "Knock-knock"
```

One for Many, and Many for One

In this chapter, I explained the fundamentals of good database design, and we learned how MySQL and, for that matter, all relational database management systems provide support for the representation of different types of relationships between entities. From your initial understanding of one-to-one relationships, you should now have expanded your knowledge to include many-to-one, one-to-many, and many-to-many relationships.

In the process, you learned a few new features of common SQL commands. In particular, you learned how to use a `SELECT` query to join data spread across multiple tables into a single set of results.

With the increased expressiveness that multiple database tables bring, you're now equipped to extend the simple "joke list" site you assembled in Chapter 4 to include authors and categories, and that's exactly what Chapter 7 will be all about. Before you tackle this project, however, you should take some time to add to your PHP skills. Just as you spent this chapter learning some of the finer points of MySQL database design, Chapter 6 will teach you some of the subtleties of PHP programming—which will make the job of building a more complete joke database site much more fun.

Structured PHP Programming

Before we plow headlong into the next enhancements of our joke database, let's spend a little time honing your "PHP-fu." Specifically, I want to show you a few techniques to better **structure your code**.

Structured coding techniques are useful in all but the simplest of PHP projects. Already in Chapter 3, you've learned how to split up your PHP code into multiple files: a controller and a set of associated templates. This lets you keep the server-side logic of your site separate from the HTML code used to display the dynamic content generated by that logic. In order to do this, you learned how to use the PHP `include` command.

The PHP language offers many such facilities to help you add structure to your code. The most powerful of these is undoubtedly its support for object oriented programming (OOP), which we touched on briefly in Chapter 4. But there's no need to learn all the complexities of OOP to build complex (and well-structured) applications with PHP;[1] thankfully, there are also opportunities for structuring your code through the more basic features of PHP.

---

[1] Indeed, possibly the most-used PHP application today, WordPress, is not written in the OOP style.

In this chapter, I'll explore some *simple* ways to keep your code manageable and maintainable without requiring you to become a total programming wizard (though you might still like to become one later on!).

Include Files

Even very simple PHP-based websites often need the same piece of code in several places. You already learned to use the PHP `include` command to load a PHP template from inside your controller; it turns out you can use the same feature to save yourself from having to write the same code again and again.

Include files (also known as just **includes**) contain snippets of PHP code that you can then load into your other PHP scripts instead of having to retype them.

Including HTML Content

The concept of include files came long before PHP. If you're an old codger like me (which, in the Web world, means you're over 25), you may have experimented with **Server-side Includes** (SSIs). A feature of just about every web server out there, SSIs let you put commonly used snippets of HTML (and JavaScript, and CSS) into include files that you can then use in multiple pages.

In PHP, include files most commonly contain either pure PHP code or, in the case of PHP templates, a mixture of HTML and PHP code. But you don't *have* to put PHP code in your include files. If you like, an include file can contain strictly static HTML. This is most useful for sharing common design elements across your site, such as a copyright notice to appear at the bottom of every page:

chapter6/static-footer/footer.inc.html.php

```
<div id="footer">
  The contents of this web page are copyright &copy; 1998&ndash;2012
  Example Pty. Ltd. All Rights Reserved.
</div>
```

This file is a **template fragment**—an include file to be used by PHP templates. To distinguish this type of file from others in your project, I recommend giving it a name ending with **.inc.html.php**.

You can then use this fragment in any of your PHP templates:

chapter6/static-footer/samplepage.html.php

```
<!DOCTYPE html>
<html lang="en">
  <head>
    <meta charset="utf-8">
    <title>A Sample Page</title>
  </head>
  <body>
    <p id="main">
      This page uses a static include to display a standard
      copyright notice below.
    </p>
    <?php include 'footer.inc.html.php'; ?>
  </body>
</html>
```

Finally, here's the controller that loads this template:

chapter6/static-footer/index.php

```
<?php
include 'samplepage.html.php';
?>
```

Figure 6.1 shows what the page looks like in the browser.

Figure 6.1. A static include displays the site's copyright notice

Now all you need to do to update your copyright notice is to edit **footer.inc.html.php**. No more time-consuming, error-prone find-and-replace operations!

Of course, if you *really* want to make your life easier, you can just let PHP do the work for you:

chapter6/dynamic-footer/footer.inc.html.php

```
<p id="footer">
  The contents of this web page are copyright &copy;
  1998&ndash;<?php echo date('Y'); ?> Example Pty. Ltd.
  All Rights Reserved.
</p>
```

Including PHP Code

On database driven websites, almost every controller script must establish a database connection as its first order of business. As we've already seen, the code for doing this is fairly substantial:

```
try
{
  $pdo = new PDO('mysql:host=localhost;dbname=ijdb', 'ijdbuser',
    'mypassword');
  $pdo->setAttribute(PDO::ATTR_ERRMODE, PDO::ERRMODE_EXCEPTION);
  $pdo->exec('SET NAMES "utf8"');
}
catch (PDOException $e)
{
  $error = 'Unable to connect to the database server.';
  include 'error.html.php';
  exit();
}
```

At some 12 lines long, it's only a slightly cumbersome chunk of code, but having to type it at the top of every controller script can quickly become annoying. Many new PHP developers will often omit essential error checking to save typing (for example, by leaving out the `try-catch` statement in this code), which can result in a lot of lost time looking for the cause when an error *does* occur. Others will make heavy use of the clipboard to copy pieces of code like this from existing scripts for use in new ones. Some even use features of their text editor software to store useful pieces of code as snippets for frequent use.

But what happens when the database password or some other detail of the code changes? Suddenly you're on a treasure hunt to find every occurrence of the code in your site to make the necessary change—a task that can be especially frustrating if you've used several variations of the code that you need to track down and update.

Figure 6.2 illustrates how include files can help in this situation. Instead of repeating the code fragment in every file that needs it, write it just once in a separate file—known as the include file. That file can then be included in any other PHP files that need to use it.

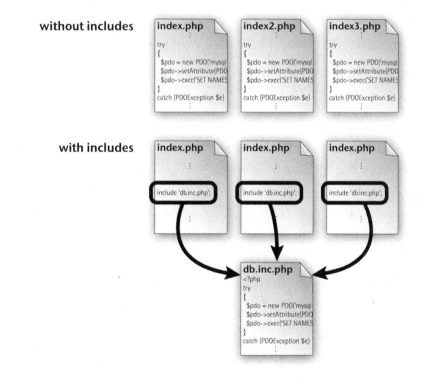

Figure 6.2. Include files allow several scripts to share common code

Let's apply this technique to create the database connection in our joke list example to see how it works in detail. First, create a file called **db.inc.php**[2] and place the database connection code inside it:

```php
<?php
try
{
  $pdo = new PDO('mysql:host=localhost;dbname=ijdb', 'ijdbuser',
    'mypassword');
  $pdo->setAttribute(PDO::ATTR_ERRMODE, PDO::ERRMODE_EXCEPTION);
  $pdo->exec('SET NAMES "utf8"');
}
catch (PDOException $e)
{
  $error = 'Unable to connect to the database server.';
  include 'error.html.php';
  exit();
}
```

As you can see, include files are just like normal PHP files, but typically they contain snippets of code that are only useful within the context of a larger script. Now you can put this **db.inc.php** file to use in your controller:

```php
<?php
if (get_magic_quotes_gpc())
{
  $process = array(&$_GET, &$_POST, &$_COOKIE, &$_REQUEST);
  while (list($key, $val) = each($process))
  {
    foreach ($val as $k => $v)
    {
```

---

[2] The current convention of naming include files with a **.inc.php** extension allows you to easily identify them among ordinary PHP scripts, while at the same time ensuring that they're identified and processed as PHP scripts by the web server and the development tools you use. In practice, though, you can name include files however you like. Previously, it was common to simply give include files an **.inc** extension, but unless the web server was specifically configured to process such files as PHP scripts or protect them from being downloaded, there was a security risk: users who guessed the names of your include files could download them as plain text and gain access to sensitive information (such as database passwords) that appeared in the source code.

```php
      unset($process[$key][$k]);
      if (is_array($v))
      {
        $process[$key][stripslashes($k)] = $v;
        $process[] = &$process[$key][stripslashes($k)];
      }
      else
      {
        $process[$key][stripslashes($k)] = stripslashes($v);
      }
    }
  }
  unset($process);
}

if (isset($_GET['addjoke']))
{
  include 'form.html.php';
  exit();
}

if (isset($_POST['joketext']))
{
  include 'db.inc.php';

  try
  {
    $sql = 'INSERT INTO joke SET
        joketext = :joketext,
        jokedate = CURDATE()';
    $s = $pdo->prepare($sql);
    $s->bindValue(':joketext', $_POST['joketext']);
    $s->execute();
  }
  catch (PDOException $e)
  {
    $error = 'Error adding submitted joke: ' . $e->getMessage();
    include 'error.html.php';
    exit();
  }

  header('Location: .');
  exit();
}
```

```php
if (isset($_GET['deletejoke']))
{
  include 'db.inc.php';

  try
  {
    $sql = 'DELETE FROM joke WHERE id = :id';
    $s = $pdo->prepare($sql);
    $s->bindValue(':id', $_POST['id']);
    $s->execute();
  }
  catch (PDOException $e)
  {
    $error = 'Error deleting joke: ' . $e->getMessage();
    include 'error.html.php';
    exit();
  }

  header('Location: .');
  exit();
}

include 'db.inc.php';

try
{
  $sql = 'SELECT joke.id, joketext, name, email
      FROM joke INNER JOIN author
        ON authorid = author.id';
  $result = $pdo->query($sql);
}
catch (PDOException $e)
{
  $error = 'Error fetching jokes: ' . $e->getMessage();
  include 'error.html.php';
  exit();
}

foreach ($result as $row)
{
  $jokes[] = array(
    'id' => $row['id'],
    'text' => $row['joketext'],
    'name' => $row['name'],
    'email' => $row['email']
```

```
    );
}

include 'jokes.html.php';
```

As you can see, wherever our controller needs a database connection, we can obtain it simply by including the **db.inc.php** file with an `include` statement. And because the code to do this is a simple one-liner, we can make our code more readable by using a separate `include` statement just before each SQL query in our controller. Previously, we established a database connection at the top of the controller, regardless of whether the code that followed would end up needing one or not.

When PHP encounters an `include` statement, it puts the current script on hold and runs the specified PHP script. When it's finished, it returns to the original script and picks up where it left off.

Include files are the simplest way to structure PHP code. Because of their simplicity, they're also the most widely used method. Even very simple web applications can benefit greatly from using include files.

Types of Includes

The `include` statement we've used so far is actually only one of four statements that can be used to include another PHP file in a currently running script:

- `include`
- `require`
- `include_once`
- `require_once`

`include` and `require` are almost identical. The only difference between them is what happens when the specified file is unable to be included (that is, if it doesn't exist, or if the web server doesn't have permission to read it). With `include`, a warning is displayed and the script continues to run. With `require`, an error is displayed and the script stops.[3]

---

[3] In production environments, warnings and errors are usually disabled in **php.ini**. In such environments, a failed `include` has no visible effect (aside from the lack of content that would normally have been generated by the include file), while a failed `require` causes the page to stop at the point of failure.

In general, you should use `require` whenever the main script is unable to work without the included script. I do recommend using `include` whenever possible, however. Even if the **db.inc.php** file for your site is unable to load, for example, you might still want to let the script for your front page continue to load. None of the content from the database will display, but the user might be able to use the **Contact Us** link at the bottom of the page to let you know about the problem!

`include_once` and `require_once` work just like `include` and `require`, respectively—but if the specified file has already been included at least once for the current page request (using *any* of the four statements described here), the statement will be ignored. This is handy for include files performing a task that only needs to be done once, like connecting to the database.

Figure 6.3 shows `include_once` in action. In the figure, **index.php** includes two files: **categories.inc.php** and **top10.inc.php**. Both files use `include_once` to include **db.inc.php**, as they both need a database connection in order to do their job. As shown, PHP will ignore the attempt to include **db.inc.php** in **top10.inc.php** because the file was already included in **categories.inc.php**. As a result, only one database connection is created.

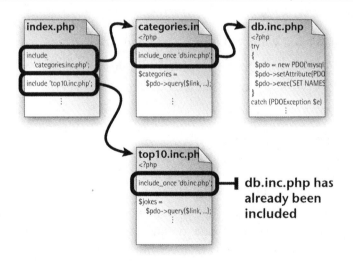

Figure 6.3. Use `include_once` to avoid opening a second database connection

When a failed `require` occurs before any content is sent to the browser, the unlucky user will see nothing but a blank page!

`include_once` and `require_once` are also useful for loading function libraries, as we'll see in the section called "Custom Functions and Function Libraries".

Shared Include Files

In all the examples I've shown you so far, I've assumed that the include file is located in the same directory on your web server as the file(s) that use it. Often, this is an invalid assumption! On many sites, you'll want to share include files among scripts that span potentially complex directory structures. A solid candidate for a shared include file would be the database connection include, **db.inc.php.**

So the question is, when the include file is in a *different* directory, how does a PHP script find it? The most obvious method is to specify the location of the include file as an **absolute path**. Here's how this would look on a Windows server:[4]

```
<?php include 'C:/Program Files/Apache Software Foundation/Apache2.2
➥/htdocs/includes/db.inc.php'; ?>
```

And here's the code on a Linux server:

```
<?php include '/usr/local/apache2/htdocs/includes/db.inc.php'; ?>
```

While this method will work, it's undesirable because it ties your site's code to your web server configuration. Ideally, you should be able to drop your PHP-based website onto any PHP-enabled web server and just watch it run. This is particularly important because many developers will build a site on one server, then deploy it publicly on a different server. That's impractical if your code refers to drives and directories that are specific to one particular server. And, even if you *do* have the luxury of working on a single server, you'll be kicking yourself if you ever need to move your website to another drive/directory on that server.

A better method is to let PHP keep track of the **document root** of your web server, then specify the path from that location. The document root is the directory on your server that corresponds to the root directory of your website. For example, to make **index.php** available at **http://www.example.com/index.php**, you'd have to place it in

---

[4] I recommend always using forward slashes in your paths, even when you're working with a Windows server. PHP is smart enough to do the conversion for you, and using forward slashes saves you from having to type double-backslashes (\ \ ) to represent single backslashes in PHP strings.

the document root directory on the www.example.com web server. In any PHP script, you can obtain the document root of your web server using $_SERVER ['DOCUMENT_ROOT']. As I briefly explained in Chapter 4, $_SERVER is an array variable that's automatically created by PHP, just like $_GET, $_POST, and $_REQUEST. $_SERVER contains a whole bunch of information supplied by your web server, including $_SERVER['DOCUMENT_ROOT'].

Here's an example:

```php
<?php include $_SERVER['DOCUMENT_ROOT'] . '/includes/db.inc.php'; ?>
```

This will work on Windows, Mac, and Linux servers with either Apache or Internet Information Services (IIS) installed.[5]

Another excellent candidate for a shared include file is the snippet of code that we used to reverse the changes to submitted values made by PHP's misguided magic quotes feature, which we looked at in Chapter 4. Simply drop this code into its own file:

chapter6/includes/magicquotes.inc.php

```php
<?php
if (get_magic_quotes_gpc())
{
  $process = array(&$_GET, &$_POST, &$_COOKIE, &$_REQUEST);
  while (list($key, $val) = each($process))
  {
    foreach ($val as $k => $v)
    {
      unset($process[$key][$k]);
      if (is_array($v))
      {
        $process[$key][stripslashes($k)] = $v;
        $process[] = &$process[$key][stripslashes($k)];
      }
```

---

[5] The one place where you're unable to count on $_SERVER['DOCUMENT_ROOT'] is on a server running the Common Gateway Interface (CGI) version of PHP. The CGI specification does not require the web server to inform PHP of the document root directory for the site, so this value will usually be absent on such configurations. Thankfully, CGI installations of PHP are increasingly rare, and should certainly be avoided in production environments. If you followed the installation instructions for PHP in this book, you can rest assured that $_SERVER['DOCUMENT_ROOT'] will work.

```
    else
    {
      $process[$key][stripslashes($k)] = stripslashes($v);
    }
  }
}
unset($process);
}
```

From this point on, you can use this include file to remove the effects of magic quotes with a single line at the top of your controller scripts:

```
<?php
include $_SERVER['DOCUMENT_ROOT'] . '/includes/magicquotes.inc.php';
```

I'll use the two shared include files discussed in this section—the database connection script and the magic quotes removal script—in many of the examples from this point forward in the book. You'll be able to follow along too, as long as the two files in question (**db.inc.php** and **magicquotes.inc.php**) can be found in a directory called **includes** situated in the document root directory of your web server.

Custom Functions and Function Libraries

By this point, you're probably quite comfortable with the idea of functions. A function in PHP that you can invoke at will, where you'd usually provide one or more **arguments** for it to use, and often receiving a **return value** as a result. You can use PHP's vast library of functions to do just about anything a PHP script could ever be asked to do, from retrieving the current date (`date`) to generating graphics on the fly (`imagecreatetruecolor`[6]).

But what you may be unaware of is that you can create functions of your own! **Custom functions**, once defined, work just like PHP's built-in functions, and they can do anything a normal PHP script can do.

Let's start with a really simple example. Say you had a PHP script that needed to calculate the area of a rectangle given its width (**3**) and height (**5**). Thinking back to

---

[6] http://www.php.net/imagecreatetruecolor

your basic geometry classes in school, you should recall that the area of a rectangle is its width multiplied by its height:

```
$area = 3 * 5;
```

But it would be nicer to have a function called **area** that simply calculated the area of a rectangle given its dimensions:

chapter6/calculate-area/index.php *(excerpt)*

```
$area = area(3, 5);
```

As it happens, PHP has no built-in **area** function, but clever PHP programmers like you and me can just roll up our sleeves and write the function ourselves:

chapter6/calculate-area/area-function.inc.php

```php
<?php
function area($width, $height)
{
  return $width * $height;
}
```

This include file defines a single custom function: **area**. The <?php marker is probably the only line that looks familiar to you in this code. What we have here is a **function declaration**; let me break it down for you one line at a time:

function area($width, $height)

The keyword `function` tells PHP that we wish to declare a new function for use in the current script. Then, we supply the function with a name (in this case, **area**). Function names operate under the same rules as variable names—they are case-sensitive, must start with a letter or an underscore (_), and may contain letters, numbers, and underscores—except, of course, that there's no dollar sign prefix. Instead, function names are always followed by a set of parentheses ((…)), which may or may not be empty.

The parentheses that follow a function name enclose the list of arguments that the function will accept. You should already be familiar with this from your experience with PHP's built-in functions. For example, when you use `date` to retrieve the current date as a PHP string, you provide a string describing the format you want the date to be written in within the parentheses.

When declaring a custom function, instead of giving a list of values for the arguments, you give a list of variable names. In this example, we list two variables: `$width` and `$height`. When the function is called, it will therefore expect to be given two arguments. The value of the first argument will be assigned to `$width`, while the value of the second will be assigned to `$height`. Those variables can then be used to perform the calculation within the function.

{

Speaking of calculations, the rest of the function declaration is the code that performs the calculation, or does whatever else the function is supposed to do. That code must be enclosed in a set of braces ({...}), so here's the opening brace.

`return $width * $height;`

You can think of the code within those braces as a miniature PHP script. This function is a simple one, because it contains just a single statement: a `return` statement.

A `return` statement can be used in the code of a function to jump back into the main script immediately. When the PHP interpreter hits a `return` statement, it immediately stops running the code of this function and goes back to where the function was called. It's sort of an ejection seat for functions!

In addition to breaking out of the function, the `return` statement lets you specify a value for the function to *return* to the code that called it. In this case, the value we're returning is `$width * $height`—the result of multiplying the first parameter by the second.

}

The closing brace marks the end of the function declaration.

In order to use this function, we must first include the file containing the function declaration:

chapter6/calculate-area/index.php

```php
<?php
include_once 'area-function.inc.php';

$area = area(3, 5);

include 'output.html.php';
```

Technically, you could write the function declaration within the controller script itself, but by putting it in an include file you can reuse the function in other scripts much more easily. It's tidier, too. To use the function in the include file, a PHP script need only include it with `include_once` (or `require_once` if the function is critical to the script).

Avoid using `include` or `require` to load include files that contain functions; as explained in the section called "Types of Includes", that would risk defining the functions in the library more than once and covering the user's screen with PHP warnings.

It's standard practice (but not required) to include your function libraries at the top of the script, so that you can quickly see which include files containing functions are used by any particular script.

What we have here are the beginnings of a **function library**—an include file that contains declarations for a group of related functions. If you wanted to, you could rename the include file to **geometry.inc.php** and add to it a whole bunch of functions to perform various geometrical calculations.

Variable Scope and Global Access

One big difference between custom functions and include files is the concept of **variable scope**. Any variable that exists in the main script will also be available and can be changed in the include file. While this is useful sometimes, more often it's a pain in the neck. Unintentionally overwriting one of the main script's variables in an include file is a common cause of error—and one that can take a long time to track down and fix! To avoid such problems, you need to remember the variable names in the script that you're working on, as well as any that exist in the include files your script uses.

Functions protect you from such problems. Variables created inside a function (including any argument variables) exist only within that function, and disappear when the function has run its course. In programmer-speak, the **scope** of these variables is the function; they're said to have **function scope**. In contrast, variables created in the main script outside of any function are unavailable inside functions. The scope of these variables is the main script, and they're said to have **global scope**.

Okay, but beyond the fancy names, what does this really *mean* for us? It means that you can have a variable called, say, $width in your main script, and another variable called $width in your function, and PHP will treat these as two entirely separate variables! Perhaps more usefully, you can have two different functions each using the same variable names, and they'll have no effect on each other because their variables are kept separate by their scope.

On some occasions, you may actually *want* to use a global-scope variable (**global variable** for short) inside one of your functions. For example, the **db.inc.php** file creates a database connection for use by your script and stores it in the global variable $pdo. You might then want to use this variable in a function that needed to access the database.

Disregarding variable scope, here's how you may write such a function:

```php
<?php
include_once $_SERVER['DOCUMENT_ROOT'] . '/includes/db.inc.php';

function totalJokes()
{
  try
  {
    $result = $pdo->query('SELECT COUNT(*) FROM joke');
  }
  catch (PDOException $e)
  {
    $error = 'Database error counting jokes!';
    include 'error.html.php';
    exit();
  }

  $row = $result->fetch();
```

```
    return $row[0];
}
```

Shared Database Include in Use!

Note that the first line of this controller script uses a shared copy of the **db.inc.php** file in the **includes** directory, as discussed earlier in the section called "Shared Include Files". Make sure you've placed a copy of this file (and the associated **error.html.php** file that it uses to display errors) in the **includes** directory in your server's document root; otherwise, PHP will complain that it's unable to find the **db.inc.php** file.

The problem here is that the global variable $pdo (shown in bold) is unavailable within the scope of the function. If you attempt to call this function as it is, you'll receive the errors shown in Figure 6.4.

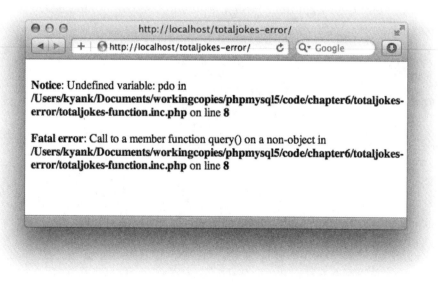

Figure 6.4. The totaljokes function cannot access $pdo

Now, of course, you could just add an argument to the totaljokes function and send it the value of $pdo that way, but having to pass this value to every function that needs database access would become quite tedious.

Instead, let's use the global variable directly within our function. There are two ways to do this. The first is to **import** the global variable into the function's scope:

chapter6/totaljokes-global1/totaljokes-function.inc.php

```php
<?php
include_once $_SERVER['DOCUMENT_ROOT'] . '/includes/db.inc.php';

function totalJokes()
{
  global $pdo;

  try
  {
    $result = $pdo->query('SELECT COUNT(*) FROM joke');
  }
  catch (PDOException $e)
  {
    $error = 'Database error counting jokes!';
    include 'error.html.php';
    exit();
  }

  $row = $result->fetch();

  return $row[0];
}
```

The global statement, shown here in bold, lets you give a list of global variables (separated by commas, if you want to import more than one) that you want to make available within the function. Programmers call this importing a variable. This is different from passing the variable as an argument, because if you modify an imported variable inside the function, the value of the variable changes outside the function, too.

The alternative to importing the variable is to use the $GLOBALS array:

chapter6/totaljokes-global2/totaljokes-function.inc.php

```php
<?php
include_once $_SERVER['DOCUMENT_ROOT'] . '/includes/db.inc.php';

function totalJokes()
```

```
{
  try
  {
    $result = $GLOBALS['pdo']->query('SELECT COUNT(*) FROM joke');
  }
  catch (PDOException $e)
  {
    $error = 'Database error counting jokes!';
    include 'error.html.php';
    exit();
  }

  $row = $result->fetch();

  return $row[0];
}
```

As you can see, all we've done here is replace $pdo with $GLOBALS['pdo']. The special PHP array $GLOBALS is available across all scopes (for this reason, it's known as a **superglobal**), and contains an entry for every variable in the global scope. You can therefore access any global variable within a function as $GLOBALS['name'], where *name* is the name of the global variable (without a dollar sign). The advantage of using $GLOBALS is that you can still create a separate function-scope variable called $pdo if you want.

Other special PHP arrays that are superglobal, and are therefore accessible inside functions, include $_SERVER, $_GET, $_POST, $_COOKIE, $_FILES, $_ENV, $_REQUEST, and $_SESSION. See the page on superglobals in the PHP Manual for full details.[7]

Structure in Practice: Template Helpers

To cap this chapter off, let's make a start on a function library you can actually use.

There are few functions more tedious to call in the PHP language than htmlspecialchars. As I explained in Chapter 3, every time you wish to output some piece of text that was submitted by a user, you need to use htmlspecialchars to prevent hackers from inserting malicious code into your page.

---

[7] http://php.net/manual/en/language.variables.superglobals.php

For example, this is the code we've used to output user-submitted jokes in our joke list examples so far:

chapter6/jokes/jokes.html.php *(excerpt)*

```php
<?php echo htmlspecialchars($joke['text'], ENT_QUOTES, 'UTF-8'); ?>
```

As well as `htmlspecialchars` being an inordinately long function name, it takes three arguments—two of which are always the same!

Because outputting text as HTML is such a common task in PHP template code, let's write a much shorter function that does this for us:

chapter6/includes/helpers.inc.php *(excerpt)*

```php
<?php
function html($text)
{
  return htmlspecialchars($text, ENT_QUOTES, 'UTF-8');
}
```

With this custom `html` function, we can call `htmlspecialchars` with a lot less typing!

```php
<?php echo html($joke['text']); ?>
```

We can take this even further by writing a second custom function, `htmlout`, that takes the value generated by the first and outputs it:

chapter6/includes/helpers.inc.php

```php
<?php
function html($text)
{
  return htmlspecialchars($text, ENT_QUOTES, 'UTF-8');
}

function htmlout($text)
{
  echo html($text);
}
```

I like to name these little convenience functions that make writing templates easier **template helpers**. Here's what our joke listing template looks like when we use these helpers:

chapter6/jokes-helpers/jokes.html.php

```php
<?php include_once $_SERVER['DOCUMENT_ROOT'] .
    '/includes/helpers.inc.php'; ?>
<!DOCTYPE html>
<html lang="en">
  <head>
    <meta charset="utf-8">
    <title>List of Jokes</title>
  </head>
  <body>
    <p><a href="?addjoke">Add your own joke</a></p>
    <p>Here are all the jokes in the database:</p>
    <?php foreach ($jokes as $joke): ?>
      <form action="?deletejoke" method="post">
        <blockquote>
          <p>
            <?php htmlout($joke['text']); ?>
            <input type="hidden" name="id" value="<?php echo
              $joke['id']; ?>">
            <input type="submit" value="Delete">
            (by <a href="mailto:<?php htmlout($joke['email']); ?>">
              <?php htmlout($joke['name']); ?></a>)
          </p>
        </blockquote>
      </form>
    <?php endforeach; ?>
  </body>
</html>
```

Helpers Belong in the Shared includes Directory

Like **db.inc.php** and **magicquotes.inc.php**, the **helpers.inc.php** file belongs in the shared **includes** directory under your server's document root, as described in the section called "Shared Include Files".

As you write templates with more and more user-submitted content in them, these little gems will come in very handy indeed!

While you're at it, update the controller script to use the shared includes **db.inc.php** and **magicquotes.inc.php**:

```php
<?php
include_once $_SERVER['DOCUMENT_ROOT'] .
➥ '/includes/magicquotes.inc.php';

if (isset($_GET['addjoke']))
{
  include 'form.html.php';
  exit();
}

if (isset($_POST['joketext']))
{
  include $_SERVER['DOCUMENT_ROOT'] . '/includes/db.inc.php';

  try
  {
    $sql = 'INSERT INTO joke SET
        joketext = :joketext,
        jokedate = CURDATE()';
    $s = $pdo->prepare($sql);
    $s->bindValue(':joketext', $_POST['joketext']);
    $s->execute();
  }
  catch (PDOException $e)
  {
    $error = 'Error adding submitted joke: ' . $e->getMessage();
    include 'error.html.php';
    exit();
  }

  header('Location: .');
  exit();
}

if (isset($_GET['deletejoke']))
{
  include $_SERVER['DOCUMENT_ROOT'] . '/includes/db.inc.php';

  try
  {
```

```php
      $sql = 'DELETE FROM joke WHERE id = :id';
      $s = $pdo->prepare($sql);
      $s->bindValue(':id', $_POST['id']);
      $s->execute();
    }
    catch (PDOException $e)
    {
      $error = 'Error deleting joke: ' . $e->getMessage();
      include 'error.html.php';
      exit();
    }

    header('Location: .');
    exit();
}

include $_SERVER['DOCUMENT_ROOT'] . '/includes/db.inc.php';

try
{
  $sql = 'SELECT joke.id, joketext, name, email
      FROM joke INNER JOIN author
        ON authorid = author.id';
  $result = $pdo->query($sql);
}
catch (PDOException $e)
{
  $error = 'Error fetching jokes: ' . $e->getMessage();
  include 'error.html.php';
  exit();
}

foreach ($result as $row)
{
  $jokes[] = array(
    'id' => $row['id'],
    'text' => $row['joketext'],
    'name' => $row['name'],
    'email' => $row['email']
  );
}

include 'jokes.html.php';
```

The Best Way

In this chapter, I have helped you to rise above the basic questions of what PHP can do for you, and begin to look for the *best* way to code a solution. Sure, you can approach many simple scripts as lists of actions you want PHP to do for you, but when you tackle site-wide issues such as database connections, shared navigation elements, visitor statistics, and access control systems, it really pays off to structure your code carefully.

We've now explored a couple of simple but effective devices for writing structured PHP code. Include files let you reuse a single piece of code across multiple pages of your site, greatly reducing the burden when you need to make changes. Writing your own functions to put in these include files lets you build powerful libraries of functions that can perform tasks as needed and return values to the scripts that call them. These new techniques will pay off in a big way in the rest of this book.

If you want to take the next step into structuring your PHP code, you'll want to explore PHP's object oriented programming (OOP) features. The section on Classes and Objects in The PHP Manual[8] has some useful information on the subject, but for a more complete guide you'll want to check out *PHP Master: Write Cutting-edge Code.*[9]

In Chapter 7, you'll use all the knowledge you've gained so far, plus a few new tricks, to build a content management system in PHP. The aim of such a system is to provide a customized, secure, web-based interface that enables you to manage the contents of your site's database, instead of requiring you to type everything into phpMyAdmin by hand.

---

[8] http://www.php.net/oop5
[9] http://www.sitepoint.com/books/phppro1/

A Content Management System

To make the leap from a web page that displays information stored in a database to a completely database driven website, we need to add a **content management system (CMS)**. Such a system usually takes the form of a series of web pages, access to which is restricted to users who are authorized to make changes to the site. These pages provide a database administration interface that allows a user to view and change the information stored in the database without bothering with the mundane details of SQL queries.

We built the beginnings of a CMS at the end of Chapter 4, where we allowed site visitors to add and delete jokes using a web-based form and a **Delete** button, respectively. While impressive, these are features that you'd normally exclude from the interface presented to casual site visitors. For example, you'd want to prevent visitors from adding offensive material to your website without your knowledge. And you *definitely* don't want just anyone to be able to delete jokes from your site.

By relegating those dangerous features to the restricted-access site administration pages, you avoid the risk of exposing your data to the average user, and you maintain the power to manage the contents of your database without having to memorize SQL queries. In this chapter, we'll expand on the capabilities of our joke management system to take advantage of the enhancements we made to our database in Chapter 5. Specifically, we'll allow a site administrator to manage authors and categories, and assign these to appropriate jokes.

As we have seen, these administration pages must be protected by an appropriate access-restriction scheme. One approach would be to configure your web server to protect the relevant PHP files by prompting users for valid usernames and passwords. On Apache servers, you can do this with an **.htaccess** file that lists authorized users.

Another method protects the administration pages with PHP itself. This option is generally more flexible and produces a much slicker result, but it takes a bit more work to set up. I'll show you how it's done in Chapter 9.

For now, let's focus on building the pages that will make up your CMS.

The Front Page

At the end of Chapter 5, your database contained tables for three types of entities: jokes, authors, and joke categories. This database layout is represented in Figure 7.1. Note that we're sticking with our original assumption that we'll have one email address per author.

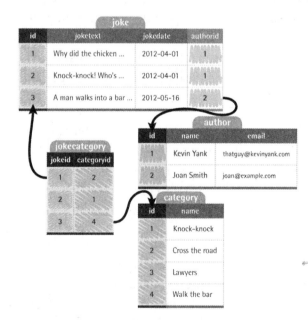

Figure 7.1. The structure of the finished `ijdb` database contains three entities

If you need to recreate this table structure from scratch, here are the SQL queries to do so, along with some sample data:

```
CREATE TABLE joke (
  id INT NOT NULL AUTO_INCREMENT PRIMARY KEY,
  joketext TEXT,
  jokedate DATE NOT NULL,
  authorid INT
) DEFAULT CHARACTER SET utf8 ENGINE=InnoDB;

CREATE TABLE author (
  id INT NOT NULL AUTO_INCREMENT PRIMARY KEY,
  name VARCHAR(255),
  email VARCHAR(255)
) DEFAULT CHARACTER SET utf8 ENGINE=InnoDB;

CREATE TABLE category (
  id INT NOT NULL AUTO_INCREMENT PRIMARY KEY,
  name VARCHAR(255)
) DEFAULT CHARACTER SET utf8 ENGINE=InnoDB;

CREATE TABLE jokecategory (
  jokeid INT NOT NULL,
  categoryid INT NOT NULL,
  PRIMARY KEY (jokeid, categoryid)
) DEFAULT CHARACTER SET utf8 ENGINE=InnoDB;

# Sample data
# We specify the IDs so they are known when we add related entries

INSERT INTO author (id, name, email) VALUES
(1, 'Kevin Yank', 'thatguy@kevinyank.com'),
(2, 'Joan Smith', 'joan@example.com');

INSERT INTO joke (id, joketext, jokedate, authorid) VALUES
(1, 'Why did the chicken cross the road? To get to the other side!',
➥ '2012-04-01', 1),
(2, 'Knock-knock! Who\'s there? Boo! "Boo" who? Don\'t cry; it\'s
➥ only a joke!', '2012-04-01', 1),
(3, 'A man walks into a bar. "Ouch."', '2012-04-01', 2),
(4, 'How many lawyers does it take to screw in a lightbulb? I can\'t
➥ say: I might be sued!', '2012-04-01', 2);
```

```
INSERT INTO category (id, name) VALUES
(1, 'Knock-knock'),
(2, 'Cross the road'),
(3, 'Lawyers'),
(4, 'Walk the bar');

INSERT INTO jokecategory (jokeid, categoryid) VALUES
(1, 2),
(2, 1),
(3, 4),
(4, 3);
```

The front page of the content management system, therefore, will contain links to pages that manage these three entities. The following HTML code produces the index page shown in Figure 7.2:

chapter7/admin/index.html

```
<!DOCTYPE html>
<html lang="en">
  <head>
    <meta charset="utf-8">
    <title>Joke CMS</title>
  </head>
  <body>
    <h1>Joke Management System</h1>
    <ul>
      <li><a href="jokes/">Manage Jokes</a></li>
      <li><a href="authors/">Manage Authors</a></li>
      <li><a href="categories/">Manage Joke Categories</a></li>
    </ul>
  </body>
</html>
```

Figure 7.2. The Joke CMS index page offers three links

Each of these links points to a different subdirectory in our code: **jokes**, **authors**, and **categories**. Each directory will contain the controller (**index.php**) and associated templates needed to manage the corresponding entities in our database.

Managing Authors

Let's begin with the code that will handle adding new authors, and deleting and editing existing ones. All of this code will go in the **authors** subdirectory.

The first information we'll present to an administrator needing to manage authors is a list of all authors currently stored in the database. Code-wise, this is the same as listing the jokes in the database. As we'll want to allow administrators to delete and edit existing authors, we'll include buttons for these actions next to each author's name. Just like the **Delete** buttons we added at the end of Chapter 4, these buttons will send the ID of the associated author, so that the controller knows which author the administrator wishes to edit or delete. Finally, we'll provide an **Add new author** link that leads to a form similar in operation to the **Add your own joke** link we created in Chapter 4.

Here's the controller code to do this:

chapter7/admin/authors/index.php *(excerpt)*

```php
// Display author list
include $_SERVER['DOCUMENT_ROOT'] . '/includes/db.inc.php';

try
{
  $result = $pdo->query('SELECT id, name FROM author');
}
catch (PDOException $e)
{
  $error = 'Error fetching authors from the database!';
  include 'error.html.php';
  exit();
}

foreach ($result as $row)
{
  $authors[] = array('id' => $row['id'], 'name' => $row['name']);
}

include 'authors.html.php';
```

There should be no surprises for you in this code, but do note that the database connection is created using the shared include file (**db.inc.php**) stored in the **includes** directory under the document root.

Here's the template that the code uses to display the list of authors:

chapter7/admin/authors/authors.html.php *(excerpt)*

```php
<?php include_once $_SERVER['DOCUMENT_ROOT'] .
    '/includes/helpers.inc.php'; ?> ❶
<!DOCTYPE html>
<html lang="en">
  <head>
    <meta charset="utf-8">
    <title>Manage Authors</title>
  </head>
  <body>
    <h1>Manage Authors</h1>
    <p><a href="?add">Add new author</a></p> ❷
    <ul>
      <?php foreach ($authors as $author): ?>
```

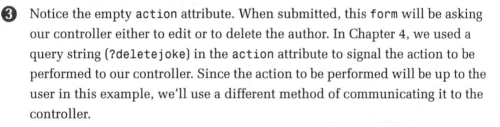

```
      <li>
        <form action="" method="post">
          <div>
            <?php htmlout($author['name']); ?>
            <input type="hidden" name="id" value="<?php
                echo $author['id']; ?>">
            <input type="submit" name="action" value="Edit">
            <input type="submit" name="action" value="Delete">
          </div>
        </form>
      </li>
      <?php endforeach; ?>
    </ul>
    <p><a href="..">Return to JMS home</a></p>
  </body>
</html>
```

Again, this code should be fairly familiar to you by now. A few points of interest:

 This template will use the same shared include file we developed in Chapter 6 to make outputting values safely with **htmlspecialchars** less tedious.

❷ This link sends a query string (?add) to our controller so that it can tell when the user wants to add a new author.

❸ Notice the empty action attribute. When submitted, this form will be asking our controller either to edit or to delete the author. In Chapter 4, we used a query string (?deletejoke) in the action attribute to signal the action to be performed to our controller. Since the action to be performed will be up to the user in this example, we'll use a different method of communicating it to the controller.

❹ Here we use our custom htmlout function to output each author's name safely.

❺ This form contains two submit buttons: one to edit the author and another to delete the author. We'll give each button the same name attribute value (action) so that our controller will be able to tell which button was clicked just by checking the submitted value for that name ($_POST['action']).

Figure 7.3 shows the list of authors produced by this template.

Figure 7.3. The maintenance of author details begins with the Manage Authors interface

Deleting Authors

When the user clicks one of the **Delete** buttons, our controller should remove the corresponding author from the database using the author's ID submitted with the form.

As we've seen before, this is frighteningly easy to do, but there's added complexity here. Remember that our joke table has an authorid column that indicates the author responsible for any given joke. When we remove an author from the database, we must also remove any references to that author in all tables. Otherwise, our database might contain jokes associated with nonexistent authors.

We have three possible ways to handle this situation:

- We prohibit users from deleting authors that are associated with jokes in the database.

- When we delete an author, we also delete any jokes attributed to that author.

- When we delete an author, we set the authorid of any jokes attributed to that author to NULL to indicate that they have no author.

When we take measures like these to preserve the relationships in our database, we are said to be protecting the database's **referential integrity**. MySQL, like most database servers, supports a feature called **foreign key constraints** that can do this automatically. By setting up these constraints, you can instruct MySQL to take any of the steps listed in order to keep your data properly related.

We'll look at foreign key constraints in Chapter 10, but we won't use them here. If we did we'd be defining some of the behavior of our CMS in our PHP code, while defining other aspects of its behavior in our database design. If we did this, and then later decided that we wanted to change how deleting an author worked (for example, preventing the user from deleting authors with any jokes to their name), we'd need to remember to make adjustments in both places. Instead, we can keep our author-deleting logic all in our PHP code, making life easier for whoever might need to make changes to your code in the future (even if it's you!).

Since most authors would like us to give credit when using their jokes, we'll choose the second option: delete all associated jokes when we delete an author. This also saves us from having to handle jokes with NULL values in the authorid column when we display our library of jokes.

As we'll be deleting jokes, there's yet another layer of complexity to consider. Jokes may be assigned to categories by means of entries in the jokecategory table. When we delete jokes, we must also ensure that such entries are removed from the database. In summary, our controller will delete an author, any jokes belonging to that author, and any category assignments that pertain to those jokes.

The code to do all this is rather lengthy, as you might imagine. Take your time to read through it and see if you can understand how it works:

chapter7/admin/authors/index.php *(excerpt)*

```php
if (isset($_POST['action']) and $_POST['action'] == 'Delete')
{
  include $_SERVER['DOCUMENT_ROOT'] . '/includes/db.inc.php';

  // Get jokes belonging to author
  try
  {
    $sql = 'SELECT id FROM joke WHERE authorid = :id';
    $s = $pdo->prepare($sql);
    $s->bindValue(':id', $_POST['id']);
    $s->execute();
  }
```

```php
catch (PDOException $e)
{
  $error = 'Error getting list of jokes to delete.';
  include 'error.html.php';
  exit();
}

$result = $s->fetchAll();

// Delete joke category entries
try
{
  $sql = 'DELETE FROM jokecategory WHERE jokeid = :id';
  $s = $pdo->prepare($sql);

  // For each joke
  foreach ($result as $row)
  {
    $jokeId = $row['id'];
    $s->bindValue(':id', $jokeId);
    $s->execute();
  }
}
catch (PDOException $e)
{
  $error = 'Error deleting category entries for joke.';
  include 'error.html.php';
  exit();
}

// Delete jokes belonging to author
try
{
  $sql = 'DELETE FROM joke WHERE authorid = :id';
  $s = $pdo->prepare($sql);
  $s->bindValue(':id', $_POST['id']);
  $s->execute();
}
catch (PDOException $e)
{
  $error = 'Error deleting jokes for author.';
  include 'error.html.php';
  exit();
}
```

```
  // Delete the author
  try
  {
    $sql = 'DELETE FROM author WHERE id = :id';
    $s = $pdo->prepare($sql);
    $s->bindValue(':id', $_POST['id']);
    $s->execute();
  }
  catch (PDOException $e)
  {
    $error = 'Error deleting author.';
    include 'error.html.php';
    exit();
  }

  header('Location: .');
  exit();
}
```

Although this code will be mostly familiar to you, there are a few new twists, which are highlighted in bold.

The first element that may seem unfamiliar is the if statement that triggers it all:

chapter7/admin/authors/index.php *(excerpt)*

```
if (isset($_POST['action']) and $_POST['action'] == 'Delete')
```

As we saw in the section called "Managing Authors", the user asks for an author to be deleted by clicking the **Delete** button next to the author name. Since the button's name attribute is set to action, we can detect this button click by checking if $_POST['action'] is set, and if so, check if its value is 'Delete'.

Next, there's this statement:

chapter7/admin/authors/index.php *(excerpt)*

```
$result = $s->fetchAll();
```

At this point in the script, we've just executed a SELECT query to retrieve all the jokes belonging to the author that we're about to delete. With this list of jokes in hand, we're going to execute a series of DELETE queries, one for each joke, to delete all the category entries for that joke. But that's the thing—we're yet to actually *have* the list of jokes in hand! Let me explain.

Normally when we perform a SELECT query, we use the condition of a while loop or a foreach loop to retrieve each row of the results, one at a time:

```
while ($row = $result->fetch())
```

```
foreach ($result as $row)
```

When we process the result of a query this way, PHP actually retrieves each row from the database as the loop requests it, and throws it away when it moves on to the next row. This saves PHP from having to use a lot of memory to hold onto all the rows of results at once.

Most of the time, we developers have no need to know that PHP is taking this clever shortcut. But every once in a while, we'll want to send another SQL query to the MySQL server before we've worked through all the results of the previous query.

That's exactly what's about to happen in this code if we aren't careful: we've just run a SELECT query to ask for a list of all jokes belonging to a particular author, and as we work through that list, we'd like to perform a DELETE query for each one. The problem is, as far as MySQL knows, it will still be busy sending us the results of the SELECT query; we can't just interrupt it and ask for it to start running DELETEs! Doing so would cause our DELETEs to fail with an error.

That's where the fetchAll method comes in. By calling this method on our prepared statement ($s), we ask PHP to retrieve the entire set of results for the query and store them in a PHP array ($result):

chapter7/admin/authors/index.php (excerpt)

```
$result = $s->fetchAll();
```

We can now loop through this array with a foreach loop just as we'd normally loop through a PDOStatement object to retrieve each row one at a time. The difference now is that PHP will hold onto all the results at once, which frees us up to send more queries to MySQL.

And that's where the third novel piece of code in our author-deleting script comes in:

```
chapter7/admin/authors/index.php (excerpt)

// Delete joke category entries
try
{
  $sql = 'DELETE FROM jokecategory WHERE jokeid = :id';
  $s = $pdo->prepare($sql);

  // For each joke
  foreach ($result as $row)
  {
    $jokeId = $row['id'];
    $s->bindValue(':id', $jokeId);
    $s->execute();
  }
}
```

With this code, we run a DELETE query to remove the jokecategory entries for each joke from the database. Your first impulse might be to begin with a foreach loop, but instead we start by creating a single prepared statement.

This code demonstrates the second big advantage of prepared statements (which we first learned about in Chapter 4).[1] Once you've prepared a statement, you can execute it over and over again, assigning its placeholders different values each time. In this case, we want to execute essentially the same DELETE query, but using a different joke ID in the WHERE clause each time. By using the same prepared statement for each of these queries, we can save MySQL the trouble of scrutinizing the SQL code for each query and coming up with a plan for how to do what we're asking. Instead, MySQL reads the SQL code once when we prepare the statement; it figures out the most efficient way to perform such a DELETE operation, and then it simply executes that same plan over and over, using each of the IDs that we send it in turn.

With this in mind, look again at this fragment of code: it should make a lot more sense now. First, it creates a prepared statement from the SQL code with a placeholder in it. Then it uses a foreach loop to work through the result set of the pre-

---

[1] In case it's slipped your mind, the first big advantage of prepared statements is that they can contain placeholders, to which you can assign values safely without worrying about SQL-injection attacks.

ceding SELECT query. It executes the newly prepared DELETE query once for each joke using bindValue to set the :id placeholder in the query to the joke's ID.

Make sense? Don't worry if you have to read all that a couple of times to understand it. It's some of the most complex PHP code you're going to see in this book!

When you're satisfied, go ahead and try deleting one of the authors from your database. Use phpMyAdmin to verify that all the author's jokes and their category entries are also deleted. The categories themselves should remain, even if they have no jokes left in them.

 Confirm on Delete

As a challenge, try adding a confirmation prompt to this process.

If you've yet to dive in and try some coding, use the code in the code archive for this chapter as a starting point. Modify your controller to respond to the **Delete** button by simply displaying another template, this one prompting the user to confirm the action. When the user submits the form in *this* page, it should trigger the code in the controller that actually deletes the data. This second form will also have to submit in a hidden field the ID of the author to be deleted.

Adding and Editing Authors

You could implement the **Add new author** link at the top of the author list page the same way you did the **Add your own joke** link in Chapter 4. Instead of prompting the user for the text of the joke, you'd instead prompt for the author's name and email address.

But our author management page includes a new, related feature: the ability to edit *existing* authors. Since both features will require the user to fill in a similar form, let's tackle both at once and kill two birds with one stone. Here's the code for the form template that will be used for both adding and editing authors:

chapter7/admin/authors/form.html.php

```php
<?php include_once $_SERVER['DOCUMENT_ROOT'] .
    '/includes/helpers.inc.php'; ?>
<!DOCTYPE html>
<html lang="en">
  <head>
```

```
    <meta charset="utf-8">
    <title><?php htmlout($pageTitle); ?></title>
  </head>
  <body>
    <h1><?php htmlout($pageTitle); ?></h1>
    <form action="?<?php htmlout($action); ?>" method="post">
      <div>
        <label for="name">Name: <input type="text" name="name"
            id="name" value="<?php htmlout($name); ?>"></label>
      </div>
      <div>
        <label for="email">Email: <input type="text" name="email"
            id="email" value="<?php htmlout($email); ?>"></label>
      </div>
      <div>
        <input type="hidden" name="id" value="<?php
            htmlout($id); ?>">
        <input type="submit" value="<?php htmlout($button); ?>">
      </div>
    </form>
  </body>
</html>
```

Note the six PHP variables that are inserted into the content of this page:

$pageTitle   sets the title and top-level heading (<h1>) for this page

$action   sets the value passed in the query string when the form is submitted

$name   sets the initial value of the form field for the author's name

$email   sets the initial value of the form field for the author's email address

$id   sets the value of the hidden form field for the author's database ID

$button   sets the label of the form's submit button

These variables enable us to use the form for two purposes: creating new authors and editing existing ones. Table 7.1 shows the values we'd like to assign to every variable in each instance.

Table 7.1. Variable values for dual-mode author form

Template variable	New author value	Existing author value
$pageTitle	'New Author'	'Edit Author'
$action	'addform'	'editform'
$name	' ' (empty string)	existing name
$email	' ' (empty string)	existing email address
$id	' ' (empty string)	existing author ID
$button	'Add author'	'Update author'

So, here's the controller code that loads the form in "new author mode" when the **Add new author** link is clicked:

```
                                    chapter7/admin/authors/index.php (excerpt)

<?php
include_once $_SERVER['DOCUMENT_ROOT'] .
    '/includes/magicquotes.inc.php';

if (isset($_GET['add']))
{
  $pageTitle = 'New Author';
  $action = 'addform';
  $name = '';
  $email = '';
  $id = '';
  $button = 'Add author';

  include 'form.html.php';
  exit();
}
```

When the user submits the form in this mode, you can detect it by watching for `$_GET['addform']`:

```
                                    chapter7/admin/authors/index.php (excerpt)

if (isset($_GET['addform']))
{
  include $_SERVER['DOCUMENT_ROOT'] . '/includes/db.inc.php';
```

```
try
{
  $sql = 'INSERT INTO author SET
      name = :name,
      email = :email';
  $s = $pdo->prepare($sql);
  $s->bindValue(':name', $_POST['name']);
  $s->bindValue(':email', $_POST['email']);
  $s->execute();
}
catch (PDOException $e)
{
  $error = 'Error adding submitted author.';
  include 'error.html.php';
  exit();
}

header('Location: .');
exit();
}
```

When the user clicks one of the **Edit** buttons in the author list, you can use the same form, but this time you need to load the author's existing details from the database:

chapter7/admin/authors/index.php *(excerpt)*

```
if (isset($_POST['action']) and $_POST['action'] == 'Edit')
{
  include $_SERVER['DOCUMENT_ROOT'] . '/includes/db.inc.php';

  try
  {
    $sql = 'SELECT id, name, email FROM author WHERE id = :id';
    $s = $pdo->prepare($sql);
    $s->bindValue(':id', $_POST['id']);
    $s->execute();
  }
  catch (PDOException $e)
  {
    $error = 'Error fetching author details.';
    include 'error.html.php';
    exit();
  }
```

```
    $row = $s->fetch();

    $pageTitle = 'Edit Author';
    $action = 'editform';
    $name = $row['name'];
    $email = $row['email'];
    $id = $row['id'];
    $button = 'Update author';

    include 'form.html.php';
    exit();
}
```

You can detect the form submitted in this mode by watching for $_GET['editform'].
The code for processing this form submission is very similar to how you add a new
author, but instead of issuing an INSERT query, it issues an UPDATE query:

chapter7/admin/authors/index.php *(excerpt)*

```
if (isset($_GET['editform']))
{
  include $_SERVER['DOCUMENT_ROOT'] . '/includes/db.inc.php';

  try
  {
    $sql = 'UPDATE author SET
        name = :name,
        email = :email
        WHERE id = :id';
    $s = $pdo->prepare($sql);
    $s->bindValue(':id', $_POST['id']);
    $s->bindValue(':name', $_POST['name']);
    $s->bindValue(':email', $_POST['email']);
    $s->execute();
  }
  catch (PDOException $e)
  {
    $error = 'Error updating submitted author.';
    include 'error.html.php';
    exit();
  }
```

```
  header('Location: .');
  exit();
}
```

That'll do the trick! Go ahead and try the completed author management system, which includes our new dual-mode form template shown in Figure 7.4. Make sure you can add, edit, and delete authors smoothly. If you see any error messages, go back and make sure you typed the code exactly as it appears here. If you become stuck, try using the completed code from the code archive and then compare it with your own.

Figure 7.4. I'll bet she's funny ...

Managing Categories

The roles of the authors and joke categories in the database really are very similar. They both reside in tables of their own, and they both serve to group jokes together in some way. As a result, categories can be handled with code very similar to what we just developed for authors, but with one important exception.

When we delete a category, we must avoid simultaneously deleting any jokes that belong to that category, because those jokes may also belong to other categories. We could check each joke to see if it belonged to any other categories, and only delete those that did not, but rather than engage in such a time-consuming process, let's allow for the possibility of including jokes in our database with no assigned category. These jokes might be invisible to our site's visitors (depending on how we decide to display jokes), but would remain in the database in case we wanted to assign them to a category later on.

Thus, to delete a category, we also need to delete any entries in the `jokecategory` table that refer to that category:

chapter7/admin/categories/index.php *(excerpt)*

```php
// Delete joke associations with this category
try
{
  $sql = 'DELETE FROM jokecategory WHERE categoryid = :id';
  $s = $pdo->prepare($sql);
  $s->bindValue(':id', $_POST['id']);
  $s->execute();
}
catch (PDOException $e)
{
  $error = 'Error removing jokes from category.';
  include 'error.html.php';
  exit();
}

// Delete the category
try
{
  $sql = 'DELETE FROM category WHERE id = :id';
  $s = $pdo->prepare($sql);
  $s->bindValue(':id', $_POST['id']);
  $s->execute();
}
catch (PDOException $e)
{
  $error = 'Error deleting category.';
  include 'error.html.php';
  exit();
}
```

Other than this one detail, category management is functionally identical to author management. The complete code for the four files involved will follow. This code also relies on the shared include files **db.inc.php**, **magicquotes.inc.php**, and **helpers.inc.php** introduced in Chapter 6:

chapter7/admin/categories/index.php

```php
<?php
include_once $_SERVER['DOCUMENT_ROOT'] .
    '/includes/magicquotes.inc.php';

if (isset($_GET['add']))
{
  $pageTitle = 'New Category';
  $action = 'addform';
  $name = '';
  $id = '';
  $button = 'Add category';

  include 'form.html.php';
  exit();
}

if (isset($_GET['addform']))
{
  include $_SERVER['DOCUMENT_ROOT'] . '/includes/db.inc.php';

  try
  {
    $sql = 'INSERT INTO category SET
        name = :name';
    $s = $pdo->prepare($sql);
    $s->bindValue(':name', $_POST['name']);
    $s->execute();
  }
  catch (PDOException $e)
  {
    $error = 'Error adding submitted category.';
    include 'error.html.php';
    exit();
  }

  header('Location: .');
  exit();
}
```

```php
if (isset($_POST['action']) and $_POST['action'] == 'Edit')
{
  include $_SERVER['DOCUMENT_ROOT'] . '/includes/db.inc.php';

  try
  {
    $sql = 'SELECT id, name FROM category WHERE id = :id';
    $s = $pdo->prepare($sql);
    $s->bindValue(':id', $_POST['id']);
    $s->execute();
  }
  catch (PDOException $e)
  {
    $error = 'Error fetching category details.';
    include 'error.html.php';
    exit();
  }

  $row = $s->fetch();

  $pageTitle = 'Edit Category';
  $action = 'editform';
  $name = $row['name'];
  $id = $row['id'];
  $button = 'Update category';

  include 'form.html.php';
  exit();
}

if (isset($_GET['editform']))
{
  include $_SERVER['DOCUMENT_ROOT'] . '/includes/db.inc.php';

  try
  {
    $sql = 'UPDATE category SET
        name = :name
        WHERE id = :id';
    $s = $pdo->prepare($sql);
    $s->bindValue(':id', $_POST['id']);
    $s->bindValue(':name', $_POST['name']);
    $s->execute();
  }
```

```php
  catch (PDOException $e)
  {
    $error = 'Error updating submitted category.';
    include 'error.html.php';
    exit();
  }

  header('Location: .');
  exit();
}

if (isset($_POST['action']) and $_POST['action'] == 'Delete')
{
  include $_SERVER['DOCUMENT_ROOT'] . '/includes/db.inc.php';

  // Delete joke associations with this category
  try
  {
    $sql = 'DELETE FROM jokecategory WHERE categoryid = :id';
    $s = $pdo->prepare($sql);
    $s->bindValue(':id', $_POST['id']);
    $s->execute();
  }
  catch (PDOException $e)
  {
    $error = 'Error removing jokes from category.';
    include 'error.html.php';
    exit();
  }

  // Delete the category
  try
  {
    $sql = 'DELETE FROM category WHERE id = :id';
    $s = $pdo->prepare($sql);
    $s->bindValue(':id', $_POST['id']);
    $s->execute();
  }
  catch (PDOException $e)
  {
    $error = 'Error deleting category.';
    include 'error.html.php';
    exit();
  }
```

```php
  header('Location: .');
  exit();
}

// Display category list
include $_SERVER['DOCUMENT_ROOT'] . '/includes/db.inc.php';

try
{
  $result = $pdo->query('SELECT id, name FROM category');
}
catch (PDOException $e)
{
  $error = 'Error fetching categories from database!';
  include 'error.html.php';
  exit();
}

foreach ($result as $row)
{
  $categories[] = array('id' => $row['id'], 'name' => $row['name']);
}

include 'categories.html.php';
```

chapter7/admin/categories/categories.html.php

```php
<?php include_once $_SERVER['DOCUMENT_ROOT'] .
    '/includes/helpers.inc.php'; ?>
<!DOCTYPE html>
<html lang="en">
  <head>
    <meta charset="utf-8">
    <title>Manage Categories</title>
  </head>
  <body>
    <h1>Manage Categories</h1>
    <p><a href="?add">Add new category</a></p>
    <ul>
      <?php foreach ($categories as $category): ?>
        <li>
          <form action="" method="post">
            <div>
              <?php htmlout($category['name']); ?>
              <input type="hidden" name="id" value="<?php
```

```
                    echo $category['id']; ?>">
            <input type="submit" name="action" value="Edit">
            <input type="submit" name="action" value="Delete">
          </div>
        </form>
      </li>
    <?php endforeach; ?>
  </ul>
  <p><a href="..">Return to JMS home</a></p>
  </body>
</html>
```

```php
<?php include_once $_SERVER['DOCUMENT_ROOT'] .
    '/includes/helpers.inc.php'; ?>
<!DOCTYPE html>
<html lang="en">
  <head>
    <meta charset="utf-8">
    <title><?php htmlout($pageTitle); ?></title>
  </head>
  <body>
    <h1><?php htmlout($pageTitle); ?></h1>
    <form action="?<?php htmlout($action); ?>" method="post">
      <div>
        <label for="name">Name: <input type="text" name="name"
            id="name" value="<?php htmlout($name); ?>"></label>
      </div>
      <div>
        <input type="hidden" name="id" value="<?php
            htmlout($id); ?>">
        <input type="submit" value="<?php htmlout($button); ?>">
      </div>
    </form>
  </body>
</html>
```

```html
<!DOCTYPE html>
<html lang="en">
  <head>
    <meta charset="utf-8">
```

```
    <title>Script Error</title>
  </head>
  <body>
    <p>
      <?php echo $error; ?>
    </p>
  </body>
</html>
```

Managing Jokes

Along with adding, deleting, and modifying jokes in our database, we also have to be able to assign categories and authors to our jokes. Furthermore, we're likely to have many more jokes than authors or categories. To try to display a complete list of jokes, as we did for the authors and categories, could result in an unmanageably long list with no easy way to spot the joke we're after. We need to create a more intelligent method of browsing our library of jokes.

Searching for Jokes

Sometimes we may know the category, author, or some of the text in a joke with which we want to work, so let's support all these methods for finding jokes in our database. When we're done, it should work like a simple search engine.

The form that prompts the administrator for information about the desired joke must present lists of categories and authors. Let's start with the controller code that fetches these details from the database:

chapter7/admin/jokes/index.php (excerpt)

```
// Display search form
include $_SERVER['DOCUMENT_ROOT'] . '/includes/db.inc.php';

try
{
  $result = $pdo->query('SELECT id, name FROM author');
}
catch (PDOException $e)
{
  $error = 'Error fetching authors from database!';
  include 'error.html.php';
```

```
  exit();
}

foreach ($result as $row)
{
  $authors[] = array('id' => $row['id'], 'name' => $row['name']);
}

try
{
  $result = $pdo->query('SELECT id, name FROM category');
}
catch (PDOException $e)
{
  $error = 'Error fetching categories from database!';
  include 'error.html.php';
  exit();
}

foreach ($result as $row)
{
  $categories[] = array('id' => $row['id'], 'name' => $row['name']);
}

include 'searchform.html.php';
```

This code builds two arrays for use by the **searchform.html.php** template: $authors
and $categories. We'll use each of these arrays to build a drop-down list in our
search form:

chapter7/admin/jokes/searchform.html.php

```php
<?php include_once $_SERVER['DOCUMENT_ROOT'] .
    '/includes/helpers.inc.php'; ?>
<!DOCTYPE html>
<html lang="en">
  <head>
    <meta charset="utf-8">
    <title>Manage Jokes</title>
  </head>
  <body>
    <h1>Manage Jokes</h1>
    <p><a href="?add">Add new joke</a></p>
    <form action="" method="get">
```

```
        <p>View jokes satisfying the following criteria:</p>
        <div>
          <label for="author">By author:</label>
          <select name="author" id="author">
            <option value="">Any author</option>
            <?php foreach ($authors as $author): ?>
              <option value="<?php htmlout($author['id']); ?>"><?php
                  htmlout($author['name']); ?></option>
            <?php endforeach; ?>
          </select>
        </div>
        <div>
          <label for="category">By category:</label>
          <select name="category" id="category">
            <option value="">Any category</option>
            <?php foreach ($categories as $category): ?>
              <option value="<?php htmlout($category['id']); ?>"><?php
                  htmlout($category['name']); ?></option>
            <?php endforeach; ?>
          </select>
        </div>
        <div>
          <label for="text">Containing text:</label>
          <input type="text" name="text" id="text">
        </div>
        <div>
          <input type="hidden" name="action" value="search">
          <input type="submit" value="Search">
        </div>
      </form>
      <p><a href="..">Return to JMS home</a></p>
    </body>
</html>
```

As you can see in each select list, we generate a series of option items using a PHP foreach loop. The value of each option is the author or category ID, and the text label of each option is the author or category name. Each of the drop-downs begins with an option with no value, which can be left alone to leave the corresponding field out of the search criteria.

Note also that the form's method attribute is set to get so that it's possible to bookmark the results of a search, since the form values will be submitted in the URL query string. You should generally apply this method to any search form you write.

The finished form appears in Figure 7.5.

It's up to the controller to use the values submitted by this form to build a list of jokes that satisfies the criteria specified. Obviously, this will be done with a SELECT query, but the exact nature of that query will depend on the search criteria specified. Because the building of this SELECT statement is a fairly complicated process, let's work through the controller code responsible a little at a time.

Figure 7.5. Search for a classic

To start, we define a few strings that, when strung together, form the SELECT query we'd need if no search criteria whatsoever had been selected in the form:

```
                                    chapter7/admin/jokes/index.php (excerpt)

if (isset($_GET['action']) and $_GET['action'] == 'search')
{
  include $_SERVER['DOCUMENT_ROOT'] . '/includes/db.inc.php';

  // The basic SELECT statement
```

```
$select = 'SELECT id, joketext';
$from   = ' FROM joke';
$where  = ' WHERE TRUE';
```

You might find the WHERE clause in this code a little confusing. The idea here is for us to be able to build on this basic SELECT statement, depending on the criteria selected in the form. These criteria will require us to add to the FROM and WHERE clauses (portions) of the SELECT query. But, if no criteria were specified (that is, the administrator wanted a list of all jokes in the database), there would be no need for a WHERE clause at all! Because it's difficult to add to a WHERE clause that's nonexistent, we need to come up with a "do nothing" WHERE clause that will have no effect on the results unless added to. Since TRUE is always true, WHERE TRUE fits the bill nicely.[2]

Our next task is to check each of the possible constraints (author, category, and search text) that may have been submitted with the form, and adjust the three components of our SQL query accordingly. First, we deal with the possibility that an author was specified. The blank option in the form was given a value of "", so if the value of that form field (stored in $_GET['author']) is not equal to '' (the empty string), an author has been specified and we must adjust our query:

chapter7/admin/jokes/index.php (excerpt)

```
$placeholders = array();

if ($_GET['author'] != '') // An author is selected
{
  $where .= " AND authorid = :authorid";
  $placeholders[':authorid'] = $_GET['author'];
}
```

As we've seen before, .= (the **append operator**) is used to tack a new string onto the end of an existing one. In this case, we add to the WHERE clause the condition that the authorid in the joke table must match the value of a placeholder, :authorid. We're going to want the value of that placeholder to be $_GET['author'], but we can't use bindValue to set it, because we're yet to have a prepared statement object to call it on; at this stage, our query is still spread across our three strings

---

[2] In fact, the "do nothing" WHERE clause could just be WHERE 1, since MySQL considers any positive number true. Feel free to change it if you like it better.

($select, $from, and $where). Eventually, we'll combine these strings together to create a prepared statement; in the meantime, we'll store our placeholders in a PHP array variable ($placeholders), with the name of each placeholder as the array index.

Next, we handle the specification of a joke category:

```
                              chapter7/admin/jokes/index.php (excerpt)

if ($_GET['category'] != '') // A category is selected
{
  $from  .= ' INNER JOIN jokecategory ON id = jokeid';
  $where .= " AND categoryid = :categoryid";
  $placeholders[':categoryid'] = $_GET['category'];
}
```

As the categories associated with a particular joke are stored in the jokecategory table, we need to add this table to the query to create a join. To do this, we simply tack INNER JOIN jokecategory ON id = jokeid onto the end of the $from variable. This joins the two tables on the condition that the id column (in the joke table) matches the jokeid column (in jokecategory).

With the join in place, we can then apply the criterion specified in the form submission—that the joke belongs to the specified category. By adding to the $where variable, we can require the categoryid column (in jokecategory) to match a particular category ID (:categoryid). Again, we store the value that we want to assign to this placeholder ($_GET['category']) in the $placeholders array.

Handling search text is fairly simple thanks to the LIKE SQL operator that we learned way back in Chapter 2:

```
                              chapter7/admin/jokes/index.php (excerpt)

if ($_GET['text'] != '') // Some search text was specified
{
  $where .= " AND joketext LIKE :joketext";
  $placeholders[':joketext'] = '%' . $_GET['text'] . '%';
}
```

We add percent signs (%) to the start and end of $_GET['text'] to get our placeholder value in this case. Remember that LIKE treats percent signs as wildcards, so in this case we're looking for joketext values that contain the value of $_GET['text'], but which may contain any other text before or after that value.

Now that we've assembled the component parts of our SQL query, we can put them together and use it to retrieve and display our jokes:

chapter7/admin/jokes/index.php *(excerpt)*

```php
try
{
  $sql = $select . $from . $where;
  $s = $pdo->prepare($sql);
  $s->execute($placeholders);
}
catch (PDOException $e)
{
  $error = 'Error fetching jokes.';
  include 'error.html.php';
  exit();
}

foreach ($s as $row)
{
  $jokes[] = array('id' => $row['id'], 'text' =>
    $row['joketext']);
}

include 'jokes.html.php';
exit();
}
```

Take particular notice of the line highlighted in bold. Because we have the values of all our placeholders stored in a PHP array variable ($placeholders), we can use a handy feature of the execute method: it lets us supply an array containing the values that we want to assign to the placeholders in our prepared statement, rather than having to use bindValue separately for each one. Slick!

The template to display these jokes will include **Edit** and **Delete** buttons for each joke. To keep the page as organized as possible, it will structure the results using an HTML table:

```php
<?php include_once $_SERVER['DOCUMENT_ROOT'] .
    '/includes/helpers.inc.php'; ?>
<!DOCTYPE html>
<html lang="en">
  <head>
    <meta charset="utf-8">
    <title>Manage Jokes: Search Results</title>
  </head>
  <body>
    <h1>Search Results</h1>
    <?php if (isset($jokes)): ?>
      <table>
        <tr><th>Joke Text</th><th>Options</th></tr>
        <?php foreach ($jokes as $joke): ?>
        <tr>
          <td><?php htmlout($joke['text']); ?></td>
          <td>
            <form action="?" method="post">
              <div>
                <input type="hidden" name="id" value="<?php
                    htmlout($joke['id']); ?>">
                <input type="submit" name="action" value="Edit">
                <input type="submit" name="action" value="Delete">
              </div>
            </form>
          </td>
        </tr>
        <?php endforeach; ?>
      </table>
    <?php endif; ?>
    <p><a href="?">New search</a></p>
    <p><a href="..">Return to JMS home</a></p>
  </body>
</html>
```

The search results will display as shown in Figure 7.6.

Figure 7.6. A classic is found

Nothing to Report

If you're up for a challenge, try adding a little code to this template to gracefully handle the case where no jokes satisfy the criteria specified in the search form. Right now, the template simply outputs nothing where the search results table should be.

Adding and Editing Jokes

At the top of the joke search form, we have our usual link to create a new joke:

```
                                    chapter7/admin/jokes/searchform.html.php (excerpt)

<p><a href="?add">Add new joke</a></p>
```

Let's implement this feature now. The code will be very similar to what we used to create new authors and categories, but in addition to specifying the joke text, the page must allow an administrator to assign an author and categories to a joke.

As with authors and categories, we can use the same form template for creating new jokes and editing existing jokes. Let's take a look at the important elements of this form. We begin with a standard text area into which we can type the text of the joke. If we're editing an existing joke, we'll populate this field with that joke's text ($text):

```
<div>
  <label for="text">Type your joke here:</label>
  <textarea id="text" name="text" rows="3" cols="40"><?php
      htmlout($text); ?></textarea>
</div>
```

Next, we'll prompt the administrator to select the author who wrote the joke:

```
<div>
  <label for="author">Author:</label>
  <select name="author" id="author">
    <option value="">Select one</option>
    <?php foreach ($authors as $author): ?>
      <option value="<?php htmlout($author['id']); ?>"<?php
        if ($author['id'] == $authorid)
        {
          echo ' selected';
        }
        ?>><?php htmlout($author['name']); ?></option>
    <?php endforeach; ?>
  </select>
</div>
```

Again, we've seen this kind of drop-down before (for example, in the joke search form), but the important difference is that we want to control the initial selection in the drop-down menu when we're editing an existing joke. The code in bold inserts the attribute selected into the <option> tag if the ID of the corresponding author ($author['id']) matches the author ID of the existing joke ($authorid).

Next, we need to prompt the administrator to select the categories the joke should belong to. A drop-down list is unsuitable because we want the administrator to be able to select *multiple* categories. Thus, we'll use a series of checkboxes (<input type="checkbox">)—one for each category. Since we have no way of knowing in advance the number of checkboxes we'll need, the matter of setting their name attribute becomes an interesting challenge.

What we'll do is use a *single* variable for all the checkboxes; thus, all the checkboxes will have the same name. To be able to receive multiple values from a single variable name, we must make that variable an **array**. Recall from Chapter 3 that an array is a single variable with compartments, each of which can hold a value. To submit a form element as part of an array variable, we simply add a pair of square brackets to the end of the `name` attribute (making it `categories[]` in this case).

A Multiple Selection List

Another way to submit an array is with a `<select multiple="multiple">` tag. Again, you'd set the `name` attribute to end with square brackets. What will be submitted is an array of all the `option` values selected from the list by the user.

Feel free to experiment with this approach by modifying the form to present the categories as a list of `option` elements; however, be aware that many users won't realize that they're able to select multiple options from the list by holding down **Ctrl** (⌘ on a Mac).

With all of our checkboxes named the same, we'll need a way to identify which particular checkboxes have been selected. To this end, we assign a different value to each checkbox—the ID of the corresponding category in the database. Thus, the form submits an array containing the IDs of all the categories to which the new joke should be added.

Again, since we need to edit an existing joke, we'll include some code to output `selected` if the joke already belongs to the corresponding category. This we'll indicate in our controller by setting `$category['selected']` to TRUE:

chapter7/admin/jokes/form.html.php *(excerpt)*

```
<fieldset>
  <legend>Categories:</legend>
  <?php foreach ($categories as $category): ?>
    <div><label for="category<?php htmlout($category['id']);
        ?>"><input type="checkbox" name="categories[]"
        id="category<?php htmlout($category['id']); ?>"
        value="<?php htmlout($category['id']); ?>"<?php
        if ($category['selected'])
        {
          echo ' checked';
        }
```

```
        ?>><?php htmlout($category['name']); ?></label></div>
    <?php endforeach; ?>
  </fieldset>
```

Other than these details, the form will work just like the other add/edit forms we've built. Here's the complete code:

```php
<?php include_once $_SERVER['DOCUMENT_ROOT'] .
    '/includes/helpers.inc.php'; ?>
<!DOCTYPE html>
<html lang="en">
  <head>
    <meta charset="utf-8">
    <title><?php htmlout($pageTitle); ?></title>
    <style type="text/css">
    textarea {
      display: block;
      width: 100%;
    }
    </style>
  </head>
  <body>
    <h1><?php htmlout($pageTitle); ?></h1>
    <form action="?<?php htmlout($action); ?>" method="post">
      <div>
        <label for="text">Type your joke here:</label>
        <textarea id="text" name="text" rows="3" cols="40"><?php
            htmlout($text); ?></textarea>
      </div>
      <div>
        <label for="author">Author:</label>
        <select name="author" id="author">
          <option value="">Select one</option>
          <?php foreach ($authors as $author): ?>
            <option value="<?php htmlout($author['id']); ?>"><?php
                if ($author['id'] == $authorid)
                {
                  echo ' selected';
                }
                ?>><?php htmlout($author['name']); ?></option>
          <?php endforeach; ?>
        </select>
```

```
    </div>
    <fieldset>
      <legend>Categories:</legend>
      <?php foreach ($categories as $category): ?>
        <div><label for="category<?php htmlout($category['id']);
            ?>"><input type="checkbox" name="categories[]"
            id="category<?php htmlout($category['id']); ?>"
            value="<?php htmlout($category['id']); ?>"<?php
            if ($category['selected'])
            {
              echo ' checked';
            }
            ?>><?php htmlout($category['name']); ?></label></div>
      <?php endforeach; ?>
    </fieldset>
    <div>
      <input type="hidden" name="id" value="<?php
          htmlout($id); ?>">
      <input type="submit" value="<?php htmlout($button); ?>">
    </div>
  </form>
 </body>
</html>
```

Figure 7.7 shows what the form will look like.

Figure 7.7. The hits just keep on coming

Let's now turn our attention back to the controller, which will display and then handle the submission of this form in both its modes.

When the user clicks the **Add new joke** link, we need to display the form with all its fields blank. None of this code should be unfamiliar. Take your time, look over it, and make sure it all makes sense to you. If you're unsure what a particular variable is for, go find it in the form template and identify its purpose:

chapter7/admin/jokes/index.php *(excerpt)*

```php
<?php
include_once $_SERVER['DOCUMENT_ROOT'] .
    '/includes/magicquotes.inc.php';

if (isset($_GET['add']))
{
  $pageTitle = 'New Joke';
  $action = 'addform';
  $text = '';
  $authorid = '';
  $id = '';
  $button = 'Add joke';

  include $_SERVER['DOCUMENT_ROOT'] . '/includes/db.inc.php';

  // Build the list of authors
  try
  {
    $result = $pdo->query('SELECT id, name FROM author');
  }
  catch (PDOException $e)
  {
    $error = 'Error fetching list of authors.';
    include 'error.html.php';
    exit();
  }

  foreach ($result as $row)
  {
    $authors[] = array('id' => $row['id'], 'name' => $row['name']);
  }

  // Build the list of categories
  try
```

```
  {
    $result = $pdo->query('SELECT id, name FROM category');
  }
  catch (PDOException $e)
  {
    $error = 'Error fetching list of categories.';
    include 'error.html.php';
    exit();
  }

  foreach ($result as $row)
  {
    $categories[] = array(
        'id' => $row['id'],
        'name' => $row['name'],
        'selected' => FALSE);
  }

  include 'form.html.php';
  exit();
}
```

Note especially that we're setting the `'selected'` item in each of the arrays stored in the `$categories` array to FALSE. As a result, none of the category checkboxes in the form will be selected by default.

When the user clicks the **Edit** button next to an existing joke, the controller must instead load the form with its fields populated with the existing values. This code is similar in structure to the code we used to generate the empty form:

chapter7/admin/jokes/index.php *(excerpt)*

```
if (isset($_POST['action']) and $_POST['action'] == 'Edit')
{
  include $_SERVER['DOCUMENT_ROOT'] . '/includes/db.inc.php';

  try
  {
    $sql = 'SELECT id, joketext, authorid FROM joke WHERE id = :id';
    $s = $pdo->prepare($sql);
    $s->bindValue(':id', $_POST['id']);
    $s->execute();
  }
```

```php
catch (PDOException $e)
{
  $error = 'Error fetching joke details.';
  include 'error.html.php';
  exit();
}
$row = $s->fetch();

$pageTitle = 'Edit Joke';
$action = 'editform';
$text = $row['joketext'];
$authorid = $row['authorid'];
$id = $row['id'];
$button = 'Update joke';

// Build the list of authors
try
{
  $result = $pdo->query('SELECT id, name FROM author');
}
catch (PDOException $e)
{
  $error = 'Error fetching list of authors.';
  include 'error.html.php';
  exit();
}

foreach ($result as $row)
{
  $authors[] = array('id' => $row['id'], 'name' => $row['name']);
}

// Get list of categories containing this joke
try
{
  $sql = 'SELECT categoryid FROM jokecategory
WHERE jokeid = :id'; ❶
  $s = $pdo->prepare($sql);
  $s->bindValue(':id', $id);
  $s->execute();
}
catch (PDOException $e)
{
  $error = 'Error fetching list of selected categories.';
  include 'error.html.php';
```

```php
    exit();
  }

  foreach ($s as $row)
  {
    $selectedCategories[] = $row['categoryid']; ❷
  }

  // Build the list of all categories
  try
  {
    $result = $pdo->query('SELECT id, name FROM category');
  }
  catch (PDOException $e)
  {
    $error = 'Error fetching list of categories.';
    include 'error.html.php';
    exit();
  }

  foreach ($result as $row)
  {
    $categories[] = array(
        'id' => $row['id'],
        'name' => $row['name'],
        'selected' => in_array($row['id'], $selectedCategories)); ❸
  }

  include 'form.html.php';
  exit();
}
```

In addition to fetching the details of the joke (ID, text, and author ID), this code fetches a list of categories to which the joke in question belongs:

 The SELECT query is straightforward, since it's simply fetching records from the jokecategory lookup table. It grabs all the category IDs associated with the joke ID for the joke that the user wishes to edit.

 This foreach loop stores all the selected category IDs into an array variable, $selectedCategories.

❸ And here's the big trick: while building the list of *all* categories for the form to display as checkboxes, we check each category's ID to see if it's listed in our $selectedCategories array. The built-in function in_array does this for us automatically. We store the return value (either TRUE or FALSE) in the 'selected' item of the array that represents each category. This value will then be used by the form template (as we've already seen) to select the appropriate checkboxes.

That takes care of generating the form in each of its two modes; now let's look at the controller code that processes the form submissions.

Since we're submitting an array for the first time (the list of selected category checkboxes), the code processing this form will feature a couple of new tricks as well. It starts off fairly simply as we add the joke to the joke table. As an author is required, we make sure that $_POST['author'] contains a value. This prevents the administrator from choosing the **Select One** option in the author select list (that choice has a value of "", the empty string):

```
                                    chapter7/admin/jokes/index.php (excerpt)

if (isset($_GET['addform']))
{
  include $_SERVER['DOCUMENT_ROOT'] . '/includes/db.inc.php';

  if ($_POST['author'] == '')
  {
    $error = 'You must choose an author for this joke.
        Click &lsquo;back&rsquo; and try again.';
    include 'error.html.php';
    exit();
  }

  try
  {
    $sql = 'INSERT INTO joke SET
        joketext = :joketext,
        jokedate = CURDATE(),
        authorid = :authorid';
    $s = $pdo->prepare($sql);
    $s->bindValue(':joketext', $_POST['text']);
    $s->bindValue(':authorid', $_POST['author']);
    $s->execute();
```

```
  }
  catch (PDOException $e)
  {
    $error = 'Error adding submitted joke.';
    include 'error.html.php';
    exit();
  }

  $jokeid = $pdo->lastInsertId();
```

The last line in the above code uses a method that we've yet to see: `lastInsertId`. This method returns the number assigned to the last inserted entry by the `AUTO_INCREMENT` feature in MySQL. In other words, it retrieves the ID of the newly inserted joke, which we'll need in a moment.

I expect you're a little foggy on how to write the code that adds the entries to `jokecategory` based on which checkboxes were checked. First of all, we've never seen how a checkbox passes its value to a PHP variable before. Additionally, we need to deal with the fact that these particular checkboxes will submit into an array variable.

A typical checkbox will pass its value to a PHP variable if it's checked, and will do nothing when it's unchecked. Checkboxes without assigned values pass `'on'` as the value of their corresponding variables when they're checked. However, we've assigned values to our checkboxes (the category IDs), so this isn't an issue.

The fact that these checkboxes submit into an array actually adds quite a measure of convenience to our code. In essence, we'll receive from the submitted form either:

- an array of category IDs to which we'll add the joke
- nothing at all (if none of the checkboxes were checked)

In the latter case, there's nothing to do—no categories were selected, so we have nothing to add to the `jokecategory` table. If we *do* have an array of category IDs to process, however, we'll use a `foreach` loop to issue an `INSERT` query for each ID (using a single prepared statement):

```
                                      chapter7/admin/jokes/index.php (excerpt)

if (isset($_POST['categories']))
{
  try
  {
    $sql = 'INSERT INTO jokecategory SET
        jokeid = :jokeid,
        categoryid = :categoryid';
    $s = $pdo->prepare($sql);

    foreach ($_POST['categories'] as $categoryid)
    {
      $s->bindValue(':jokeid', $jokeid);
      $s->bindValue(':categoryid', $categoryid);
      $s->execute();
    }
  }
  catch (PDOException $e)
  {
    $error = 'Error inserting joke into selected categories.';
    include 'error.html.php';
    exit();
  }
}

header('Location: .');
exit();
}
```

Note the use of the $jokeid variable, which we obtained from lastInsertId.

That takes care of adding new jokes. The form processing code for editing existing jokes is predictably similar, with two important differences:

- It uses an UPDATE query instead of an INSERT query to store the joke's details in the joke table.

- It removes all existing entries for the joke from the jokecategory table before INSERTing entries for the selected checkboxes in the form.

Here's the code. Take the time to read through it and make sure it all makes sense to you:

```php
if (isset($_GET['editform']))
{
  include $_SERVER['DOCUMENT_ROOT'] . '/includes/db.inc.php';

  if ($_POST['author'] == '')
  {
    $error = 'You must choose an author for this joke.
        Click &lsquo;back&rsquo; and try again.';
    include 'error.html.php';
    exit();
  }

  try
  {
    $sql = 'UPDATE joke SET
        joketext = :joketext,
        authorid = :authorid
        WHERE id = :id';
    $s = $pdo->prepare($sql);
    $s->bindValue(':id', $_POST['id']);
    $s->bindValue(':joketext', $_POST['text']);
    $s->bindValue(':authorid', $_POST['author']);
    $s->execute();
  }
  catch (PDOException $e)
  {
    $error = 'Error updating submitted joke.';
    include 'error.html.php';
    exit();
  }

  try
  {
    $sql = 'DELETE FROM jokecategory WHERE jokeid = :id';
    $s = $pdo->prepare($sql);
    $s->bindValue(':id', $_POST['id']);
    $s->execute();
  }
  catch (PDOException $e)
  {
    $error = 'Error removing obsolete joke category entries.';
    include 'error.html.php';
    exit();
```

```
  }

  if (isset($_POST['categories']))
  {
    try
    {
      $sql = 'INSERT INTO jokecategory SET
          jokeid = :jokeid,
          categoryid = :categoryid';
      $s = $pdo->prepare($sql);

      foreach ($_POST['categories'] as $categoryid)
      {
        $s->bindValue(':jokeid', $_POST['id']);
        $s->bindValue(':categoryid', $categoryid);
        $s->execute();
      }
    }
    catch (PDOException $e)
    {
      $error = 'Error inserting joke into selected categories.';
      include 'error.html.php';
      exit();
    }
  }

  header('Location: .');
  exit();
}
```

Deleting Jokes

The last feature to implement is the **Delete** button displayed next to each joke. The controller code responsible for this feature mirrors the code we wrote for the author and category **Delete** buttons, with only minor adjustments. For example, besides deleting the selected joke from the joke table, it must also remove any entries in the jokecategory table for that joke.

Here's the code. There's nothing new here, but take a look and make sure you're comfortable with everything that's going on:

chapter7/admin/jokes/index.php *(excerpt)*

```php
if (isset($_POST['action']) and $_POST['action'] == 'Delete')
{
  include $_SERVER['DOCUMENT_ROOT'] . '/includes/db.inc.php';

  // Delete category assignments for this joke
  try
  {
    $sql = 'DELETE FROM jokecategory WHERE jokeid = :id';
    $s = $pdo->prepare($sql);
    $s->bindValue(':id', $_POST['id']);
    $s->execute();
  }
  catch (PDOException $e)
  {
    $error = 'Error removing joke from categories.';
    include 'error.html.php';
    exit();
  }

  // Delete the joke
  try
  {
    $sql = 'DELETE FROM joke WHERE id = :id';
    $s = $pdo->prepare($sql);
    $s->bindValue(':id', $_POST['id']);
    $s->execute();
  }
  catch (PDOException $e)
  {
    $error = 'Error deleting joke.';
    include 'error.html.php';
    exit();
  }

  header('Location: .');
  exit();
}
```

Summary

There are still a few minor tasks that our content management system is incapable of. For example, it's unable to provide a listing of just the jokes that don't belong to *any* category—and this listing could be very handy as the number of jokes in the database grows. You might also like to sort the joke lists by various criteria. These particular capabilities require a few more advanced SQL tricks that we'll see in Chapter 11.

Some Code We've Left Behind

If you were to scrutinize closely the code archive for this chapter, you might notice that I've also tweaked the joke list page (in the **joke** folder) to remove the **Add your own joke** link and the **Delete** buttons. Because these features weren't designed to work with the new database structure we developed in this chapter, I've removed them for now.

In the section called "A Challenge: Joke Moderation" in Chapter 9, I challenge you to find a way to handle user-submitted jokes in an elegant way.

If we ignore these little details for the moment, you'll see that you now have a system that allows a person without SQL or database knowledge to administer your database of jokes with ease! Together with a set of PHP-powered pages through which regular site visitors can view the jokes, this CMS allows us to set up a complete database driven website that can be maintained by a user with absolutely no database knowledge. And if you think that sounds like a valuable commodity to businesses looking to be on the Web today, you're right!

In fact, only one aspect of our site requires users to have special knowledge (beyond the use of a web browser): content formatting. If we wanted to enable administrators to include rich-text formatting in the jokes they entered, we could invite them to type the necessary HTML code directly into the **New Joke** form. To preserve this formatting, we'd then `echo` out the content of our jokes "raw" instead of using our `htmlout` function.

This is unacceptable for two reasons: first, we'd have to stop accepting joke submissions from the general public, otherwise we'd be opening the door to attackers submitting harmful code in their jokes; our site would then display these unfiltered, since we'd no longer be passing our content through `htmlspecialchars`.

Second, as we stated way back in the introduction to this book, one of the most desirable features of a database driven website is that people can be responsible for adding content despite being unfamiliar with technical *mumbo jumbo* like HTML.

If we require knowledge of HTML for a task as simple as dividing a joke into paragraphs, or applying italics to a word or two, we'll have failed to achieve our goal.

In Chapter 8, I'll show you how to use some of the features of PHP that make it simpler for your users to format content without knowing the ins and outs of HTML. We'll also revisit the **Submit your own joke** form, and discover how we can safely accept content submissions from casual site visitors.

Content Formatting with Regular Expressions

We're almost there! We've designed a database to store jokes, organized them into categories, and tracked their authors. We've learned how to create a web page that displays this library of jokes to site visitors. We've even developed a set of web pages that a site administrator can use to manage the joke library without knowing anything about databases.

In so doing, we've built a site that frees the resident webmaster from continually having to plug new content into tired HTML page templates, and from maintaining an unmanageable mass of HTML files. The HTML is now kept completely separate from the data it displays. If you want to redesign the site, you simply have to make the changes to the HTML contained in the PHP templates that you've constructed. A change to one file (for example, modifying the footer) is immediately reflected in the page layouts of all pages in the site. Only one task still requires knowledge of HTML: **content formatting**.

On any but the simplest of websites, it will be necessary to allow content (in our case, jokes) to include some sort of formatting. In a simple case, this might merely be the ability to break text into paragraphs. Often, however, content providers will expect facilities such as **bold** or *italic* text, hyperlinks, and so on.

Supporting these requirements with our current code is deceptively easy. In the past couple of chapters, we've used `htmlout` to output user-submitted content:

```
chapter7/jokes/jokes.html.php (excerpt)

<?php htmlout($joke['text']); ?>
```

If, instead, we just `echo` out the raw content pulled from the database, we can enable administrators to include formatting in the form of HTML code in the joke text:

```
<?php echo $joke['text']; ?>
```

Following this simple change, a site administrator could include HTML tags that would have their usual effect on the joke text when inserted into a page.

But is this really what we want? Left unchecked, content providers can do a lot of damage by including HTML code in the content they add to your site's database. Particularly if your system will be enabling nontechnical users to submit content, you'll find that invalid, obsolete, and otherwise inappropriate code will gradually infest the pristine website you set out to build. With one stray tag, a well-meaning user could tear apart the layout of your site.

In this chapter, you'll learn about several new PHP functions that specialize in finding and replacing patterns of text in your site's content. I'll show you how to use these capabilities to provide a simpler markup language for your users that's better suited to content formatting. By the time we've finished, we'll have completed a content management system that anyone with a web browser can use—no knowledge of HTML required.

Regular Expressions

To implement our own markup language, we'll have to write some PHP code to spot our custom tags in the text of jokes and then replace them with their HTML equivalents. For tackling this sort of task, PHP includes extensive support for regular expressions.

A **regular expression** is a short piece of code that describes a pattern of text that may occur in content like our jokes. We use regular expressions to search for and replace patterns of text. They're available in many programming languages and environments, and are especially prevalent in web development languages like PHP.

The popularity of regular expressions has everything to do with how useful they are, and absolutely nothing to do with how easy they are to use—because they're not at all easy. In fact, to most people who encounter them for the first time, regular expressions look like what might eventuate if you fell asleep with your face on the keyboard.

Here, for example, is a relatively simple (yes, really!) regular expression that will match any string that might be a valid email address:

```
/^[\w\.\-]+@([\w\-]+\.)+[a-z]+$/i
```

Scary, huh? By the end of this section, you'll actually be able to make sense of that.

The language of a regular expression is cryptic enough that, once you master it, you may feel as if you're able to weave magical incantations with the code that you write. To begin with, let's start with some very simple regular expressions.

This is a regular expression that searches for the text "PHP" (without the quotes):

```
/PHP/
```

Fairly simple, right? It's the text for which you want to search surrounded by a pair of matching delimiters. Traditionally, slashes (/) are used as regular expression delimiters, but another common choice is the hash character (#). You can actually use any character as a delimiter except letters, numbers, or backslashes (\). I'll use slashes for all the regular expressions in this chapter.

Escape Delimiter Characters

To include a forward slash as part of a regular expression that uses forward slashes as delimiters, you must escape it with a preceding backslash (\/); otherwise, it will be interpreted as marking the end of the pattern.

The same goes for other delimiter characters: if you use hash characters as delimiters, you'll need to escape any hashes within the expression with backslashes (\#).

To use a regular expression, you must be familiar with the regular expression functions available in PHP. preg_match is the most basic, and can be used to determine whether a regular expression is **matched** by a particular text string.

Consider this code:

chapter8/preg_match1/index.php

```php
<?php
$text = 'PHP rules!';

if (preg_match('/PHP/', $text))
{
  $output = '$text contains the string &ldquo;PHP&rdquo;.';
}
else
{
  $output = '$text does not contain the string &ldquo;PHP&rdquo;.';
}

include 'output.html.php';
```

In this example, the regular expression finds a match because the string stored in the variable $text contains "PHP". This example will therefore output the message shown in Figure 8.1 (note that the single quotes around the strings in the code prevent PHP from filling in the value of the variable $text).

Figure 8.1. The regular expression finds a match

By default, regular expressions are case-sensitive; that is, lowercase characters in the expression only match lowercase characters in the string, and uppercase characters only match uppercase characters. If you want to perform a case-insensitive search instead, you can use a pattern modifier to make the regular expression ignore case.

Pattern modifiers are single-character flags following the ending delimiter of an expression. The modifier for performing a case-insensitive match is i. So while /PHP/ will only match strings that contain "PHP", /PHP/i will match strings that contain "PHP", "php", or even "pHp".

Here's an example to illustrate this:

chapter8/preg_match2/index.php

```php
<?php
$text = 'What is Php?';

if (preg_match('/PHP/i', $text))
{
  $output = '$text contains the string &ldquo;PHP&rdquo;.';
}
else
{
  $output = '$text does not contain the string &ldquo;PHP&rdquo;.';
}

include 'output.html.php';
```

Again, as shown in Figure 8.2, this outputs the same message despite the string actually containing "Php".

Figure 8.2. No need to be picky ...

Regular expressions are almost a programming language unto themselves. A dazzling variety of characters have a special significance when they appear in a regular expression. Using these special characters, you can describe in great detail the pattern of characters that a PHP function like `preg_match` will search for. To show you what I mean, let's look at a slightly more complex regular expression:

```
/^PH.*/
```

The caret (^), the dot (.), and the asterisk (*) are all special characters that have a specific meaning inside a regular expression. Specifically, the caret means "the start of the string," the dot means "any character," and the asterisk means "zero or more of the preceding character."

Therefore, the pattern `/^PH.*/` matches not only the string "PH", but "PHP", "PHX", "PHP: Hypertext Preprocessor", and any other string beginning with "PH".

When you first encounter it, regular expression syntax can be downright confusing and difficult to remember, so if you intend to make extensive use of it, a good reference might come in handy. The PHP Manual includes a very thorough regular expression reference,[1] but let's start with the basics.

Here are some of the most commonly used regular expression special characters (try not to lose too much sleep memorizing these), and some simple examples to illustrate how they work:

^ **(caret)**   The caret matches the start of the string. This excludes any characters—it considers merely the position itself.

$ **(dollar)**   A dollar character matches the end of the string. This excludes any characters—it considers merely the position itself:

```
/PHP/       Matches 'PHP rules!' and 'What is PHP?'
/^PHP/      Matches 'PHP rules!' but not 'What is PHP?'
/PHP$/      Matches 'I love PHP' but not 'What is PHP?'
/^PHP$/     Matches 'PHP' and no other string.
```

---

[1] http://php.net/manual/en/reference.pcre.pattern.syntax.php

| . (dot) | This is the wildcard character. It matches any single character except a newline (\n):[2] |

| /^...$/ | *Matches any three-character string (no newlines).* |

| * (asterisk) | An asterisk requires that the preceding character appears zero or more times. |

When matching, the asterisk will be **greedy**, including as many characters as possible. For example, for the string 'a word here, a word there', the pattern /a.*word/ will match 'a word here, a word'. In order to make a minimal match (just 'a word'), use the question mark character (explained shortly).

| + (plus) | This character requires that the preceding character appears one or more times. When matching, the plus will be greedy (just like the asterisk) unless you use the question mark character. |

| ? (question mark) | This character makes the preceding character optional. |

If placed after a plus or an asterisk, it instead dictates that the match for this preceding symbol will be a **minimal match** (also known as non-greedy or lazy matching), including as few characters as possible:

/bana?na/	*Matches 'banana' and 'banna', but not 'banaana'.*
/bana+na/	*Matches 'banana' and 'banaana', but not 'banna'.*
/bana*na/	*Matches 'banna', 'banana', and 'banaaana', but not 'bnana'.*
/^[a-zA-Z]+$/	*Matches any string of one or more letters only.*

| | (pipe) | The pipe causes the regular expression to match either the pattern on the left of the pipe, or the pattern on the right. |

---

[2] If you put an **S** pattern modifier at the end of your regular expression, the dot character will also match newlines.

(...) (round brackets)   Round brackets define a group of characters that must occur together, to which you can then apply a modifier like *, +, or ? by placing it after the closing bracket.

You can also refer to a bracketed portion of a regular expression later to obtain the *portion* of the string that it matched:

```
/^(yes|no)$/   Matches the strings 'yes' and 'no' only.
/ba(na)+na/    Matches 'banana' and 'banananana',
               but not 'bana' or 'banaana'.
/ba(na|ni)+/   Matches 'bana' and 'banina',
               but not 'naniba'.
```

[...] (square brackets)   Square brackets define a **character class**. A character class matches *one* character out of those listed within the square brackets.

A character class can include an explicit list of characters (for instance, [aqz], which is the same as (a|q|z)), or a range of characters (such as [a-z], which is the same as (a|b|c|...|z).

A character class can also be defined so that it matches one character that's *not* listed in the brackets. To do this, simply insert a caret (^) after the opening square bracket (so [^a] will match any single character except 'a').

Let's see all these in action:

```
/[12345]/    Matches '1a' (contains '1') and '39' (contains '3'),
             but doesn't match 'a' or '76'.
/[^12345]/   Matches '1a' (contains 'a') and '39' (contains '9'),
             but not '1', or '54'.
/[1-5]/      Equivalent to /[12345]/.
/^[a-z]$/    Matches any single lowercase letter.
/^[^a-z]$/   Matches any single character not a lowercase letter.
/[0-9a-zA-Z]/ Matches any string containing a letter or number.
```

If you want to use one of these special characters as a literal character to be matched by the regular expression pattern, escape it by placing a backslash (\) before it:

```
/1\+1=2/        Matches any string containing '1+1=2'.
/\$\$\$/        Matches any string containing '$$$'.
```

There are also a number of so-called **escape sequences** that will match a character that's either not easily typed, or a certain type of character:

\n   This sequence matches a newline character.

\r   This matches a carriage-return character.

\t   This matches a tab character.

\s   This sequence matches any **whitespace character**, which includes any newline, carriage-return, or tab character; it's the same as [\n\r\t].

\S   This matches any nonwhitespace character, and is the same as [^ \n\r\t].

\d   This matches any digit; it's the same as [0-9].

\D   This sequence matches anything but a digit, and is the same as [^0-9].

\w   This matches any "word" character. It's the same as [a-zA-Z0-9_].

\W   This sequence matches any "non-word" character, and is the same as [^a-zA-Z0-9_].

\b   This code is a little special because it doesn't actually match a character. Instead, it matches a word boundary—the start or end of a word.

\B   Like \b, this won't match a character. Rather, it matches a position in the string that is *not* a word boundary.

****   This matches an actual backslash character. So if you want to match the string "\n" exactly, your regular expression would be /\\n/, not /\n/ (which matches a newline character). Similarly, if you wanted to match the string "\\" exactly, your regular expression would be /\\\\/.

> ## \\ becomes \\\\
>
> To use your regular expression with a PHP function like `preg_match`, you need to write it as a PHP string. Just like regular expressions, however, PHP uses \\ to indicate a single backslash in a PHP string. A regular expression like /\\n/ must therefore be written in PHP as '/\\\\n/' to work properly. PHP takes the four backslashes to mean two backslashes, which is what you want your regular expression to contain.

Believe it or not, we now have everything we need to be able to understand the email address regular expression I showed you at the start of this section:

```
/^[\w\.\-]+@([\w\-]+\.)+[a-z]+$/i
```

/	The slash is the starting delimiter that marks the beginning of the regular expression.
^	We match the beginning of the string to make sure that nothing appears before the email address.
[\w\.\-]+	The name portion of the email address is made up of one or more (+) characters that are either "word" characters, dots, or hyphens ([\w\.\-]).
@	The name is followed by the @ character.
([\w\-]+\.)+	Then we have one or more (+) subdomains (such as "sitepoint."), each of which is one or more "word" characters or hyphens ([\w\-]+) followed by a dot (\.).
[a-z]+	Next, there's the top-level domain (for example, "com"), which is simply one or more letters ([a-z]+).
$	Finally, we match the end of the string, to make sure that nothing appears after the email address.
/i	The slash is the ending delimiter marking the end of the regular expression. The pattern modifier i following the slash indicates

that the letters in the regular expression (such as [a-z]) should
be treated case-insensitively.

Got all that? If you're feeling anything like I was when I first learned regular expressions, you're probably a little nervous. Okay, so you can follow along with a breakdown of a regular expression that someone else wrote for you, but can you really come up with this gobbledygook yourself? Don't sweat it: in the rest of this chapter, we'll look at a bunch more regular expressions, and before you know it you'll be writing expressions of your own with confidence.

String Replacement with Regular Expressions

As you may recall, we're aiming in this chapter to make it easier for non-HTML-savvy users to add formatting to the jokes on our website. For example, if a user puts asterisks around a word in the text of a joke (for example, 'Knock *knock*…'), we'd like to display that joke with HTML emphasis tags around that word (Knock knock…').

We can detect the presence of plain-text formatting such as this in a joke's text using preg_match with the regular expression syntax we've just learned; however, what we *need* to do is pinpoint that formatting and *replace* it with appropriate HTML tags. To achieve this, we need to look at another regular expression function offered by PHP: preg_replace.

preg_replace, like preg_match, accepts a regular expression and a string of text, and attempts to match the regular expression in the string. In addition, preg_replace takes another string of text and replaces every match of the regular expression with that string.

The syntax for preg_replace is as follows:

```
$newString = preg_replace(regExp, replaceWith, oldString);
```

Here, *regExp* is the regular expression, and *replaceWith* is the string that will replace matches in *oldString*. The function returns the new string with all the replacements made. In that code, this newly generated string is stored in $newString.

We're now ready to build our joke formatting function.

Emphasized Text

In Chapter 6, we wrote a helper function, htmlout, for outputting arbitrary text as HTML. This function is housed in a shared include file, **helpers.inc.php.** Since we'll now want to output text containing plain-text formatting as HTML, let's add a new helper function to the file for this purpose:

```
                                          chapter8/includes/helpers.inc.php (excerpt)

function markdown2html($text)
{
  $text = html($text);

  : Convert plain-text formatting to HTML

  return $text;
}
```

The plain-text formatting syntax we'll support is a simplified form of **Markdown,** created by John Gruber.

> Markdown is a text-to-HTML conversion tool for web writers. Markdown allows you to write using an easy-to-read, easy-to-write plain-text format, then convert it to structurally valid XHTML (or HTML).
>
> —the Markdown home page[3]

Since this helper function will convert Markdown to HTML, it's named markdown2html.

This function's first action is to use the html helper function to convert any HTML code present in the text into HTML text. We want to avoid any HTML code appearing in the output except that which is generated from plain-text formatting.[4]

---

[3] http://daringfireball.net/projects/markdown/

[4] Technically, this breaks one of the features of Markdown: support for inline HTML. "Real" Markdown can contain HTML code, which will be passed through to the browser untouched. The idea is that you can use HTML to produce any formatting that is too complex to create using Markdown's plain-text formatting syntax. Since we don't want to allow this, it might be more accurate to say we'll support Markdown-*style* formatting.

Let's start with formatting that will create **bold** and *italic* text.

In Markdown, you can emphasize text by surrounding it with a pair of asterisks (*), or a pair of underscores (_). Obviously, we'll replace any such pair with an <em> and </em> tag.[5]

To achieve this, we'll use two regular expressions: one that handles a pair of asterisks and one that handles a pair of underscores.

Let's start with the underscores:

```
/_[^_]+_/
```

Breaking this down:

/   We choose our usual slash character to begin (and therefore delimit) our regular expression.

_   There's nothing special about underscores in regular expressions, so this will simply match an underscore character in the text.

[^_]   A sequence of one or more characters that aren't underscores.

_   The second underscore, which marks the end of the italicized text.

/   The end of the regular expression.

Now, it's easy enough to feed this regular expression to `preg_replace`, but we have a problem:

```php
$text = preg_replace('/_[^_]+_/', '<em>emphasized text</em>',
➥$text);
```

The second argument we pass to `preg_replace` needs to be the text that we want to replace each match with. The problem is, we have no idea what the text that goes

---

[5] You may be more accustomed to using <b> and <i> tags for bold and italic text; however, I've chosen to respect the most recent HTML standards, which recommend using the more meaningful <strong> and <em> tags, respectively. If bold text doesn't necessarily indicate strong emphasis in your content, and italic text isn't representative of emphasis, you might want to use <b> and <i> instead.

between the <em> and </em> tags should be—it's part of the text that's being matched by our regular expression!

Thankfully, another feature of `preg_replace` comes to our rescue. If you surround a portion of the regular expression with round brackets (or parentheses), you can **capture** the corresponding portion of the matched text and use it in the replacement string. To do this, you'll use the code $*n*, where *n* is 1for the first parenthesized portion of the regular expression, 2 for the second, and so on, up to 99 for the 99th. Consider this example:

```
$text = 'banana';
$text = preg_replace('/(.*)(nana)/', '$2$1', $text);
echo $text; // outputs 'nanaba'
```

So $1 is replaced with the text matched by the first round-bracketed portion of the regular expression ((.*)—zero or more non-newline characters), which is ba in this case. $2 is replaced by nana, which is the text matched by the second round-bracketed portion of the regular expression ((nana)). The replacement string '$2$1', therefore, produces 'nanaba'.

We can use the same principle to create our emphasized text, adding a pair of round brackets to our regular expression:

```
/_([^_]+)_/
```

These brackets have no effect on how the expression works at all, but they create a **group** of matched characters that we can reuse in our replacement string:

chapter8/includes/helpers.inc.php *(excerpt)*

```
$text = preg_replace('/_([^_]+)_/', '<em>$1</em>', $text);
```

The pattern to match and replace pairs of asterisks looks much the same, except we need to escape the asterisks with backslashes, since the asterisk character normally has a special meaning in regular expressions:

chapter8/includes/helpers.inc.php *(excerpt)*

```
$text = preg_replace('/\*([^\*]+)\*/', '<em>$1</em>', $text);
```

That takes care of emphasized text, but Markdown also supports creating strong emphasis (`<strong>` tags) by surrounding text with a pair of *double* asterisks or underscores (`**strong emphasis**` or `__strong emphasis__`). Here's the regular expression to match pairs of double underscores:

```
/__(.+?)__/s
```

The double underscores at the start and end are straightforward enough, but what's going on inside the round brackets?

Previously, in our single-underscore pattern, we used `[^_]+` to match a series of one or more characters, none of which could be underscores. That works fine when the end of the emphasized text is marked by a single underscore, but when the end is a *double* underscore we want to allow for the emphasized text to contain single underscores (for example, `__text_with_strong_emphasis__`). "No underscores allowed," therefore, won't cut it—we must come up with some other way to match the emphasized text.

You might be tempted to use `.+` (one or more characters, any kind), giving us a regular expression like this:[6]

```
/__(.+)__/s
```

The problem with this pattern is that the `+` is **greedy**—it will cause this portion of the regular expression to gobble up as many characters as it can. Consider this joke, for example:

```
__Knock-knock.__ Who's there? __Boo.__ Boo who? __Aw, don't cry
➥ about it!__
```

When presented with this text, the regular expression above will see just a single match, beginning with two underscores at the start of the joke and ending with two underscores at the end. The rest of the text in between (including all the other double underscores) will be gobbled up by the greedy `.+` as the text to be emphasized!

---

[6] The `s` pattern modifier at the end of the regular expression ensures that the dot (`.`) will truly match any character, including newlines.

To fix this problem, we can ask the + to be *non-greedy* by adding a question mark after it. Instead of matching as many characters as possible, .+? will match as few characters as possible while still matching the rest of the pattern, ensuring we'll match each piece of emphasized text (and the double-underscores that surround it) individually. This gets us to our final regular expression:

```
/__(.+?)__/s
```

Using the same technique, we can also come up with a regular expression for double-asterisks. This is how the finished code for applying strong emphasis ends up looking:

chapter8/includes/helpers.inc.php *(excerpt)*

```
$text = preg_replace('/__(.+?)__/s', '<strong>$1</strong>',
➥ $text);
$text = preg_replace('/\*\*(.+?)\*\*/s', '<strong>$1</strong>',
➥ $text);
```

One last point: we must avoid converting pairs of single asterisks and underscores into <em> and </em> tags until after we've converted the pairs of double asterisks and underscores in the text into <strong> and </strong> tags. Our markdown2html function, therefore, will apply strong emphasis first, then regular emphasis:

chapter8/includes/helpers.inc.php *(excerpt)*

```
function markdown2html($text)
{
  $text = html($text);

  // strong emphasis
  $text = preg_replace('/__(.+?)__/s', '<strong>$1</strong>',
➥ $text);
  $text = preg_replace('/\*\*(.+?)\*\*/s', '<strong>$1</strong>',
➥ $text);

  // emphasis
  $text = preg_replace('/_([^_]+)_/', '<em>$1</em>', $text);
  $text = preg_replace('/\*([^\*]+)\*/', '<em>$1</em>', $text);
  ⋮
  return $text;
}
```

Paragraphs

While we could choose characters to mark the start and end of paragraphs just as we did for emphasized text, a simpler approach makes more sense. Since your users will type the content into a form field that allows them to create paragraphs using the **Enter** key, we'll take a single newline to indicate a line break (<br>) and a double newline to indicate a new paragraph (</p><p>).

As I explained earlier, you can represent a newline character in a regular expression as \n. Other whitespace characters you can write this way include a carriage return (\r) and a tab space (\t).

Exactly which characters are inserted into text when the user hits **Enter** depends on the user's operating system. In general, Windows computers represent a line break as a carriage return followed by a newline (\r\n), whereas Mac computers used to represent it as a single carriage return character (\r). These days, Macs and Linux computers use a single newline character (\n) to indicate a new line.[7]

To deal with these different line-break styles, any of which may be submitted by the browser, we must do some conversion:

```
// Convert Windows (\r\n) to Unix (\n)
$text = preg_replace('/\r\n/', "\n", $text);
// Convert Macintosh (\r) to Unix (\n)
$text = preg_replace('/\r/', "\n", $text);
```

Regular Expressions in Double Quoted Strings

All the regular expressions we've seen so far in this chapter have been expressed as single-quoted PHP strings. The automatic variable substitution provided by PHP strings is sometimes more convenient, but they can cause headaches when used with regular expressions.

Double-quoted PHP strings and regular expressions share a number of special character escape codes. "\n" is a PHP string containing a newline character.

---

[7] In fact, the type of line breaks used can vary between software programs on the same computer. If you've ever opened a text file in Notepad to see all the line breaks missing, you've experienced the frustration this can cause. Advanced text editors used by programmers usually let you specify the type of line breaks to use when saving a text file.

Likewise, /\n/ is a regular expression that will match any string containing a newline character. We can represent this regular expression as a single-quoted PHP string ('/\n/') and all is well, because the code \n has no special meaning in a single-quoted PHP string.

If we were to use a double-quoted string to represent this regular expression, we'd have to write "/\\n/"—with a double-backslash. The double-backslash tells PHP to include an actual backslash in the string, rather than combining it with the n that follows it to represent a newline character. This string will therefore generate the desired regular expression, /\n/.

Because of the added complexity it introduces, it's best to avoid using double-quoted strings when writing regular expressions. Note, however, that I *have* used double quotes for the replacement strings ("\n") passed as the second parameter to preg_replace. In this case, we actually do want to create a string containing a newline character, so a double-quoted string does the job perfectly.

With our line breaks all converted to newline characters, we can convert them to paragraph breaks (when they occur in pairs) and line breaks (when they occur alone):

```
// Paragraphs
$text = '<p>' . preg_replace('/\n\n/', '</p><p>', $text) . '</p>';
// Line breaks
$text = preg_replace('/\n/', '<br>', $text);
```

Note the addition of <p> and </p> tags surrounding the joke text. Because our jokes may contain paragraph breaks, we must make sure the joke text is output within the context of a paragraph to begin with.

This code does the trick: the line breaks in the text will now become the natural line- and paragraph-breaks expected by the user, removing the requirement to learn anything new to create this simple formatting.

It turns out, however, that there's a simpler way to achieve the same result in this case—there's no need to use regular expressions at all! PHP's str_replace function works a lot like preg_replace, except that it only searches for strings instead of regular expression patterns:

```
$newString = str_replace(searchFor, replaceWith, oldString);
```

We can therefore rewrite our line-breaking code as follows:

```php
// Convert Windows (\r\n) to Unix (\n)
$text = str_replace("\r\n", "\n", $text);
// Convert Macintosh (\r) to Unix (\n)
$text = str_replace("\r", "\n", $text);

// Paragraphs
$text = '<p>' . str_replace("\n\n", '</p><p>', $text) . '</p>';
// Line breaks
$text = str_replace("\n", '<br>', $text);
```

str_replace is much more efficient than preg_replace because there's no need for it to apply the complex rules that govern regular expressions. Whenever str_replace (or str_ireplace, if you need a case-insensitive search) can do the job, you should use it instead of preg_replace.

Hyperlinks

While supporting the inclusion of hyperlinks in the text of jokes may seem unnecessary, such a feature makes plenty of sense in other applications.

Here's what a hyperlink looks like in Markdown:[8]

```
[linked text](link URL)
```

Simple, right? You put the text of the link in square brackets, and follow it with the URL for the link in round brackets.

As it turns out, you've already learned everything you need to match and replace links like this with HTML links. If you're feeling up to the challenge, you should stop reading right here and try to tackle the problem yourself!

First, we need a regular expression that will match links of this form. The regular expression is as follows:

---

[8] Markdown also supports a more advanced link syntax where you put the link URL at the end of the document, as a footnote. But we won't be supporting that kind of link in our simplified Markdown implementation.

```
/\[([^\]]+)]\(([-a-z0-9._~:\/?#@!$&'()*+,;=%]+)\)/i
```

This is a rather complicated regular expression. You can see how regular expressions have gained a reputation for being indecipherable!

Squint at it for a little while, and see if you can figure out how it works. Grab a pen and break it into parts if you need to. If you have a highlighter pen handy, you might use it to mark the two pairs of parentheses (()) used to capture portions of the matched string: the linked text ($1) and the link URL ($1).

Let me break it down for you:

/

As with all our regular expressions, we choose to mark its beginning with a slash.

\[

This matches the opening square bracket ([). Since square brackets have a special meaning in regular expressions, we must escape it with a backslash to have it interpreted literally.

([^\]]+)

First of all, this portion of the regular expression is surrounded with round brackets, so the matching text will be available to us as $1 when we write the replacement string.

Inside the round brackets, we're after the linked text. Because the end of the linked text is marked with a closing square bracket (]), we can describe it as one or more characters, none of which is a closing square bracket ([^\]]+).

]\(

This will match the closing square bracket that ends the linked text, followed by the opening round bracket that signals the start of the link URL. The round bracket needs to be escaped with a backslash to prevent it from having its usual grouping effect. (The square bracket doesn't need to be escaped with a backslash because there is no unescaped opening square bracket currently in play.)

```
([-a-z0-9._~:\/?#@!$&'()*+,;=%]+)
```

Again, the round brackets make the matching text available to us as $2 in the replacement string.

As for the gobbledygook inside the brackets, it will match any URL.[9] The square brackets contain a list of characters that may appear in a URL, which is followed by a + to indicate that one or more of these acceptable characters must be present.

Within a square-bracketed list of characters, many of the characters that normally have a special meaning within regular expressions lose that meaning. ., ?, +, *, (, and) are all listed here without the need to be escaped by backslashes. The only character that *does* need to be escaped in this list is the slash (/), which must be written as \/ to prevent it from being mistaken for the end-of-regular-expression delimiter.

Note also that to include the hyphen (-) in the list of characters, you have to list it first. Otherwise, it would have been taken to indicate a range of characters (as in a-z and 0-9).

```
\)
```

This escaped round bracket matches the closing round bracket ()) at the end of the link URL.

```
/i
```

We mark the end of the regular expression with a slash, followed by the case-insensitivity flag, i.

We can therefore convert links with the following PHP code:

chapter8/includes/helpers.inc.php *(excerpt)*

```php
$text = preg_replace(
    '/\[([^\]]+)\]\(([-a-z0-9._~:\/?#@!$&\'()*+,;=%]+)\)/i',
    '<a href="$2">$1</a>', $text);
```

---

[9] It will also match some strings that are invalid URLs, but it's close enough for our purposes. If you're especially intrigued by regular expressions, you might want to check out RFC 3986, [http://tools.ietf.org/html/rfc3986#appendix-B] the official standard for URLs. Appendix B of this specification demonstrates how to parse a URL with a rather impressive regular expression.

As you can see, $1 is used in the replacement string to substitute the captured link text, and $2 is used for the captured URL.

Additionally, because we're expressing our regular expression as a single-quoted PHP string, you have to escape the single quote that appears in the list of acceptable characters with a backslash.

Putting It All Together

Here's our finished helper function for converting Markdown to HTML:

chapter8/includes/helpers.inc.php *(excerpt)*

```php
function markdown2html($text)
{
  $text = html($text);

  // strong emphasis
  $text = preg_replace('/__(.+?)__/s', '<strong>$1</strong>',
➡ $text);
  $text = preg_replace('/\*\*(.+?)\*\*/s', '<strong>$1</strong>',
➡ $text);

  // emphasis
  $text = preg_replace('/_([^_]+)_/', '<em>$1</em>', $text);
  $text = preg_replace('/\*([^\*]+)\*/', '<em>$1</em>', $text);

  // Convert Windows (\r\n) to Unix (\n)
  $text = str_replace("\r\n", "\n", $text);
  // Convert Macintosh (\r) to Unix (\n)
  $text = str_replace("\r", "\n", $text);

  // Paragraphs
  $text = '<p>' . str_replace("\n\n", '</p><p>', $text) . '</p>';
  // Line breaks
  $text = str_replace("\n", '<br>', $text);

  // [linked text](link URL)
  $text = preg_replace(
      '/\[([^\]]+)]\](([-a-z0-9._~:\/?#@!$&\'()*+,;=%]+)\)/i',
      '<a href="$2">$1</a>', $text);

  return $text;
}
```

For added convenience when using this in a PHP template, we'll add a markdownout function that calls markdown2html and then echoes out the result:

chapter8/includes/helpers.inc.php (excerpt)

```php
function markdownout($text)
{
  echo markdown2html($text);
}
```

We can then use this helper in our two templates that output joke text. First, in the admin pages, we have the joke search results template:

chapter8/admin/jokes/jokes.html.php

```php
<?php include_once $_SERVER['DOCUMENT_ROOT'] .
    '/includes/helpers.inc.php'; ?>
<!DOCTYPE html>
<html lang="en">
  <head>
    <meta charset="utf-8">
    <title>Manage Jokes: Search Results</title>
  </head>
  <body>
    <h1>Search Results</h1>
    <?php if (isset($jokes)): ?>
      <table>
        <tr><th>Joke Text</th><th>Options</th></tr>
        <?php foreach ($jokes as $joke): ?>
        <tr valign="top">
          <td><?php markdownout($joke['text']); ?></td>
          <td>
            <form action="?" method="post">
              <div>
                <input type="hidden" name="id" value="<?php
                    htmlout($joke['id']); ?>">
                <input type="submit" name="action" value="Edit">
                <input type="submit" name="action" value="Delete">
              </div>
            </form>
          </td>
        </tr>
        <?php endforeach; ?>
      </table>
```

```
      <?php endif; ?>
      <p><a href="?">New search</a></p>
      <p><a href="..">Return to JMS home</a></p>
   </body>
</html>
```

Second, we have the public joke list page:

chapter8/jokes/jokes.html.php

```
<?php include_once $_SERVER['DOCUMENT_ROOT'] .
   '/includes/helpers.inc.php'; ?>
<!DOCTYPE html>
<html lang="en">
  <head>
    <meta charset="utf-8">
    <title>List of Jokes</title>
  </head>
  <body>
    <p>Here are all the jokes in the database:</p>
    <?php foreach ($jokes as $joke): ?>
      <blockquote>
        <p>
          <?php markdownout($joke['text']); ?>
          (by <a href="mailto:<?php htmlout($joke['email']); ?>">
            <?php htmlout($joke['name']); ?></a>)
        </p>
      </blockquote>
    <?php endforeach; ?>
  </body>
</html>
```

With these changes made, take your new plain-text formatting for a spin! Edit a few of your jokes to contain Markdown syntax and verify that the formatting is correctly displayed.

Use the PHP Markdown Library

What's nice about adopting a formatting syntax like Markdown for your own website is that there's often plenty of open-source code out there to help you deal with it.

Your newfound regular expression skills will serve you well in your career as a web developer, but if you want to support Markdown formatting on your site, the easiest way to do it would be to *not* write all the code to handle Markdown formatting yourself!

Instead, a quick Google search will find you the PHP Markdown project,[10] from which you can download a **markdown.php** file that you can drop in your site's **includes** folder. You can then use the `Markdown` function it contains in your `markdown2html` helper function:

```
function markdown2html($text)
{
  $text = html($text);

  include_once $_SERVER['DOCUMENT_ROOT'] .
➥ '/includes/markdown.php';
  return Markdown($text);
}
```

Go ahead and give this a try. Make sure your formatting still works, and then curse me for dragging you through the ordeal of regular expressions when you could have avoided it. (Seriously, it's a handy skill.)

Real World Content Submission

It seems a shame to have spent so much time and effort on a content management system that's really easy to use, when the only people who are actually *allowed* to use it are the site administrators. Furthermore, while it's extremely convenient for an administrator not having to edit HTML when making updates to the site's content, submitted documents still need to be transcribed into the "Add new joke" form, and any formatted text converted into Markdown—a tedious and mind-numbing task, to say the least.

What if we put the "Add new joke" form in the hands of casual site visitors? If you recall, we actually did this in Chapter 4 when we put an **Add your own joke** link on our public joke list page, through which users could submit their own jokes. At the time, this was simply a device that demonstrated how `INSERT` statements could be made from within PHP scripts, and we've since removed it (because it was incom-

---

[10] http://michelf.com/projects/php-markdown/

patible with some changes we made to our database structure), but given how easy Markdown is to write, it sure would be nice to put a joke submission form back in the hands of our visitors.

In the next chapter, we'll introduce access control to your joke database, making your website one that could survive in the real world. Most importantly, you'll limit access to the admin pages for the site to authorized users only. But perhaps more excitingly, we will revisit the idea of accepting joke submissions from your visitors.

Cookies, Sessions, and Access Control

Cookies and sessions are two of those mysterious technologies that are almost always made out to be more intimidating and complex than they really are. In this chapter, I'll debunk those myths by explaining in simple language what they are, how they work, and what they can do for you. I'll also provide practical examples to demonstrate each.

Finally, we'll use these new tools to provide sophisticated access control to the administration features of your Internet Joke Database site.

Cookies

Most computer programs these days preserve some form of **state** when you close them. Whether it be the position of the application window, or the names of the last five files that you worked with, the settings are usually stored in a small file on your system so that they can be read back the next time the program is run. When web developers took web design to the next level, and moved from static pages to complete, interactive online applications, there was a need for similar functionality in web browsers—so cookies were born.

A **cookie** is a name-value pair associated with a given website, and stored on the computer that runs the client (browser). Once a cookie is set by a website, all future page requests to that same site will also include the cookie until it **expires** or becomes out of date. Other websites are unable to access the cookies set by your site, and vice versa, so, contrary to popular belief, they're a relatively safe place to store personal information. Cookies in and of themselves are incapable of compromising a user's privacy.

Illustrated in Figure 9.1 is the life cycle of a PHP-generated cookie.

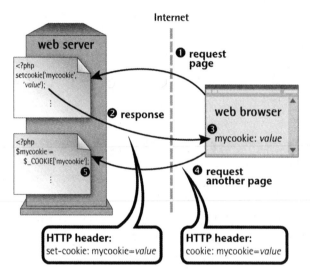

Figure 9.1. The life cycle of a cookie

❶ First, a web browser requests a URL that corresponds to a PHP script. Within that script is a call to the `setcookie` function that's built into PHP.

❷ The page produced by the PHP script is sent back to the browser, along with an HTTP `set-cookie` header that contains the name (for example, `mycookie`) and value of the cookie to be set.

❸ When it receives this HTTP header, the browser creates and stores the specified value as a cookie named `mycookie`.

❹ Subsequent page requests to that website contain an HTTP `cookie` header that sends the name/value pair (`mycookie=value`) to the script requested.

Upon receipt of a page request with a `cookie` header, PHP automatically creates an entry in the `$_COOKIE` array with the name of the cookie (`$_COOKIE['mycookie']`) and its value.

In other words, the PHP `setcookie` function lets you set a variable that will automatically be set by subsequent page requests from the same browser. Before we examine an actual example, let's take a close look at the `setcookie` function:

```
setcookie(name[, value[, expiryTime[, path[, domain[, secure[,
    httpOnly]]]]]])
```

 Square Brackets Indicate Optional Code

The square brackets (`[…]`) indicate portions of the code that are optional. Leave out the square brackets when using the syntax in your code.

Like the `header` function we saw in Chapter 4, the `setcookie` function adds HTTP headers to the page, and thus *must be called before any of the actual page content is sent*. Any attempt to call `setcookie` after page content has been sent to the browser will produce a PHP error message. Typically, therefore, you'll use these functions in your controller script before any actual output is sent (by an included PHP template, for example).

The only required parameter for this function is *name*, which specifies the name of the cookie. Calling `setcookie` with only the *name* parameter will actually delete the cookie that's stored on the browser, if it exists. The *value* parameter allows you to create a new cookie, or modify the value stored in an existing one.

By default, cookies will remain stored by the browser, and thus will continue to be sent with page requests until the browser is closed by the user. If you want the cookie to persist beyond the current browser session, you must set the *expiryTime* parameter to specify the number of seconds from January 1, 1970 to the time at which you want the cookie to be deleted automatically. The current time in this format can be obtained using the PHP `time` function. Thus, a cookie could be set to expire in one hour, for example, by setting *expiryTime* to `time() + 3600`. To delete a cookie that has a preset expiry time, change this expiry time to represent a point in the past (such as one year ago: `time() - 3600 * 24 * 365`). Here are two examples showing these techniques in practice:

```
// Set a cookie to expire in 1 year
setcookie('mycookie', 'somevalue', time() + 3600 * 24 * 365);
```

```
// Delete it
setcookie('mycookie', '', time() - 3600 * 24 * 365);
```

The *path* parameter lets you restrict access to the cookie to a given path on your server. For instance, if you set a path of ' /admin/ ' for a cookie, only requests for pages in the **admin** directory (and its subdirectories) will include the cookie as part of the request. Note the trailing /, which prevents scripts in other directories beginning with /admin (such as /**adminfake**/) from accessing the cookie. This is helpful if you're sharing a server with other users, and each user has a web home directory. It allows you to set cookies without exposing your visitors' data to the scripts of other users on your server.

The *domain* parameter serves a similar purpose: it restricts the cookie's access to a given domain. By default, a cookie will be returned only to the host from which it was originally sent. Large companies, however, commonly have several host names for their web presence (for example, www.example.com and support.example.com). To create a cookie that's accessible by pages on both servers, you would set the *domain* parameter to ' .example.com '. Note the leading ., which prevents another site at fakeexample.com from accessing your cookies on the basis that their domain ends with example.com.

The *secure* parameter, when set to 1, indicates that the cookie should be sent only with page requests that happen over a secure (SSL) connection (that is, with a URL that starts with https://).

The *httpOnly* parameter, when set to 1, tells the browser to prevent JavaScript code on your site from seeing the cookie that you're setting. Normally, the JavaScript code you include in your site can read the cookies that have been set by the server for the current page. While this can be useful in some cases, it also puts the data stored in your cookies at risk should an attacker figure out a way to inject malicious JavaScript code into your site. This code could then read your users' potentially sensitive cookie data and do unspeakable things with it. If you set *httpOnly* to 1, the cookie you're setting will be sent to your PHP scripts as usual, but will be invisible to JavaScript code running on your site.

While all parameters except *name* are optional, you must specify values for earlier parameters if you want to specify values for later ones. For instance, to call setcookie with a *domain* value, you also need to specify a value for the *expiryTime* parameter. To omit parameters that require a value, you can set string parameters (*value*, *path*, *domain*) to ' ' (the empty string) and numerical parameters (*expiryTime*, *secure*) to 0.

Let's now look at an example of cookies in use. Imagine you want to display a special welcome message to people on their first visit to your site. You could use a cookie to count the number of times a user had been to your site before, and only display the message when the cookie was not set. Here's the code:

chapter9/cookiecounter/index.php

```php
<?php

if (!isset($_COOKIE['visits']))
{
  $_COOKIE['visits'] = 0;
}
$visits = $_COOKIE['visits'] + 1;
setcookie('visits', $visits, time() + 3600 * 24 * 365);

include 'welcome.html.php';
```

This code starts by checking if $_COOKIE['visits'] is set. If it isn't, it means the visits cookie has yet to be set in the user's browser. To handle this special case, we set $_COOKIE['visits'] to 0. The rest of our code can then safely assume that $_COOKIE['visits'] contains the number of previous visits the user has made to the site.

Next, to work out the number of *this* visit, we take $_COOKIE['visits'] and add the value 1. This variable, $visits, will be used by our PHP template.

Finally, we use setcookie to set the visits cookie to reflect the new number of visits. We set this cookie to expire in one year's time.

With all the work done, our controller includes the PHP template **welcome.html.php**:

```
                                        chapter9/cookiecounter/welcome.html.php
<?php include_once $_SERVER['DOCUMENT_ROOT'] .
    '/includes/helpers.inc.php'; ?>
<!DOCTYPE html>
<html lang="en">
  <head>
    <meta charset="utf-8">
    <title>Cookie counter</title>
  </head>
  <body>
    <p>
      <?php
      if ($visits > 1)
      {
        echo "This is visit number $visits.";
      }
      else
      {
        // First visit
        echo 'Welcome to my website! Click here for a tour!';
      }
      ?>
    </p>
  </body>
</html>
```

Figure 9.2 shows what this example looks like the first time a browser visits the page. Subsequent visits look like Figure 9.3.

Figure 9.2. The first visit

Figure 9.3. The second visit

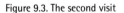

Before you go overboard using cookies, be aware that browsers place a limit on the number and size of cookies allowed per website. Some browsers will start deleting old cookies to make room for new ones after you've set 20 cookies from your site. Other browsers will allow up to 50 cookies per site, but will *reject* new cookies beyond this limit. Browsers also enforce a maximum combined size for all cookies from all websites, so an especially cookie-heavy site might cause your own site's cookies to be deleted.

For these reasons, do your best to keep the number and size of the cookies your site creates to a minimum.

PHP Sessions

Because of the limitations I've just described, cookies are inappropriate for storing large amounts of information. If you run an ecommerce website that uses cookies to store items in shopping carts as users make their way through your site, it can be a huge problem; the bigger a customer's order, the more likely it will run afoul of a browser's cookie restrictions.

Sessions were developed in PHP as the solution to this issue. Instead of storing all your (possibly large) data as cookies in your visitor's web browser, sessions let you store the data on your web server. The only value that's stored in the browser is a single cookie containing the user's **session ID**—a long string of letters and numbers that serves to identify that user uniquely for the duration of their visit to your site. It's a variable for which PHP watches on subsequent page requests, and uses to load the stored data that's associated with that session.

Unless configured otherwise, a PHP session automatically sets a cookie in the user's browser that contains the session ID. The browser then sends that cookie, along with every request for a page from your site, so that PHP can determine to which of potentially numerous sessions-in-progress the request belongs. Using a set of temporary files that are stored on the web server,[1] PHP keeps track of the variables that have been registered in each session, and their values.

Before you can go ahead and use the spiffy session-management features in PHP, you should ensure that the relevant section of your **php.ini** file has been set up properly. If you're using one of the all-in-one packages described in Chapter 1 (like XAMPP or MAMP), or if you're using a server that belongs to your web host, it's probably safe to assume this has been done for you. Otherwise, open your **php.ini** file in a text editor and look for the section marked [Session] (say *that* ten times fast!). Beneath it, you'll find around 20 options that begin with the word session. Most of them are fine as they are, but there are a few crucial ones you'll want to check:

---

[1] PHP can also be configured to store sessions in your MySQL database; however, this is only necessary if you need to share session data between multiple web servers.

```
session.save_handler    = files
session.save_path       = "C:\WINDOWS\TEMP"
session.use_cookies     = 1
```

session.save_path tells PHP where to create the temporary files used to track sessions. It must be set to a directory that exists on the system, or you'll receive ugly error messages when you try to create a session on one of your pages. On Mac OS X and Linux systems, **/tmp** is a popular choice. In Windows, you could use **C:\WINDOWS\TEMP**, or some other directory if you prefer (**D:\PHP\SESSIONS**, for example). With these adjustments made, restart your web server software to allow the changes to take effect.

You're now ready to start working with PHP sessions. Before we jump into an example, let's quickly look at the most common session management functions in PHP. To tell PHP to look for a session ID, or start a new session if none is found, you simply call session_start. If an existing session ID is found when this function is called, PHP restores the variables that belong to that session. Since this function attempts to create a cookie, it must come before any page content is sent to the browser, just as we saw for setcookie above:

```
session_start();
```

To create a session variable that will be available on all pages in the site when accessed by the current user, set a value in the special $_SESSION array. For example, the following will store the variable called password in the current session:

```
$_SESSION['password'] = 'mypassword';
```

To remove a variable from the current session, use PHP's unset function:

```
unset($_SESSION['password']);
```

Finally, should you want to end the current session and delete all registered variables in the process, clear all the stored values and use session_destroy:

```
$_SESSION = array();
session_destroy();
```

For more detailed information on these and the other session-management functions in PHP, see the relevant section of the PHP Manual.[2]

Now that we have these basic functions under our belt, let's put them to work in a simple example.

A Simple Shopping Cart

This example will consist of a controller script feeding two PHP templates:

- a product catalog, through which you can add items to your shopping cart
- a checkout page, which displays the contents of the user's shopping cart for confirmation

From the checkout page, the order could then be submitted to a processing system that would handle the details of payment acceptance and shipping arrangements. That system is beyond the scope of this book, but if you'd like to try one I'd recommend playing with PayPal,[3] which is quite easy to set up. The documentation page should be well within reach of your PHP skills at this point.

Let's start with the controller code that sets up the list of items we'll have for sale in our online store. For each item, we wish to list a description and a price per unit. For this example, we'll code these details as a PHP array. In a real-world system, you would probably store these details in a database, but I'm using this method so that we can focus on the session code. You should already have all the knowledge to put together a database driven product catalog, so if you're feeling ambitious, go ahead and write it now.

Here's the code for our list of products:

chapter9/shoppingcart/index.php *(excerpt)*

```php
<?php
include_once $_SERVER['DOCUMENT_ROOT'] .
    '/includes/magicquotes.inc.php';

$items = array(
    array('id' => '1', 'desc' => 'Canadian-Australian Dictionary',
```

[2] http://www.php.net/session
[3] http://www.paypal.com/

```
                'price' => 24.95),
    array('id' => '2', 'desc' => 'As-new parachute (never opened)',
                'price' => 1000),
    array('id' => '3', 'desc' => 'Songs of the Goldfish (2CD set)',
                'price' => 19.99),
    array('id' => '4', 'desc' => 'Simply JavaScript (SitePoint)',
                'price' => 39.95));
```

Each item in this array is itself an associative array of three items: a unique item ID, the item description, and the price. It's no coincidence that this looks like an array of results we might build from querying a database.

Now we're going to store the list of items the user placed in the shopping cart in yet another array. Because we'll need this variable to persist throughout a user's visit to your site, we'll store it using PHP sessions. Here's the code that's responsible:

chapter9/shoppingcart/index.php (excerpt)

```
session_start();
if (!isset($_SESSION['cart']))
{
  $_SESSION['cart'] = array();
}
```

session_start either starts a new session (and sets the session ID cookie), or restores the variables registered in the existing session, if one exists. The code then checks if $_SESSION['cart'] exists, and, if it doesn't, initializes it to an empty array to represent the empty cart.

That's all we need to display a product catalog using a PHP template:

chapter9/shoppingcart/index.php (excerpt)

```
include 'catalog.html.php';
```

Let's look at the code for this template:

chapter9/shoppingcart/catalog.html.php

```
<?php include_once $_SERVER['DOCUMENT_ROOT'] .
    '/includes/helpers.inc.php'; ?>
<!DOCTYPE html>
```

```
<html lang="en">
  <head>
    <meta charset="utf-8">
    <title>Product Catalog</title>
    <style>
    table {
      border-collapse: collapse;
    }
    td, th {
      border: 1px solid black;
    }
    </style>
  </head>
  <body>
    <p>Your shopping cart contains <?php
        echo count($_SESSION['cart']); ?> items.</p> ❶
    <p><a href="?cart">View your cart</a></p> ❷
    <table border="1">
      <thead>
        <tr>
          <th>Item Description</th>
          <th>Price</th>
        </tr>
      </thead>
      <tbody>
        <?php foreach ($items as $item): ?>
          <tr>
            <td><?php htmlout($item['desc']); ?></td>
            <td>
              $<?php echo number_format($item['price'], 2); ?> ❸
            </td>
            <td>
              <form action="" method="post"> ❹
                <div>
                  <input type="hidden" name="id" value="<?php
                      htmlout($item['id']); ?>">
                  <input type="submit" name="action" value="Buy">
                </div>
              </form>
            </td>
          </tr>
        <?php endforeach; ?>
      </tbody>
    </table>
```

```
    <p>All prices are in imaginary dollars.</p>
  </body>
</html>
```

Here are the highlights:

 We use the built-in PHP function `count` to output the number of items in the array stored in the `$_SESSION['cart']`.

 We provide a link to let the user view the contents of the shopping cart. In a system that provided checkout facilities, you might label this link **Proceed to Checkout**.

 We use PHP's built-in `number_format` function to display the prices with two digits after the decimal point (see the PHP Manual[4] for more information about this function).

 For each item in the catalog, we provide a form with a **Buy** button that submits the unique ID of the item.

Figure 9.4 shows the product catalog produced by this template.

Figure 9.4. The completed product catalog

---

[4] http://www.php.net/number_format

Now, when a user clicks one of the **Buy** buttons, our controller will receive a form submission with `$_POST['action']` set to `'Buy'`. Here's how we process this in the controller:

```
                                    chapter9/shoppingcart/index.php (excerpt)

if (isset($_POST['action']) and $_POST['action'] == 'Buy')
{
  // Add item to the end of the $_SESSION['cart'] array
  $_SESSION['cart'][] = $_POST['id'];
  header('Location: .');
  exit();
}
```

We add the product ID of the item to the `$_SESSION['cart']` array before redirecting the browser back to the same page, but without submitted form data, thereby ensuring that the user can refresh the page without adding the item to the cart again.

When the user clicks the **View your cart** link, our controller will receive a request with `$_GET['cart']` set. Here's how our controller will handle this:

```
                                    chapter9/shoppingcart/index.php (excerpt)

if (isset($_GET['cart']))
{
  $cart = array();
  $total = 0;
  foreach ($_SESSION['cart'] as $id)
  {
    foreach ($items as $product)
    {
      if ($product['id'] == $id)
      {
        $cart[] = $product;
        $total += $product['price'];
        break;
      }
    }
  }

  include 'cart.html.php';
  exit();
}
```

What this code does is build an array ($cart) much like the $items array, except that the items in $cart reflect the items the user has added to the shopping cart. To do this, it uses two nested foreach loops. The first loops through the IDs in $_SESSION['cart']. For each of these IDs, it uses the second foreach loop to search through the $items array looking for a product whose ID ($product['id']) is equal to the $id from the cart. When it finds the product, it adds it to the $cart array.

At the same time, this code tallies the total price of the items in the shopping cart. Each time the second foreach loop finds the product in the cart, it adds its price ($product['price']) to the $total.

The break command tells PHP to stop executing the second foreach loop, since it's found the product it has been searching for.

Once the $cart array is built, we load the second of our two PHP templates, **cart.html.php**.

The code for **cart.html.php** is very similar to the product catalog template. All it does is list the items in the $cart array instead of the $items array. It also outputs the total in the footer of the table:

chapter9/shoppingcart/cart.html.php

```php
<?php include_once $_SERVER['DOCUMENT_ROOT'] .
    '/includes/helpers.inc.php'; ?>
<!DOCTYPE html>
<html lang="en">
  <head>
    <meta charset="utf-8">
    <title>Shopping Cart</title>
    <style>
    table {
      border-collapse: collapse;
    }
    td, th {
      border: 1px solid black;
    }
    </style>
  </head>
  <body>
    <h1>Your Shopping Cart</h1>
    <?php if (count($cart) > 0): ?>
```

```
    <table>
      <thead>
        <tr>
          <th>Item Description</th>
          <th>Price</th>
        </tr>
      </thead>
      <tfoot>
        <tr>
          <td>Total:</td>
          <td>$<?php echo number_format($total, 2); ?></td>
        </tr>
      </tfoot>
      <tbody>
        <?php foreach ($cart as $item): ?>
          <tr>
            <td><?php htmlout($item['desc']); ?></td>
            <td>
              $<?php echo number_format($item['price'], 2); ?>
            </td>
          </tr>
        <?php endforeach; ?>
      </tbody>
    </table>
    <?php else: ?>
    <p>Your cart is empty!</p>
    <?php endif; ?>
    <form action="?" method="post">
      <p>
        <a href="?">Continue shopping</a> or
        <input type="submit" name="action" value="Empty cart">
      </p>
    </form>
  </body>
</html>
```

Once you have filled your cart with goodies, Figure 9.5 shows the output of this template.

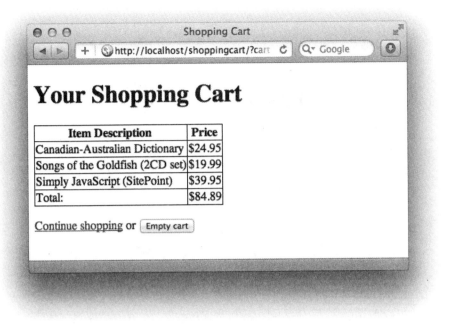

Figure 9.5. A full cart

This template also provides an **Empty cart** button that causes the controller script to unset the $_SESSION['cart'] variable, which results in a new, empty shopping cart. Here's the code:

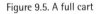

```
                                    chapter9/shoppingcart/index.php (excerpt)

if (isset($_POST['action']) and $_POST['action'] == 'Empty cart')
{
  // Empty the $_SESSION['cart'] array
  unset($_SESSION['cart']);
  header('Location: ?cart');
  exit();
}
```

And Figure 9.6 shows what the cart looks like once emptied.

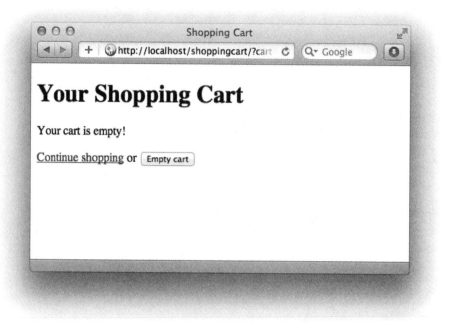

Figure 9.6. Avoid going home empty-handed!

That's it! Here's the complete code for the controller, with all the pieces assembled:

```
                                    chapter9/shoppingcart/index.php
<?php
include_once $_SERVER['DOCUMENT_ROOT'] .
    '/includes/magicquotes.inc.php';

$items = array(
    array('id' => '1', 'desc' => 'Canadian-Australian Dictionary',
        'price' => 24.95),
    array('id' => '2', 'desc' => 'As-new parachute (never opened)',
        'price' => 1000),
    array('id' => '3', 'desc' => 'Songs of the Goldfish (2CD set)',
        'price' => 19.99),
    array('id' => '4', 'desc' => 'Simply JavaScript (SitePoint)',
        'price' => 39.95));

session_start();
if (!isset($_SESSION['cart']))
{
```

```php
    $_SESSION['cart'] = array();
}

if (isset($_POST['action']) and $_POST['action'] == 'Buy')
{
  // Add item to the end of the $_SESSION['cart'] array
  $_SESSION['cart'][] = $_POST['id'];
  header('Location: .');
  exit();
}

if (isset($_POST['action']) and $_POST['action'] == 'Empty cart')
{
  // Empty the $_SESSION['cart'] array
  unset($_SESSION['cart']);
  header('Location: ?cart');
  exit();
}

if (isset($_GET['cart']))
{
  $cart = array();
  $total = 0;
  foreach ($_SESSION['cart'] as $id)
  {
    foreach ($items as $product)
    {
      if ($product['id'] == $id)
      {
        $cart[] = $product;
        $total += $product['price'];
        break;
      }
    }
  }

  include 'cart.html.php';
  exit();
}

include 'catalog.html.php';
```

Access Control

One of the most common reasons for building a database driven website is that it allows the site owner to update the site from any web browser, anywhere! But, in a world where roaming bands of jubilant hackers will fill your site with viruses and pornography, you need to stop and think about the security of your administration pages.

At the very least, you'll want to require username and password authentication before a visitor to your site can access the administration area. There are two main ways of doing this:

- configure your web server software to require a valid login for the relevant pages
- use PHP to prompt the user and check the login credentials as appropriate

If you have access to your web server's configuration, the first option is often the easiest to set up, but the second is by far the more flexible. With PHP, you can design your own login form, even embed it into the layout of your site if you wish. PHP also makes it easy to change the credentials required to gain access, or manage a database of authorized users, each with their own credentials and privileges.

In this section, you'll enhance your joke database site to protect sensitive features with username/password-based authentication. In order to control which users can do what, you'll build a sophisticated **role-based access control** system.

"What does all this have to do with cookies and sessions?" you might wonder. Well, rather than prompting your users for login credentials every time they wish to view a confidential page or perform a sensitive action, you can use PHP sessions to hold onto those credentials throughout their visit to your site.

Database Design

Depending on the type of application you're working on, you may need to create a new database table to store the list of authorized users and their passwords. In the case of the joke database site, you already have a table to do the job—the author table shown in Figure 9.7.

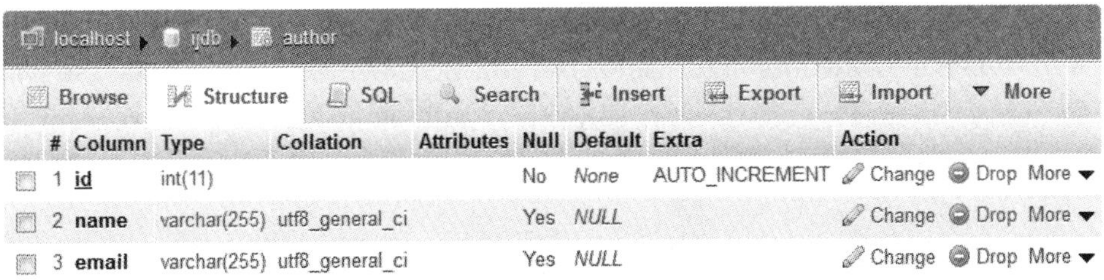

Figure 9.7. The existing structure of the `author` table

Rather than track authors and users separately, let's extend this existing database table so that authors can log in to your site. Some authors in the database may never log in, and may exist only to be given credit for jokes. Other authors may never write a joke, existing only to give a person administrative access to the site. But for those users who do both, it will be more elegant to have their details stored in this one table, rather than spread across two different tables.

We can use each author's email address as a username, but to do this, we'll want to ensure that each author in the database has a unique email address. We can achieve this with an `ALTER TABLE ADD UNIQUE` command. Use phpMyAdmin's Query window to run this command:[5]

```
ALTER TABLE author ADD UNIQUE (email)
```

With this change made, MySQL will now generate an error if you try to create a new author with the same email address as an existing author.

Now all this table needs is an extra column to store each author's password:

```
ALTER TABLE author ADD COLUMN password CHAR(32)
```

Note that we refrain from using the `NOT NULL` modifier on this column, so some authors may have no password. When we write the PHP code that uses this column, we'll simply prevent authors with no password from logging in.

Note the column type: `CHAR(32)`. It's a big no-no to store users' actual passwords in your database. Many users share a bad habit of reusing the same password across

---

[5] In this chapter, I'll show you the SQL commands needed to modify the database we've built up to this point. If you need to recreate the database from scratch, the necessary commands are provided in the **ijdb.sql** file in the code archive for this chapter.

many different websites. It's an expected courtesy, therefore, as a site administrator, to *scramble* the passwords your users give you, so that even if your database were stolen out from under you, those passwords would be useless to an attacker trying to gain access to your users' accounts on other websites.

A typical method of scrambling passwords is to use the md5 function built into PHP:

```
$scrambled = md5($password . 'ijdb');
```

Adding 'ijdb' to the end of the password supplied by the user before scrambling it ensures that the scrambled password in your site's database is different to the scrambled version of the same password in another site's database. Security experts call this **salt**, as in "add a dash of salt before you scramble the eggs."

A Note from the Security Experts

Security experts will tell you that using the same salt for every password in your database is asking for trouble, since an attacker who's able to figure out your salt (by obtaining a copy of your site's code, for example) will be one step closer to guessing the original passwords based on the scrambled versions in your database. Of course, those same security experts will tell you that rather than write your own password-handling code, you should rely on a proven solution developed by security experts like themselves.

This example provides a basic level of security with plenty of room for improvement if you're interested in doing a little research.

The md5 function creates a string exactly 32 characters long made up of apparently random letters and numbers. Although the same password will always generate the same string of 32 characters, it's effectively impossible to guess the password that was used to generate a given 32-character string. By storing only these strings in your database, you'll be able to check if a user has entered the correct password.

Unlike the VARCHAR column type, a column of type CHAR(32) will only store values exactly 32 characters long. This added regularity makes your database perform faster. Since the md5 function always generates a string 32 characters long, we can safely take advantage of this speed boost.

It turns out that MySQL has an MD5 function that performs the same task. Go ahead and store a password for your own author entry—or create one from scratch if you need to—now:

```
UPDATE author SET password = MD5('passwordijdb')
WHERE id = 1
```

Note that you have to tack onto your desired password the same suffix ('ijdb' in this example) that you're using in your PHP code.

Next, we need to store the list of sensitive actions each author is permitted to do. While you *could* simply give every logged-in user *carte blanche*—blanket permission to do absolutely anything—on most sites it will make greater sense to have more granular control over what each user's able to do.

Let's build a new table that will contain a list of **roles** that you'll be able to assign to each of your authors. Each author may have one or more of these roles assigned to them. An author who's assigned the role of Content Editor, for example, would be able to edit jokes in your CMS. This type of system is called **role-based access control**:

```
CREATE TABLE role (
  id VARCHAR(255) NOT NULL PRIMARY KEY,
  description VARCHAR(255)
) DEFAULT CHARACTER SET utf8 ENGINE=InnoDB
```

Each role will have a short string ID and a longer description. Let's fill in a few roles now:

```
INSERT INTO role (id, description) VALUES
('Content Editor', 'Add, remove, and edit jokes'),
('Account Administrator', 'Add, remove, and edit authors'),
('Site Administrator', 'Add, remove, and edit categories')
```

Finally, we will need a lookup table to assign roles to users in a many-to-many relationship:

```
CREATE TABLE authorrole (
  authorid INT NOT NULL,
  roleid VARCHAR(255) NOT NULL,
  PRIMARY KEY (authorid, roleid)
) DEFAULT CHARACTER SET utf8 ENGINE=InnoDB
```

While you're at it, assign yourself the Account Administrator role:

```
INSERT INTO authorrole (authorid, roleid) VALUES
(1, 'Account Administrator')
```

That takes care of the database. Now let's turn our attention to the PHP code that will use these new database structures.

Controller Code

Obviously, access control is a feature that will be handy in many different PHP projects. Therefore, like our database connection code and view helpers, it makes sense to write as much of our access control code as possible as a shared include file, so that we can then reuse it in future projects.

Rather than try to guess what functions our shared include file should contain, let's start by modifying our controller code as if we already had the include file written.

You'll recall that our administration pages start with an ordinary HTML page that displays the menu shown in Figure 9.8.

Figure 9.8. No protection required on this page

Your instinct might be to protect this page, but in fact it contains no sensitive information, so we can safely leave it alone. Each of the three links, however, point to a PHP controller script that performs all sorts of sensitive operations:

/admin/jokes/index.php

Searches for, displays, adds, edits, and removes jokes from the system. Only users with the Content Editor role should be able to perform these actions.

/admin/authors/index.php

Lists, adds, edits, and removes authors from the system. Users with the Account Administrator role only should be able to perform these actions.

/admin/categories/index.php

Lists, adds, edits, and removes categories from the system. Only users with the Site Administrator role should be able to perform these actions.

Each of these controllers, therefore, should check if the user is currently logged in and assigned the required role before proceeding. If the user has yet to log in, a login form should be displayed. If the user is logged in but lacks the required role, it should display an appropriate error message.

If we imagine that we already have functions to achieve all these actions, here's what the code might look like:

```php
<?php
include_once $_SERVER['DOCUMENT_ROOT'] .
    '/includes/magicquotes.inc.php';

require_once $_SERVER['DOCUMENT_ROOT'] . '/includes/access.inc.php';

if (!userIsLoggedIn())
{
  include '../login.html.php';
  exit();
}

if (!userHasRole('Account Administrator'))
{
  $error = 'Only Account Administrators may access this page.';
  include '../accessdenied.html.php';
  exit();
}
```

: *The rest of the controller code is unchanged.*

We add similar code to each of our other two controllers, but with the appropriate role specified for each:

```php
<?php
include_once $_SERVER['DOCUMENT_ROOT'] .
    '/includes/magicquotes.inc.php';

require_once $_SERVER['DOCUMENT_ROOT'] . '/includes/access.inc.php';

if (!userIsLoggedIn())
{
  include '../login.html.php';
  exit();
}

if (!userHasRole('Site Administrator'))
```

```
{
  $error = 'Only Site Administrators may access this page.';
  include '../accessdenied.html.php';
  exit();
}
```

: *The rest of the controller code is unchanged.*

chapter9/admin/jokes/index.php *(excerpt)*

```php
<?php
include_once $_SERVER['DOCUMENT_ROOT'] .
    '/includes/magicquotes.inc.php';

require_once $_SERVER['DOCUMENT_ROOT'] . '/includes/access.inc.php';

if (!userIsLoggedIn())
{
  include '../login.html.php';
  exit();
}

if (!userHasRole('Content Editor'))
{
  $error = 'Only Content Editors may access this page.';
  include '../accessdenied.html.php';
  exit();
}
```

: *The rest of the controller code is unchanged.*

From each of these blocks of code, we can see that we have the following tasks ahead of us:

- Write the login form, **login.html.php**.
- Write the "access denied" error page, **accessdenied.html.php**.
- Write the shared include file **access.inc.php** containing the following functions:

  userIsLoggedIn   Checks if the user's already logged in, or if the user has just submitted the login form with a correct email address and password.

userHasRole   Checks if the user who's logged in has been assigned the specified role in the database.

Since the login form and the error page will be shared by all three of our controllers, we'll put them in the **admin** directory alongside **index.html**.

The code for the error page is completely straightforward. All it does is output the $error variable set by the controller:

chapter9/admin/accessdenied.html.php

```php
<?php include_once $_SERVER['DOCUMENT_ROOT'] .
    '/includes/helpers.inc.php'; ?>
<!DOCTYPE html>
<html lang="en">
  <head>
    <meta charset="utf-8">
    <title>Access Denied</title>
  </head>
  <body>
    <h1>Access Denied</h1>
    <p><?php htmlout($error); ?></p>
  </body>
</html>
```

The login form takes a little more thought. Here's the code:

chapter9/admin/login.html.php

```php
<?php include_once $_SERVER['DOCUMENT_ROOT'] .
    '/includes/helpers.inc.php'; ?>
<!DOCTYPE html>
<html lang="en">
  <head>
    <meta charset="utf-8">
    <title>Log In</title>
  </head>
  <body>
    <h1>Log In</h1>
    <p>Please log in to view the page that you requested.</p>
    <?php if (isset($loginError)): ?> ❶
      <p><?php htmlout($loginError); ?></p>
    <?php endif; ?>
    <form action="" method="post"> ❷
```

```
    <div>
      <label for="email">Email: <input type="text" name="email"
        id="email"></label>
    </div>
    <div>
      <label for="password">Password: <input type="password"
        name="password" id="password"></label>
    </div>
    <div>
      <input type="hidden" name="action" value="login">
      <input type="submit" value="Log in">
    </div>
  </form>
  <p><a href="/admin/">Return to JMS home</a></p>
  </body>
</html>
```

The form takes an email address and a password, as you might expect.

① If the user submits the login form with an incorrect email address or password, the user will be denied access, simply being presented with the login form again. We need a way to tell the user what went wrong in this situation; this template will check if a variable named `$loginError` exists, and if so, will display it above the form.

② The `<form>` tag has an empty `action` attribute, so this form will be submitted back to the same URL that produced it. Thus, if the user's login attempt is successful, the controller will display the page that the browser originally requested.

③ Notice the second `<input>` tag has its `type` attribute set to `password`. This tells the browser to hide the value that the user types in, to shield the password from prying eyes.

④ This hidden field will be submitted with the form, to act as a signal to the `userIsLoggedIn` function that the user has submitted this form in an attempt to log in. You might be tempted simply to put the `name="action"` attribute on the submit button's `<input>` tag and watch for that—but if the user submits the form by hitting **Enter** while editing one of the two text fields, the submit button will not be sent with the form. Using a hidden field like this ensures that the `action` variable will be submitted no matter how the submission is triggered.

 A user might request a protected page by accident, or might be unaware that a page is protected until they see the login form. We therefore provide a link back to an unprotected page as a way out.

This form will take care of people logging in, but we also want to provide a way for a logged-in user to log out. Just as our `userIsLoggedIn` function will detect submissions of the login form to log users in, we can also make it detect the submission of a logout form to log users out. Let's add this form to the bottom of each protected page:

chapter9/admin/logout.inc.html.php

```
<form action="" method="post">
  <div>
    <input type="hidden" name="action" value="logout">
    <input type="hidden" name="goto" value="/admin/">
    <input type="submit" value="Log out">
  </div>
</form>
```

Again, we use a hidden `action` field to signal the user's intentions. The `goto` field indicates where we wish to send the user who's just logged out.

To add this form to all our protected pages, simply add the necessary `include` command to the bottom of each template:

chapter9/admin/authors/authors.html.php (excerpt)

```
    ⋮
    <p><a href="..">Return to JMS home</a></p>
    <?php include '../logout.inc.html.php'; ?>
  </body>
</html>
```

chapter9/admin/categories/categories.html.php *(excerpt)*

```
      ⋮
    <p><a href="..">Return to JMS home</a></p>
    <?php include '../logout.inc.html.php'; ?>
  </body>
</html>
```

chapter9/admin/jokes/jokes.html.php *(excerpt)*

```
      ⋮
    <p><a href="..">Return to JMS home</a></p>
    <?php include '../logout.inc.html.php'; ?>
  </body>
</html>
```

chapter9/admin/jokes/searchform.html.php *(excerpt)*

```
      ⋮
    <p><a href="..">Return to JMS home</a></p>
    <?php include '../logout.inc.html.php'; ?>
  </body>
</html>
```

Function Library

Finally, we can look at writing the shared include file, **access.inc.php**. Our code demands a lot from this humble file, but having written all the code that depends on it ahead of time, we have a fairly good idea of what it needs to do.

Let's review. This file must define two custom functions:

userIsLoggedIn

This function should return TRUE if the user is logged in, or FALSE if not.

This function should also detect and handle a couple of special cases:

- If the current request contains a submission of the login form, as indicated by the hidden field in the form (which sets $_POST['action'] to 'login'), it should check if the submitted username and password are correct. If they are, it should log in the user and return TRUE. Otherwise, it should set the global variable $loginError to an appropriate error message, and return FALSE.

■ If the current request contains a submission of the logout form, as indicated by the hidden field in the form (which sets $_POST['action'] to 'logout'), it should log out the user and redirect the browser to the URL specified by $_POST['goto'].

userHasRole

This function should look in the database and check if the currently logged-in user has been assigned the role that's passed to the function. If the role has been assigned, the function should return TRUE; if not, it should return FALSE.

Let's work through these two functions a few lines at a time:

```
chapter9/includes/access.inc.php (excerpt)

<?php

function userIsLoggedIn()
{
  if (isset($_POST['action']) and $_POST['action'] == 'login')
  {
```

We start with the userIsLoggedIn function. The first deed it does is check if the login form has been submitted:

```
chapter9/includes/access.inc.php (excerpt)

    if (!isset($_POST['email']) or $_POST['email'] == '' or
        !isset($_POST['password']) or $_POST['password'] == '')
    {
      $GLOBALS['loginError'] = 'Please fill in both fields';
      return FALSE;
    }
```

Next, before we go looking in the database, we should make sure that the user has filled in a value for both the email address and password. If either of these were not submitted, or were submitted as an empty string, we set the global $loginError variable (using the special $GLOBALS array we looked at in Chapter 6) and return FALSE.

Now that we've checked that an email address and password were actually submitted, we can look for a matching author in the database. Our first task is to scramble the submitted password to match the scrambled version that will be stored in the database:

chapter9/includes/access.inc.php *(excerpt)*

```php
$password = md5($_POST['password'] . 'ijdb');
```

Next, we'll query the database for a matching author record. Since this is an undertaking we'll have to do more than once in this code, we'll write another custom function to do it:

chapter9/includes/access.inc.php *(excerpt)*

```php
function databaseContainsAuthor($email, $password)
{
  include 'db.inc.php';

  try
  {
    $sql = 'SELECT COUNT(*) FROM author
        WHERE email = :email AND password = :password';
    $s = $pdo->prepare($sql);
    $s->bindValue(':email', $email);
    $s->bindValue(':password', $password);
    $s->execute();
  }
  catch (PDOException $e)
  {
    $error = 'Error searching for author.';
    include 'error.html.php';
    exit();
  }

  $row = $s->fetch();

  if ($row[0] > 0)
  {
    return TRUE;
  }
  else
  {
```

```
      return FALSE;
  }
}
```

This code should be quite familiar to you by now. We start by connecting to the database using our shared **db.inc.php** include file.[6] We then use our usual approach to execute a prepared SELECT query containing our two submitted values—the email address and the scrambled password. This database query will count the number of records in the author table that have a matching email address and password. If the number returned is greater than zero, we return TRUE; if not, we return FALSE.

Back in the userIsLoggedIn function, we can call our new databaseContainsAuthor function:

chapter9/includes/access.inc.php (excerpt)

```
if (databaseContainsAuthor($_POST['email'], $password))
{
```

If the database contains a matching author, it means the user filled out the login form correctly and we have to log in the user. But what exactly does "log in the user" mean? There are two approaches to this, both of which involve using PHP sessions:

▨ You can log in the user by setting a session variable as a "flag" (for example, $_SESSION['loggedIn'] = TRUE). On future requests, you can just check if this variable is set. If it is, the user is logged in, and the isUserLoggedIn function can return TRUE.

▨ You can store the "flag" variable as well as the submitted email address and scrambled password in two additional session variables. On future requests, you can check if these variables are set. If they are, you can use the databaseContainsAuthor function to check if they still match an author stored in the database. If they do, the isUserLoggedIn function can return TRUE.

---

[6] We use include instead of include_once here, since the $pdo variable that **db.inc.php** creates will be unavailable outside this function. Code elsewhere in our application that requires a database connection will therefore have to include **db.inc.php** again.

The first option will give better performance, since the user's credentials are only checked once—when the login form is submitted. The second option offers greater security, since the user's credentials are checked against the database every time a sensitive page is requested.

In general, the more secure option is preferable, since it allows you to remove authors from the site even while they're logged in. Otherwise, once a user is logged in, they'll stay logged in for as long as their PHP session remains active. That's a steep price to pay for a little extra performance.

So, here's the code for the second option:

chapter9/includes/access.inc.php (excerpt)

```
    session_start();
    $_SESSION['loggedIn'] = TRUE;
    $_SESSION['email'] = $_POST['email'];
    $_SESSION['password'] = $password;
    return TRUE;
  }
```

And finally, of course, if the user submits a login form with incorrect values, we need to ensure the user is logged out, set an appropriate error message, and return FALSE:

chapter9/includes/access.inc.php (excerpt)

```
  else
  {
    session_start();
    unset($_SESSION['loggedIn']);
    unset($_SESSION['email']);
    unset($_SESSION['password']);
    $GLOBALS['loginError'] =
        'The specified email address or password was incorrect.';
    return FALSE;
  }
}
```

That takes care of processing the login form. The second special case we need to handle is the logout form. This one's much simpler—so much so that the code should be self-explanatory:

chapter9/includes/access.inc.php *(excerpt)*

```php
if (isset($_POST['action']) and $_POST['action'] == 'logout')
{
  session_start();
  unset($_SESSION['loggedIn']);
  unset($_SESSION['email']);
  unset($_SESSION['password']);
  header('Location: ' . $_POST['goto']);
  exit();
}
```

Finally, if neither of the two special cases are detected, we simply check if the user is logged in using the session variables we've already discussed:

chapter9/includes/access.inc.php *(excerpt)*

```php
  session_start();
  if (isset($_SESSION['loggedIn']))
  {
    return databaseContainsAuthor($_SESSION['email'],
      $_SESSION['password']);
  }
}
```

That takes care of userIsLoggedIn. Now let's look at userHasRole. This function really just performs a complex database query: Given an author's email address (stored in the session), and a role ID (passed to the function), we need to check if the specified author has been assigned that role. This query will involve three database tables, so let's look at the SQL code in isolation:

```sql
SELECT COUNT(*) FROM author
INNER JOIN authorrole ON author.id = authorid
INNER JOIN role ON roleid = role.id
WHERE email = :email AND role.id = :roleId
```

We join the author table to the authorrole table by matching up the author table's id field with the authorrole table's authorid field. We then join *those* with the role table by matching up the authorrole table's roleid field with the role table's id field. Finally, with our three tables joined, we use the WHERE clause to look for records with the email address and role ID we're after.

From there, it's just a matter of writing the PHP code to execute this query and interpret the results:

```php
function userHasRole($role)
{
  include 'db.inc.php';

  try
  {
    $sql = "SELECT COUNT(*) FROM author
        INNER JOIN authorrole ON author.id = authorid
        INNER JOIN role ON roleid = role.id
        WHERE email = :email AND role.id = :roleId";
    $s = $pdo->prepare($sql);
    $s->bindValue(':email', $_SESSION['email']);
    $s->bindValue(':roleId', $role);
    $s->execute();
  }
  catch (PDOException $e)
  {
    $error = 'Error searching for author roles.';
    include 'error.html.php';
    exit();
  }

  $row = $s->fetch();

  if ($row[0] > 0)
  {
    return TRUE;
  }
  else
  {
    return FALSE;
  }
}
```

Understand all that? Save your changes, and try visiting some of the protected pages. If you gave yourself the Account Administrator role as I suggested, you should be able to visit and use the **Manage Authors** section of the admin pages. The other sections should display the appropriate "access denied" errors. Also try clicking the **Log out** button on any of the protected admin pages. These should return you to the admin index, and prompt you to log in again if you try to access a protected page afterwards.

If you have any problems, check your code using whatever error messages you see as a guide. For easy reference, here's the completed **access.inc.php** file:

```
                                        chapter9/includes/access.inc.php
<?php

function userIsLoggedIn()
{
  if (isset($_POST['action']) and $_POST['action'] == 'login')
  {
    if (!isset($_POST['email']) or $_POST['email'] == '' or
      !isset($_POST['password']) or $_POST['password'] == '')
    {
      $GLOBALS['loginError'] = 'Please fill in both fields';
      return FALSE;
    }

    $password = md5($_POST['password'] . 'ijdb');

    if (databaseContainsAuthor($_POST['email'], $password))
    {
      session_start();
      $_SESSION['loggedIn'] = TRUE;
      $_SESSION['email'] = $_POST['email'];
      $_SESSION['password'] = $password;
      return TRUE;
    }
    else
    {
      session_start();
      unset($_SESSION['loggedIn']);
      unset($_SESSION['email']);
      unset($_SESSION['password']);
      $GLOBALS['loginError'] =
          'The specified email address or password was incorrect.';
      return FALSE;
    }
  }

  if (isset($_POST['action']) and $_POST['action'] == 'logout')
  {
```

```php
    session_start();
    unset($_SESSION['loggedIn']);
    unset($_SESSION['email']);
    unset($_SESSION['password']);
    header('Location: ' . $_POST['goto']);
    exit();
  }

  session_start();
  if (isset($_SESSION['loggedIn']))
  {
    return databaseContainsAuthor($_SESSION['email'],
      $_SESSION['password']);
  }
}

function databaseContainsAuthor($email, $password)
{
  include 'db.inc.php';

  try
  {
    $sql = 'SELECT COUNT(*) FROM author
        WHERE email = :email AND password = :password';
    $s = $pdo->prepare($sql);
    $s->bindValue(':email', $email);
    $s->bindValue(':password', $password);
    $s->execute();
  }
  catch (PDOException $e)
  {
    $error = 'Error searching for author.';
    include 'error.html.php';
    exit();
  }

  $row = $s->fetch();

  if ($row[0] > 0)
  {
    return TRUE;
  }
  else
  {
    return FALSE;
```

```php
    }
}

function userHasRole($role)
{
  include 'db.inc.php';

  try
  {
    $sql = "SELECT COUNT(*) FROM author
        INNER JOIN authorrole ON author.id = authorid
        INNER JOIN role ON roleid = role.id
        WHERE email = :email AND role.id = :roleId";
    $s = $pdo->prepare($sql);
    $s->bindValue(':email', $_SESSION['email']);
    $s->bindValue(':roleId', $role);
    $s->execute();
  }
  catch (PDOException $e)
  {
    $error = 'Error searching for author roles.';
    include 'error.html.php';
    exit();
  }

  $row = $s->fetch();

  if ($row[0] > 0)
  {
    return TRUE;
  }
  else
  {
    return FALSE;
  }
}
```

Managing Passwords and Roles

Now that we've added passwords and roles to the database, we should update our author admin pages so that they can manipulate these aspects of authors.

First, let's add to the author add/edit form a **Set password** field, as well as a set of checkboxes for choosing the roles that the user should be assigned:

```php
<?php include_once $_SERVER['DOCUMENT_ROOT'] .
    '/includes/helpers.inc.php'; ?>
<!DOCTYPE html>
<html lang="en">
  <head>
    <meta charset="utf-8">
    <title><?php htmlout($pageTitle); ?></title>
  </head>
  <body>
    <h1><?php htmlout($pageTitle); ?></h1>
    <form action="?<?php htmlout($action); ?>" method="post">
      <div>
        <label for="name">Name: <input type="text" name="name"
            id="name" value="<?php htmlout($name); ?>"></label>
      </div>
      <div>
        <label for="email">Email: <input type="text" name="email"
            id="email" value="<?php htmlout($email); ?>"></label>
      </div>
      <div>
        <label for="password">Set password: <input type="password"
            name="password" id="password"></label>
      </div>
      <fieldset>
        <legend>Roles:</legend>
        <?php for ($i = 0; $i < count($roles); $i++): ?>
          <div>
            <label for="role<?php echo $i; ?>"><input
              type="checkbox"
              name="roles[]" id="role<?php echo $i; ?>"
              value="<?php htmlout($roles[$i]['id']); ?>"<?php
              if ($roles[$i]['selected'])
              {
                echo ' checked';
              }
              ?>><?php htmlout($roles[$i]['id']); ?></label>:
              <?php htmlout($roles[$i]['description']); ?>
          </div>
        <?php endfor; ?>
      </fieldset>
      <div>
        <input type="hidden" name="id" value="<?php
            htmlout($id); ?>">
```

```
            <input type="submit" value="<?php htmlout($button); ?>">
        </div>
    </form>
  </body>
</html>
```

The **Set password** field is a little special because, when it's left blank, it should cause the controller to leave the user's current password alone. Remember that because we store only scrambled passwords in the database, we're unable to display a user's existing password in the form for editing.

The role checkboxes are a lot like the category checkboxes we created for the joke add/edit form in Chapter 7, with one notable difference. Since we're using strings instead of numbers for our role IDs in the database, we're unable to use the IDs to generate the `<input>` tags' `id` attributes. The `id` attribute can't contain spaces. We therefore have to go a little out of our way to generate a unique number for each role. Instead of using a `foreach` loop to step through our array of roles, we use an old-fashioned `for` loop:

chapter9/admin/authors/form.html.php *(excerpt)*

```php
<?php for ($i = 0; $i < count($roles); $i++): ?>
```

The counter variable `$i` starts at 0 and each time through the loop it's incremented by one. We can therefore access each role within the loop as `$roles[$i]`, and we can also use `$i` to build our unique `id` attributes:

chapter9/admin/authors/form.html.php *(excerpt)*

```php
id="role<?php echo $i; ?>"
```

Now you can update the controller to handle these new fields. The code for the password field is straightforward, and the code for the role checkboxes is nearly identical to what we wrote to process joke categories. I've highlighted the changes in bold below. Take a look, and satisfy yourself that you understand everything that's going on:

```php
<?php
include_once $_SERVER['DOCUMENT_ROOT'] .
    '/includes/magicquotes.inc.php';

require_once $_SERVER['DOCUMENT_ROOT'] . '/includes/access.inc.php';

if (!userIsLoggedIn())
{
  include '../login.html.php';
  exit();
}

if (!userHasRole('Account Administrator'))
{
  $error = 'Only Account Administrators may access this page.';
  include '../accessdenied.html.php';
  exit();
}

if (isset($_GET['add']))
{
  include $_SERVER['DOCUMENT_ROOT'] . '/includes/db.inc.php';

  $pageTitle = 'New Author';
  $action = 'addform';
  $name = '';
  $email = '';
  $id = '';
  $button = 'Add author';

  // Build the list of roles
  try
  {
    $result = $pdo->query('SELECT id, description FROM role');
  }
  catch (PDOException $e)
  {
    $error = 'Error fetching list of roles.';
    include 'error.html.php';
    exit();
  }

  foreach ($result as $row)
```

```php
  {
    $roles[] = array(
      'id' => $row['id'],
      'description' => $row['description'],
      'selected' => FALSE);
  }

  include 'form.html.php';
  exit();
}

if (isset($_GET['addform']))
{
  include $_SERVER['DOCUMENT_ROOT'] . '/includes/db.inc.php';

  try
  {
    $sql = 'INSERT INTO author SET
        name = :name,
        email = :email';
    $s = $pdo->prepare($sql);
    $s->bindValue(':name', $_POST['name']);
    $s->bindValue(':email', $_POST['email']);
    $s->execute();
  }
  catch (PDOException $e)
  {
    $error = 'Error adding submitted author.';
    include 'error.html.php';
    exit();
  }

  $authorid = $pdo->lastInsertId();

  if ($_POST['password'] != '')
  {
    $password = md5($_POST['password'] . 'ijdb');

    try
    {
      $sql = 'UPDATE author SET
          password = :password
          WHERE id = :id';
      $s = $pdo->prepare($sql);
      $s->bindValue(':password', $password);
```

```php
      $s->bindValue(':id', $authorid);
      $s->execute();
    }
    catch (PDOException $e)
    {
      $error = 'Error setting author password.';
      include 'error.html.php';
      exit();
    }
  }

  if (isset($_POST['roles']))
  {
    foreach ($_POST['roles'] as $role)
    {
      try
      {
        $sql = 'INSERT INTO authorrole SET
            authorid = :authorid,
            roleid = :roleid';
        $s = $pdo->prepare($sql);
        $s->bindValue(':authorid', $authorid);
        $s->bindValue(':roleid', $role);
        $s->execute();
      }
      catch (PDOException $e)
      {
        $error = 'Error assigning selected role to author.';
        include 'error.html.php';
        exit();
      }
    }
  }

  header('Location: .');
  exit();
}

if (isset($_POST['action']) and $_POST['action'] == 'Edit')
{
  include $_SERVER['DOCUMENT_ROOT'] . '/includes/db.inc.php';

  try
  {
    $sql = 'SELECT id, name, email FROM author WHERE id = :id';
```

```php
  $s = $pdo->prepare($sql);
  $s->bindValue(':id', $_POST['id']);
  $s->execute();
}
catch (PDOException $e)
{
  $error = 'Error fetching author details.';
  include 'error.html.php';
  exit();
}

$row = $s->fetch();

$pageTitle = 'Edit Author';
$action = 'editform';
$name = $row['name'];
$email = $row['email'];
$id = $row['id'];
$button = 'Update author';

// Get list of roles assigned to this author
try
{
  $sql = 'SELECT roleid FROM authorrole WHERE authorid = :id';
  $s = $pdo->prepare($sql);
  $s->bindValue(':id', $id);
  $s->execute();
}
catch (PDOException $e)
{
  $error = 'Error fetching list of assigned roles.';
  include 'error.html.php';
  exit();
}

$selectedRoles = array();
foreach ($s as $row)
{
  $selectedRoles[] = $row['roleid'];
}

// Build the list of all roles
try
{
  $result = $pdo->query('SELECT id, description FROM role');
```

```php
    }
    catch (PDOException $e)
    {
      $error = 'Error fetching list of roles.';
      include 'error.html.php';
      exit();
    }

    foreach ($result as $row)
    {
      $roles[] = array(
        'id' => $row['id'],
        'description' => $row['description'],
        'selected' => in_array($row['id'], $selectedRoles));
    }

    include 'form.html.php';
    exit();
}

if (isset($_GET['editform']))
{
  include $_SERVER['DOCUMENT_ROOT'] . '/includes/db.inc.php';

  try
  {
    $sql = 'UPDATE author SET
        name = :name,
        email = :email
        WHERE id = :id';
    $s = $pdo->prepare($sql);
    $s->bindValue(':id', $_POST['id']);
    $s->bindValue(':name', $_POST['name']);
    $s->bindValue(':email', $_POST['email']);
    $s->execute();
  }
  catch (PDOException $e)
  {
    $error = 'Error updating submitted author.';
    include 'error.html.php';
    exit();
  }

  if ($_POST['password'] != '')
  {
```

```php
  $password = md5($_POST['password'] . 'ijdb');

  try
  {
    $sql = 'UPDATE author SET
        password = :password
        WHERE id = :id';
    $s = $pdo->prepare($sql);
    $s->bindValue(':password', $password);
    $s->bindValue(':id', $_POST['id']);
    $s->execute();
  }
  catch (PDOException $e)
  {
    $error = 'Error setting author password.';
    include 'error.html.php';
    exit();
  }
}

try
{
  $sql = 'DELETE FROM authorrole WHERE authorid = :id';
  $s = $pdo->prepare($sql);
  $s->bindValue(':id', $_POST['id']);
  $s->execute();
}
catch (PDOException $e)
{
  $error = 'Error removing obsolete author role entries.';
  include 'error.html.php';
  exit();
}

if (isset($_POST['roles']))
{
  foreach ($_POST['roles'] as $role)
  {
    try
    {
      $sql = 'INSERT INTO authorrole SET
          authorid = :authorid,
          roleid = :roleid';
      $s = $pdo->prepare($sql);
      $s->bindValue(':authorid', $_POST['id']);
```

```php
      $s->bindValue(':roleid', $role);
      $s->execute();
    }
    catch (PDOException $e)
    {
      $error = 'Error assigning selected role to author.';
      include 'error.html.php';
      exit();
    }
  }
}

header('Location: .');
exit();
}

if (isset($_POST['action']) and $_POST['action'] == 'Delete')
{
  include $_SERVER['DOCUMENT_ROOT'] . '/includes/db.inc.php';

  // Delete role assignments for this author
  try
  {
    $sql = 'DELETE FROM authorrole WHERE authorid = :id';
    $s = $pdo->prepare($sql);
    $s->bindValue(':id', $_POST['id']);
    $s->execute();
  }
  catch (PDOException $e)
  {
    $error = 'Error removing author from roles.';
    include 'error.html.php';
    exit();
  }

  // Get jokes belonging to author
  try
  {
    $sql = 'SELECT id FROM joke WHERE authorid = :id';
    $s = $pdo->prepare($sql);
    $s->bindValue(':id', $_POST['id']);
    $s->execute();
  }
  catch (PDOException $e)
  {
```

```php
    $error = 'Error getting list of jokes to delete.';
    include 'error.html.php';
    exit();
  }

  $result = $s->fetchAll();

  // Delete joke category entries
  try
  {
    $sql = 'DELETE FROM jokecategory WHERE jokeid = :id';
    $s = $pdo->prepare($sql);

    // For each joke
    foreach ($result as $row)
    {
      $jokeId = $row['id'];
      $s->bindValue(':id', $jokeId);
      $s->execute();
    }
  }
  catch (PDOException $e)
  {
    $error = 'Error deleting category entries for joke.';
    include 'error.html.php';
    exit();
  }

  // Delete jokes belonging to author
  try
  {
    $sql = 'DELETE FROM joke WHERE authorid = :id';
    $s = $pdo->prepare($sql);
    $s->bindValue(':id', $_POST['id']);
    $s->execute();
  }
  catch (PDOException $e)
  {
    $error = 'Error deleting jokes for author.';
    include 'error.html.php';
    exit();
  }

  // Delete the author
  try
```

```
  {
    $sql = 'DELETE FROM author WHERE id = :id';
    $s = $pdo->prepare($sql);
    $s->bindValue(':id', $_POST['id']);
    $s->execute();
  }
  catch (PDOException $e)
  {
    $error = 'Error deleting author.';
    include 'error.html.php';
    exit();
  }

  header('Location: .');
  exit();
}

// Display author list
include $_SERVER['DOCUMENT_ROOT'] . '/includes/db.inc.php';

try
{
  $result = $pdo->query('SELECT id, name FROM author');
}
catch (PDOException $e)
{
  $error = 'Error fetching authors from the database!';
  include 'error.html.php';
  exit();
}

foreach ($result as $row)
{
  $authors[] = array('id' => $row['id'], 'name' => $row['name']);
}

include 'authors.html.php';
```

That's it! Take your enhancements for a spin and give yourself ultimate power by assigning yourself all the roles! Make sure everything works, and if it doesn't, fix it. Just for kicks, try changing your own password while you're logged in. You should be kicked out to the login form with the next link or button you click, where you can enter your new password to log back in.

A Challenge: Joke Moderation

It's all well and good to follow along with the code that I present, but it's quite another to write a significant new feature yourself. Now is a good time to try your hand at planning and building a major feature for the joke database website.

For the past few chapters, we've been so focused on the administration pages that the public side of the site hasn't progressed much. In fact, it's gone backwards. Before we removed the **Add your own joke** link and **Delete** buttons, the main page of our joke database site looked like Figure 9.9.

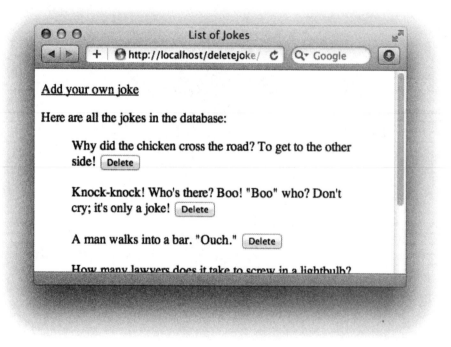

Figure 9.9. The joke list we left behind

Obviously, those **Delete** buttons had to go, but what about that **Add your own joke** link? Originally, this link went to the form shown in Figure 9.10.

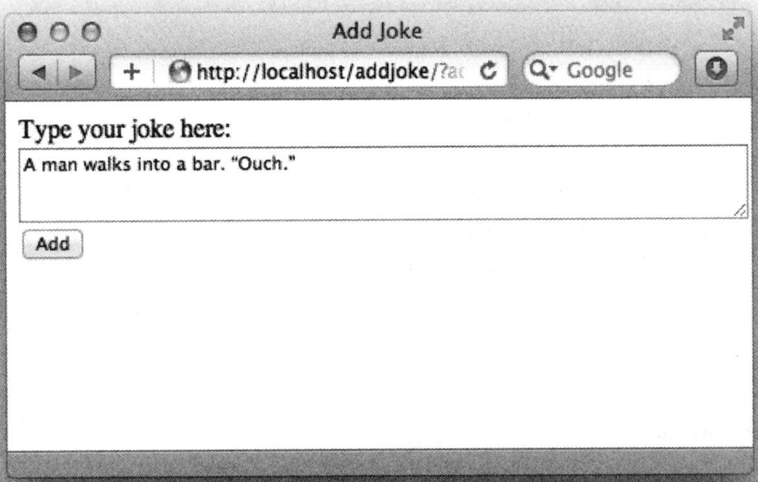

Figure 9.10. Another nugget of comic genius is added to the database

When submitted, this form inserted a new joke into the database with no associated author or categories (because our database didn't contain those features at the time). Those features would be easy enough for you to add if you wanted to, however; what's not easy to deal with is the possibility of abuse. Launch the site with a publicly accessible joke submission form like this, and spammers will be filling up your database with junk in no time!

How would you deal with this problem? Remove the feature? Force authors to email their submissions to a content editor? Think about it: there must be a way to preserve this "easy submission" feature without having your front page filled with spam.

Is it necessary for new joke submissions to appear on the site immediately? What if you add a new column to the `joke` table called `visible` that could take one of two values: `'YES'` and `'NO'`? Newly submitted jokes could automatically be set to `'NO'`, and be prevented from appearing on the site if you simply added `WHERE visible='YES'` to any query of the `joke` table where the results are intended for public viewing. Jokes with `visible` set to `'NO'` would wait in the database for review by a Content Editor, who could edit each joke and assign it an author and categories before making it visible, or just delete it as unwanted.

To create a column that can contain either of two values, of which one is the default, you'll need a new MySQL column type called ENUM:

```
ALTER TABLE joke ADD COLUMN
visible ENUM('NO', 'YES') NOT NULL
```

Since we declared this column as required (NOT NULL), the first value listed within the parentheses ('NO' in this case) is the default value, which is assigned to new entries if no value is specified in the INSERT command. All that's left for you to do is modify the administration system, enabling Content Editors to make hidden jokes visible. A simple checkbox in the joke add/edit form should do the trick. You also may want to modify the joke search form to allow Content Editors to search only for visible or hidden jokes.

If you begin with the code as we left it in Chapter 6, newly submitted jokes won't have an author associated with them. How to deal with that I'll leave up to you. The **Add your own joke** form could prompt visitors to include contact information with their submissions, which Content Editors could then use to identify and assign authors to submitted jokes. A more challenging solution might be to invite authors to sign up, set a password, and then log in before submitting new jokes.

There's no right answer, but I challenge you to find a way to deal with the issue, and build that into your Internet Joke Database site. You have all the tools you need: set aside some time and see what you can build if you put your mind to it. If you get stuck, the SitePoint PHP Forum[7] is a friendly place to gain answers to your questions.

The Sky's the Limit

In this chapter, you learned about the two main methods of creating persistent variables—those variables that continue to exist from page to page in PHP. The first stores the variable in the visitor's browser in the form of a cookie. By default, cookies terminate at the end of the browser session, but by specifying an expiry time, they can be preserved indefinitely. Unfortunately, cookies are fairly unreliable because you have no way of knowing when the browser might delete your cookies,

---

[7] http://www.sitepoint.com/forums/forumdisplay.php?34-PHP

and because some users occasionally clear their cookies out of concern for their privacy.

Sessions, on the other hand, free you from all the limitations of cookies. They let you store an unlimited number of potentially large variables. Sessions are an essential building block in modern ecommerce applications, as we demonstrated in our simple shopping cart example. They're also a critical component of systems that provide access control, like the one we built for your joke content management system.

At this point, you should be equipped with all the basic skills and concepts you need to build your very own database driven website. While you may be tempted to skip the challenge of building a complete system for safely accepting public submissions, I encourage you to give it a try. You already have all the skills necessary to build it, and there is no better way to learn than to make a few mistakes of your own to learn from. At the very least, set this challenge aside for now and come back to it when you've finished this book.

If you can tackle it with confidence, you may wish to try another challenge. Want to let users rate the jokes on the site? How about letting joke authors make changes to their jokes, but with the backup of requiring an administrator to approve the changes before they go live on the site? The power and complexity of the system is limited only by your imagination.

In the rest of this book, I'll cover more advanced topics that will help optimize your site's performance and solve some complex problems using less code. Oh, and of course we'll explore more exciting features of PHP and MySQL!

In Chapter 10, we'll take a step away from our joke database and have a close-up look at MySQL server maintenance and administration. We'll learn how to make backups of our database (a critical task for any web-based company), to administer MySQL users and their passwords, and to log in to a MySQL server if you've forgotten your password.

MySQL Administration

At the core of most well-designed content-driven sites is a relational database. In this book, we've used the MySQL Relational Database Management System (RDBMS) to create our database. MySQL is a popular choice among web developers because it's free, and because MySQL servers are fairly simple to set up. As I demonstrated in Chapter 1, armed with proper instructions a new user can have a MySQL server up and running in less than five minutes—under two if you practice a little!

If all you want is a MySQL server to play with a few examples and experiment a little, the initial installation process we went through in Chapter 1 is likely to be all you'll need. If, on the other hand, you want to set up a database back end to a real live website—perhaps a site your company depends on—there are a few more fundamentals you'll need to learn before you can rely on a MySQL server day-in, day-out.

First, we'll look at backups. Backing up data that's important to you or your business should be an essential item on any administrator's list of priorities. Because administrators usually have more interesting work to do, though, backup procedures are often arranged once out of necessity and deemed "good enough" for all applications. If, until now, your answer to the question, "Should we back up our databases?" has been, "It's okay; they'll be backed up along with everything else," you really should read on. I'll show you why a generic file-backup solution is inadequate for many MySQL installations, and I'll demonstrate the *right* way to back up and restore a MySQL database.

Next, it's time we looked more closely at how to control access to your MySQL database. I showed you the basics early in this book, but it turns out there are some tricky details that can make your life difficult if you don't understand them. Oh, and I'll show you how to regain control of your MySQL server should you forget your password!

Then we'll turn our attention to performance, and how to keep your SELECT queries running quickly. With the careful application of database indexes (a skill many working PHP developers lack, surprisingly), you can keep your database speedy even as it grows to contain thousands (or even hundreds of thousands) of rows.

Finally, I'll show you how to use a relatively new feature of MySQL—foreign keys—to express the structure of your database, and how each of the tables it contains are related to one another.

As you can see, this chapter's a real mixed bag, but by the end of it you'll understand MySQL a whole lot better!

Backing Up MySQL Databases

Like web servers, most MySQL servers are expected to remain online 24 hours a day, seven days a week. This makes backups of MySQL database files problematic. Because the MySQL server uses memory caches and buffers to improve the efficiency of updates to the database files stored on disk, these files may be in an inconsistent state at any given time. Since standard backup procedures involve merely copying system and data files, backups of MySQL data files are unreliable, as there's no guarantee the files that are copied are in a fit state to be used as replacements in the event of a crash.

Furthermore, as many website databases receive new information at all hours of the day, standard backups can provide only periodic snapshots of database data. Any information stored in the database that's changed after the last backup will be lost in the event that the live MySQL data files are destroyed or become unusable.

In many situations, such as when a MySQL server is used to track customer orders on an ecommerce site, this is an unacceptable loss.

Facilities exist in MySQL to keep up-to-date backups that are largely unaffected by server activity at the time at which the backups are generated. Unfortunately, they require you to set up a backup scheme specifically for your MySQL data, completely apart from whatever backup measures you've established for the rest of your data. As with any good backup system, however, you'll appreciate it when the time comes to use it.

Database Backups Using phpMyAdmin

The browser-based MySQL administration tool we've been using throughout this book, phpMyAdmin, also offers a convenient facility for obtaining a backup of your site's database. Once you've selected your database, click the **Export** tab as shown in Figure 10.1.

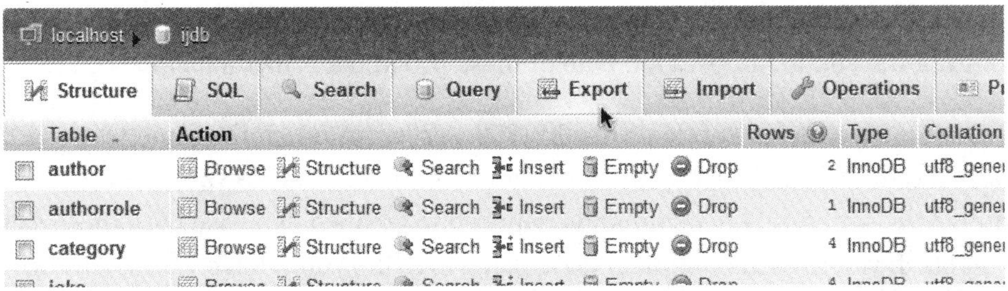

Figure 10.1. Click **Export** to save a backup of your database

The default Export options, to perform a **Quick** export in SQL format, are perfect for our needs. Just click **Go** and your browser will download an **ijdb.sql** file (assuming your database is named ijdb).

If you open this file in a text editor, you'll find it contains a series of SQL CREATE TABLE and INSERT commands that, if run on a blank database, would reproduce the current contents of your database. Yes, a MySQL database backup is just a series of SQL commands!

To restore your database from a backup file like this one, first make sure your database is empty (select all the tables on the **Structure** tab and from the **With selected** menu choose **Drop**); then just click the **Import** tab and select the backup file from your computer (as before, the other default options on this page are fine). Moments later, the contents of your database will be restored to their previous state.

In this way, we can use phpMyAdmin to create backups of our databases. phpMyAdmin connects to the MySQL server to perform backups, rather than accessing directly the MySQL database data files. The backup it produces is therefore guaranteed to be a valid copy of the database, instead of merely a point-in-time snapshot of the database files stored on disk, which may be in a state of flux as long as the MySQL server is running.

Database Backups Using `mysqldump`

phpMyAdmin makes it really easy to obtain a database backup whenever the mood strikes you, but the best backups are automated, and an automated backup tool phpMyAdmin is not.

As you'll already know if you've ever worked with MySQL on Linux, the MySQL database server software comes with a handful of utility programs designed to be run from the command prompt. One of these programs is **mysqldump**.

When run, **mysqldump** connects to a MySQL server (in much the same way as PHP does) and downloads the complete contents of the database(s) you specify. It then outputs the series of SQL commands required to create a database with those same contents. If you save the output of **mysqldump** to a file, you'll have yourself the same kind of backup file that phpMyAdmin can generate for you!

New to the Command Prompt?

If you're unfamiliar with your operating system's command prompt, some of the instructions that follow may likely confuse you. Don't sweat it! If you find yourself floundering, feel free to skip ahead to the next section of this chapter.

Practically speaking, there's no real need to set up automated MySQL backups on your development server. When you shut down XAMPP at the end of the day, whatever backup software you run on your computer (you *do* back up your computer, don't you?) will be able to back up your MySQL database files in their dormant state. As for the production MySQL server you use when you launch your website to the Internet at large, any good web host will handle your MySQL backups for you.

You'll probably only need to set up automated MySQL backups if you launch and manage your own production database server. I'm going to assume that if that's a job you're tackling, you're already familiar with using the command prompt on your operating system of choice.

That said, if you're a Windows user especially keen to learn this stuff, I wrote an article back in 2002 called *Kev's Command Prompt Cheat Sheet*[1] that will fill you in on the basics.

The following command (typed all on one line) connects to the MySQL server running on the local machine as user `root` with password *password*, and saves a backup of the `ijdb` database into the file **ijdb.sql**:[2]

```
mysqldump -u root -ppassword ijdb > ijdb.sql
```

To restore this database after a server crash, you could again feed this SQL file to phpMyAdmin;[3] alternatively, you could use the **mysql** utility program:

```
mysql -u root -ppassword ijdb < ijdb.sql
```

This command connects to the MySQL server, selects the `ijdb` database, and feeds in our backup file as a list of SQL commands to be executed.

But how do we bridge the gap between these snapshots to maintain a database backup that's always up to date?

Incremental Backups Using Binary Logs

As I mentioned, many situations in which MySQL databases are used would make the loss of data—any data—unacceptable. In cases like these, we need a way to bridge the gaps between the backups we made using phpMyAdmin or **mysqldump** as recently described.

---

[1] http://www.sitepoint.com/command-prompt-cheat-sheet/

[2] To run **mysqldump** and the other MySQL utility programs, you need to be in the **bin** directory of your MySQL installation (or the **/Applications/MAMP/Library/bin** folder on a Mac with MAMP installed, or the **mysql** subdirectory of your XAMPP installation), or that directory must be added to the system path.

[3] Unlike the SQL files created by phpMyAdmin's Export facility, **mysqldump** backups include commands to drop the tables if they happen to exist before creating them, so you don't have to worry if your database isn't empty first.

The solution is to configure the MySQL server to keep a **binary log**, a record of all SQL queries that were received by the database, and which modified the contents of the database in some way. This includes INSERT, UPDATE, and DELETE statements (among others), but excludes SELECT statements.

The basic idea of a binary log is that you should be able to restore the contents of the database at the very moment at which a disaster occurs. This restoration involves applying a backup (made using phpMyAdmin or **mysqldump**), and then applying the contents of the binary logs that were generated after that backup was made.

You can also edit binary logs to undo mistakes that might have been made. For example, if a co-worker comes to you after accidentally issuing a DROP TABLE command, you can export your binary log to a text file and then edit that file to remove the command. You can then restore the database using your last backup and then running the edited binary log. In this way, you can even preserve database changes that were made *after* the accident. And, as a precaution, you should probably also revoke your co-worker's DROP privileges.

To tell your MySQL server to keep binary logs, you need to edit the server's **my.ini** (Windows) or **my.cnf** (OS X or Linux) configuration file. This is a simple text file with a list of options that control some of the finer points of how your MySQL server works. In many cases, MySQL is installed without a configuration file, and simply runs with the default settings. In this situation, you'll need to create a new file and set the appropriate option.

 Where does my.ini/my.cnf belong?

On Windows, XAMPP comes with a **my.ini** file already made for you: **C:\xampp\mysql\bin\my.ini**. You can open it in Notepad to make changes.

On OS X, the MySQL server built into MAMP will look for a **/etc/my.cnf** file to read when it starts up. You may have some trouble creating this file (Finder generally keeps you from messing with files in sensitive locations like this); you'll need to create it elsewhere, and then use a sudo mv command in Terminal to move it to **/etc** with administrator privileges:

```
sudo mv my.cnf /etc/
```

To enable binary logging, you add a `log-bin` setting to the `[mysqld]` section of your configuration file. If you're creating a new configuration file from scratch, you'll have to type the `[mysqld]` section heading yourself on the first line before adding the setting on the next line.

The `log-bin` setting tells MySQL where to store the binary log files and what name to give them. On Windows, for example, you might want it to store them in your MySQL data directory:[4]

```
[mysqld]
log-bin="C:/xampp/mysql/data/binlog"
```

On OS X, MAMP's **logs** folder is a good place for them:

```
[mysqld]
log-bin=/Applications/MAMP/logs/binlog
```

Both these examples tell MySQL to create files named **binlog.000001**, **binlog.000002**, and so on. A new file will be created each time the server flushes its log files; in practice, this occurs whenever the server is restarted.

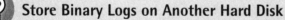 **Store Binary Logs on Another Hard Disk**

If possible, you should store your binary logs on a hard disk other than the one where your MySQL database files are stored. That way, if a hard disk goes bad, you won't lose both your database and your backups!

With your new configuration file in place, restart your MySQL server. From now on, the server will create binary log files. To make sure, check the location you specified to verify that a new log file was created when the server started up.

Obviously, binary logs can take up a lot of space on an active server. For this reason, it's important to tell MySQL to delete obsolete binary logs whenever you perform a full backup. This is easy to do if you use **mysqldump** to perform your backup:

```
mysqldump -u root -ppassword --flush-logs
➥ --master-data=2 --delete-master-logs ijdb > ijdb.sql
```

---

[4] Note that MySQL configuration files use slashes (/) instead of backslashes (\) in Windows filepaths.

The `--flush-logs` option tells the MySQL server to close the current binary log file and start a new one, as if the MySQL server had been restarted. The `--master-data=2` option instructs **mysqldump** to include a comment at the end of the **ijdb.sql** file that indicates the name of the new binary log file; this will contain the first changes that are made to the database following the full backup. Finally, the `--delete-master-logs` command tells **mysqldump** to delete the binary log files that are no longer needed, now that a full backup has taken place.

In the event of a disaster, as long as you have a full backup and the binary log files that were generated after the backup was made, restoring your database should be fairly simple. Set up a new, empty MySQL server, then apply the full backup as described in the previous section. All that's left is to apply the binary logs using the **mysqlbinlog** utility program.

mysqlbinlog's job is to convert the data format of MySQL binary logs into SQL commands that you can run on your database. Say you had two binary log files that you needed to apply after restoring your most recent full backup. You can generate an SQL text file from the two files using **mysqlbinlog**, and then apply that file to your MySQL server just as you would a file generated by **mysqldump**:

```
mysqlbinlog binlog.000041 binlog.000042 > binlog.sql
mysql -u root -ppassword < binlog.sql
```

MySQL Access Control Tips

In Chapter 2, I mentioned that the database called `mysql`, which appears on every MySQL server, is used to keep track of users, their passwords, and what they're allowed to do. In Chapter 4, I showed you how to use phpMyAdmin to create another user account, with access only to your website's database.

The MySQL access control system is fully documented in Chapter 5 of the MySQL Reference Manual.[5] In essence, user access is governed by the contents of five tables in the `mysql` database: `user`, `db`, `host`, `tables_priv`, and `columns_priv`. If you plan to edit these tables directly using INSERT, UPDATE, and DELETE statements, I suggest you read the relevant section of the MySQL manual first. But, for us mere mortals,

---

[5] http://dev.mysql.com/doc/refman/5.5/en/privilege-system.html

phpMyAdmin provides all the tools you'll need to manage access to your MySQL server.

As a result of the way the access control system in MySQL works, there are a couple of idiosyncrasies of which you should be aware if you're going to be responsible for controlling access to a MySQL server.

Host Name Issues

When you create users that can log in to the MySQL server only from the computer on which that server is running (for example, you require them to log in to the server and run the **mysql** command prompt utility from there, or to communicate using server-side scripts like PHP), you may ask yourself what to enter in the **Host** field of phpMyAdmin's **Add a new User** form. Imagine the server is running on www.example.com. Should you specify the **Host** as **www.example.com** or **localhost**?

The answer is that both are unreliable to handle all connections. In theory, if, when connecting, the user specifies the host name either with the **mysql** command prompt utility program, or with PHP's PDO class, that host name will have to match the entry in the access control system. However, as you probably want to avoid forcing your users to specify the host name a particular way (in fact, users of the **mysql** utility program are likely to want to steer clear of stating the host name at all), it's best to use a workaround.

For users who need the ability to connect from the machine on which the MySQL server is running, it's best to create two user entries in the MySQL access system: one with the actual host name of the machine (**www.example.com**, for example), the other with **localhost**. Of course, you'll have to grant/revoke all privileges to both user entries individually, but it's the only workaround that you can really rely upon.

Another problem commonly faced by MySQL administrators is that user entries whose host names contain wild cards (for example, %.example.com) may fail to work. When MySQL's access control system behaves unexpectedly, it's usually due to the way MySQL prioritizes the user entries. In particular, it orders entries so that more specific host names appear first (for example, www.example.com is absolutely specific, %.example.com is less specific, and % is totally unspecific).

In a fresh installation,[6] the MySQL access control system contains two anonymous user entries (these allow connections to be made from the local host using any username—the two entries support connections from `localhost` and the server's actual host name, as described before), and two root user entries. The problem just described occurs when the anonymous user entries take precedence over our new entry because their host name is more specific.

Let's look at the abridged contents of the user table on `www.example.com`, a fictitious MySQL server, where we've just added a new account for a user named Jess. The rows are sorted in the order in which the MySQL server considers them when it validates a connection:

Host	User	Password
`localhost`	`root`	*encrypted value*
`www.example.com`	`root`	*encrypted value*
`localhost`		
`www.example.com`		
`%.example.com`	`jess`	*encrypted value*

As you can see, since Jess's entry has the least specific host name, it comes last in the list. When Jess attempts to connect from `www.example.com`, the MySQL server matches her connection attempt to one of the anonymous user entries (a blank `User` value matches anyone). Since a password is unnecessary for these anonymous entries, and presumably Jess enters her password, MySQL rejects the connection attempt. Even if Jess managed to connect without a password, she would be given the very limited privileges that are assigned to anonymous users, as opposed to the privileges assigned to her entry in the access control system.

The solution is either to make your first order of business as a MySQL administrator the deletion of those anonymous user entries (`DELETE FROM mysql.user WHERE User=""`), or to give two more entries to all users who need to connect from localhost (that is, entries for `localhost` and the actual host name of the server):

---

[6] All-in-one installers like XAMPP and MAMP tend to differ in this respect.

Host	User	Password
localhost	root	*encrypted value*
www.example.com	root	*encrypted value*
localhost	jess	*encrypted value*
www.example.com	jess	*encrypted value*
localhost		
www.example.com		
%.example.com	jess	*encrypted value*

As it's excessively burdensome to maintain three user entries (and three sets of privileges) for each user, I recommend that you remove the anonymous users, unless you have a particular need for them:

Host	User	Password
localhost	root	*encrypted value*
www.example.com	root	*encrypted value*
%.example.com	jess	*encrypted value*

Locked Out?

Like locking your keys in the car, forgetting your password after you've spent an hour installing and tweaking a new MySQL server can be an embarrassment—to say the least! Fortunately, if you have administrator access to the computer on which the MySQL server is running, or if you can log in as the user you set up to run the MySQL server, all is well. The following procedure will let you regain control of the server.

Command Prompt Knowledge Assumed

Again, I'm going to go ahead and assume in this section that if you're locked out of your MySQL server, you know how to use your system's command prompt.

If you're using the MySQL server bundled with XAMPP or MAMP on your development machine, there's probably no mission-critical data stored in your database, and the easiest way to recover from a lost root password will usually be just to reinstall your server and start from scratch.

That said, if you're a Windows user, my trusty old *Kev's Command Prompt Cheat Sheet*[7] article should provide everything you need to get going.

First, you must shut down the MySQL server. If you normally do this using the **mysqladmin** command prompt utility, which requires your forgotten password, you'll instead need to kill the server process to shut it down. Under Windows, use Task Manager to find and end the MySQL process, or simply stop the MySQL service if you've installed it as such. Under OS X or Linux, use the `ps` command, or look in the server's PID file in the MySQL data directory to determine the process ID of the MySQL server; then terminate it with this command:

```
kill pid
```

pid is the process ID of the MySQL server.

This should be enough to stop the server. Do *not* use `kill -9` (a forced kill) unless absolutely necessary, as this may damage your data files. If you're forced to do so, however, the next section provides instructions on how to check and repair those files.

Now that the server's down, you must restart it using the `skip-grant-tables` option. You can do this by adding the option to your MySQL server's **my.ini** or **my.cnf** configuration file (see the instructions for setting up such a file in the section called "Incremental Backups Using Binary Logs"):

```
[mysqld]
skip-grant-tables
```

This instructs the MySQL server to allow unrestricted access to anyone. Obviously, you'll want to run the server in this mode as briefly as possible, to avoid the inherent security risks.

Once you're connected to your server (using phpMyAdmin or the **mysql** command prompt utility), change your root password to a memorable one:

---

[7] http://www.sitepoint.com/command-prompt-cheat-sheet/

```
UPDATE mysql.user SET Password=PASSWORD("newpassword")
WHERE User="root"
```

Finally, disconnect, shut down your MySQL server, and remove the skip-grant-tables option.

That does it—and nobody ever has to know what you did. As for locking your keys in your car, you're on your own there.

Indexes

Just like the index in this book makes it a lot easier to find every mention of a particular topic in its pages, a **database index** can make it much easier for MySQL to find the records you've asked for in a SELECT query. Let me give you an example.

As the Internet Joke Database grows, the joke table might grow to contain thousands, if not hundreds of thousands of rows. Now let's say PHP asks for the text of a particular joke:

```
SELECT joketext FROM joke WHERE id = 1234
```

In the absence of an index, MySQL must look at the value of the id column in each and every row of the joke table, one by one, until it finds the one with the value 1234. Worse yet, without an index, MySQL has no way of knowing that there is only *one* row with that value, so it must also scan the rest of the table for more matching rows to make sure it gets them all!

Computers are fast, and good at menial labor, but in the web development game where half seconds count, large tables and complex WHERE clauses can easily combine to create delays of 30 seconds or more!

Fortunately for us, this query will always run quickly, and that's because the id column of the joke table has an index. To see it, open phpMyAdmin, select the joke table, and click the **Structure** tab. There, below the list of columns in the table, you'll see the list of indexes shown in Figure 10.2.

Indexes: ⊙

Action	Keyname	Type	Unique	Packed	Column	Cardinality	Collation	Null	Comment
✏ Edit ⊖ Drop	**PRIMARY**	BTREE	Yes	No	id	4	A		

Figure 10.2. Each of our tables already has a single index

Take a look at the **Column** column; this index lists the values of the id column. From the name in the **Keyname** column, PRIMARY, you might even guess where this index came from: it was created automatically when we told MySQL to make the id column the primary key of this table.

Remember how we defined the id column of the table:

```
CREATE TABLE joke (
  id INT NOT NULL AUTO_INCREMENT PRIMARY KEY,
  joketext TEXT,
  jokedate DATE NOT NULL,
  authorid INT
) DEFAULT CHARACTER SET utf8 ENGINE=InnoDB;
```

In fact, "key" is just a fancy way to say "index" in database parlance, and a primary key is just an index named PRIMARY that requires each value in the table for that particular column to be unique. Note in Figure 10.2 that the **Unique** property of the index is **Yes**.

What all this boils down to is that every database table we've created so far has an index on its id column. Any WHERE clause that seeks a particular id value will be able to find the record with that value quickly, because it will be able to look it up in the index.

You can confirm this by asking MySQL to explain how it performs a particular SE-LECT query. To do this, just add the command EXPLAIN at the start of the query:

```
EXPLAIN SELECT joketext FROM joke WHERE id = 1
```

Use Real Values to See Real Results

Note that I've specified a joke ID of 1 in this query, which actually exists in my database. Had I used a made-up value like 1234, MySQL is smart enough to know that this ID didn't exist in the joke table and wouldn't even try to fetch results from the table.

If you run this EXPLAIN query in phpMyAdmin, you will have a similar view to Figure 10.3.

id	select_type	table	type	possible_keys	key	key_len	ref	rows	Extra
1	SIMPLE	joke	const	PRIMARY	PRIMARY	4	const	1	

Figure 10.3. These results confirm that the SELECT query will use the PRIMARY index

By the same mechanism, an SQL query that joins two tables together using id values (for example, finding the author that goes with each joke using the value of the authorid column) will be able to find related records quickly.

Now consider this SELECT query, which fetches all jokes by a particular author:

```
SELECT * FROM joke WHERE authorid = 2
```

Ask MySQL to EXPLAIN this SELECT, and Figure 10.4 shows the result.

id	select_type	table	type	possible_keys	key	key_len	ref	rows	Extra
1	SIMPLE	joke	ALL	NULL	NULL	NULL	NULL	4	Using where

Figure 10.4. Those NULLs indicate slowness

As you can see, MySQL is unable to find an index to assist with this query, so it is forced to perform a complete scan of the table for results. We can speed up this query by adding an index to the table for the authorid column.

But surely author IDs are already indexed?

Yes, the id column of the author table has an index by virtue of it being the primary key for that table. This won't help in the case of this query, however, which has no involvement with the author table at all.

The WHERE clause in this case is looking for a value in the authorid field of the joke table, which is without an index.

In phpMyAdmin, select the joke table, click the **Structure** tab, then under **Indexes** use the form to "Create an index on **1** columns." This will give you the **Create a new index** form shown in Figure 10.5.

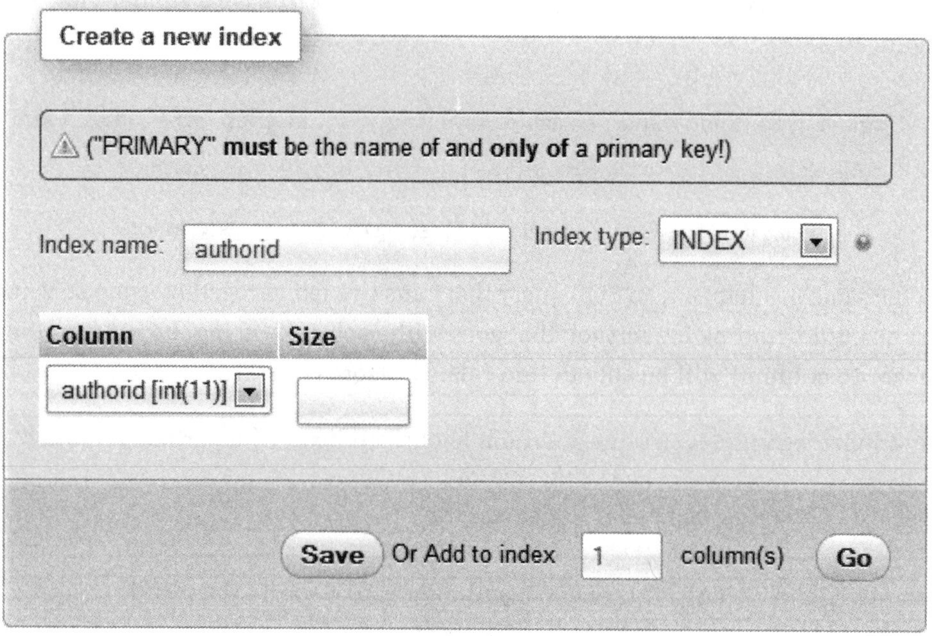

Figure 10.5. Creating a new index for the authorid column

Fill out the form as shown:

▪ Set the **Index name** to match the name of the column it will index (although you could actually call it anything you like).

▪ Choose to create a plain **INDEX** as opposed to a **PRIMARY** index (the table already has one), a **UNIQUE** index (there's no requirement for each joke to have a unique author), or **FULLTEXT** index (an index used for searching large amounts of text).

▪ Select the column to index—authorid in this case. Leave the **Size** field blank to index the full value of the column (as opposed to, say, just the first few characters of a text column).

Click **Save**, and you should see the second index listed along with the `PRIMARY` index. Ask MySQL to `EXPLAIN` the `SELECT` query again to confirm that it will use your new `authorid` index this time.

It might be tempting to index each and every column in your database, but I'd advise against it. Not only do indexes require extra disk space, but every time you make a change to the contents of your database (with an `INSERT` or `UPDATE` query, for example), MySQL has to spend time rebuilding all affected indexes!

For this reason, you should usually add the indexes required to keep your website's `SELECT` queries speedy and no more.

Multicolumn Indexes

But wait! Not *every* table we've created so far has an `id` column. What about the `jokecategory` table?

```
CREATE TABLE jokecategory (
  jokeid INT NOT NULL,
  categoryid INT NOT NULL,
  PRIMARY KEY (jokeid, categoryid)
) DEFAULT CHARACTER SET utf8 ENGINE=InnoDB;
```

This table's primary key is made up of two columns: `jokeid` and `categoryid`. Figure 10.6 shows what this index looks like in phpMyAdmin.

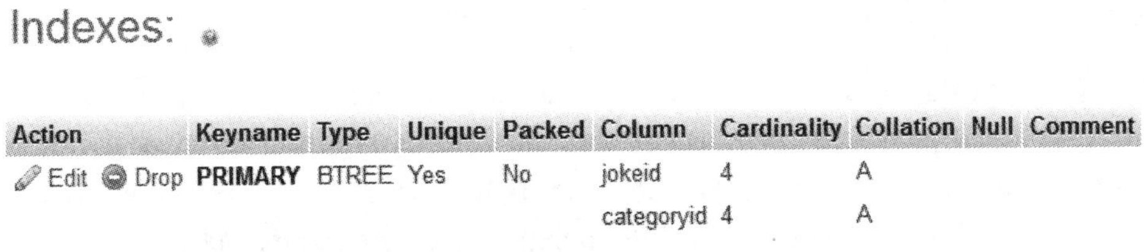

Indexes:

Action	Keyname	Type	Unique	Packed	Column	Cardinality	Collation	Null	Comment
✎ Edit ⊘ Drop	PRIMARY	BTREE	Yes	No	jokeid	4	A		
					categoryid	4	A		

Figure 10.6. Indexes can contain multiple columns

A multicolumn index like this is called a **composite index**. It's great at speeding up queries that involve both indexed columns, like this one that checks if joke ID 3 is in category ID 4 (it is):

```
SELECT * FROM jokecategory WHERE jokeid = 3 AND categoryid = 4
```

A two-column index like this one can also be used as a one-column index on the first column in the list. In this case, that's the `jokeid` field, so this query will also use the index to list the categories that joke ID 1 belongs to:

```sql
SELECT name
FROM jokecategory
  INNER JOIN category ON categoryid = category.id
WHERE jokeid = 1
```

Foreign Keys

By now, you should be used to the concept of a column in one table pointing to the `id` column in another table to represent a relationship between the two tables. For example, the `authorid` column in `joke` points to the `id` column in `author` to record which author wrote each joke.

In database design lingo, a column that contains values that match those in another table is called a **foreign key**. That is, we say that `authorid` is a foreign key that references the `id` column in `author`.

Up to this point, we've simply designed tables with foreign key relationships in mind, but these relationships have not been enforced by MySQL. That is, we've made sure to only store values in `authorid` that correspond to entries in the `author` table. But if we carelessly inserted an `authorid` value without any matches for an `author` record, MySQL would do nothing to stop us; as far as MySQL is concerned, `authorid` is just a column that contains whole numbers.

MySQL supports a feature called **foreign key constraints**, which you can use to record relationships between tables like this one explicitly and have MySQL enforce them. You can include foreign key constraints in your `CREATE TABLE` commands, or you can add foreign key constraints to existing tables using `ALTER TABLE`:

chapter10/sql/ijdb.sql *(excerpt)*

```sql
CREATE TABLE joke (
  id INT NOT NULL AUTO_INCREMENT PRIMARY KEY,
  joketext TEXT,
  jokedate DATE NOT NULL,
```

```
  authorid INT,
  FOREIGN KEY (authorid) REFERENCES author (id)
) DEFAULT CHARACTER SET utf8 ENGINE=InnoDB
```

```
ALTER TABLE joke
ADD FOREIGN KEY (authorid) REFERENCES author (id)
```

You can also use phpMyAdmin to create foreign key constraints. First, you must make sure the foreign key column (authorid in this case) has an index. MySQL will create this index for you automatically if you use either of these two queries, but phpMyAdmin requires you to do it yourself. Thankfully, we already added an index to authorid. Next, on the **Structure** tab for the joke table, click **Relation view** as shown in Figure 10.7.

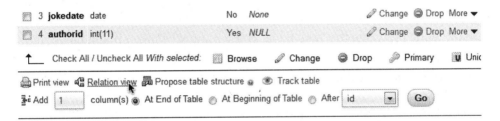

Figure 10.7. Clicking **Relation view** to edit the foreign keys in a table

The resulting page shows each of the columns in the table, and lets you configure a foreign key constraint for each one that has an index. For the authorid column, under **Foreign key constraint (INNODB)** choose `` `ijdb`.`author`.`id` `` (where *ijdb* is the name of your database). Leave the **Internal relation** option blank,[8] and leave the **ON DELETE** and **ON UPDATE** menus set to **RESTRICT** as shown in Figure 10.8, then click **Save**.

---

[8] The **Internal relation** setting lets you record a relationship between tables in phpMyAdmin without actually creating a foreign key constraint (or even an index for the column) in the database. This enables you to navigate from table to table more easily in phpMyAdmin, but MySQL won't enforce the relationship in any way.

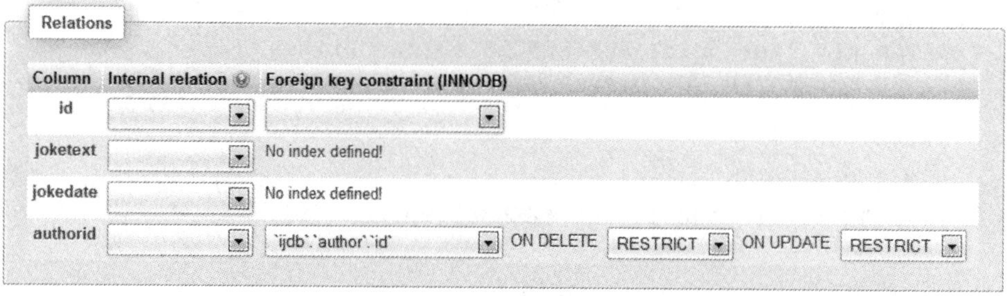

Figure 10.8. Setting up a foreign key in phpMyAdmin

With this foreign key constraint in place, MySQL will reject any attempt to insert into joke an authorid value that fails to correspond to an entry in the author table; furthermore, it will stop you from deleting an entry in the author table unless you first remove any joke records that point to it.

Perhaps best of all, however, in phpMyAdmin if you click on a value in the authorid column while browsing the joke table, you will now be taken immediately to the corresponding row in the author table! Because MySQL (and therefore phpMyAdmin) now understands the structure of your database, it can help you navigate it.

To make sure you've got the hang of it, go ahead and create a foreign key constraint to represent each of the relationships between your tables. See if you can do it without peeking at the list of ALTER TABLE commands following (hint: there are four others):

```
ALTER TABLE jokecategory
ADD FOREIGN KEY (jokeid) REFERENCES joke (id)
```

```
ALTER TABLE jokecategory
ADD FOREIGN KEY (categoryid) REFERENCES category (id)
```

```
ALTER TABLE authorrole
ADD FOREIGN KEY (authorid) REFERENCES author (id)
```

```
ALTER TABLE authorrole
ADD FOREIGN KEY (roleid) REFERENCES role (id)
```

A Word on Referential Actions

Instead of rejecting attempts to delete or update records that have foreign keys pointing to them (for example, preventing you from deleting authors who still have jokes associated with them), you can perform a **referential action**. This involves configuring a foreign key constraint in MySQL to automatically resolve the conflict.

It can do this either by **cascading** the operation (that is, deleting any jokes associated with the author that you're deleting), or by setting the values of any affected foreign key columns to NULL (setting the authorid of the author's jokes to NULL). That's what the **ON RESTRICT** and **ON UPDATE** options for the foreign key constraint in phpMyAdmin are all about.

It can be tempting to use this feature to let MySQL take care of what happens to affected jokes when a user deletes an author or a category. It's certainly easier to select an option in phpMyAdmin than it is to write the PHP code to automatically delete related jokes before removing an author.

The problem with doing this is that it splits the logic of your website into two places: your PHP code and the foreign key constraints. No longer will you be able to see and control everything that happens when you delete a joke by just looking at the PHP controller responsible for doing that job.

For this reason, most experienced PHP developers (myself included) prefer to avoid using referential actions in foreign key constraints. In fact, some developers prefer to avoid using foreign key constraints altogether!

Better Safe than Sorry

Admittedly, this chapter hasn't been the usual nonstop, action–packed codefest to which you may have become accustomed by now. But our concentration on these topics—the backup and restoration of MySQL data, the inner workings of the MySQL access control system, the improvement of query performance with indexes, and the enforcement of the structure of your database with foreign keys—has armed you with the tools you'll need to set up a MySQL database server that will stand the test of time, as well as endure the constant traffic your site will attract.

In Chapter 11, we'll return to the fun stuff and learn some advanced SQL techniques that can make a relational database server perform tricks you may never have thought possible.

Advanced SQL Queries

As you've worked through the construction of the Internet Joke Database website, you've had opportunities to explore most aspects of Structured Query Language (SQL). From the basic form of a `CREATE TABLE` query to the two syntaxes of `INSERT` queries, you probably know many of these commands by heart now.

In an effort to tie up some loose ends in this chapter, we'll look at a few more SQL tricks that we've yet to come across—some having been a bit too advanced to delve into before now. As is typical, most of these will expand on your knowledge of what's already the most complex and potentially confusing SQL command available to you: the `SELECT` query.

Sorting `SELECT` Query Results

Long lists of information are always easier to use when they're presented in some kind of order. To find a single author in a list from your `author` table, for example, could become an exercise in frustration if you had more than a few dozen registered authors in your database.

Fortunately, there's an optional part of the SELECT query that lets you specify a column by which your table of results should be sorted. Let's say you wanted to print out a listing of the entries in your author table for future reference. Here's a short list of a table of authors, with the result in Figure 11.1:

```
SELECT id, name, email FROM author
```

id	name	email
1	Kevin Yank	thatguy@kevinyank.com
2	Jessica Graham	jess@example.com
3	Michael Yates	yatesy@example.com
4	Amy Mathieson	amym@example.com

Figure 11.1. An unsorted list of authors

The entries are unsorted, which is fine for a short list like this; it would be easier, though, to find a particular author's email address (that of Amy Mathieson, for example) in a very long list of authors—say a few hundred or so—if the authors' names appeared in alphabetical order. Here's how you'd create that ordering (as seen in Figure 11.2):

```
SELECT id, name, email FROM author ORDER BY name
```

id	name	email
4	Amy Mathieson	amym@example.com
2	Jessica Graham	jess@example.com
1	Kevin Yank	thatguy@kevinyank.com
3	Michael Yates	yatesy@example.com

Figure 11.2. Authors sorted by name

The entries now appear sorted alphabetically by their names. Just as you can add a WHERE clause to a SELECT statement to narrow down the list of results, you can also add an ORDER BY clause to specify a column by which a set of results should be sorted. Adding the keyword DESC after the name of the column allows you to sort the entries in descending order, as shown in Figure 11.3:

```
SELECT id, name, email FROM author ORDER BY name DESC
```

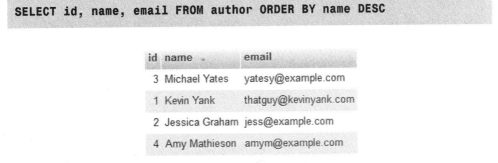

id	name	email
3	Michael Yates	yatesy@example.com
1	Kevin Yank	thatguy@kevinyank.com
2	Jessica Graham	jess@example.com
4	Amy Mathieson	amym@example.com

Figure 11.3. Authors in descending name order

You can actually use a comma-separated list of several column names in the ORDER BY clause to have MySQL sort the entries by the first column, then sort any sets of tied entries by the second, and so on. Any of the columns listed in the ORDER BY clause may use the DESC keyword to reverse the sort order.

Obviously in a large table, MySQL must do a lot of work to sort the result set. You can ease this burden by setting up indexes for columns (or sets of columns) that you expect to use to sort result sets, as we learned in Chapter 10.

Setting LIMITs

Often, you might work with a large database table but only be interested in a few entries within it. Let's say you wanted to track the popularity of different jokes on your site. You could add a column named timesviewed to your joke table. Start it with a value of zero for new jokes, and add one to the value of the requested joke every time the joke is viewed, to keep count of the number of times each joke in your database has been read.

The query that adds one to the timesviewed column of a joke with a given ID is as follows:

```
try
{
  $sql = 'UPDATE joke SET
      timesviewed = timesviewed + 1
      WHERE id = :id';
  $s = $pdo->prepare($sql);
  $s->bindValue(':id', $id);
  $s->execute();
```

```
}
catch (PDOException $e)
{
  $error = 'Error updating joke view count.';
  include 'error.html.php';
  exit();
}
```

You might use this joke view counter to present a "Top 10 Jokes" list on the front page of your site, for example. Using `ORDER BY timesviewed DESC` to list the jokes from highest `timesviewed` to lowest, you'd just have to pick the first ten values from the top of the list. But if you have thousands of jokes in your database, retrieving that entire list to gain a mere ten results would be quite wasteful in terms of the processing time and server system resources required, such as memory and CPU load.

However, if you use a `LIMIT` clause, you can specify a certain number of results to be returned. As stated, in this example you need only the first ten:

```
$sql = 'SELECT joke.id, joketext, name, email
    FROM joke INNER JOIN author
      ON authorid = author.id
    ORDER BY timesviewed DESC
    LIMIT 10';
```

Although it's much less interesting, you could eliminate the word `DESC` and retrieve the ten *least* popular jokes in the database.

Often, you'll want to let users view a long list of entries—for example, the results of a search—but display only a few at a time.[1] Think of the last time you went looking through pages of search engine results to find a particular website. You can use a `LIMIT` clause to do this sort of action; simply specify the result with which the list will begin, and the maximum number of results to display. The query below, for example, will list the 21st to 25th most popular jokes in the database:

---

[1] I've written an article that explores this technique in greater detail at sitepoint.com, entitled *Object Oriented PHP: Paging Result Sets*. [http://www.sitepoint.com/php-paging-result-sets/]

```
$sql = 'SELECT joke.id, joketext, name, email
    FROM joke INNER JOIN author
      ON authorid = author.id
    ORDER BY timesviewed DESC
    LIMIT 20, 5';
```

Remember, the first entry in the list of results is entry number zero. Thus, the 21st entry in the list is entry number 20.

Database Transactions

In some situations, you may wish to perform a series of multiple SQL queries and have them take effect all at once. An advanced feature called **transactions** makes this possible.

Let's say your site's database contained tables listing the products for sale on your site, the number of each product available in inventory, and the orders placed by visitors to your site. When a visitor places an order, you'd like to update your inventory to reflect the purchased item(s) at the same time as you add to the list of orders. If one of these updates occurred before the other, there's a risk that another visitor to your site might view a page and see an inconsistent state: for example, your site might show that the ten widgets you had for sale are now sold out, but only nine have been ordered.

Transactions let you perform complex multiquery operations as a group to take effect simultaneously. To begin a transaction, just send a START TRANSACTION SQL command:

```
START TRANSACTION
```

You can then perform your series of SQL queries as you normally would. When you're done and ready for all the changes to be committed to the database at once, send a COMMIT SQL command:

```
COMMIT
```

Transactions also let you change your mind. If you're partway through your group of queries and decide you don't want to perform the queries after all, just use a ROLLBACK command:

ROLLBACK

ROLLBACK is especially useful for dealing with errors. If you've run a first query in a transaction successfully but the second one gives you an error, you can use ROLLBACK to cancel the effects of the first query, in order to rethink your strategy.

In a PHP script, your PDO object offers methods to make working with transactions very convenient. Begin a transaction with the beginTransaction method, then commit it with the commit method or cancel it with the rollBack method:

```
try
{
  $pdo->beginTransaction();

  : perform a series of queries…

  $pdo->commit();
}
catch (PDOException $e)
{
  $pdo->rollBack();

  $error = 'Error performing the transaction.';
  include 'error.html.php';
  exit();
}
```

Transactions Require InnoDB

Support for transactions is one of the reasons we've always used the newer InnoDB table type (ENGINE=InnoDB) when creating database tables in this book. MySQL's older MyISAM table type does not support transactions.

Column and Table Name Aliases

In some situations, it may be more convenient to refer to MySQL columns and tables using different names. Let's take the example of a database used by an airline's online booking system; this example actually came up in the SitePoint Forums when I was first writing this book. The database structure can be found in **airline.sql** in the code archive if you want to follow along.

To represent the flights offered by the airline, the database contains two tables: flight and city. Each entry in the flight table represents an actual flight between two cities—the origin and destination of the flight. Obviously, origincityid and destinationcityid are columns in the flight table; other columns record inform- ation like the date and time of the flight, the type of aircraft, the flight numbers, and the various fares.

The city table contains a list of all the cities to which the airline flies. Thus, both the origincityid and destinationcityid columns in the flight table will just contain IDs referring to entries in the city table.

Now, consider these queries. To retrieve a list of flights with their origins, here's what you do:

```
SELECT flight.number, city.name
FROM flight INNER JOIN city
  ON flight.origincityid = city.id
```

Figure 11.4 shows the results.

number	name
CP110	Montreal
QF2026	Melbourne
CP226	Sydney
QF2027	Sydney

Figure 11.4. Flights with their origins

To obtain a list of flights with their destinations, the query is very similar:

```
SELECT flight.number, city.name
FROM flight INNER JOIN city
  ON flight.destinationcityid = city.id
```

Again, Figure 11.5 shows the results.

number	name
CP226	Montreal
QF2027	Melbourne
CP110	Sydney
QF2026	Sydney

Figure 11.5. Flights with their destinations

Now, what if you wanted to list both the origin and destination of each flight with a single query? That's reasonable, right? Here's a query you might try:

```
SELECT flight.number, city.name, city.name
FROM flight INNER JOIN city
   ON flight.origincityid = city.id
INNER JOIN city
   ON flight.destinationcityid = city.id
```

Try this query, and phpMyAdmin will display an error: **#1066 - Not unique table/alias 'city'**.

Why does this fail? Have another look at the query, and this time focus on what it actually says, rather than what you expect it to do. It tells MySQL to join the `flight`, `city`, and `city` (yes, twice!) tables. This attempt at joining the same table twice is what produces the error message.

But even without this error, the query lacks sense. It attempts to list the flight number, city name, and city name (twice again) of all entries obtained, by matching up the `origincityid` with the city `id`, and the `destinationcityid` with the city `id`. In other words, the `origincityid`, `destinationcityid`, and city `id` must all be equal. Even if this query worked, it would result in a list of all flights where the origin and the destination are the same. Unless your airline offers scenic flights, it's unlikely there'll be any entries that match this description.

What we need is a way to use the `city` table twice without confusing MySQL. We want to be able to return two different entries from the `city` table—one for the origin and one for the destination—for each result. If we had two copies of the table—one called `origin` and one called `destination`—this would be much easier to do, but why maintain two tables that contain the same list of cities? The solution is to give the `city` table two unique **aliases** (temporary names) for the purposes of this query.

If we follow the name of a table with AS *alias* in the FROM portion of the SELECT query, we can give it a temporary name by which we can refer to it elsewhere in the query. Here's that first query again (to display flight numbers and origins only), but this time we've given the city table origin as its alias:

```
SELECT flight.number, origin.name
FROM flight INNER JOIN city AS origin
  ON flight.origincityid = origin.id
```

The query still works the same way and the results remain unchanged, but for long table names it can save some typing. Consider, for example, if we'd given aliases of f and o to flight and origin, respectively. The query would be much shorter as a result.

Let's now return to our problem query. If we refer to the city table twice using different aliases, we can use a three-table join (in which two of the tables are actually one and the same) to achieve the effect we want:

```
SELECT flight.number, origin.name, destination.name
FROM flight INNER JOIN city AS origin
  ON flight.origincityid = origin.id
INNER JOIN city AS destination
  ON flight.destinationcityid = destination.id
```

You can see the expected results in Figure 11.6.

number	name	name
CP110	Montreal	Sydney
CP226	Sydney	Montreal
QF2026	Melbourne	Sydney
QF2027	Sydney	Melbourne

Figure 11.6. Flights with origins and destinations

You can also define aliases for column names. We could use this to differentiate the two name columns in our table of results:

```
SELECT f.number, o.name AS origin, d.name AS destination
FROM flight AS f INNER JOIN city AS o
  ON f.origincityid = o.id
INNER JOIN city AS d
  ON f.destinationcityid = d.id
```

The very readable result is in Figure 11.7.

number	origin	destination
CP110	Montreal	Sydney
CP226	Sydney	Montreal
QF2026	Melbourne	Sydney
QF2027	Sydney	Melbourne

Figure 11.7. Flights with origins and destinations clearly labeled

You could use this same technique to add a messaging system to the Internet Joke Database website, whereby one author could send a message to another author on the site. The table of sent messages would reference the author table twice: once for the sender of the message, and another for the recipient. If you're keen for a fresh challenge, try building this system.

GROUPing SELECT Results

In Chapter 2, you saw the following query, which tells you how many jokes are stored in your joke table:

```
SELECT COUNT(*) FROM joke
```

The MySQL function COUNT used in this query belongs to a special class of functions called **aggregate functions** or **group-by functions**, depending on where you look. A complete list of these functions is provided in Chapter 11 of the MySQL Manual[2] and in Appendix C. Unlike other functions, which affect each entry individually in the result of the SELECT query, summary functions group together all the results and return a single result. In the aforementioned example, for instance, COUNT returns the total number of result rows.

---

[2] http://dev.mysql.com/doc/mysql/en/group-by-functions.html

Let's say you want to display a list of authors along with the number of jokes they have to their names. Your first instinct might be to retrieve a list of all the authors' names and IDs, then use COUNT to count the number of results when you SELECT the jokes with each author's ID. The PHP code (presented without error handling, for simplicity) would look a little like this:

```php
// Get a list of all the authors
$result = $pdo->query('SELECT id, name FROM author');

// Read all of the authors
foreach ($result as $row)
{
  $authors[] = array(
      'id' => $row['id'],
      'name' => $row['name']
  );
}

// Get count of jokes attributed to an author
$sql = 'SELECT COUNT(*) AS numjokes FROM joke WHERE authorid = :id';
$s = $pdo->prepare($sql);

// Process each author
foreach ($authors as $author)
{
  $s->bindValue(':id', $author['id']);
  $s->execute();
  $row = $s->fetch();
  $numjokes = $row['numjokes'];

  // Display the author & number of jokes
  $output .= htmlspecialchars($author['name'], ENT_QUOTES, 'UTF-8')
      . " ($numjokes jokes)<br>";
}
```

Note the use of AS in the second query to give a friendlier name (numjokes) to the result of COUNT(*).

This technique will work, but will require n+1 separate queries (where n is the number of authors in the database). Having the number of queries depend on a number of entries in the database is always worth avoiding, as a large number of authors would make this script unreasonably slow and resource-intensive. Fortunately, another advanced feature of SELECT comes to the rescue!

If you add a GROUP BY clause to a SELECT query, you can tell MySQL to group the query results into sets, the results in each set sharing a common value in the specified column. Aggregate functions like COUNT then operate on those groups, rather than the entire result set as a whole. The next query, for example, lists the number of jokes attributed to each author in the database:

```
SELECT author.name, COUNT(*) AS numjokes
FROM joke INNER JOIN author
  ON authorid = author.id
GROUP BY authorid
```

The results shown in Figure 11.8 confirm that we've obtained our per-author joke count with a single SELECT query.

name	numjokes
Kevin Yank	3
Jessica Graham	1

Figure 11.8. Number of jokes per author

Note that you could have specified GROUP BY author.id and achieved the same result (since, as stipulated in the FROM clause, these columns must be equal). GROUP BY author.name would also work in most cases, but as there's always the possibility, however slight, that two different authors might have the same name (in which case their results would be lumped together), it's best to stick to the ID columns, which are guaranteed to be unique for each author.

LEFT JOINs

You can see from the results just shown that Kevin Yank has three jokes to his name, and Jessica Graham has one. What they conceal is that there's a third and fourth author, Amy Mathieson and Michael Yates, who have *no* jokes. Since there are no entries in the joke table with authorid values that match either of the absent authors' ID, there will be no results that satisfy the ON clause in the aforementioned query and they'll be excluded from the table of results.

About the only practical way to overcome this challenge with the tools we've seen so far would be to add another column to the author table and store the number of jokes attributed to each author in that column. Keeping that column up to date, however, would be a real pain, because we'd have to remember to update it each time a joke was added, removed, or changed (for example, if the value of `authorid` was changed) in the `joke` table. To keep it all synchronized, we'd have to use transactions whenever we made such changes as well. Quite a mess, to say the least!

Besides the `INNER JOIN`s we've used so far, MySQL provides another type of join. Called a **left join**, it's designed for this type of situation. To understand how left joins differ from standard joins, we must first recall how inner joins work.

As shown in Figure 11.9, MySQL performs a standard join of two tables by listing all possible combinations of the rows of those tables. In a simple case, a standard join of two tables with two rows apiece will contain four rows: row 1 of table 1 with row 1 of table 2, row 1 of table 1 with row 2 of table 2, row 2 of table 1 with row 1 of table 2, and row 2 of table 1 with row 2 of table 2. With all these result rows calculated, MySQL then looks to the `ON` condition for guidance on which rows should be kept (for example, those where the `id` column from table 1 matches the `authorid` column from table 2).

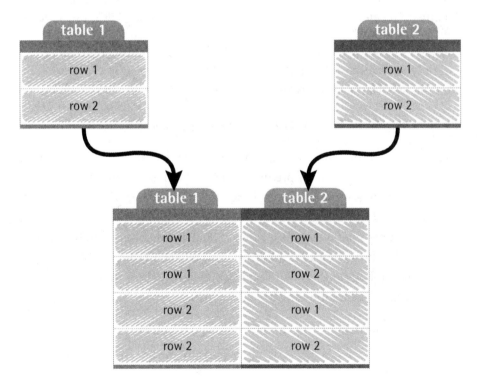

Figure 11.9. Inner joins take all possible combinations of rows

The reason why this solution is unsuitable for our purposes is that we'd like to also include rows in table 1 (that is, author) that don't match any rows in table 2 (joke). A left join does exactly what we need: it forces a row to appear in the results for each row in the first (left-hand) table, even if no matching entries are found in the second (right-hand) table. Such **forced rows** are given NULL values for all columns in the right-hand table.

To perform a left join between two tables in MySQL, simply type LEFT JOIN instead of INNER JOIN within the FROM clause. Here's our revised query for listing authors and the number of jokes to their credit:

```
SELECT author.name, COUNT(*) AS numjokes
FROM author LEFT JOIN joke
  ON authorid = author.id
GROUP BY author.id
```

A couple of important points to note about this query:

- We must type author LEFT JOIN joke, rather than joke LEFT JOIN author.

  The order in which we list the tables to be joined is significant. A LEFT JOIN will only force all rows from the table on the *left* to appear in the results. In this example, we want every row in the author table to appear in the results.

- We must use GROUP BY author.id, rather than GROUP BY authorid.

  author.id is the id field of the author table, whereas authorid is the authorid field of the joke table. In all previous SELECT queries, our join has guaranteed that these would always have matching values; however, when the LEFT JOIN creates a forced row based on a row in the author table that has no matching row in the joke table, it assigns a value of NULL to all columns in the joke table. This includes the authorid field. If we used GROUP BY authorid, the query would group all our authors with no jokes together, since they all share an authorid value of NULL following the LEFT JOIN.[3]

If you type that query right, you should achieve the results shown in Figure 11.10.

---

[3] You may find you have to read this a few times to understand it. That's because this is by far the subtlest aspect of the SQL language you'll find in the book.

name	numjokes
Kevin Yank	3
Jessica Graham	1
Michael Yates	1
Amy Mathieson	1

Figure 11.10. Something's not quite right ...

Wait just a minute! Suddenly Amy Mathieson and Michael Yates have one joke apiece. That can't be right, surely? In fact, it is—but only because the query is still wrong. COUNT(*) counts the number of rows returned for each author. If we look at the ungrouped results of the LEFT JOIN, we can see what's happened:

```
SELECT author.name, joke.id AS jokeid
FROM author LEFT JOIN joke
  ON authorid = author.id
```

Figure 11.11 reveals that Amy Mathieson and Michael Yates *do* have rows—the rows that are forced because there are no matching rows in the right-hand table of the LEFT JOIN (joke). The fact that the joke ID value is NULL has no effect on COUNT(*); it still counts it as a row.

name	jokeid
Kevin Yank	1
Kevin Yank	2
Kevin Yank	3
Jessica Graham	4
Michael Yates	NULL
Amy Mathieson	NULL

Figure 11.11. Ungrouped results

If, instead of *, you specify an actual column name (say, joke.id) for the COUNT function to look at, it will ignore NULL values in that column and give us the count we want:

```
SELECT author.name, COUNT(joke.id) AS numjokes
FROM author LEFT JOIN joke
  ON authorid = author.id
GROUP BY author.id
```

The long-awaited results are shown in Figure 11.12.

name	numjokes
Kevin Yank	3
Jessica Graham	1
Michael Yates	0
Amy Mathieson	0

Figure 11.12. At last!

Limiting Results with HAVING

What if we wanted a list of *only* those authors that had no jokes to their name? Once again, let's look at the query that many developers would try first:

```
SELECT author.name, COUNT(joke.id) AS numjokes
FROM author LEFT JOIN joke
   ON authorid = author.id
WHERE numjokes = 0
GROUP BY author.id
```

This will cause phpMyAdmin to spit out the error **#1054 - Unknown column 'numjokes' in 'where clause'**.

By now, you're probably unfazed that it failed to work as expected. The reason why WHERE numjokes = 0 caused an error has to do with the way MySQL processes result sets. First, MySQL produces the raw, combined list of authors and jokes from the author and joke tables. Next, it processes the ON portion of the FROM clause and the WHERE clause so that only the relevant rows in the list are returned (in this case, rows that match authors with their jokes, and which have a numjokes value of 0). Finally, MySQL processes the GROUP BY clause by grouping the results according to their authorid, COUNTing the number of entries in each group that have non-NULL joke.id values, and producing the numjokes column as a result.

Notice that the numjokes column is actually created after the GROUP BY clause is processed, and *that* happens only after the WHERE clause does its stuff. Hence the error message—the WHERE clause is looking for a numjokes column that is yet to be created.

If you wanted to exclude jokes that contained the word "chicken" from the count, you could use the WHERE clause without a problem, because that exclusion doesn't rely on a value that the GROUP BY clause is responsible for producing. Conditions that affect the results *after* grouping takes place, however, must appear in a special HAVING clause. Here's the corrected query:

```
SELECT author.name, COUNT(joke.id) AS numjokes
FROM author LEFT JOIN joke
  ON authorid = author.id
GROUP BY author.id
HAVING numjokes = 0
```

The expected results are shown in Figure 11.13.

name	numjokes
Michael Yates	0
Amy Mathieson	0

Figure 11.13. Our least prolific authors

Some conditions work both in the HAVING and the WHERE clauses. For example, if we wanted to exclude a particular author by name, we could do this by using author.name != 'Author Name' in either the WHERE or HAVING clause; that's because, regardless of whether you filter out the author before or after you group the results, the same results are returned. In such cases, it's always best to use the WHERE clause, because MySQL is better at optimizing such queries internally so they happen faster.

Further Reading

In this chapter, you rounded out your knowledge of Structured Query Language (SQL) as supported by MySQL. We focused predominantly on features of SELECT that allow you to view information stored in a database with an unprecedented level of flexibility and power. With judicious use of the advanced features of SELECT, you can have MySQL do what it does best, lightening the load on PHP in the process.

There are still a few isolated query types that we've yet to see, and MySQL offers a whole library of built-in functions to do tasks like calculate dates and format text strings (see Appendix C). To become truly proficient with MySQL, you should also have a firm grasp on the various column types offered by MySQL. The TIMESTAMP type, for example, can be a real time-saver (no pun intended). All of these are fully documented in the MySQL Manual,[4] and briefly covered in Appendix D.

For more detailed coverage of the features of SQL covered in this chapter—and a whole lot more that wasn't—I highly recommend the book *Simply SQL* by Rudy Limeback.[5]

---

[4] http://dev.mysql.com/doc/refman/5.5/en/datetime.html
[5] http://www.sitepoint.com/books/sql1/

Chapter

Binary Data

All the examples of database driven websites we've seen so far have dealt with sites based around textual data. Jokes, authors, categories … all these elements can be fully represented with strings of text. But what if you ran, say, an online digital photo gallery to which people could upload pictures taken with digital cameras? For this idea to work, visitors need to be able to upload their photos to our site, and we need the ability to keep track of them.

In this chapter, you will develop a system whereby users can upload binary files (images, documents … whatever!) and have them stored on your web server for display on your site. There are several techniques you'll need to learn on the way, though, and I'll cover all of these in this chapter: working with files in PHP, handling uploaded files in PHP, and storing and retrieving binary data in MySQL.

As we learn to juggle files with PHP, we'll also take the opportunity to relieve some of the load on your web server with the help of semidynamic pages.

Semidynamic Pages

As the owner of a successful—or soon-to-be successful—website, site traffic is probably worth encouraging. Unfortunately, high site traffic can be just what a web server administrator dreads—especially when that site's primarily composed of dynamically generated, database driven pages. Such pages use a great deal more horsepower on the computer that runs the web server software than do plain old HTML files, because every page request is like a miniature program that runs on that computer.

While some pages of a database driven site must always display current-to-the-second data taken from the database, others do not. Consider the front page of a website like sitepoint.com. Typically, it presents a digest of what's new and fresh on the site. But how often does that information actually change? Once an hour? Once a *day*? And how important is it that visitors to your site see those changes the instant they occur? Would your site really suffer if changes took effect after a slight delay?

By converting high-traffic dynamic pages into **semidynamic** equivalents—static pages that are regenerated dynamically at regular intervals to freshen their content—you can significantly reduce the toll that the database driven components of your site take on your web server's performance.

Say that you have a controller script—**index.php**—that uses a PHP template to generate your front page, which provides a summary of new content on your site. Through examining the server logs, you'll probably find that this is one of the most requested pages on your site. If you ask yourself some of the questions just mentioned, you'll realize that there's no need to dynamically generate this page for every request. As long as it's updated every time new content is added to your site, it'll be as dynamic as it needs to be. Instead of using a controller script to handle every request for the front page of your site, you can use the PHP code to generate a static snapshot of the PHP template's output and put this snapshot online—in place of the dynamic version—as **index.html**.

This little trick will require some reading, writing, and juggling of files. PHP is perfectly capable of accomplishing this task, but we're yet to cover the functions we'll need:

file_get_contents

This function opens a file and reads the contents, returning them in the form of a PHP string. The file can be stored on the server's hard disk, or PHP can load it from a URL just like a web browser would. If an error occurs, the function returns FALSE instead.

file_put_contents

This function opens a file and writes the specified data into it. You can option-ally specify settings such as whether the data should be added to the end of the existing file, rather than replacing the file completely (the default).[1]

file_exists

This function checks if a file with a specific name exists or not. If the file exists, the function returns TRUE; otherwise, it returns FALSE.

copy

This function performs a run-of-the-mill file copy operation.

unlink

This function deletes a file from the hard disk.

Do you see where we're headed? If not, I assure you that you will in a moment.

Let's begin with a dead-simple controller script and template for displaying a list of the three most recent jokes in the databases of the Internet Joke Database, as we last left it in Chapter 10:

chapter12/recentjokes/controller.php

```php
<?php

include_once $_SERVER['DOCUMENT_ROOT'] . '/includes/db.inc.php';

try
{
  $sql = 'SELECT id, joketext FROM joke
      ORDER BY jokedate DESC
      LIMIT 3';
  $result = $pdo->query($sql);
```

[1] For full details of the available options, check out the PHP Manual [http://php.net/file_put_contents].

```
}
catch (PDOException $e)
{
  $error = 'Error fetching jokes.';
  include $_SERVER['DOCUMENT_ROOT'] . '/includes/error.html.php';
  exit();
}

foreach ($result as $row)
{
  $jokes[] = array('text' => $row['joketext']);
}

include 'jokes.html.php';
```

chapter12/recentjokes/jokes.html.php

```
<?php include_once $_SERVER['DOCUMENT_ROOT'] .
    '/includes/helpers.inc.php'; ?>
<!DOCTYPE html>
<html lang="en">
  <head>
    <meta charset="utf-8">
    <title>Recent Jokes</title>
    <link rel="canonical" href="/recentjokes/">
  </head>
  <body>
    <p>Here are the most recent jokes in the database:</p>
    <?php foreach ($jokes as $joke): ?>
      <?php markdownout($joke['text']); ?>
    <?php endforeach; ?>
  </body>
</html>
```

Normally, you'd name the controller script **index.php**, so that a browser request for http://www.example.com/recentjokes/ would run the controller script and build the list of jokes on the fly. However, the controller is named **controller.php** in this case. A browser that knew this filename could still request the controller, but as indicated by the <link rel="canonical"> tag[2] in the **jokes.html.php** template, we still expect most visitors to access the page as http://www.example.com/recentjokes/.

---

[2] For a full description of the <link rel="canonical"> tag, check out the Google Webmaster Central Blog [http://googlewebmastercentral.blogspot.com/2009/02/specify-your-canonical.html].

Instead of triggering the controller, though, browsers that request this URL will hit a static version of the page that's been prepared in advance.

To generate this static version, we'll write another script: **generate.php**. It will be the responsibility of this script to load **controller.php**—the dynamic version of your front page—as a web browser would, then to write an up-to-date static snapshot of the page as **index.html**. If anything goes wrong in this process, you'll want to hold onto the existing version of **index.html**; we'll make this script write the new static version into a temporary file (**tempindex.html**), then copy it over **index.html** if all is well.

We start out by setting some PHP variables to configure the URL of the PHP script we wish to load, the temporary filename to use in the process, and the name of the static page we wish to create:

```
chapter12/recentjokes/generate.php (excerpt)

<?php
$srcurl = 'http://localhost/recentjokes/controller.php';
$tempfilename = $_SERVER['DOCUMENT_ROOT'] .
    '/recentjokes/tempindex.html';
$targetfilename = $_SERVER['DOCUMENT_ROOT'] .
    '/recentjokes/index.html';
```

$srcurl Must Be a URL

Resist the temptation to set $srcurl to the filename of **controller.php** on your web server. In order for this script to retrieve the page *produced* by the **controller.php** script, it must request the script using a URL that points to your web server. If you pointed the script directly at the file, it would receive the code of the **controller.php** script itself rather than the HTML output it produces.

Now, to do the work. We start out by deleting the temporary file, in case it was previously left lying around by a failed execution of this script. We use `file_exists` to check if the file exists, then `unlink` to delete it if it does:

```
chapter12/recentjokes/generate.php (excerpt)
```

```php
if (file_exists($tempfilename))
{
  unlink($tempfilename);
}
```

Now we can load the dynamic page (**controller.php**) by requesting its URL with
`file_get_contents`. Since we're requesting the file as a URL rather than directly
using its filename, the PHP script will be processed by the web server before we
receive it, so what we'll end up with is essentially a static HTML page:

```
chapter12/recentjokes/generate.php (excerpt)
```

```php
$html = file_get_contents($srcurl);
if (!$html)
{
  $error = "Unable to load $srcurl. Static page update aborted!";
  include $_SERVER['DOCUMENT_ROOT'] . '/includes/error.html.php';
  exit();
}
```

With the page contents tucked away in the `$html` variable, we now want to write
them into a static HTML file. The `file_put_contents` function makes this a piece
of cake:

```
chapter12/recentjokes/generate.php (excerpt)
```

```php
if (!file_put_contents($tempfilename, $html))
{
  $error = "Unable to write $tempfilename. Static page update
➥ aborted!";
  include $_SERVER['DOCUMENT_ROOT'] . '/includes/error.html.php';
  exit();
}
```

The static page has now been written into a temporary file, so we should copy the
temporary file and paste over the previous version of the static file using `copy`. We
can then delete the temporary file with `unlink`:

```
copy($tempfilename, $targetfilename);
unlink($tempfilename);
```

Now, whenever **generate.php** is executed, a fresh copy of **index.html** will be generated from **controller.php**. Go ahead and request **generate.php** with your browser, then load the **recentjokes** directory (for example, http://localhost/recentjokes/). You should see the contents of the generated **index.html** file.

 Errors Due to File Permissions

Particularly on Mac OS X and Linux servers, the script could be tripped up if it has insufficient privileges to copy and delete files in this directory on your server. If **generate.php** outputs errors that indicate this, you'll need to make the directory containing these files writable by your web server. Usually, this can be done with a simple `chmod` command:

```
chmod 777 /path/to/recentjokes/
```

Check with your web host if you need help setting permissions to make a directory PHP-writable on your site.

Of course, it would be a pain to have to manually request the **generate.php** script whenever the content of your site changes. The easiest way to automate this process is to `include` the **generate.php** script from within the code of your site's content management system whenever a joke is added, updated, or removed from the site.

If a page is quite complex, it may be difficult to find all the right places within your CMS to regenerate its static version. Alternatively, you may simply wish to set up your server to run **generate.php** at regular intervals—say, every hour. Under Windows, you can use the Task Scheduler to run **php.exe** (a standalone version of PHP included with XAMPP and other distributions of PHP for Windows) automatically every hour. Just create a batch file called **generate.bat** that contains this line of text:

```
@C:\xampp\php\php.exe generate.php
```

Adjust the paths and filenames as necessary, then set up Task Scheduler to run **generate.bat** every hour. Done!

Under OS X or Linux, you can do a similar thing with **cron**—a system-level utility that lets you define tasks to be run at regular intervals. Type `man crontab` at your system's Terminal prompt to read about how you can set up tasks for **cron**.

The task you'll set **cron** to run will be very similar to the Windows task just discussed. MAMP includes a standalone version of PHP that you can run with **cron** (it's **/Applications/MAMP/bin/php/php5.3.6/bin/php** in the version I'm using).

For experienced **cron** users in a hurry, here's what the line in your **crontab** file should look like:

```
0 0-23 * * * /Applications/MAMP/bin/php/php5.3.6/bin/php
➥/path/to/generate.php > /dev/null
```

Handling File Uploads

Okay, we can now juggle files we've created ourselves. The next piece of the puzzle is to accept files uploaded by visitors to your site, and handle them just as deftly.

We'll start with the basics: let's write an HTML form that allows users to upload files. HTML makes this quite easy with its `<input type="file">` tag. By default, however, only the name of the file selected by the user is sent. To have the file itself submitted with the form data, we need to add `enctype="multipart/form-data"` to the `<form>` tag:

```
<form action="index.php" method="post"
    enctype="multipart/form-data">
  <div><label for="upload">Select file to upload:
    <input type="file" id="upload" name="upload"></label></div>
  <div>
    <input type="hidden" name="action" value="upload">
    <input type="submit" value="Submit">
  </div>
</form>
```

As we can see, a PHP script (**index.php**, in this case) will handle the data submitted with this form. Information about uploaded files appears in a array called $_FILES that's automatically created by PHP. As you'd expect, an entry in this array called $_FILES['upload'] (from the name attribute of the <input> tag) will contain information about the file uploaded in this example. However, instead of storing the contents of the uploaded file, $_FILES['upload'] contains yet another array. We therefore use a second set of square brackets to select the information we want:

$_FILES['*upload*']['tmp_name']

Provides the name of the file stored on the web server's hard disk in the system temporary file directory, unless another directory has been specified using the upload_tmp_dir setting in your **php.ini** file. This file is only kept as long as the PHP script responsible for handling the form submission is running. So, if you want to use the uploaded file later on (for example, store it for display on the site), you need to make a copy of it elsewhere. To do this, use the copy function described in the section called "Semidynamic Pages".

$_FILES['*upload*']['name']

Provides the name of the file on the client machine before it was submitted. If you make a permanent copy of the temporary file, you might want to give it its original name instead of the automatically generated temporary filename that's described.

$_FILES['*upload*']['size']

Provides the size (in bytes) of the file.

$_FILES['*upload*']['type']

Provides the **MIME type** of the file. (It is sometimes referred to as **file type** or **content type**, an identifier used to describe the file format; for example, text/plain, image/png, and so on.)

Remember, 'upload' is just the name attribute of the <input> tag that submitted the file, so the actual array index will depend on that attribute.

You can use these variables to decide whether to accept or reject an uploaded file. For example, in a photo gallery we'd only really be interested in JPEG, and possibly GIF and PNG files. These files have MIME types of image/jpeg, image/gif, and image/png, respectively, but to cater for differences between browsers,[3] you should use regular expressions to validate the uploaded file's type:

```
if (preg_match('/^image\/p?jpeg$/i', $_FILES['upload']['type']) or
    preg_match('/^image\/gif$/i', $_FILES['upload']['type']) or
    preg_match('/^image\/(x-)?png$/i', $_FILES['upload']['type']))
{
  : Handle the file…
}
else
{
  $error = 'Please submit a JPEG, GIF, or PNG image file.';
  include $_SERVER['DOCUMENT_ROOT'] . '/includes/error.html.php';
  exit();
}
```

See Chapter 8 for help with regular expression syntax.

While you can use a similar technique to disallow files that are too large (by checking the $_FILES['upload']['size'] variable), I advise against it. Before this value can be checked, the file is already uploaded and saved in the temporary directory. If you try to reject files because you have limited disk space and/or bandwidth, the fact that large files can still be uploaded (even though they're deleted almost immediately) may be a problem for you.

Instead, you can tell PHP in advance the maximum file size you'll accept. There are two ways to do this. The first is to adjust the upload_max_filesize setting in your **php.ini** file. The default value is 2MB, so if you want to accept uploads larger than that, you'll need to change that value immediately.[4]

The second method is to include a hidden <input> field in your form with the name MAX_FILE_SIZE, and the actual maximum file size you want to accept with this form as its value. For security reasons, this value can't exceed the upload_max_filesize setting in your **php.ini**, but it does provide a way for you to accept different maximum

---

[3] The exact MIME type depends on the browser in use. Internet Explorer uses image/pjpeg for JPEG images and image/x-png for PNG images, while Firefox and other browsers use image/jpeg and image/png, respectively.

[4] A second restriction, affecting the total size of form submissions, is enforced by the post_max_size setting in **php.ini**. Its default value is 8MB, so if you want to accept *really* big uploads you'll need to modify that setting, too.

sizes on different pages. The following form, for example, will allow uploads of up to one kilobyte (1024 bytes):

```
<form action="upload.php" method="post"
    enctype="multipart/form-data">
  <p><label id="upload">Select file to upload:
  <input type="hidden" name="MAX_FILE_SIZE" value="1024">
    <input type="file" id="upload" name="upload"></label></p>
  <p>
    <input type="hidden" name="action" value="upload">
    <input type="submit" value="Submit">
  </p>
</form>
```

Note that the hidden MAX_FILE_SIZE field must come before any <input type="file"> tags in the form, so that PHP is apprised of this restriction before it receives any submitted files. Note also that this restriction can easily be circumvented by malicious users who simply write their own form without the MAX_FILE_SIZE field. For fail-safe security against large file uploads, use the upload_max_filesize setting in **php.ini**.

Assigning Unique Filenames

As I explained, to keep an uploaded file you need to copy it to another directory. And while you have access to the name of each uploaded file with its $_FILE['upload']['name'] variable, there's no guarantee that two files with the same name will not be uploaded. In such a case, storage of the file with its original name may result in newer uploads overwriting older ones.

For this reason, you'll usually want to adopt a scheme that allows you to assign a unique filename to every uploaded file. Using the system time (which you can access using the PHP time function), you can easily produce a name based on the number of seconds since January 1, 1970. But what if two files happen to be uploaded within one second of each other? To help guard against this possibility, we'll also use the client's IP address (automatically stored in $_SERVER['REMOTE_ADDR'] by PHP) in the filename. Since you're unlikely to receive two files from the same IP address within one second of each other, it's acceptable for most purposes:

```php
// Pick a file extension
if (preg_match('/^image\/p?jpeg$/i', $_FILES['upload']['type']))
{
  $ext = '.jpg';
}
else if (preg_match('/^image\/gif$/i', $_FILES['upload']['type']))
{
  $ext = '.gif';
}
else if (preg_match('/^image\/(x-)?png$/i',
    $_FILES['upload']['type']))
{
  $ext = '.png';
}
else
{
  $ext = '.unknown';
}

// The complete path/filename
$filename = 'C:/uploads/' . time() . $_SERVER['REMOTE_ADDR'] . $ext;

// Copy the file (if it is deemed safe)
if (!is_uploaded_file($_FILES['upload']['tmp_name']) or
    !copy($_FILES['upload']['tmp_name'], $filename))
{
  $error = "Could not save file as $filename!";
  include $_SERVER['DOCUMENT_ROOT'] . '/includes/error.html.php';
  exit();
}
```

Important to note in this code is the use of the is_uploaded_file function to check if the file is "safe." All this function does is return TRUE if the filename it's passed as a parameter ($_FILES['upload']['tmp_name'] in this case) was uploaded as part of a form submission. If a malicious user loaded this script and manually specified a filename such as **/etc/passwd** (the system password store on Linux servers), and you had failed to use is_uploaded_file to check that $_FILES['upload'] really referred to an uploaded file, your script might be used to copy sensitive files on your server into a directory where they'd become publicly accessible over the Web! Thus, before you ever trust a PHP variable that you expect to contain the filename of an uploaded file, be sure to use is_uploaded_file to check it.

A second trick I've used in the aforementioned code is to combine `is_uploaded_file` and `copy` together as the condition of an `if` statement. If the result of `is_uploaded_file($_FILES['upload']['tmp_name'])` is FALSE (making `!is_uploaded_file($_FILES['upload']['tmp_name'])` TRUE), PHP will know immediately that the entire condition will be TRUE when it sees the or operator separating the two function calls. To save time, it will refrain from bothering to run `copy`, so the file won't be copied when `is_uploaded_file` returns FALSE. On the other hand, if `is_uploaded_file` returns TRUE, PHP goes ahead and copies the file. The result of `copy` then determines whether or not an error message is displayed. Similarly, if we'd used the and operator instead of or, a FALSE result in the first part of the condition would cause PHP to skip evaluating the second part. This characteristic of `if` statements is known as **short-circuit evaluation**, and it works in other conditional structures such as `while` and `for` loops, too.

Finally, note that I've used UNIX-style forward slashes (/) in the path, despite it being a Windows path. If I'd used backslashes, I would've had to replace them with double-backslashes (\\) to stop PHP from interpreting them as escaped characters. PHP is smart enough to convert forward slashes in a filepath to backslashes when it's running on a Windows system. Since we can also use single slashes (/) as usual on non-Windows systems, adopting forward slashes in general for filepaths in PHP will make your scripts more portable.

Recording Uploaded Files in the Database

So, you've created a system whereby visitors can upload JPEG, GIF, and PNG images and have them saved on your server … but this book was supposed to be about database driven websites—right? If we used the system as it stands now, the submitted images would need to be collected from the folder in which they're saved, then added to the website by hand! If you think back to the end of Chapter 9 when I suggested you develop a system that enabled site visitors to submit jokes to be stored in the database ready for quick approval by a content administrator, you'll know there must be a better way!

MySQL has several column types that allow you to store binary data. In database parlance, these column types let us store **BLOBs (Binary Large OBjects)**; however, the storage of potentially large files in a relational database is often a bad idea. While there's convenience in having all the data located in one place, large files lead to large databases, and large databases lead to reduced performance and humongous backup files.

The best alternative is usually to store the *filenames* in the database. As long as you remember to delete files when you delete their corresponding entries in the database, everything should work the way you need it to. Since we've seen all the SQL code involved in this time and again, I'll leave the details to you. As usual, the SitePoint Forum community is there to offer a helping hand if necessary.

In cases where you're dealing with relatively small files—for example, head shots for use in a staff directory—the storage of data in MySQL is quite practical. In the rest of this chapter, I'll demonstrate how to use PHP to store binary files uploaded over the Web in a MySQL database, and how to retrieve those files for download or display.

Binary Column Types

As with most database driven web applications, the first factor to consider is the layout of the database. To keep this example separate from the Internet Joke Database, I recommend creating a new database for it:

```
CREATE DATABASE filestore
```

If this isn't possible (for example, if you're working on a hosted MySQL server where you're only allowed a single database), go ahead and stick with your existing database.

For each file that's stored in our database, we'll store the filename, the MIME type (for example, image/jpeg for JPEG image files), a short description of the file, and the binary data itself. Here's the CREATE TABLE statement to create the table:

chapter12/sql/filestore.sql (excerpt)

```
CREATE TABLE filestore (
  id INT NOT NULL PRIMARY KEY AUTO_INCREMENT,
  filename VARCHAR(255) NOT NULL,
  mimetype VARCHAR(50) NOT NULL,
  description VARCHAR(255) NOT NULL,
  filedata MEDIUMBLOB
) DEFAULT CHARACTER SET utf8 ENGINE=InnoDB
```

Most of this syntax should be familiar to you; however, the MEDIUMBLOB column type is new. If you consult the MySQL Column Type Reference in Appendix D, you'll find that MEDIUMBLOB is the same as MEDIUMTEXT, except that it performs case-sensitive searches and sorts. In fact, there's no difference between binary data and blocks of text from MySQL's point of view—both are just long strings of bytes to be stored in the database. MySQL just applies a bunch of extra rules to text column types to ensure that the expected sorting behavior and character encoding conversions are performed transparently.

Aside from the increased performance you gain from avoiding these extra rules, MySQL provides BLOB column types like MEDIUMBLOB to support situations in which you might need to compare the contents of one binary file with another. In such cases, you'd want the comparison to be case-sensitive, as binary files may use byte patterns that are the equivalent to alphabetical letters; for example, you'd want to distinguish the byte pattern that represents "A" from that representing "a," which a MEDIUMTEXT column would consider equal.

MEDIUMBLOB is one of several BLOB column types designed to store variable-length binary data. These column types differ from one another only in two aspects: the maximum size of the data a particular value in the column can contain, and the number of bytes used to store the length of each data value. The different binary column types are listed with these details in Table 12.1.

Table 12.1. Binary Column Types in MySQL

Column type	Maximum size	Space required per entry
TINYBLOB	255B	Data size + 1 byte
BLOB	65KB	Data size + 2 bytes
MEDIUMBLOB	16.7MB	Data size + 3 bytes
LONGBLOB	4.3GB	Data size + 4 bytes

As you can see, the table we've created will be able to store files up to 16.7MB in size. If you think you'll need larger files, you can bump the filedata column up to a LONGBLOB. Each file will occupy one more byte in the database, because MySQL will require that extra byte in order to record larger file sizes, but you'll be able to store files up to 4.3GB (assuming that your operating system allows files of this size)!

If you took my advice to create this table in a separate database, you'll need a new **db.inc.php** file to enable this example to connect to the database:

```php
<?php
try
{
  $pdo = new PDO('mysql:host=localhost;dbname=filestore',
      'filestoreuser', 'mypassword');
  $pdo->setAttribute(PDO::ATTR_ERRMODE, PDO::ERRMODE_EXCEPTION);
  $pdo->exec('SET NAMES "utf8"');
}
catch (PDOException $e)
{
  $error = 'Unable to connect to the database server.';
  include 'error.html.php';
  exit();
}
```

Storing Files

With the database ready and waiting, the next step is to create a PHP controller script and template that lets users upload files and store them in the database. You can hold off copying the code in the next two sections; I'll present the completed code at the end of the chapter. Here's the code for the form—there should be no surprises here:

```html
<form action="" method="post" enctype="multipart/form-data">
  <div>
    <label for="upload">Upload File:
    <input type="file" id="upload" name="upload"></label>
  </div>
  <div>
    <label for="desc">File Description:
    <input type="text" id="desc" name="desc"
        maxlength="255"></label>
  </div>
  <div>
    <input type="hidden" name="action" value="upload">
```

```
      <input type="submit" value="Upload">
   </div>
</form>
```

As you'll know from your reading in this chapter, this form will create a temporary file on the server and store the name of that file in $_FILES['upload']['tmp_name']. It also creates $_FILES['upload']['name'] (the original name of the file), $_FILES['upload']['size'] (the file size measured in bytes), and finally, $_FILES['upload']['type'] (the MIME type of the file).

Inserting the file into the database is a relatively straightforward process: read the data from the temporary file into a PHP variable, then use that variable in a standard MySQL INSERT query. Again, we make use of is_uploaded_file to make sure the filename we use does, in fact, correspond to an uploaded file before we start any of this. Here's the code:

chapter12/filestore/index.php (excerpt)

```php
<?php
include_once $_SERVER['DOCUMENT_ROOT'] .
    '/includes/magicquotes.inc.php';

if (isset($_POST['action']) and $_POST['action'] == 'upload')
{
  // Bail out if the file isn't really an upload
  if (!is_uploaded_file($_FILES['upload']['tmp_name']))
  {
    $error = 'There was no file uploaded!';
    include $_SERVER['DOCUMENT_ROOT'] . '/includes/error.html.php';
    exit();
  }
  $uploadfile = $_FILES['upload']['tmp_name'];
  $uploadname = $_FILES['upload']['name'];
  $uploadtype = $_FILES['upload']['type'];
  $uploaddesc = $_POST['desc'];
  $uploaddata = file_get_contents($uploadfile);

  include 'db.inc.php';

  try
  {
    $sql = 'INSERT INTO filestore SET
```

```
        filename = :filename,
        mimetype = :mimetype,
        description = :description,
        filedata = :filedata';
    $s = $pdo->prepare($sql);
    $s->bindValue(':filename', $uploadname);
    $s->bindValue(':mimetype', $uploadtype);
    $s->bindValue(':description', $uploaddesc);
    $s->bindValue(':filedata', $uploaddata);
    $s->execute();
  }
  catch (PDOException $e)
  {
    $error = 'Database error storing file!';
    include $_SERVER['DOCUMENT_ROOT'] . '/includes/error.html.php';
    exit();
  }

  header('Location: .');
  exit();
}
```

Viewing Stored Files

Armed with the code that accepts file uploads and stores them in a database, you're halfway home. But you still need to be able to pull that data out of the database to use it. For our purposes, this will mean sending the file to a requesting browser.

Once again, this turns out to be a relatively straightforward process. We simply retrieve the data for the requested file from the database and send it to the web browser. The only tricky part is to send the browser information *about* the file:

the file size   so that the browser can display accurate download-progress information to the user

the file type   so that the browser knows what to do with the data it receives; that is, display it as a web page, text file, or image, or offer to save the file

the filename   without specifying this, the browser will assume all files downloaded from our script have the same filename as our controller script

All this information is sent to the browser using **HTTP headers**, which is information that precedes the transmission of the file data itself. As we've already seen, sending HTTP headers via PHP is quite easy using the `header` function, but as headers must be sent before plain content, any calls to this function must come before anything is output by your script.

The file size is specified with a `Content-length` header:

chapter12/filestore/index.php *(excerpt)*

```
header('Content-length: ' . strlen($filedata));
```

`strlen` is a built–in PHP function that returns the length of the given string. Since binary data is just a string of bytes as far as PHP is concerned, you can use this function to count the length (in bytes) of the file data.

The file type is specified with a `Content-type` header:

chapter12/filestore/index.php *(excerpt)*

```
header("Content-type: $mimetype");
```

Finally, the filename is specified with a `Content-disposition` header:

```
header("Content-disposition: inline; filename=$filename");
```

You could use the following code to fetch a file with a given ID from the database, and send it to the browser:

```
include 'db.inc.php';

try
{
  $sql = 'SELECT filename, mimetype, filedata
      FROM filestore
      WHERE id = :id';
  $s = $pdo->prepare($sql);
  $s->bindValue(':id', $_GET['id']);
  $s->execute();
}
catch (PDOException $e)
```

```php
{
  $error = 'Database error fetching requested file.';
  include $_SERVER['DOCUMENT_ROOT'] . '/includes/error.html.php';
  exit();
}

$file = $s->fetch();
if (!$file)
{
  $error = 'File with specified ID not found in the database!';
  include $_SERVER['DOCUMENT_ROOT'] . '/includes/error.html.php';
  exit();
}

$filename = $file['filename'];
$mimetype = $file['mimetype'];
$filedata = $file['filedata'];

header('Content-length: ' . strlen($filedata));
header("Content-type: $mimetype");
header("Content-disposition: inline; filename=$filename");

echo $filedata;
exit();
```

One final trick we can add to this code is to allow a file to be downloaded, instead of viewed, if the user so desires. Web standards suggest that the way to do this is to send a Content-disposition of attachment instead of inline. Here's the modified code. It checks if $_GET['action'] equals 'download', which would indicate that this special file type should be sent:

```php
include 'db.inc.php';

try
{
  $sql = 'SELECT filename, mimetype, filedata
      FROM filestore
      WHERE id = :id';
  $s = $pdo->prepare($sql);
  $s->bindValue(':id', $_GET['id']);
  $s->execute();
}
catch (PDOException $e)
```

```php
{
  $error = 'Database error fetching requested file.';
  include $_SERVER['DOCUMENT_ROOT'] . '/includes/error.html.php';
  exit();
}

$file = $s->fetch();
if (!$file)
{
  $error = 'File with specified ID not found in the database!';
  include $_SERVER['DOCUMENT_ROOT'] . '/includes/error.html.php';
  exit();
}

$filename = $file['filename'];
$mimetype = $file['mimetype'];
$filedata = $file['filedata'];
$disposition = 'inline';

if ($_GET['action'] == 'download')
{
  $disposition = 'attachment';
}

header('Content-length: ' . strlen($filedata));
header("Content-type: $mimetype");
header("Content-disposition: $disposition; filename=$filename");

echo $filedata;
exit();
```

Unfortunately, many older browsers generally ignore the Content-disposition header, deciding what to do with a file based on the Content-type header instead—especially when it comes after the Content-disposition header.

To achieve the desired download behavior in as many browsers as possible, make sure the Content-type header comes before the Content-disposition header. Then replace the file's actual MIME type with a generic Content-type of application/octet-stream (which is required to force a download in older browsers):

```php
include 'db.inc.php';

try
{
  $sql = 'SELECT filename, mimetype, filedata
      FROM filestore
      WHERE id = :id';
  $s = $pdo->prepare($sql);
  $s->bindValue(':id', $_GET['id']);
  $s->execute();
}
catch (PDOException $e)
{
  $error = 'Database error fetching requested file.';
  include $_SERVER['DOCUMENT_ROOT'] . '/includes/error.html.php';
  exit();
}

$file = $s->fetch();
if (!$file)
{
  $error = 'File with specified ID not found in the database!';
  include $_SERVER['DOCUMENT_ROOT'] . '/includes/error.html.php';
  exit();
}

$filename = $file['filename'];
$mimetype = $file['mimetype'];
$filedata = $file['filedata'];
$disposition = 'inline';

if ($_GET['action'] == 'download')
{
  $mimetype = 'application/octet-stream';
  $disposition = 'attachment';
}

// Content-type must come before Content-disposition
header('Content-length: ' . strlen($filedata));
header("Content-type: $mimetype");
header("Content-disposition: $disposition; filename=$filename");
```

```
echo $filedata;
exit();
```

Putting It All Together

You'll find the complete file store example following. It combines all the elements given previously with some simple code that will list the files in the database, and allow them to be viewed, downloaded, or deleted. As always, this code is available in the code archive.

First, the controller script:

chapter12/filestore/index.php

```php
<?php
include_once $_SERVER['DOCUMENT_ROOT'] .
    '/includes/magicquotes.inc.php';

if (isset($_POST['action']) and $_POST['action'] == 'upload')
{
  // Bail out if the file isn't really an upload
  if (!is_uploaded_file($_FILES['upload']['tmp_name']))
  {
    $error = 'There was no file uploaded!';
    include $_SERVER['DOCUMENT_ROOT'] . '/includes/error.html.php';
    exit();
  }
  $uploadfile = $_FILES['upload']['tmp_name'];
  $uploadname = $_FILES['upload']['name'];
  $uploadtype = $_FILES['upload']['type'];
  $uploaddesc = $_POST['desc'];
  $uploaddata = file_get_contents($uploadfile);

  include 'db.inc.php';

  try
  {
    $sql = 'INSERT INTO filestore SET
        filename = :filename,
        mimetype = :mimetype,
        description = :description,
        filedata = :filedata';
```

```php
    $s = $pdo->prepare($sql);
    $s->bindValue(':filename', $uploadname);
    $s->bindValue(':mimetype', $uploadtype);
    $s->bindValue(':description', $uploaddesc);
    $s->bindValue(':filedata', $uploaddata);
    $s->execute();
  }
  catch (PDOException $e)
  {
    $error = 'Database error storing file!';
    include $_SERVER['DOCUMENT_ROOT'] . '/includes/error.html.php';
    exit();
  }

  header('Location: .');
  exit();
}

if (isset($_GET['action']) and
    ($_GET['action'] == 'view' or $_GET['action'] == 'download') and
    isset($_GET['id']))
{
  include 'db.inc.php';

  try
  {
    $sql = 'SELECT filename, mimetype, filedata
        FROM filestore
        WHERE id = :id';
    $s = $pdo->prepare($sql);
    $s->bindValue(':id', $_GET['id']);
    $s->execute();
  }
  catch (PDOException $e)
  {
    $error = 'Database error fetching requested file.';
    include $_SERVER['DOCUMENT_ROOT'] . '/includes/error.html.php';
    exit();
  }

  $file = $s->fetch();
  if (!$file)
  {
    $error = 'File with specified ID not found in the database!';
    include $_SERVER['DOCUMENT_ROOT'] . '/includes/error.html.php';
```

```
    exit();
  }

  $filename = $file['filename'];
  $mimetype = $file['mimetype'];
  $filedata = $file['filedata'];
  $disposition = 'inline';

  if ($_GET['action'] == 'download')
  {
    $mimetype = 'application/octet-stream';
    $disposition = 'attachment';
  }

  // Content-type must come before Content-disposition
  header('Content-length: ' . strlen($filedata));
  header("Content-type: $mimetype");
  header("Content-disposition: $disposition; filename=$filename");

  echo $filedata;
  exit();
}

if (isset($_POST['action']) and $_POST['action'] == 'delete' and
    isset($_POST['id']))
{
  include 'db.inc.php';

  try
  {
    $sql = 'DELETE FROM filestore
        WHERE id = :id';
    $s = $pdo->prepare($sql);
    $s->bindValue(':id', $_POST['id']);
    $s->execute();
  }
  catch (PDOException $e)
  {
    $error = 'Database error deleting requested file.';
    include $_SERVER['DOCUMENT_ROOT'] . '/includes/error.html.php';
    exit();
  }

  header('Location: .');
  exit();
```

```php
}

include 'db.inc.php';

try
{
  $result = $pdo->query(
      'SELECT id, filename, mimetype, description
      FROM filestore');
}
catch (PDOException $e)
{
  $error = 'Database error fetching stored files.';
  include $_SERVER['DOCUMENT_ROOT'] . '/includes/error.html.php';
  exit();
}

$files = array();
foreach ($result as $row)
{
  $files[] = array(
      'id' => $row['id'],
      'filename' => $row['filename'],
      'mimetype' => $row['mimetype'],
      'description' => $row['description']);
}

include 'files.html.php';
```

Next, the PHP template that includes the upload form and list of files:

chapter12/filestore/files.html.php

```php
<?php include_once $_SERVER['DOCUMENT_ROOT'] .
    '/includes/helpers.inc.php'; ?>
<!DOCTYPE html>
<html lang="en">
  <head>
    <meta charset="utf-8">
    <title>PHP/MySQL File Repository</title>
  </head>
  <body>
    <h1>PHP/MySQL File Repository</h1>

    <form action="" method="post" enctype="multipart/form-data">
```

```
   <div>
     <label for="upload">Upload File:
     <input type="file" id="upload" name="upload"></label>
   </div>
   <div>
     <label for="desc">File Description:
     <input type="text" id="desc" name="desc"
        maxlength="255"></label>
   </div>
   <div>
     <input type="hidden" name="action" value="upload">
     <input type="submit" value="Upload">
   </div>
</form>

<?php if (count($files) > 0): ?>

<p>The following files are stored in the database:</p>

<table>
  <thead>
    <tr>
      <th>Filename</th>
      <th>Type</th>
      <th>Description</th>
    </tr>
  </thead>
  <tbody>
    <?php foreach($files as $f): ?>
    <tr>
      <td>
        <a href="?action=view&amp;id=<?php htmlout($f['id']); ?>
          "><?php htmlout($f['filename']); ?></a>
      </td>
      <td><?php htmlout($f['mimetype']); ?></td>
      <td><?php htmlout($f['description']); ?></td>
      <td>
        <form action="" method="get">
          <div>
            <input type="hidden" name="action"
              value="download"/>
            <input type="hidden" name="id"
              value="<?php htmlout($f['id']); ?>"/>
            <input type="submit" value="Download"/>
          </div>
```

```
          </form>
        </td>
        <td>
          <form action="" method="post">
            <div>
              <input type="hidden" name="action" value="delete"/>
              <input type="hidden" name="id"
                value="<?php htmlout($f['id']); ?>"/>
              <input type="submit" value="Delete"/>
            </div>
          </form>
        </td>
      </tr>
      <?php endforeach; ?>
    </tbody>
  </table>

  <?php endif; ?>
  </body>
</html>
```

And just to be thorough, the database connection include file:

```
                                          chapter12/filestore/db.inc.php
<?php
try
{
  $pdo = new PDO('mysql:host=localhost;dbname=filestore',
      'filestoreuser', 'mypassword');
  $pdo->setAttribute(PDO::ATTR_ERRMODE, PDO::ERRMODE_EXCEPTION);
  $pdo->exec('SET NAMES "utf8"');
}
catch (PDOException $e)
{
  $error = 'Unable to connect to the database server.';
  include 'error.html.php';
  exit();
}
```

Note that this uses a different database (filestore) than the Internet Joke Database site and user (filestoreuser). If you prefer to put the filestore table in the ijdb database along with everything else that's in there, you can just use the shared **db.inc.php** include file instead.

With all these files in place and the database set up, fire up your browser and take a look. The empty repository should produce a page like the one in Figure 12.1.

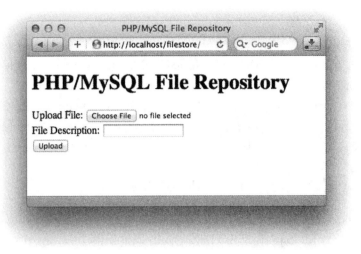

Figure 12.1. The Empty Repository

Upload a few files and you should see them listed in a table, as shown in Figure 12.2.

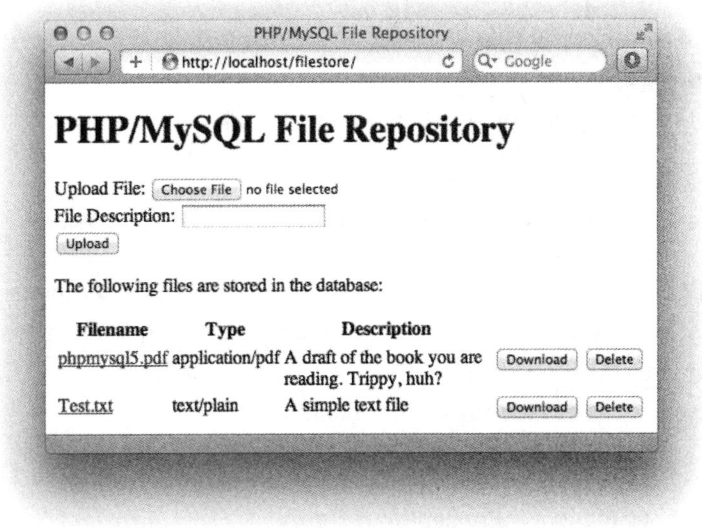

Figure 12.2. A couple of files on board

Click on a filename and the file should be displayed in the browser (assuming the file is of a type that your browser supports). In addition, try out the **Download** and **Delete** buttons provided for each file. They should work as you would expect.

This example demonstrates all the techniques you need in order to juggle binary files with PHP and MySQL, and I invite you to think of some creative uses of this code. Consider, for example, a file archive to which users must provide a username and password before they're allowed to view or download the files. If a user enters an incorrect username/password combination, your script can display an error page instead of sending the file data. Another possibility would be a script that sends different files depending on the details submitted by the form.

Large File Considerations

In systems like those we've just developed, large files present some unique challenges to the developer. I'll explain these here briefly, but fully developed solutions to these problems are beyond the scope of this book.

MySQL Packet Size

By default, MySQL rejects commands (packets) that are longer than 1MB. This default puts a reasonably severe limit on the maximum file size you can store, unless you're prepared to write your file data in 1MB chunks using an INSERT followed by several UPDATEs. Increase the maximum packet size by setting the max_allowed_packet option in your **my.cnf** or **my.ini** file. Refer to the MySQL manual[5] for more information on this issue.

PHP Memory Limit

PHP is configured by default to consume no more than 8MB of memory for the processing of any particular request. If your script needs to read a file whose size is close to or even larger than that limit, your browser will likely display an ugly error message about PHP having been unable to allocate memory.

To fix this issue, edit your server's **php.ini** file and change the value of the memory_limit setting to a more generous figure.

---

[5] http://dev.mysql.com/doc/refman/5.1/en/packet-too-large.html

PHP Script Timeout

PHP is configured by default to kill PHP scripts that run for more than 30 seconds. Needless to say, for large downloads over slow connections, this limit will be reached fairly quickly. Use PHP's `set_time_limit` function to set an appropriate time limit for the download, or simply set the time limit to zero, which allows the script to run to completion, however long it takes. But only do this if you're positive your script will always terminate, and not run forever!

The End

In this chapter, we completed our exploration of PHP and MySQL with a practical look at handling file uploads and storing binary data in MySQL databases. Admittedly, this is a rather arbitrary place to end this book; there are plenty of other aspects of PHP and MySQL that you could explore, some of which could be called no less basic or essential than binary data.

PHP in particular—with its "batteries included" philosophy of packing as much functionality as possible directly into the language in the form of built-in functions—could fill *ten* books this size. Exactly which aspects you'll need to learn before tackling any particular project will vary wildly. Having worked as a professional PHP developer for many years now, I have to admit that I remain unfamiliar with *most* of the functionality that PHP has to offer. There's just so much available to explore. That's why very few people bother to print out the PHP Manual[6] in its entirety.

By far the best way to cement your newfound knowledge of PHP and MySQL is to put it to work: build your own database driven website from scratch using the techniques covered in this book. Publish it on the Web, and ask for feedback from real, live users. Chances are they'll push you to make improvements to the site that you might lack the knowhow to implement right away. These real-world requirements should direct your further exploration of PHP and MySQL—and there's plenty more to be learned!

A great resource on your adventures would be a copy of SitePoint's *PHP Master: Write Cutting-edge Code.*[7] Beginning with an exploration of PHP's object oriented

---

[6] http://php.net/docs.php
[7] http://www.sitepoint.com/books/phppro1/

programming features, it builds on that foundation to demonstrate efficient ways of tackling some of the problems we looked at in this book, and many more that we didn't.

If you end up tackling more than one project, you may find yourself writing the same pieces of code over and over again. Rather than spending time perfecting your own collection of shared include files, you might like to spend some time learning a PHP framework such as Zend Framework,[8] CakePHP,[9] or Symfony.[10]

Each of these frameworks represent many thousands of hours' work by PHP experts who've developed ready-made solutions for the most common problems tackled by PHP developers. By using these solutions in your own projects, you can focus on writing the code to solve the problems that are unique to your project and waste less time reinventing the wheel. Each framework has its own philosophy, strengths, and weaknesses, and finding the right one for you will take some work. If you plan on becoming a professional PHP developer, however, you'll find it time well spent.

However you proceed from this point, rest assured you're starting out with a solid grounding in the essentials. That's more than can be said for many developers working today. Take that advantage and use it.

Most importantly, go out there and write some code!

---

[8] http://framework.zend.com/
[9] http://cakephp.org/
[10] http://www.symfony-project.org/

Appendix A: Manual Installation Instructions

In Chapter 1, I recommended using a packaged solution like XAMPP or MAMP to set up a PHP-capable web server and MySQL database server on your computer. Especially when you're just starting out, it's useful to have your development web server bundled together so that you can switch it on and off—even throw it away and start from scratch all at once, whenever you need to.

That said, the time may come when you want to do it all yourself, if only to understand how all the parts fit together. In this appendix, I'll walk you through a manual installation process on each of the three major platforms that PHP and MySQL support: Windows, OS X, and Linux.

Windows

Installing MySQL

You can download MySQL free of charge. Simply proceed to the MySQL Downloads page[1] and click the **Download** link for the free MySQL Community Server. This will take you to a page with a list of download links for the current recommended version of MySQL (as of this writing, it's MySQL 5.5.22).

At the top of the list you'll see links for Windows 64-bit and Windows 32-bit. If you're positive you're running a 64-bit version of Windows, go ahead and click the **Download** button next to **Windows (x86, 64-bit), MSI Installer** to download the package (about 33MB in size). If you know you're running a 32-bit version of Windows, or if you're at all unsure, click the **Download** button next to **Windows (x86, 32-bit), MSI Installer** to download that package (about 31MB); it will work even if it turns out you're running a 64-bit version of Windows.

Once you've downloaded the file, double-click it and go through the installation as you would for any other program. Choose the **Typical** option when prompted for the setup type, unless you have a particular preference for the directory in which MySQL

---

[1] http://dev.mysql.com/downloads/

is installed. When you reach the end, you'll be prompted to choose whether you want to **Launch the MySQL Instance Configuration Wizard**. Go ahead and launch it, and choose **Detailed Configuration**, which we'll use to specify a number of options that are vital to ensuring compatibility with PHP. For each step in the wizard, select the options indicated here:

1. **Server Type**

    Assuming you're setting up MySQL for development purposes on your desktop computer, choose **Developer Machine**.

2. **Database Usage**

    Although any of these options will work fine with the examples in this book, go with the default **Multifunctional Database** option.

3. **InnoDB Tablespace Settings**

    This lets you control where your database files are stored. The default option of storing them in your MySQL **Installation Path** is perfect for a development server. No need to touch anything here.

4. **Connection Limit**

    Select **Decision Support (DSS)/OLAP** to optimize MySQL for a relatively modest number of connections.

5. **Networking Options**

    Uncheck the **Enable Strict Mode** option to ensure MySQL's compatibility with older PHP code that you might need to use in your own work.

6. **Default Character Set**

    Select **Best Support For Multilingualism** to tell MySQL to assume you want to use UTF-8 encoded text, which supports the full range of characters in use on the Web today.

7. **Windows Options**

Allow MySQL to be installed as a Windows Service that's launched automatic-ally. Select **Include Bin Directory in Windows PATH** to make it easier to run MySQL's administration tools from the command prompt.

8. **Security Options**

Go ahead and set a password for the MySQL `root` user account, which grants full access to all databases stored in your MySQL server. Leave the other options alone.

Once the wizard has completed, your system should now be fully equipped with a running MySQL server!

To verify that the MySQL server is running properly, type **Ctrl+Alt+Del** and choose the option to open the Task Manager. On the **Processes** tab, click the **Show processes from all users** button unless it's already selected. If all is well, the server program (**mysqld.exe**) should be listed. It will also start up automatically whenever you restart your system.

Installing PHP

The next step is to install PHP, so head over to the PHP Downloads page.[2] There are two versions of PHP 5.4.x for Windows: VC9 Non Thread Safe and VC9 Thread Safe. Talk about confusing! You definitely want a Thread Safe version of PHP. The Non Thread Safe versions are unsuitable for use as a plugin for Apache.

Download the **Zip** package of the VC9 Thread Safe release of PHP.

PHP was designed to run as a plugin for existing web server software such as Apache or Internet Information Services, so before you can install PHP, you must first set up a web server.

Many versions of Windows come with Microsoft's powerful Internet Information Services (IIS) web server, but not all do. Windows XP Home, Windows Vista Home, and Windows 7 Home Basic (among others) are without IIS, so you need to install your own web server on these versions of Windows if you want to develop database

---

[2] http://windows.php.net/download/

driven websites. On top of that, assorted versions of Windows come with different versions of IIS, some of which vary dramatically in how you configure them to work with PHP.

With that in mind, if you're still considering IIS, you should know it's relatively uncommon to host websites built using PHP with IIS in the real world. It's generally less expensive and more reliable to host PHP-powered sites on servers running some flavor of the Linux operating system, with the free Apache web server installed. About the only reason for hosting a PHP site on IIS is if your company has already invested in Windows servers to run applications built using ASP.NET (a Microsoft technology built into IIS), and you want to reuse that existing infrastructure to host a PHP application as well.

Although it's by no means a requirement, it's generally easiest to set up your development server to match the environment your website will be deployed in publicly as closely as possible. For this reason, I recommend using the Apache web server —even for development on a Windows computer. If you insist (or your boss insists) on hosting your PHP-based site using IIS, you'll find the necessary installation instructions in the **install.txt** file contained in the PHP zip package you downloaded from the PHP website.

If you need to install Apache on your computer, surf on over to the Apache Lounge[3] website and download the latest version of Apache (as of writing it's version 2.4.1).

Once the ZIP file has downloaded, right-click it and choose **Extract All...** to extract the file's contents into a folder. Inside, you'll find a couple of text files containing installation instructions. The first is a reminder to download and install the latest Microsoft Visual C++ Redistributable Package. Go ahead and do that now. When you're done, drag the **.exe** file you downloaded to the **Recycle Bin**.

Next, the installation instructions will tell you to drag the **Apache24** folder that you extracted from the ZIP file to the root of your **C:** drive, so that Apache will be installed in **C:\Apache24**. (It's possible to change this path if you really want to, but it's a bit of a pain to edit the relevant configuration files so I recommend just going with it.)

---

[3] http://www.apachelounge.com/

Now Apache is installed, but to launch it for the first time (and configure it to run automatically at system startup), you'll need to open a Command Prompt. On your Start Menu, find **All Programs** > **Accessories** > **Command Prompt**, then right-click on **Command Prompt** and choose **Run as administrator**. This will drop you in a window showing the current directory (**C:\Windows\system32** on my system):

```
C:\Windows\system32>
```

At the end of this prompt, you'll see a cursor blinking away. Type C: and hit **Enter** to make sure you're working on **C:** drive, then type cd \Apache24\bin and hit **Enter** to switch to the **C:\Apache24\bin** folder:

```
C:\Windows\system32>C:

C:\Windows\system32>cd \Apache24\bin

C:\Apache24\bin>
```

Now, to launch Apache for the first time, type httpd.exe and hit **Enter**:

```
C:\Apache24\bin>httpd.exe
```

If all goes well, it should look like nothing is happening. There won't be another prompt; your command will just sit there running.

On the other hand, you might receive an error message like this:

```
C:\Apache24\bin>httpd.exe
(OS 10013)An attempt was made to access a socket in a way forbidden
by its access permissions.  : AH00072: make_sock: could not bind to
address [::]:80(OS 10013)An attempt was made to access a socket in a
way forbidden by its access permissions.  : AH00072: make_sock:
could not bind to address 0.0.0.0:80AH00451: no listening sockets
available, shutting downAH00015: Unable to open logs

C:\Apache24\bin>
```

This overwhelming error is Apache's way of telling you that you already have a web server running on your computer, listening for web browsers to connect on port 80 (the standard port for web servers). Check if you have IIS running, or another copy of Apache (perhaps bundled in a package like XAMPP?). Shut it down, then try launching Apache from the Command Prompt again.

With Apache up and running, open your web browser of choice and type http://localhost into the location bar. Hit **Enter**, and you should see a page like that shown in Figure A.1, confirming Apache is working correctly.

Figure A.1. You can take my word for it!

Close your browser and return to the Command Prompt. Shut down Apache by hitting **Ctrl+C**. After a moment, there'll be another prompt:

```
C:\Apache24\bin>httpd.exe

C:\Apache24\bin>
```

You probably don't want to have to open a Command Prompt every time you need to run Apache. Instead, type `httpd.exe -k install` to install Apache as a system service. Here's what you should see:

```
C:\Apache24\bin>httpd.exe -k install
Installing the Apache2.4 service
The Apache2.4 service is successfully installed.
Testing httpd.conf....
Errors reported here must be corrected before the service can be
➥started.
```

But you might see this instead:

```
C:\Apache24\bin>httpd.exe -k install
Installing the Apache2.4 service
(OS 5)Access is denied.  : AH00369: Failed to open the WinNT service
➥ manager, perhaps you forgot to log in as Adminstrator?yoss
```

If that's the case, it means you neglected to right-click and choose **Run as administrator** when launching Command Prompt above. Try again with a Command Prompt window running as administrator.

With Apache set up as a system service, close the Command Prompt and navigate to **C:\Apache24\bin** in Windows Explorer. In that folder, you'll find a file named **ApacheMonitor.exe**. This is a program that will help you monitor and control your Apache server now that it's set up as a service. Pin it to your Start Menu (or, if you prefer, create a shortcut to it and put that wherever you like in your **All Programs** menu), then launch it. A new Apache Monitor icon will appear in your system tray (you may need to customize your system tray to keep it visible).

Click the icon, and you'll see the **Apache2.4** system service listed. Hover over that service and a fly-out menu will appear with options to **Start**, **Stop**, and **Restart** the server. Choose **Start** to fire up Apache. The icon will change to show a tiny green arrow that indicates Apache is running.

Figure A.2. The green light means Apache is up and running

You can also use the Apache Monitor icon to stop Apache running, once you've finished your web development work for the day.

With Apache standing on its own two feet, you can now install PHP. Follow these steps:

1. Unzip the file you downloaded from the PHP website into a directory of your choice. I recommend **C:\php** and will refer to this directory from this point forward, but feel free to choose another directory if you like.

2. Find the file called **php.ini-development** in the PHP folder and make a duplicate copy of it. The easiest way to do it is to right-click and drag the file's icon, drop it in the same Explorer window, and choose **Copy Here** from the pop-up menu. You'll be left with a new file named along the lines of **php - Copy.ini-development** (depending on the version of Windows you're using). Find this new file and

rename it to **php.ini**. Windows will ask if you're sure about changing the filename extension (from *.ini-dist* to *.ini*); click **Yes**.

Windows Hides Known Filename Extensions by Default

When you rename the file to **php.ini**, you might notice that the new filename appearing next to the icon is actually just **php**. If this happens, it's because your copy of Windows is set up to hide the filename extension if it recognizes it. Since Windows knows that **.ini** files are Configuration Settings files, it hides this filename extension.

As you can imagine, this feature can cause a certain amount of confusion. When you return to edit the **php.ini** file in the future, it would help to be able to see its full filename so that you could tell it apart from the **php.gif** and **php.exe** files in the same folder.

To switch off filename extension hiding, open the Windows Control Panel and search for Folder Options. Open the Folder Options window and switch to the **View** tab. Under **Files and Folders**, uncheck the **Hide extensions for known file types** checkbox, as shown in Figure A.3.

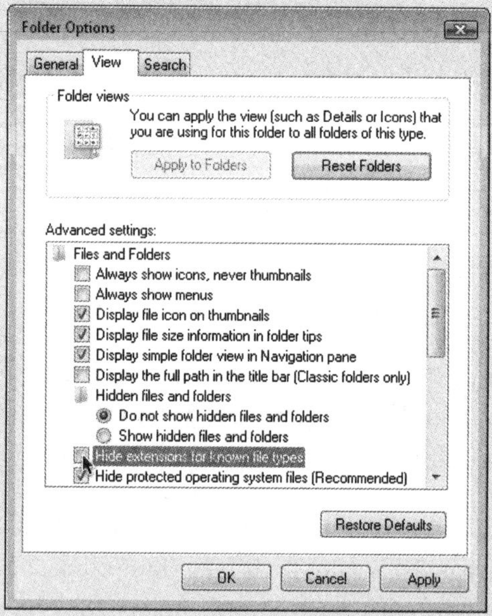

Figure A.3. Make filename extensions visible for all files

3. Open the **php.ini** file in your favorite text editor. If you have no particular preference, just double-click the file to open it in Notepad. It's a large file with a lot of confusing options, but look for the line that begins with doc_root (Notepad's **Edit > Find...** feature will help). Out of the box, the line looks like this:

```
doc_root =
```

To the end of this line, add the path to your web server's document root directory. For the Apache server, this is the **htdocs** folder in the main Apache web server directory. If you installed Apache in the default location, the path should be "**C:\Apache24\htdocs**". If you installed it elsewhere, find the **htdocs** folder and type its path:

```
doc_root = "C:\Apache24\htdocs"
```

Just a little further down in the file, look for the line that begins with ; extension_dir, remove the semicolon from the start of the line, and set it so that it points to the **ext** subfolder of your PHP folder:

```
extension_dir = "C:\php\ext"
```

Scroll further down in the file and you'll see a bunch of lines beginning with ;extension=. These are optional extensions to PHP, disabled by default. We want to enable the MySQL extension so that PHP can communicate with MySQL. To do this, remove the semicolon from the start of the **php_mysqli.dll** line:

```
extension=php_mysqli.dll
```

php_mysqli, not php_mysql

Just above the line for php_mysqli.dll there is a line for php_mysql.dll. The *i* in php_mysqli stands for *improved*. You want to enable the new improved MySQL extension. The one without the *i* is obsolete, and some of its features are incompatible with current versions of MySQL.

Keep scrolling even further down in the file, and look for a line that starts with ;session.save_path. Once again, remove the semicolon to enable this line, and set it to your Windows **Temp** folder:

```
session.save_path = "C:\Windows\Temp"
```

Save the changes you made and close your text editor.

That takes care of setting up PHP. Now you can set up your Apache server to use it as a plugin:

1. Launch Notepad (or your text editor of choice) and choose **File** > **Open**.... Browse to the **conf** subfolder in your Apache installation folder (by default, **C:\Apache24\conf**), and select the **httpd.conf** file located there. In order to make this file visible for selection, you'll need to select **All Files (*.*)** from the file type drop-down menu at the bottom of the **Open** window.

2. Look for the existing line in this file that begins with `DirectoryIndex`, shown here:

```
<IfModule dir_module>
    DirectoryIndex index.html
</IfModule>
```

This line tells Apache which filenames to use when it looks for the default page for a given directory. Add **index.php** to the end of this line:

```
<IfModule dir_module>
    DirectoryIndex index.html index.php
</IfModule>
```

3. The remaining options in this long and intimidating configuration file should be fine as is. All you need to do is add the following lines to the very end of the file:

```
LoadModule php5_module "C:/php/php5apache2_4.dll"
AddType application/x-httpd-php .php
PHPIniDir "C:/php"
```

Make sure the `LoadModule` and `PHPIniDir` lines point to your PHP installation directory, and note the use of forward slashes (/) instead of backslashes (\) in the paths.

PHP and Apache Versions

Historically, major new versions of the Apache server have required new versions of the .dll file you see referenced in the LoadModule line, and sometimes PHP lags behind new Apache releases. At the time of this writing, for example, the Windows PHP distribution doesn't actually *include* a **php5apache2_4.dll** file!

If you take another look in your PHP installation directory, you'll probably see there are files named **php5apache2_2.dll** and **php5apache2_3.dll** in there. These files were provided for use with Apache 2.2 and 2.3, respectively.

By the time you read this, it's possible that Apache has undergone another major release, which might need yet another new .dll file. For example, Apache 2.5 might require you to use a new file named **php5apache2_5.dll**.

If indeed there is no file to match the version of Apache you've installed, return to the Apache Lounge download page;[4] you should find it available for download there (for example, **php5apache2_4.dll-php-5.4-win32.zip**). Download the ZIP file, extract it, and drop the missing .dll file in your PHP installation folder. Apache will now be able to find it where your LoadModule command says it should be.

4. Save your changes and close Notepad.

5. Restart Apache using the Apache Monitor system tray icon. If all is well, Apache will start up again without complaint. If Apache fails to start, try launching it from the Command Prompt again (as previously); this will give you a more detailed error message. Chances are you made a small mistake when editing **httpd.conf.**

6. Double-click the Apache Monitor icon to open the Apache Service Monitor window. If PHP is installed correctly, the status bar of this window should indicate the version of PHP you've installed, as shown in Figure A.4.

7. Click **OK** to close the Apache Service Monitor window.

---

[4] http://www.apachelounge.com/download/

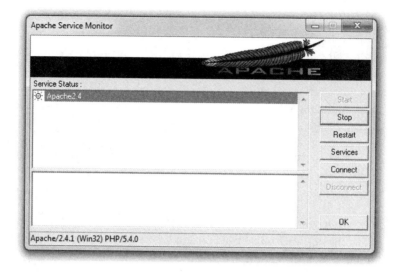

Figure A.4. The PHP version number indicates Apache is configured to support PHP

With MySQL, Apache, and PHP installed, you're ready to start working with your new web server!

OS X

The following instructions assume you're running Mac OS X 10.6 (Snow Leopard) or later. If you're running an earlier version of OS X, you should stick with the all-in-one option.

Installing MySQL

Start by visiting the The MySQL Downloads page.[5] Click the **Download** link for the free MySQL Community Server. This will take you to a page with a long list of download links for the current recommended version of MySQL (as of this writing, it's MySQL 5.5.22).

You'll be presented with the list of downloads shown in Figure A.5. Which one you need to choose depends on your operating system version and platform architecture. If you know your Mac has a 64-bit processor, you can safely pick the **Mac OS X ver. 10.6 (x86, 64-bit), DMG Archive** version. If you're at all unsure, your best bet is the **Mac OS X ver. 10.6 (x86, 32-bit), DMG Archive** version; all it requires is that you have

---

[5] http://dev.mysql.com/downloads/

an Intel-based Mac (to be sure, check the processor information in the **About This Mac** window, which you can access from the Apple menu). The 32-bit version is the safe bet, since it will run on 64-bit systems too.

Figure A.5. The 32-bit version of MySQL for Intel processors will work on most current Macs

Once you've downloaded the **mysql-*version*-osx*version*-*platform*.dmg** file, double-click it to mount the disk image. As shown in Figure A.6, it contains the installer in **.pkg** format, as well as a **MySQLStartupItem.pkg** file. Double-click the installer, which will guide you through the installation of MySQL.

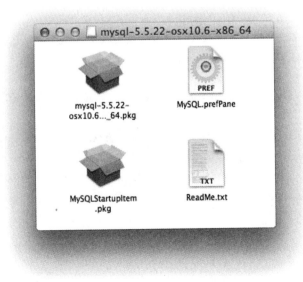

Figure A.6. The MySQL Mac OS X package contains lots of goodies

With MySQL is installed, you can launch the MySQL server. Open a Terminal window[6] and type this command:

```
Machine:~ user$ sudo /usr/local/mysql/bin/mysqld_safe
```

What to Type

The `Machine:~ user$` portion (where *Machine* is your computer's name) represents the prompt that's already displayed. You only need to type the command, which is shown in bold.

When you've typed the command, hit **Enter**.

This command runs the **mysqld_safe** script with administrator privileges, which will require you to input your password. A status message will confirm that MySQL is running.

Once MySQL is running, you can switch it to background execution by typing **Ctrl+Z** to stop the process, and then typing this command to let it continue running in the background:

```
Machine:~ user$ bg
```

You can then quit the Terminal application and MySQL will continue to run as a server on your system. When you want to shut down the MySQL server, open a new Terminal window and type this command:

```
Machine:~ user$ sudo /usr/local/mysql/bin/mysqladmin shutdown
```

Though you'll gain plenty of geek cred for memorizing these commands, there's a much less tedious way to control your MySQL server. Back in the installation disk image shown in Figure A.6, you'll notice a file named **MySQL.prefPane**. Double-click this to install a new pane in Mac OS X's System Preferences, and the window shown in Figure A.7 will open.

---

[6] To open a Terminal window, launch the **Terminal** application, which you can find in the **Utilities** folder in the **Applications** folder.

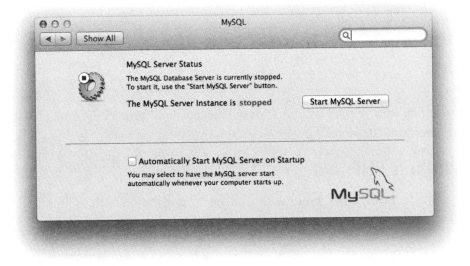

Figure A.7. The MySQL System Preferences pane

This window will tell you if your MySQL server is running or not, and lets you start it up and shut it down with the click of a button!

Presumably, you'll want your system to launch the MySQL server at startup automatically, so that you can avoid having to repeat the above process whenever you restart your system. The system preferences pane has a checkbox that does this, but for this checkbox to do anything you must first install the **MySQLStartupItem.pkg** from the installation disk image.

When you have everything set up the way you want it, you can safely drag the MySQL installation disk icon on your desktop to the trash, then delete the **.dmg** file you downloaded.

One last task you'll want to do is add the **/usr/local/mysql/bin** directory to your system path. Doing this enables you to run programs like **mysqladmin** and **mysql** in the Terminal without typing out their full paths. Pop open a new Terminal window and type these commands:

```
Machine:~ user$ sudo su
Password: (type your password)
sh-3.2# echo '/usr/local/mysql/bin' >> /etc/paths.d/mysql
sh-3.2# exit
```

Close the Terminal window and open a new one to allow this change to take effect. Then, with your MySQL server running, try running the **mysqladmin** program from your home directory:

```
Machine:~ user$ mysqladmin status
```

If everything worked the way it's supposed to, you should see a brief list of statistics about your MySQL server.

Installing PHP

Mac OS X 10.5 (Leopard) comes with Apache 2.2 and PHP 5 built right in! All you need to do is switch them on:

1. Open System Preferences (**System Preferences…** on the Apple menu).

2. In the main System Preferences menu, click **Sharing** under **Internet & Wireless**.

3. Make sure that **Web Sharing** is checked, as shown in Figure A.8.

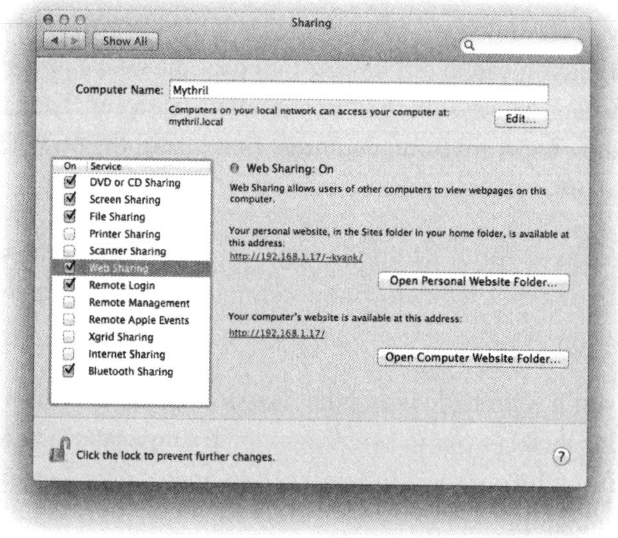

Figure A.8. Enable Web Sharing in Mac OS X

4. Quit System Preferences.

5. Open your browser, type http://localhost into the address bar, and hit **Enter**. Your browser should display the standard Apache welcome message shown in Figure A.9.

Figure A.9. The standard Apache welcome page

With this procedure complete, Apache will be run at startup automatically on your system. You're now ready to enhance this server by enabling PHP support:

1. In the Finder menu bar, choose **Go > Go to folder** (⇧+⌘+G), and type **/private/etc/apache2/** before clicking **Go**.

2. In the Finder window that opens, there should be a file named **httpd.conf**. This is the Apache configuration file. By default, it's read-only. Right-click the file and choose **Get Info** (⌘+I) to open the file's properties. Scroll down to the bottom of the **httpd.conf Info** window to find the **Sharing & Permissions** setting.

    By default, the settings in this section are disabled. Click the little lock icon shown in Figure A.10 to enable them. Enter your password when prompted.

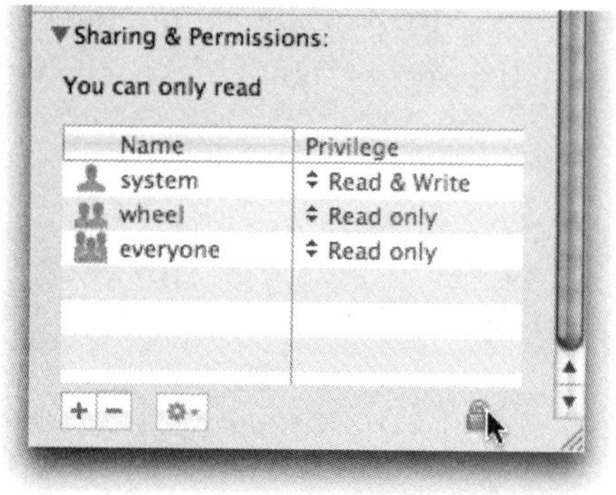

Figure A.10. Click the lock to make changes to these settings

To make this file editable, change the value in the **Privilege** column for **everyone** to **Read & Write**, as shown in Figure A.11.

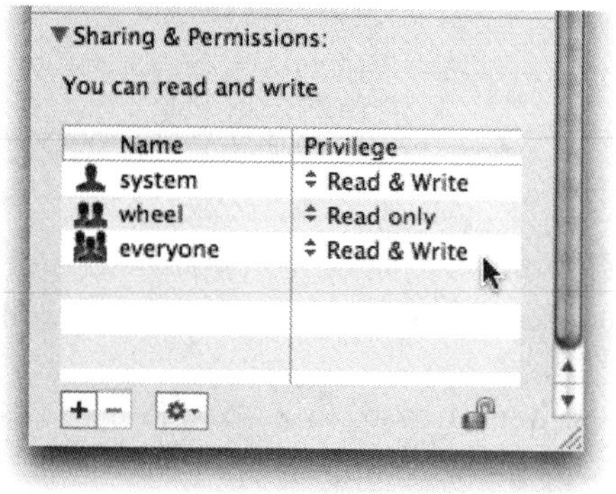

Figure A.11. Set the permissions for **everyone** to **Read & Write**

3. Back in the Finder window for the **apache2** folder, right-click in the background of the folder window and choose **Get Info** to open the folder's properties. As in the previous step, set the **Sharing & Permissions** settings from **everyone** to **Read & Write**.

4. Finally, double-click the `httpd.conf` file to open it in TextEdit.

5. In the **httpd.conf** file, search for this line:

```
#LoadModule php5_module        libexec/apache2/libphp5.so
```

Enable this command by deleting the hash (#) character at the start of the line.

6. Save your changes, and close the file.

7. If you like to tidy up after yourself, you can go back and reset the privileges on the **httpd.conf** file and the **apache2** folder. This will keep other users of your computer from making changes to the Apache configuration.

8. Open a Terminal window and type this command to restart Apache:

```
Machine:~ user$ sudo /usr/sbin/apachectl restart
```

Type your password when prompted.

9. Load http://localhost in your browser again to ensure that Apache is still running. Give it a minute if it's not available right away.

If it fails to come back up, open Console (in the **Utilities** subfolder of **Applications**). In the sidebar under **/var/log**, select **apache2** > **error_log** to view the Apache error log and look for clues as to what went wrong. If you're still stuck, you could head over to the SitePoint Forums for help.

Your computer is now equipped with an Apache web server with PHP support. If you need to make changes to Apache's configuration, you know how to edit its **httpd.conf** file using the instructions above. The PHP plugin, however, has its own configuration file, named **php.ini**. You need to edit that file to tell PHP how to connect to your MySQL server.

With the version of PHP built into Mac OS X, there is no **php.ini** file by default—PHP just runs with the default settings. In order to modify those settings, you'll need to open Terminal and copy the **/private/etc/php.ini.default** file to **/private/etc/php.ini**:

```
Machine:~ user$ cd /private/etc
Machine:etc user$ sudo cp php.ini.default php.ini
Password: (type your password)
```

To make this new **php.ini** file editable by users like yourself, use the same procedure described above for editing **httpd.conf**: in Finder use **Go** > **Go to folder** to open **/private/etc**, modify the permissions of both the **php.ini** file and the folder that contains it, then open the file with TextEdit.

Scroll down through the file or use **Edit** > **Find** > **Find...** (⌘+F) to locate the `mysql.default_socket` option. Edit this line of the **php.ini** file so that it looks like this:

```
mysql.default_socket = /tmp/mysql.sock
```

You should only have to add the portion in bold.

Scroll down further to locate the `mysqli.default_socket` option (`mysqli`, not `mysql`), and make the same change:

```
mysqli.default_socket = /tmp/mysql.sock
```

Save your changes, quit TextEdit, and restore the file and directory permissions if you want to. Finally, open a Terminal window and type this command to restart Apache once more:

```
Machine:~ user$ sudo /usr/sbin/apachectl restart
```

Type your password when prompted. Once Apache is up and running again, load http://localhost in your browser once more to make sure that all is well.

And we're done! With MySQL, Apache, and PHP installed, you're ready to get to work.

Linux

This section will show you the procedure for manually installing Apache, PHP, and MySQL under most current distributions of Linux. These instructions were tested under Ubuntu 10.04.4;[7] however, they should work on other distributions such as Fedora,[8] Debian,[9] openSUSE,[10] and Gentoo[11] without much trouble. The steps involved will be very similar, almost identical.

---

[7] http://www.ubuntu.com
[8] http://fedoraproject.org
[9] http://www.debian.org
[10] http://www.opensuse.org
[11] http://www.gentoo.org

Most Linux distributions come with a **package manager** of one kind or another. Ubuntu's Synaptic Package Manager[12] is a graphical front end to APT,[13] the Debian package manager. Other distributions use the older RPM package manager. Regardless of which distribution you use, prepackaged versions of Apache, PHP, and MySQL should be readily available. These prepackaged versions of software are really easy to install; unfortunately, they also limit the software configuration options available to you. For this reason—and because any attempt to document the procedures for installing the packaged versions across all popular Linux distributions would be doomed to failure—I will instead show you how to install them manually.

If you already have Apache, PHP, and MySQL installed in packaged form, feel free to use those versions. If you encounter any problems, you can always uninstall the packaged versions and return here to install them by by hand.

Installing MySQL

Start by downloading MySQL. Simply proceed to the MySQL Downloads page[14] and click the **Download** link for the free MySQL Community Server. This will take you to a page with a long list of download links for the current recommended version of MySQL (as of this writing, it's MySQL 5.5.22).

Make sure **Linux – Generic** is selected from the menu near the top of the list of files to download. Now you need to choose the package that corresponds to your system architecture. If you're positive you're running a 64-bit version of Linux, go ahead and download the **Linux – Generic 2.6 (x86, 64-bit), Compressed TAR Archive** package (about 177MB in size). If you're running a 32-bit version of Linux, download the **Linux – Generic 2.6 (x86, 32-bit), Compressed TAR Archive** package (about 171MB); this will still work even if it turns out you're running a 64-bit version of Linux. Click the **Download** button next to whichever version is right for you.

Once you've downloaded the file, open a Terminal and log in as the root user:

```
user@machine:~$ sudo su
```

You will, of course, be prompted for your password.

---

[12] https://help.ubuntu.com/community/SynapticHowto
[13] http://www.debian.org/doc/user-manuals#apt-howto
[14] http://dev.mysql.com/downloads/

Change directories to **/usr/local** and unpack the downloaded file:

```
root@machine:/home/user# cd /usr/local
root@machine:/usr/local# tar xfz ~user/Desktop/mysql-version-linux2.
➥6-platform.tar.gz
```

The second command assumes you left the downloaded file on your desktop, which is the **Desktop** directory in your home directory. You'll need to replace *user* with your username, *version* with the MySQL version you downloaded, and *platform* with the architecture and compiler version of the release you downloaded; this is so that the command matches the path and filename of the file you downloaded exactly. On my computer, for example, the exact command looks like this:

```
root@mythril:/usr/local# tar xfz ~kyank/Desktop/mysql-5.5.22-linux2.
➥6-x86_64.tar.gz
```

After a minute or two, you'll be returned to the command prompt. A quick ls will confirm that you now have a directory named **mysql-*version*-linux-*platform***. This is what it looks like on my computer:

```
root@mythril:/usr/local# ls
bin   games    lib   mysql-5.5.22-linux2.6-x86_64   share
etc   include  man   sbin                           src
```

Next, create a symbolic link to the new directory with the name **mysql** to make accessing the directory easier. Then enter the directory:

```
root@machine:/usr/local# ln -s mysql-version-linux-platform mysql
root@machine:/usr/local# cd mysql
```

While you can run the server as the root user, or even as yourself (for example, if you were to install the server in your home directory), you should normally set up a special user on the system whose sole purpose is to run the MySQL server. This will remove any possibility of an attacker using the MySQL server as a way to break into the rest of your system. To create a special MySQL user, type the following commands (still logged in as root):

```
root@machine:/usr/local/mysql# groupadd mysql
root@machine:/usr/local/mysql# useradd -g mysql mysql
```

Now give ownership of your MySQL directory to this new user:

```
root@machine:/usr/local/mysql# chown -R mysql .
root@machine:/usr/local/mysql# chgrp -R mysql .
```

MySQL is now installed, but before it can do anything useful, its database files need to be installed, too. Still in the new **mysql** directory, type the following command:

```
root@machine:/usr/local/mysql# scripts/mysql_install_db --user=mysql
```

If this command generates an error about **libaio.so**, you'll need to install that library before trying again. On Ubuntu Linux, you can do that with a simple apt-get:

```
root@machine:/usr/local/mysql# apt-get install libaio1
root@machine:/usr/local/mysql# scripts/mysql_install_db --user=mysql
```

Now everything's prepared for you to launch the MySQL server for the first time. From the same directory, type the following command:

```
root@machine:/usr/local/mysql# bin/mysqld_safe --user=mysql &
```

If you see the message mysql daemon ended, the MySQL server was prevented from starting. The error message should have been written to a file called *hostname*.err (where *hostname* is your machine's host name) in MySQL's **data** directory. You'll usually find that this happens because another MySQL server is already running on your computer.

If the MySQL server was launched without complaint, the server will run (just like your web or FTP server) until your computer is shut down. To test that the server is running properly, type the following command:

```
root@machine:/usr/local/mysql# bin/mysqladmin -u root status
```

A little blurb with some statistics about the MySQL server should be displayed. If you receive an error message, check the *hostname*.err file to see if the fault lies with the MySQL server upon starting up. If you retrace your steps to ensure you followed the process described above, and this fails to solve the problem, a post to the Site-Point Forums[15] will help you pin it down in little time.

If you want your MySQL server to run automatically whenever the system is running, you'll have to set it up to do so. In the **support-files** subdirectory of the **mysql** directory, there's a script called **mysql.server** that can be added to your system startup routines to do this. For most versions of Linux, you can do this by creating a link to the **mysql.server** script in the **/etc/init.d** directory, then create two links to that: **/etc/rc2.d/S99mysql** and **/etc/rc0.d/K01mysql**. Here are the commands to type:

```
root@machine:/usr/local/mysql# cd /etc
root@machine:/etc# ln -s /usr/local/mysql/support-files/mysql.server
➥ init.d/
root@machine:/etc# ln -s /etc/init.d/mysql.server rc2.d/S99mysql
root@machine:/etc# ln -s /etc/init.d/mysql.server rc0.d/K01mysql
```

That's it! To test that this works, reboot your system, and request the status of the server with `mysqladmin` as you did earlier.

You should now take a moment to set a `root` user password. Run the **bin/mysql_secure_installation** program to do this:

```
root@machine:/usr/local/mysql# ./bin/mysql_secure_installation
```

Having trouble removing test database?

If the **mysql_secure_installation** program appears to struggle dropping the `test` database, don't worry about it. This is a problem in the packaging of the MySQL database for Linux: the **data/test** folder (where the `test` database files are stored) contains a file named **.empty** that MySQL fails to recognize, and therefore will not delete.

If you delete this file yourself, MySQL will be able to drop the `test` database.

One final task you might like to do for the sake of convenience is to place the MySQL client programs—which you'll use to administer your MySQL server later on—in the system path. To this end, you can place symbolic links to **mysql**, **mysqladmin**, and **mysqldump** in your **/usr/local/bin** directory:

---

[15] http://www.sitepoint.com/forums/

```
root@machine:/etc# cd /usr/local/bin
root@machine:/usr/local/bin# ln -s /usr/local/mysql/bin/mysql .
root@machine:/usr/local/bin# ln -s /usr/local/mysql/bin/mysqladmin .
root@machine:/usr/local/bin# ln -s /usr/local/mysql/bin/mysqldump .
```

Once you've done this, you can log out of the root account. From this point on, you can administer MySQL from any directory on your system:

```
root@machine:/usr/local/bin# exit
user@machine:~$ mysqladmin -u root -p status
```

Installing PHP

As mentioned, PHP is more a web server plugin module than a program. There are actually three ways to install the PHP plugin for Apache:

- as a CGI program that Apache runs every time it needs to process a PHP-enhanced web page
- as an Apache module compiled right into the Apache program
- as an Apache module loaded by Apache each time it starts up

The first option is the easiest to install and set up, but it requires Apache to launch PHP as a program on your computer every time a PHP page is requested. This activity can really slow down the response time of your web server, especially if more than one request needs to be processed at a time.

The second and third options are almost identical in terms of performance, but the third option is the most flexible, since you can add and remove Apache modules without having to recompile it each time. For this reason, we'll use the third option.

Assuming you don't already have Apache running on your computer (and don't simply want to install it automatically with, say, sudo apt-get install apache2 on Ubuntu Linux), surf on over to the Apache HTTP Server Project[16] and look for the version of Apache described as "the best available version" (as of this writing it's version 2.4.1).

Once you get to the Download page, scroll down to find the links to the various versions available. The one you want is **Unix Source**, shown in Figure A.12. Both

---

[16] http://httpd.apache.org/

the .tar.gz or the .tar.bz2 are the same; just grab whichever archive format you're used to extracting.

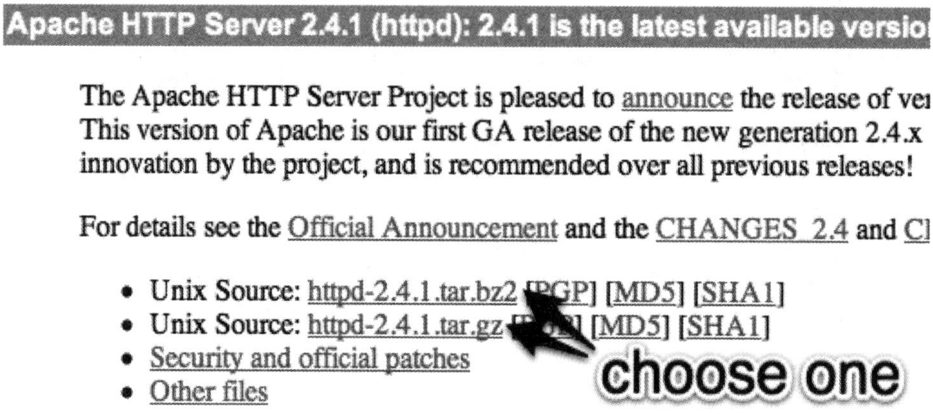

Apache HTTP Server 2.4.1 (httpd): 2.4.1 is the latest available versio

The Apache HTTP Server Project is pleased to announce the release of ver This version of Apache is our first GA release of the new generation 2.4.x innovation by the project, and is recommended over all previous releases!

For details see the Official Announcement and the CHANGES_2.4 and Cl

- Unix Source: httpd-2.4.1.tar.bz2 [PGP] [MD5] [SHA1]
- Unix Source: httpd-2.4.1.tar.gz [PGP] [MD5] [SHA1]
- Security and official patches
- Other files

choose one

Figure A.12. This is the one you need

What you've just downloaded is actually the source code for the Apache server. The first step, then, is to compile it into an executable binary installation. Pop open a Terminal, navigate to the directory where the downloaded file is located, extract it, and then navigate into the resulting directory:

```
user@machine:~$ cd Desktop
user@machine:~/Desktop$ tar xfz httpd-version.tar.gz
user@machine:~/Desktop$ cd httpd-version
```

The first step in compiling Apache is to configure it to your requirements. Most of the defaults will be fine for your purposes, but you'll need to enable dynamic loading of Apache modules (like PHP), which is off by default. Additionally, you should probably enable the URL rewriting feature, upon which many PHP applications rely (although it's unnecessary for the examples in this book). To make these configuration changes, type this command:

```
user@machine:~/Desktop/httpd-version$ ./configure --enable-so
➥ --enable-rewrite
```

A long stream of status messages will scroll up your screen. If the process stops with an error message, your system may be missing some critical piece of software that's required to compile Apache. Some Linux distributions lack the essential development libraries or even a C compiler installed by default. Installing these should enable you to return and run this command successfully. Current versions of Ubuntu, however, should come with everything that's needed.

After several minutes, the stream of messages should come to an end:

```
⋮
config.status: creating build/rules.mk
config.status: creating build/pkg/pkginfo
config.status: creating build/config_vars.sh
config.status: creating include/ap_config_auto.h
config.status: executing default commands
user@machine:~/Desktop/httpd-version$
```

You're now ready to compile Apache. The one-word command make is all it takes:

```
user@machine:~/Desktop/httpd-version$ make
```

Again, this process will take several minutes to complete, and should end with the following message:

```
⋮
make[1]: Leaving directory `/home/user/Desktop/httpd-version'
user@machine:~/Desktop/httpd-version$
```

To install your newly compiled copy of Apache, type sudo make install (the sudo is required, since you need root access to write to the installation directory).

```
user@machine:~/Desktop/httpd-version$ sudo make install
```

Enter your password when prompted.

As soon as this command has finished copying files, your installation of Apache is complete. Navigate to the installation directory and launch Apache using the apachectl script:

```
user@machine:~/Desktop/httpd-version$ cd /usr/local/apache2
user@machine:/usr/local/apache2$ sudo bin/apachectl -k start
```

You'll likely see a warning message from Apache complaining that it was unable to determine the server's fully qualified domain name. That's because most personal computers come without one. Don't sweat it.

If instead you elected to use your Linux distribution's package installer to install Apache, you should be able to fire it up with a command like this (on Ubuntu):

```
user@machine:~$ sudo service apache2 start
```

Fire up your browser and type http://localhost into the address bar. If Apache is up and running, you should see a welcome message like the one in Figure A.13.

Figure A.13. You can take my word for it!

As with your MySQL server, you'll probably want to configure Apache to start automatically when your system boots. If you installed Apache with a package installer, it's likely to be already set up for you.

The procedure to set this up is similar to that for MySQL; just copy and link the **apachectl** script from your Apache installation:

```
user@machine:/usr/local/apache2$ sudo su
root@machine:/usr/local/apache2# cd /etc
root@machine:/etc# ln -s /usr/local/apache2/bin/apachectl init.d/
root@machine:/etc# ln -s /etc/init.d/apachectl rc2.d/S99httpd
root@machine:/etc# ln -s /etc/init.d/apachectl rc0.d/K01httpd
```

To test that this works, restart your computer and then hit the http://localhost page in your browser again.

With a shiny new Apache installation up and running, you're now ready to add PHP support to it. To start, download the PHP Complete Source Code package from the PHP Downloads page.[17] Again, the **.tar.gz** and **.tar.bz2** versions are identical; just download whichever one you're used to extracting.

The file you downloaded should be called **php-*version*.tar.gz** (or **.bz2**). Pop open a new Terminal window, navigate to the directory containing the downloaded file, extract it, and move into the resulting directory:

```
user@machine:~$ cd Desktop
user@machine:~/Desktop$ tar xfz php-version.tar.gz
user@machine:~/Desktop$ cd php-version
```

To install PHP as an Apache module, you'll need to use the Apache **apxs** program. This will have been installed along with the Apache server if you followed the instructions to compile it yourself. But if you used your distribution's package manager to install Apache, you may need to install the Apache development package to access Apache **apxs**. You should be able to install this package by using the same package manager you used to install Apache. For example, on Ubuntu, you can use `apt-get` to install it as follows:

```
user@machine:~$ sudo apt-get install apache2-dev
```

Now, to install PHP you must be logged in as root:

```
user@machine:~/Desktop/php-version$ sudo su
[sudo] password for user: (type your password)
root@machine:/home/user/Desktop/php-version#
```

The first step is to configure the PHP installation program by telling it which options you want to enable, and where it should find the programs it needs to know about (such as Apache **apxs** and MySQL). The command should look like this (all on one line):

```
root@machine:/home/user/Desktop/php-version# ./configure
➥ --prefix=/usr/local/php --with-apxs2=/usr/local/apache2/bin/apxs
➥ --with-mysqli=/usr/local/mysql/bin/mysql_config
```

---

[17] http://www.php.net/downloads.php

The - -prefix option tells the installer where you want PHP to be installed (/usr/local/php is a good choice).

The - -with-apxs2 option tells the installer where to find the Apache **apxs** program mentioned. When installed using your Linux distribution's package manager, the program is usually found at **/usr/bin/apxs2**. If you compiled and installed Apache yourself as described before, however, it will be in the Apache binary directory, at **/usr/local/apache2/bin/apxs**.

The - -with-mysqli option tells the installer where to find your MySQL installation. More specifically, it must point to the **mysql_config** program in your MySQL install-ation's **bin** directory (**/usr/local/mysql/bin/mysql_config**).

Again, a parade of status messages will appear on your screen. When it stops, check for error messages and install any files it identifies as missing. On a default Ubuntu 10.04.4 installation, for example, you're likely to see an error complaining about an incomplete libxml2 installation. To correct this particular error, open Synaptic Package Manager, then locate and install the **libxml2-dev** package (**libxml2** should already be installed). Alternatively, at the Terminal prompt, just run apt-get in-stall libxml2-dev. Once it's installed, try the configure command again.

After you watch several screens of tests scroll by, you'll be returned to the command prompt with the comforting message "Thank you for using PHP." The following two commands will compile and then install PHP:

```
root@machine:/home/user/Desktop/php-version# make
root@machine:/home/user/Desktop/php-version# make install
```

Take a coffee break. This will take some time.

Upon completion of the make install command, PHP will be installed in /usr/local/php (unless you specified a different directory with the - -prefix option of the **configure** script). Now you just need to configure it.

The PHP configuration file is called **php.ini**. PHP comes with two sample **php.ini** files called **php.ini-development** and **php.ini-production**. Copy these files from your installation work directory to the **/usr/local/php/lib** directory, then make a copy of the **php.ini-development** file and call it **php.ini**:

```
root@machine:/home/user/Desktop/php-version# cp php.ini* /usr/local/
➥php/lib/
root@machine:/home/user/Desktop/php-version# cd /usr/local/php/lib
root@machine:/usr/local/php/lib# cp php.ini-development php.ini
```

You may now delete the directory from which you compiled PHP—it's no longer needed.

We'll worry about fine-tuning **php.ini** shortly. For now, we need to tweak Apache's configuration to make it more PHP-friendly, so locate your Apache configuration file. It can usually be found in the **conf** subdirectory of your Apache installation (**/usr/local/apache2/conf/httpd.conf**), or in **/etc/apache2/apache2.conf** if you installed Apache with a package manager.

To edit this file you must be logged in as root, so launch your text editor from the Terminal window where you're still logged in as root:

```
root@machine:/usr/local/php/lib# cd /usr/local/apache2/conf
root@machine:/usr/local/apache2/conf# gedit httpd.conf
```

Go right to the bottom of the file and add these lines to tell Apache that files with names ending in **.php** should be treated as PHP scripts:

```
<FilesMatch \.php$>
  SetHandler application/x-httpd-php
</FilesMatch>
```

That should do it. Save your changes and restart your Apache server:

```
root@machine:/usr/local/apache2/conf# /usr/local/apache2/bin/
➥apachectl -k restart
```

If it all goes according to plan, Apache should start up without any error messages. If you run into any trouble, the helpful individuals in the SitePoint Forums[18] (myself included) will be happy to help.

---

[18] http://www.sitepoint.com/forums/

Appendix B: MySQL Syntax Reference

This appendix describes the syntax of the most commonly used SQL statements in MySQL, as of version 5.5.22 (current as of this writing).

The following conventions are used in this reference:

- Commands are listed in alphabetical order for easy reference.

- Optional portions of each command are surrounded by square brackets ([]).

- Lists of elements from which one element must be chosen are surrounded by braces ({}), with the elements separated by vertical bars (|).

- An ellipsis (...) means that the preceding element may be repeated.

The query syntax documented in this appendix has been simplified in several places by the omission of the alternative syntax, and of keywords that performed no function, but which were originally included for compatibility with other database systems. Query features having to do with some advanced features such as transactions have also been omitted. For a complete, up-to-date reference to supported MySQL syntax, see the MySQL Reference Manual.[1]

SQL Statements Implemented in MySQL

ALTER TABLE

```
ALTER [IGNORE] TABLE tbl_name action[, action …]
```

In this code, *action* refers to an action as defined as follows.

ALTER TABLE queries may be used to change the definition of a table without losing any of the information in that table (except in obvious cases, such as the deletion of a column). Here are the main actions that are possible:

---

[1] http://dev.mysql.com/doc/mysql/en/

ADD [COLUMN] *create_definition* **[FIRST | AFTER** *column_name*]

This action adds a new column to the table. The syntax for *create_definition* is as described for the section called "CREATE TABLE". By default, the column will be added to the end of the table, but by specifying FIRST or AFTER *column_name*, you can place the column wherever you like. The optional word COLUMN performs no actual function—leave it off unless you particularly like to see it there.

ADD INDEX [*index_name***] (***index_col_name*, ...**)**

This action creates a new index to speed up searches based on the column(s) specified. You may assign a name to your indexes by specifying the *index_name*; otherwise, a default name based on the first column in the index will be used. When creating an index based on CHAR and/or VARCHAR columns, you can specify a number of characters to index as part of *index_col_name* (for example, my-Column(5) will index the first five characters of myColumn). This number must be specified when indexing BLOB and TEXT columns.

ADD FULLTEXT [*index_name***] (***index_col_name*, ...**)**

This action creates a full-text index on the column(s) specified. This special type of index allows you to perform complex searches for text in CHAR, VARCHAR, or TEXT columns using the MATCH MySQL function. For full details, see the MySQL Reference Manual.[2]

ADD FOREIGN KEY [*index_name***] (***index_col_name*, ...**)** *reference_definition*

On InnoDB tables, this creates a foreign key constraint, requiring the values in this index to correspond to matching entries in another table.

reference_definition specifies the table and column(s) that are referenced by the constraint:

```
REFERENCES tbl_name (index_col_name, ...)
        [ON DELETE { RESTRICT | CASCADE | SET NULL | NO ACTION }]
        [ON UPDATE { RESTRICT | CASCADE | SET NULL | NO ACTION }]
```

The optional ON DELETE and ON UPDATE portions of *reference_definition* specify what should happen to entries in this table when the corresponding entry in

---

[2] http://dev.mysql.com/doc/mysql/en/fulltext-search.html

the referenced table is deleted or updated. For full details, see the MySQL Reference Manual.[3]

ADD PRIMARY KEY (*index_col_name*, …)

This action creates an index for the specified row(s) with the name PRIMARY, identifying it as the primary key for the table. All values (or combinations of values) must be unique, as described for the ADD UNIQUE action below. This action will cause an error if a primary key already exists for the table. *index_col_name* is defined as it is for the ADD INDEX action before.

ADD UNIQUE [*index_name*] (*index_col_name*, …)

This action creates an index on the specified columns, but with a twist: all values in the designated column—or all combinations of values if more than one column is included in the index—must be unique. The parameters *index_name* and *index_col_name* are defined as they are for the ADD INDEX action.

ALTER [COLUMN] *col_name* {SET DEFAULT *value* | DROP DEFAULT}

This action assigns a new default value to a column (SET DEFAULT), or removes the existing default value (DROP DEFAULT). Again, the word COLUMN is completely optional and has no effect.

CHANGE [COLUMN] *col_name* *create_definition*

This action replaces an existing column (*col_name*) with a new column, as defined by *create_definition* (the syntax of which is as specified for the section called "CREATE TABLE"). The data in the existing column is converted, if necessary, and placed in the new column. Note that *create_definition* includes a new column name, so this action may be used to rename a column. If you want to leave the name of the column unchanged, however, remember to include it twice (once for *col_name* and once for *create_definition*), or use the MODIFY action below.

DISABLE KEYS
ENABLE KEYS

When you insert a large number of records into a table, MySQL can spend a lot of time updating the index(es) of the table to reflect the new entries. Executing ALTER TABLE … DISABLE KEYS before you perform the inserts will instruct MySQL to postpone those index updates. Once the inserts are complete, execute

---

[3] http://dev.mysql.com/doc/mysql/en/innodb-foreign-key-constraints.html

ALTER TABLE ... ENABLE KEYS to update the indexes for all the new entries at once. This will usually save time over performing the updates one at a time.

DROP [COLUMN] col_name

Fairly self-explanatory, this action completely removes a column from the table. The data in that column is irretrievable after this query completes, so be sure of the column name you specify. COLUMN, as usual, can be left off; it just makes the query sound better when read aloud.

DROP PRIMARY KEY
DROP INDEX index_name
DROP FOREIGN KEY index_name

These actions are quite self-explanatory: they remove from the table the primary key, index, or foreign key constraint, respectively.

MODIFY [COLUMN] create_definition

Nearly identical to the aforementioned CHANGE action, this action lets you specify a new declaration for a column in the table, but assumes the name will remain the same. Thus, you simply have to re-declare the column with the same name in the create_definition parameter (as defined for the section called "CREATE TABLE"). As before, COLUMN is completely optional and does nothing. Although convenient, this action is not standard SQL syntax, and was added for compatibility with an identical extension in Oracle database servers.

ORDER BY col_name

This action lets you sort a table's entries by a particular column. However, as soon as new entries are added to the table or existing entries modified, ordering can no longer be guaranteed. The only practical use of this action would be to increase performance of a table that you sorted regularly in a certain way in your application's SELECT queries. Under some circumstances, arranging the rows in (almost) the right order to begin with will make sorting quicker.

RENAME [TO] new_tbl_name

This action renames the table. The word TO is completely optional, and does nothing. Use it if you like it.

table_options

Using the same syntax as in the `CREATE TABLE` query, this action allows you to set and change advanced table options. These options are fully documented in the MySQL Reference Manual.[4]

ANALYZE TABLE

```
ANALYZE TABLE tbl_name[, tbl_name …]
```

This function updates the information used by the `SELECT` query in the optimization of queries that take advantage of table indexes. It pays in performance to run this query periodically on tables whose contents change a lot over time. The table(s) in question are locked as "read-only" while the analysis runs.

BEGIN

```
BEGIN
```

`BEGIN` performs the same action as `START TRANSACTION`.

COMMIT

```
COMMIT
```

Once a transaction has been started (that is, autocommit mode has been disabled) with `START TRANSACTION`, MySQL collects the changes made to the database so that they may be applied simultaneously. A `COMMIT` query applies all those changes at once, ending the transaction.

CREATE DATABASE

```
CREATE DATABASE [IF NOT EXISTS] db_name
```

This action simply creates a new database with the given name (*db_name*). This query will fail if the database already exists (unless `IF NOT EXISTS` is specified), or if you lack the required privileges.

---

[4] http://dev.mysql.com/doc/refman/5.5/en/create-table.html

CREATE INDEX

```
CREATE [UNIQUE | FULLTEXT] INDEX index_name ON tbl_name
    (col_name[(length)], …)
```

This query creates a new index on an existing table. It works identically to ALTER
TABLE ADD {INDEX | UNIQUE | FULLTEXT}, described in the section called "ALTER
TABLE".

CREATE TABLE

```
CREATE [TEMPORARY] TABLE [IF NOT EXISTS] [db_name.]tbl_name
    {   [(create_definition, …)]
        [table_options] [[IGNORE | REPLACE] select_statement]

    | LIKE [db_name.]old_tbl_name }
```

Where *create_definition* is:

```
{   col_name type [NOT NULL] [DEFAULT default_value]
        [AUTO_INCREMENT] [PRIMARY KEY]

    | PRIMARY KEY (index_col_name, …)

    | INDEX [index_name] (index_col_name, …)

    | UNIQUE [INDEX] [index_name] (index_col_name, …)

    | FULLTEXT [index_name] (index_col_name, …)

    | FOREIGN KEY [index_name] (index_col_name, …)
        REFERENCES tbl_name (index_col_name, …)
        [ON DELETE { RESTRICT | CASCADE | SET NULL | NO ACTION }]
        [ON UPDATE { RESTRICT | CASCADE | SET NULL | NO ACTION }]}
```

In this code, *type* is a MySQL column type (see Appendix D), and *index_col_name*
is as described for ALTER TABLE ADD INDEX in the section called "ALTER TABLE".

CREATE TABLE is used to create a new table called *tbl_name* in the current database
(or in a specific database if *db_name* is specified). If TEMPORARY is specified, the
table disappears when the connection that created it is terminated. A temporary

table created with the same name as an existing table will hide the existing table from the current client session until the temporary table is deleted or the session ends; however, other clients will continue to see the original table.

Assuming TEMPORARY is not specified, this query will fail if a table with the given name already exists, unless IF NOT EXISTS is specified (in which case the query is ignored). A CREATE TABLE query will also fail if you lack the required privileges.

Most of the time, the name of the table will be followed by a series of column declarations (*create_definition* above). Each column definition includes the name and data type for the column, and any of the following options:

NOT NULL

This specifies that the column may not be left empty (NULL). Note that NULL is a special "no value" value, which is quite different from, say, an empty string (' '). A column of type VARCHAR, for instance, which is set NOT NULL may be set to ' ' but will not be NULL. Likewise, a NOT NULL column of type INT may contain zero (0), which is a value, but it may not contain NULL, as this is not a value.

DEFAULT *default_value*

DEFAULT lets you specify a value to be given to a column when no value is assigned in an INSERT statement. When there's no value given in an INSERT statement, NULL columns (that is, columns where the NOT NULL option isn't set) are normally assigned a value of NULL. When DEFAULT is specified, NOT NULL columns will instead be assigned a "default default value": an empty string (' '), zero (0), '0000-00-00', or a current timestamp, depending on the data type of the column.

AUTO_INCREMENT

As described in Chapter 2, an AUTO_INCREMENT column will automatically insert a number that is one greater than the current highest number in that column when NULL is inserted. AUTO_INCREMENT columns must also be NOT NULL, and be either a PRIMARY KEY or UNIQUE.

PRIMARY KEY

This option specifies that the column in question should be the primary key for the table; that is, the values in the column must identify uniquely each of the rows in the table. This forces the values in this column to be unique, and speeds up searches for items based on this column by creating an index of the values it contains.

UNIQUE

Very similar to PRIMARY KEY, this option requires all values in the column to be unique, and indexes the values for high-speed searches.

In addition to column definitions, you can list additional indexes you wish to create on the table using the PRIMARY KEY, INDEX, UNIQUE, FULLTEXT, and FOREIGN KEY forms of *create_definition*. See the descriptions of the equivalent forms of ALTER TABLE in the section called "ALTER TABLE" for details.

The *table_options* portion of the CREATE TABLE query is used to specify advanced properties of the table, such as DEFAULT CHARACTER SET utf8 and the ENGINE=InnoDB, and is described in detail in the MySQL Reference Manual.[5]

The *select_statement* portion of the CREATE TABLE query allows you to create a table from the results of a SELECT query (see the section called "SELECT"). When you create this table, it's unnecessary to declare separately the columns that correspond to those results. This type of query is useful if you want to obtain the result of a SELECT query, store it in a temporary table, and then perform a number of SELECT queries upon it.

Instead of defining a table from scratch, you can instead instruct MySQL to create the new table using the same structure as another table. Rather than a list of *create_definition*s and the *table_options*, simply end the CREATE TABLE query with LIKE, followed by the name of the existing table.

DELETE

```
DELETE [LOW_PRIORITY] [QUICK] [IGNORE]
    {   FROM tbl_name
            [WHERE where_clause]
            [ORDER BY order_by_expr]
            [LIMIT rows]

      | tbl_name[, tbl_name …]
            FROM table_references
```

---

[5] http://dev.mysql.com/doc/mysql/en/create-table.html

```
      [WHERE where_clause]

  | FROM tbl_name[, tbl_name …]
      USING table_references
      [WHERE where_clause] }
```

The first form of this query deletes all rows from the specified table, unless the optional (but desirable) WHERE or LIMIT clauses are specified. The WHERE clause works the same way as its twin in the SELECT query (see the section called "SELECT"). The LIMIT clause simply lets you specify the maximum number of rows to be deleted. The ORDER BY clause lets you specify the order in which the entries are deleted, which, in combination with the LIMIT clause, allows you to perform actions such as delete the ten oldest entries from the table.

The second and third forms are equivalent, and enable you to delete rows from multiple tables in a single operation, in much the same way as you can retrieve entries from multiple tables using a join in a SELECT query (see the section called "SELECT"). The *table_references* work the same way as they do for SELECT queries (you can create simple joins or outer joins), while the WHERE clause lets you narrow down the rows that are considered for deletion. The first list of tables (*tbl_name*[, *tbl_name* …]), however, identifies from the *table_references* the tables where rows will actually be deleted. In this way, you can use a complex join involving a number of tables to isolate a set of results, then delete the rows from only one of those tables.

The LOW_PRIORITY option causes the query to wait until there are no clients reading from the table before performing the operation. The QUICK option attempts to speed up lengthy delete operations by changing the way it updates the table's index(es). The IGNORE option instructs MySQL to refrain from reporting any errors that occur while the delete is performed.

DESCRIBE/DESC

```
{DESCRIBE | DESC} tbl_name [col_name | wild]
```

This command supplies information about the columns, a specific column (*col_name*), or any columns that match a pattern containing the wild cards % and _ (*wild*) that make up the specified table. The information returned includes the column name, its type, whether it accepts NULL as a value, whether the column has an index, the default value for the column, and any extra features it has (for example, AUTO_INCREMENT).

DROP DATABASE

```
DROP DATABASE [IF EXISTS] db_name
```

This is a dangerous command. It will immediately delete a database, along with all its tables. This query will fail with an error if the database does not exist (unless IF EXISTS is specified, in which case it will fail silently), or if you lack the required privileges.

DROP INDEX

```
DROP INDEX index_name ON tbl_name
```

DROP INDEX has exactly the same effect as ALTER TABLE DROP INDEX, described in the section called "ALTER TABLE".

DROP TABLE

```
DROP TABLE [IF EXISTS] tbl_name[, tbl_name, …]
```

This query completely deletes one or more tables. *This is a dangerous query*, since the data can never be retrieved once this action is executed. Be very careful with it!

The query will fail with an error if the table doesn't exist (unless IF EXISTS is specified, in which case it will fail silently) or if you lack the required privileges.

EXPLAIN

The explain query has two very different forms. The first,

```
EXPLAIN tbl_name
```

is equivalent to DESCRIBE tbl_name or SHOW COLUMNS FROM tbl_name.

The second format,

```
EXPLAIN select_statement
```

where *select_statement* can be any valid SELECT query, will produce an explanation of how MySQL would determine the results of the SELECT statement. This query is useful for finding out where indexes will help speed up your SELECT queries, and for determining if MySQL is performing multi-table queries in optimal order. See the STRAIGHT_JOIN option of the SELECT query in the section called "SELECT" for information on how to override the MySQL optimizer and control this order manually. See the MySQL Reference Manual[6] for complete information on how to interpret the results of an EXPLAIN query.

GRANT

```
GRANT priv_type [(column_list)], …
    ON {tbl_name | * | *.* | db_name.*}
    TO username [IDENTIFIED BY 'password'], …
    [WITH GRANT OPTION]
```

GRANT adds new access privileges to a user account, and creates a new account if the specified *username* does not yet exist. It may also change the password if IDENTIFIED BY 'password' is used on an account that already has a password.

See the MySQL Reference Manual[7] for a complete description of this and other queries that may be used to manage user accounts.

INSERT

```
INSERT [LOW_PRIORITY | DELAYED] [IGNORE] [INTO] tbl_name

    {   [(col_name, …)] VALUES (expression, …), …

      | SET col_name=expression, col_name=expression, …

      | [(col_name, …)] SELECT … }

      [ON DUPLICATE KEY UPDATE col_name=expression[, …]]
```

---

[6] http://dev.mysql.com/doc/mysql/en/explain.html
[7] http://dev.mysql.com/doc/mysql/en/account-management-sql.html

The INSERT query is used to add new entries to a table. It supports three general options:

LOW_PRIORITY

The query will wait until there are no clients reading from the table before it proceeds.

DELAYED

The query completes immediately from the client's point of view, and the INSERT operation is performed in the background. This option is useful when you wish to insert a large number of rows without waiting for the operation to complete. Be aware that the client will not know the last inserted ID on an AUTO_INCREMENT column when a DELAYED insert is performed (for example, PHP's PDO lastInsertId method will fail to work correctly).

IGNORE

Normally, when an insert operation causes a clash in a PRIMARY KEY or UNIQUE column, the insert fails and produces an error message. This option allows the insert to fail silently; the new row is not inserted, but no error message is displayed.

The word INTO is entirely optional, and has no effect on the operation of the query.

As you can see above, INSERT queries may take three forms. The first form lets you insert one or more rows by specifying the values for the table columns in parentheses. If the optional list of column names is omitted, the list(s) of column values must include a value for every column in the table, in the order in which they appear in the table.

The second form of INSERT can be used only to insert a single row, but, very intuitively, it allows you to assign values to the columns in that row by giving them in *col_name=value* format.

In the third and final form of INSERT, the rows to be inserted result from a SELECT query. Again, if the list of column names is omitted, the result set of the SELECT must contain values for each and every column in the table, in the correct order. A SELECT query that makes up part of an insert statement may not contain an ORDER BY clause, and you're unable to use the table into which you're inserting in the FROM clause.

Columns to which you assign no value (for example, if you leave them out of the column list) are assigned their default. By default, inserting a NULL value into a NOT NULL field will also cause that field to be set to its default value; however, if MySQL is configured with the DONT_USE_DEFAULT_FIELDS option enabled, this sort of INSERT operation will cause an error. For this reason, it's best to avoid them.

The optional ON DUPLICATE KEY UPDATE clause takes effect when the INSERT query attempts to add a new entry to the table that would introduce a duplicate value disallowed by a unique index or primary key. Instead of the query failing with an error, this clause specifies how the existing entry in the table should be updated. The form of this clause is very similar to an UPDATE statement: it specifies one or more columns and the new value that should be assigned to each. See the section called "UPDATE" for more information.

LOAD DATA INFILE

```
LOAD DATA [LOW_PRIORITY | CONCURRENT] [LOCAL] INFILE
     'file_name.txt' [REPLACE | IGNORE] INTO TABLE tbl_name
     [FIELDS
       [TERMINATED BY 'string']
       [[OPTIONALLY] ENCLOSED BY 'char']
       [ESCAPED BY 'char'] ]
     [LINES [STARTING BY ''] [TERMINATED BY 'string']]
     [IGNORE number LINES]
     [(col_name, …)]
```

The LOAD DATA INFILE query is used to import data from a text file either on the MySQL server, or on the LOCAL (client) system (for example, a text file created with a SELECT INTO OUTFILE query). The syntax of this command is in the code, but I'd refer you to the MySQL Reference Manual[8] for a complete explanation of this query and the issues that surround its use.

OPTIMIZE TABLE

```
OPTIMIZE TABLE tbl_name[, tbl_name …]
```

---

[8] http://dev.mysql.com/doc/mysql/en/load-data.html

Much like a hard-disk partition becomes fragmented if existing files are deleted or resized, MySQL tables become fragmented as you delete rows and modify variable-length columns (such as VARCHAR or BLOB) over time. This query performs the database equivalent of a defrag on the table, reorganizing the data it contains to eliminate wasted space.

It's important to note that a table is *locked* while an optimize operation occurs, so if your application relies on a large table being constantly available, that application will grind to a halt while the optimization takes place. In such cases, it's better to copy the table, optimize the copy, and then replace the old table with the newly optimized version using a RENAME query. Changes made to the original table in the interim will be lost, so this technique is only appropriate for some applications.

RENAME TABLE

```
RENAME TABLE tbl_name TO new_table_name[, tbl_name2 TO …, …]
```

This query quickly and conveniently renames one or more tables. This differs from ALTER TABLE tbl_name RENAME in that all the tables being renamed in the query are locked for the duration of the query, so that no other connected clients may access them. As the MySQL Reference Manual explains,[9] this assurance of atomicity lets you replace a table with an empty equivalent; for example, if you wanted to safely start a new table once a certain number of entries was reached:

```
CREATE TABLE new_table (…);
RENAME TABLE old_table TO backup_table, new_table TO old_table;
```

You can also move a table from one database to another by specifying the table name as db_name.tbl_name, as long as both tables are stored on the same physical disk, which is usually the case.

You must have ALTER and DROP privileges on the original table, as well as CREATE and INSERT privileges on the new table, in order to perform this query. A RENAME TABLE query that fails to complete halfway through will automatically be reversed, so that the original state is restored.

---

[9] http://dev.mysql.com/doc/mysql/en/rename-table.html

REPLACE

```
REPLACE [LOW_PRIORITY | DELAYED] [INTO] tbl_name

  {   [(col_name, …)] VALUES (expression, …), …

    | [(col_name, …)] SELECT …

    | SET col_name=expression, col_name=expression, … }
```

REPLACE is identical to INSERT, except that if an inserted row clashes with an existing row in a PRIMARY KEY or UNIQUE column, the old entry is replaced with the new.

REVOKE

```
REVOKE priv_type [(column_list)], …
       ON {tbl_name | * | *.* | db_name.*}
       FROM user, …
```

This function removes access privileges from a user account. If all privileges are removed from an account, the user will still be able to log in but unable to access any information.

See the section called "MySQL Access Control Tips" in Chapter 10 for a complete description of this query.

ROLLBACK

```
ROLLBACK
```

Once a transaction has been started (that is, autocommit mode has been disabled) with START TRANSACTION, MySQL collects the changes made to the database so that they may be applied all at once. A ROLLBACK query discards all those changes, canceling the transaction.

SELECT

```
SELECT [select_options]
    select_expression, …
    [INTO {OUTFILE | DUMPFILE} 'file_name' export_options]
    [FROM table_references
      [WHERE where_definition]
      [GROUP BY {col_name | col_pos } [ASC | DESC], …]
      [HAVING where_definition]
      [ORDER BY {col_name | col_pos } [ASC | DESC], …]
      [LIMIT [offset,] rows]]
```

SELECT is the most complex query in SQL, and is used to perform all data retrieval operations. This query supports the following *select_options*, which may be specified in any sensible combination simply by listing them, separated by spaces:

ALL

DISTINCT

DISTINCTROW

> Any one of these options may be used to specify the treatment of duplicate rows in the result set. ALL (the default) specifies that all duplicate rows appear in the result set, while DISTINCT and DISTINCTROW (they have the same effect) specify that duplicate rows should be eliminated from the result set.

HIGH_PRIORITY

> This option does exactly what it says: it assigns a high priority to the SELECT query. Normally, if a query is waiting to update a table, all read-only queries (such as SELECT) must yield to it. A SELECT HIGH_PRIORITY, however, will go first.

STRAIGHT_JOIN

> Forces MySQL to join multiple tables specified in the *table_references* portion of the query in the order specified there. If you think MySQL's query optimizer is doing it the *slow* way, this argument lets you override it. See the section called "Joins" for more information.

SQL_BUFFER_RESULT

This option forces MySQL to store the result set in a temporary table. This frees up the tables employed in the query for use by other processes, while the result set is transmitted to the client.

SQL_CACHE

This option instructs MySQL to store the result of this query in the **query cache**, an area of memory set aside by the server to store the results of frequently run queries so that there's no need to recalculate them from scratch if the contents of the relevant tables are still the same. MySQL can be configured so that only queries with the SQL_CACHE option are cached. If the query cache is disabled, this option will have no effect.

SQL_NO_CACHE

This option instructs MySQL to avoid storing the result of this query in the query cache (see the previous option). MySQL can be configured so that every query is cached unless it has the SQL_NO_CACHE option. If the query cache is disabled, this option will have no effect.

SQL_CALC_FOUND_ROWS

For use in conjunction with a LIMIT clause, this option calculates and sets aside the total number of rows that would be returned from the query if no LIMIT clause were present. You can then retrieve this number using SELECT FOUND_ROWS() (see Appendix C).

select_expression defines a column of the result set to be returned by the query. Typically, this is a table column name, and may be specified as *col_name*, *tbl_name.col_name*, or *db_name.tbl_name.col_name*, depending on how specific you need to be for MySQL to identify the column that you're referring to. *select_expressions* can refer to other expressions apart from the database column; simple mathematical formulas including column names as variables, and complex expressions calculated with MySQL functions may also be used. Here's an example of the latter, which will give the date one month from now in the form "January 1, 2010":

```
SELECT DATE_FORMAT(DATE_ADD(CURDATE(), INTERVAL 1 MONTH), '%M %D,
    %Y')
```

select_expressions may also contain an alias or assigned name for the result column, if the expression is followed with [AS] `alias` (the AS is entirely optional). This expression must be used when referring to that column elsewhere in the query (for example, in WHERE and ORDER BY clauses), as follows:

```
SELECT jokedate AS jd FROM joke ORDER BY jd ASC
```

MySQL lets you use an INTO clause to output the results of a query into a file instead of returning them to the client. The most typical use of this clause is to export the contents of a table into a text file containing comma-separated values (CSV). Here's an example:

```
SELECT * INTO OUTFILE '/home/user/myTable.txt'
    FIELDS TERMINATED BY ',' OPTIONALLY ENCLOSED BY '"'
    LINES TERMINATED BY '\n'
    FROM myTable
```

The file to which the results are dumped must not exist beforehand, or this query will fail. This restriction prevents an SQL query from being used to overwrite critical operating system files. The created file will also be world-readable on systems that support file security, so consider this before you export sensitive data to a text file that anyone on the system can read.

DUMPFILE may be used instead of OUTFILE to write only a single row to the file, without row or column delimiters. It can be used, for example, to dump a BLOB stored in the table to a file (SELECT *blobCol* INTO DUMPFILE ...). For complete information on the INTO clause, see the MySQL Reference Manual.[10] For information on reading data back from a text file, see the section called "LOAD DATA INFILE".

The FROM clause contains a list of tables from which the rows composing the result set should be formed, along with instructions on how they should be joined together. At its most basic, *table_references* is the name of a single database table, which may be assigned an alias with or without using AS as described for *select_expression* beforehand. If you specify more than one table name, you're performing a **join**. These are discussed in the section called "Joins" shortly.

---

[10] http://dev.mysql.com/doc/mysql/en/select.html

The *where_definition* in the WHERE clause sets the condition for a row to be included in the table of results sent in response to the SELECT query. This may be a simple condition (for example, id = 5), or a complex expression that makes use of MySQL functions and combines multiple conditions using Boolean operators (AND, OR, NOT).

The GROUP BY clause lets you specify one or more columns (by name, alias, or column position, where 1 is the first column in the result set) for which rows with equal values should be collapsed into single rows in the result set. This clause should normally be used in combination with the MySQL grouping functions such as COUNT, MAX, and AVG, described in Appendix C, to produce result columns that give summary information about the groups created. By default, the grouped results are sorted in ascending order of the grouped column(s); however, the ASC or DESC argument may be added following each column reference to explicitly sort that column's results in ascending or descending order, respectively. Results are sorted by the first column listed, then tying sets of rows are sorted by the second, and so on.

Note that the WHERE clause is processed before GROUP BY grouping occurs, so conditions in the WHERE clause may not refer to columns that depend on the grouping operation. To impose conditions on the post-grouping result set, you should use the HAVING clause instead. This clause's syntax is identical to that of the WHERE clause, except the conditions specified here are processed just prior to returning the set of results, and are not optimized. For this reason, you should use the WHERE clause whenever possible. For more information on GROUP BY and the HAVING clause, see Chapter 11.

The ORDER BY clause lets you sort results according to the values in one or more rows before they're returned. As for the GROUP BY clause, each column may be identified by a column name, alias, or position (where 1 is the first column in the result set), and each column may have an ASC or DESC argument to specify that sorting occurs in ascending or descending order, respectively (ascending is the default). Rows are sorted initially by the first column listed, then tying sets of rows are sorted by the second, and so on.

The LIMIT clause instructs the query to return only a portion of the results it would normally generate. In the simplest case, LIMIT *n* returns only the first *n* rows of the complete result set. You can also specify an offset by using the form LIMIT *x*, *n*.

In this case, up to *n* rows will be returned, beginning from the xth row of the complete result set. The first row corresponds to $x = 0$, the second to $x = 1$, and so on.

Joins

As recently described, the FROM clause of a SELECT query lets you specify the tables that are combined to create the result set. When multiple tables are combined in this way, it's called a **join**. MySQL supports several types of joins, as defined by the following supported syntaxes for the *table_references* component of the FROM clause:

```
table_ref
```

```
table_references, table_ref
```

```
table_references [CROSS] JOIN table_ref
```

```
table_references INNER JOIN table_ref join_condition
```

```
table_references STRAIGHT_JOIN table_ref
```

```
table_references LEFT [OUTER] JOIN table_ref join_condition
    { OJ table_ref LEFT OUTER JOIN table_ref ON cond_expr }
```

```
table_references NATURAL [LEFT [OUTER]] JOIN table_ref
```

```
table_references RIGHT [OUTER] JOIN table_ref join_condition
```

```
table_references NATURAL [RIGHT [OUTER]] JOIN table_ref
```

where *table_ref* is defined as:

```
table_name [[AS] alias] [USE INDEX (key_list)]
        [IGNORE INDEX (key_list)]
```

and *join_condition* is defined as one of the following:

```
ON cond_expr
```

```
USING (column_list)
```

Don't be disheartened by the sheer variety of join types; I'll be explaining how each of them works.

The most basic type of join, an **inner join**, produces rows made up of all possible pairings of the rows from the first table with the second. You can perform an inner join in MySQL either by separating the table names with a comma (,) or with the words JOIN, CROSS JOIN, or INNER JOIN (these are all equivalent).

It's common—especially in older PHP code—to use the comma (,) form to create an inner join, and then use the WHERE clause of the SELECT query to specify a condition, in order to narrow down which of the combined rows are actually returned (for example, to match up a primary key in the first table with a column in the second); however, this is generally considered untidy and bad practice today.

Instead, the INNER JOIN syntax followed by a *join_condition* should be used. The ON form of the *join_condition* puts the condition(s) required to join two tables right next to the names of those tables, keeping the WHERE clause for conditions unrelated to the join operations.

As a final alternative, the USING (*column_list*) form of *join_condition* lets you specify columns that must match between the two tables. For example:

```
SELECT * FROM t1 INNER JOIN t2 USING (tid)
```

This is equivalent to:

```
SELECT * FROM t1 INNER JOIN t2 ON t1.tid = t2.tid
```

STRAIGHT_JOIN works in the same way as an inner join, except that the tables are processed in the order listed (left first, then right). Normally, MySQL selects the order that will produce the shortest processing time, but if you think you know better, you can use a STRAIGHT_JOIN.

The second type of join is an **outer join**, which is accomplished in MySQL with LEFT/RIGHT [OUTER] JOIN (OUTER is completely optional, and has no effect). In a LEFT outer join, any row in the left-hand table that has no matching rows in the right-hand table (as defined by the *join_condition*), will be listed as a single row in the result set. NULL values will appear in all the columns that come from the right-hand table.

The { OJ … } syntax is equivalent to a standard left outer join; it's included for compatibility with other ODBC (Open Database Connectivity) databases.

RIGHT outer joins work in the same way as LEFT outer joins, except in this case, it's the table on the right whose entries are always included, even if they lack a matching entry in the left-hand table. Since RIGHT outer joins are nonstandard, it's usually best to stick to LEFT outer joins for cross-database compatibility.

For some practical examples of outer joins and their uses, see Chapter 11.

Natural joins are "automatic" in that they automatically match up rows based on column names that are found to match between the two tables. Thus, if a table called joke has an authorid column referring to entries in an author table whose primary key is another authorid column, you can perform a join of these two tables on that column very simply (assuming there are no other columns with identical names in the two tables):

```
SELECT * FROM joke NATURAL JOIN author
```

Unions

A union combines the results from a number of SELECT queries to produce a single result set. Each of the queries must produce the same number of columns, and these columns must be of the same type. The column names produced by the first query are used for the union's result set:

```
SELECT …
    UNION [ALL | DISTINCT]
    SELECT …
        [UNION [ALL | DISTINCT]
        SELECT …] …
```

By default, duplicate result rows in the union will be eliminated so that each row in the result set is unique. The DISTINCT option can be used to make this clear, but it has no actual effect. The ALL option, on the other hand, allows duplicate results through to the final result set.

SET

```
SET option = value, …
```

The SET query allows you to set a number of options both on your client and on the server.

For example, you can SET autocommit = 0 to disable autocommit mode for the current session. In effect, this is like running START TRANSACTION, and then running it again automatically after every COMMIT or ROLLBACK. With autocommit off, you always have a transaction open, and queries like INSERT, UPDATE, and DELETE will not take effect until you COMMIT them.

For a complete list of the options that may be SET, refer to the MySQL Reference Manual.[11]

SHOW

The SHOW query may be used in a number of forms to obtain information about the MySQL server, the databases, and the tables it contains. Many of these forms have an optional LIKE wild component, where wild is a string that may contain wildcard characters (% for multiple characters, _ for just one) to filter the list of results. Each of the forms of the SHOW query are described here:

SHOW DATABASES [LIKE wild]

This query lists the databases that are available on the MySQL server.

SHOW [OPEN] TABLES [FROM db_name] [LIKE wild]

This query lists the tables (or, optionally, the currently OPEN tables) in the default or specified database.

SHOW [FULL] COLUMNS FROM tbl_name [FROM db_name] [LIKE wild]

When FULL is not used, this query provides the same information as a DESCRIBE query (see the section called "DESCRIBE/DESC"). The FULL option adds a listing of the privileges you have on each column to this information. SHOW FIELDS is equivalent to SHOW COLUMNS.

---

[11] http://dev.mysql.com/doc/mysql/en/set-option.html

SHOW INDEX FROM *tbl_name* [FROM *db_name*]

This query provides detailed information about the indexes that are defined on the specified table. See the MySQL Reference Manual[12] for a guide to the results produced by this query. SHOW KEYS is equivalent to SHOW INDEX.

SHOW TABLE STATUS [FROM *db_name*] [LIKE *wild*]

This query displays detailed information about the tables in the specified or default database.

SHOW STATUS [LIKE *wild*]

This query displays detailed statistics for the server. See the MySQL Reference Manual[13] for details on the meaning of each figure.

SHOW VARIABLES [LIKE *wild*]

This query lists the MySQL configuration variables and their settings. See the MySQL Reference Manual[14] for a complete description of these options.

SHOW [FULL] PROCESSLIST

This query displays all threads running on the MySQL server and the queries being executed by each. If you lack the process privilege, you'll only see threads executing your own queries. The FULL option causes complete queries to be displayed, rather than only the first 100 characters of each (the default).

SHOW GRANTS FOR *user*

This query lists the GRANT queries that would be required to recreate the privileges of the specified user.

SHOW CREATE TABLE *table_name*

This query displays the CREATE TABLE query that would be required to reproduce the specified table.

START TRANSACTION

```
START TRANSACTION
```

---

[12] http://dev.mysql.com/doc/en/show-index.html
[13] http://dev.mysql.com/doc/en/show-status.html
[14] http://dev.mysql.com/doc/en/show-variables.html

Once a transaction has been started (that is, autocommit mode has been disabled) with START TRANSACTION, MySQL collects the changes made to the database so that they may be applied all at once (with COMMIT) or discarded (with ROLLBACK).

TRUNCATE

```
TRUNCATE [TABLE] tbl_name
```

A TRUNCATE command deletes all the rows in a table, just like a DELETE command with no WHERE clause. TRUNCATE, however, takes a number of shortcuts to make the process go much faster, especially with large tables. In effect, TRUNCATE performs a DROP TABLE query, followed by a CREATE TABLE query to re-create an empty table.

UPDATE

```
UPDATE [LOW_PRIORITY] [IGNORE] tbl_name
     SET col_name = expr[, …]
     [WHERE where_definition]
     [ORDER BY …]
     [LIMIT #]
```

The UPDATE query updates existing table entries by assigning new values to the specified columns. Columns that aren't listed are left alone, except columns with the TIMESTAMP type (see Appendix D). The WHERE clause lets you specify a condition (*where_definition*) that rows must satisfy if they're to be updated, while the LIMIT clause lets you specify a maximum number of rows to be updated.

 Avoid Omitting WHERE or LIMIT

If WHERE and LIMIT are unspecified, every row in the table will be updated!

The ORDER BY clause lets you specify the order in which entries are updated. This is most useful when combined with the LIMIT clause; together they let you create queries like "update the ten most recent rows."

An UPDATE operation will fail with an error if the new value assigned to a row clashes with an existing value in a PRIMARY KEY or UNIQUE column, unless the IGNORE option is specified; in this case the query will simply have no effect on that particular row.

The LOW_PRIORITY option instructs MySQL to wait until there are no other clients reading the table before it performs the update.

Like the DELETE query (see the section called "DELETE"), UPDATE has an alternate form that can affect multiple tables in a single operation:

```
UPDATE [LOW_PRIORITY] [IGNORE] tbl_name[, tbl_name …]
    SET col_name = expr[, …]
    [WHERE where_definition]
```

USE

```
USE db_name
```

This simple query sets the default database for MySQL queries in the current session. Tables in other databases may still be accessed as db_name.tbl_name.

Appendix C: MySQL Functions

MySQL provides a sizeable library of functions to format and combine data within SQL queries in order to produce the desired results in the preferred format. This appendix provides a reference to the most useful of these functions, as implemented in MySQL as of version 5.5.22 (current this writing).

For a complete, up-to-date reference to supported SQL functions, see the MySQL Reference Manual.[1]

Control Flow Functions

IFNULL(*expr1*, *expr2*)

> This function returns *expr1* unless it's NULL, in which case it returns *expr2*.

NULLIF(*expr1*, *expr2*)

> This function returns *expr1* unless it equals *expr2*, in which case it returns NULL.

IF(*expr1*, *expr2*, *expr3*)

> If *expr1* is TRUE (that is, not NULL or 0), this function returns *expr2*; otherwise, it returns *expr3*.

CASE *value* WHEN [*compare-value1*] THEN *result1* [WHEN …] [ELSE *else-result*] END

> This function returns *result1* when *value=compare-value1* (note that several compare-value/result pairs can be defined); otherwise, it returns *else-result*, or NULL if none is defined.

CASE WHEN [*condition1*] THEN *result1* [WHEN …] [ELSE *else-result*] END

> This function returns *result1* when *condition1* is TRUE (note that several condition/result pairs can be defined); otherwise, it returns *else-result*, or NULL if none is defined.

---

[1] http://dev.mysql.com/doc/mysql/en/functions.html

Mathematical Functions

ABS(*expr*)

This function returns the absolute (positive) value of *expr*.

SIGN(*expr*)

This function returns -1, 0, or 1 depending on whether *expr* is negative, zero, or positive, respectively.

MOD(*expr1*, *expr2*)
expr1 % *expr2*

This function returns the remainder of dividing *expr1* by *expr2*.

FLOOR(*expr*)

This function rounds down *expr* (that is, it returns the largest integer value that is less than or equal to *expr*).

CEILING(*expr*)
CEIL(*expr*)

This function rounds up *expr* (that is, it returns the smallest integer value that's greater than or equal to *expr*).

ROUND(*expr*)

This function returns *expr* rounded to the nearest integer. Note that this function's behavior when the value is exactly an integer plus 0.5 is system-dependent. Thus, you should avoid relying on any particular outcome when migrating to a new system.

ROUND(*expr*, *num*)

This function rounds *expr* to a number with *num* decimal places, leaving trailing zeros in place. Use a *num* of 2, for example, to format a number as dollars and cents. Note that the same uncertainty about the rounding of 0.5 applies as discussed for ROUND.

EXP(*expr*)

This function returns e^{expr}, the base of natural logarithms raised to the power of *expr*.

LOG(*expr*)

This function returns ln(*expr*), or log_e(*expr*), the natural logarithm of *expr*.

LOG(*B, expr*)

This function returns the logarithm of *expr* with the arbitrary base *B*.

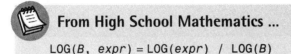

From High School Mathematics ...

LOG(*B, expr*) = LOG(*expr*) / LOG(*B*)

LOG10(*expr*)

This function returns the base-10 logarithm of *expr*.

POW(*expr1, expr2*)
POWER(*expr1, expr2*)

This function returns *expr1* raised to the power of *expr2*.

SQRT(*expr*)

This function returns the square root of *expr*.

PI()

This function returns the value of π (pi).

COS(*expr*)

This function returns the cosine of *expr* in radians (for example, COS(PI()) = -1).

SIN(*expr*)

This function returns the sine of *expr* in radians (for example, SIN(PI()) = 0).

TAN(*expr*)

This function returns the tangent of *expr* in radians (for example, TAN(PI()) = 0).

ACOS(*expr*)

This function returns the arc cosine ($\cos^{-1}$ or inverse cosine) of *expr* (for example, ACOS(-1) = PI()).

ASIN(*expr*)

This function returns the arc sine (sin^{-1} or inverse sine) of *expr* (for example, ASIN(0) = PI()).

ATAN(*expr*)

This function returns the arc tangent (tan^{-1} or inverse tangent) of *expr* (for example, ATAN(0) = PI()).

ATAN(*y*, *x*)
ATAN2(*y*, *x*)

This function returns the angle (in radians) made at the origin between the positive *x* axis and the point (*x*,*y*); for example, ATAN(1, 0) = PI() / 2.

COT(*expr*)

This function returns the cotangent of *expr* (for example, COT(PI() / 2) = 0).

RAND()
RAND(*expr*)

This function returns a random, floating point number between 0.0 and 1.0. If *expr* is specified, a random number will be generated based on that value, which will always be the same.

LEAST(*expr1*, *expr2*, …)

This function returns the smallest of the values specified.

GREATEST(*expr1*, *expr2*, …)

This function returns the largest of the values specified.

DEGREES(*expr*)

This function returns the value of *expr* (in radians) in degrees.

RADIANS(*expr*)

This function returns the value of *expr* (in degrees) in radians.

TRUNCATE(*expr*, *num*)

This function returns the value of floating point number *expr* truncated to *num* decimal places (that is, rounded down).

BIN(*expr*)

This function converts decimal *expr* to binary, equivalent to CONV(*expr*, 10, 2).

OCT(*expr*)

This function converts decimal *expr* to octal, equivalent to CONV(*expr*, 10, 8).

HEX(*expr*)

This function converts decimal *expr* to hexadecimal, equivalent to CONV(*expr*, 10, 16).

CONV(*expr*, *from_base*, *to_base*)

This function converts a number (*expr*) in base *from_base* to a number in base *to_base*. Returns NULL if any of the arguments are NULL.

String Functions

ASCII(*str*)

This function returns the ASCII code value of the left-most character in *str*, 0 if *str* is an empty string, or NULL if *str* is NULL.

ORD(*str*)

This function returns the ASCII code of the left-most character in *str*, taking into account the possibility that it might be a multibyte character.

CHAR(*expr*, …)

This function creates a string composed of characters, the ASCII code values of which are given by the expressions passed as arguments.

CONCAT(*str1*, *str2*, …)

This function returns a string made up of the strings passed as arguments joined end to end. If any of the arguments are NULL, NULL is returned instead.

CONCAT_WS(*separator*, *str1*, *str2*, …)

This is CONCAT "with separator" (WS). This function is the same as CONCAT, except that the first argument is placed between each of the additional arguments when they're combined.

LENGTH(*str*)
OCTET_LENGTH(*str*)
CHAR_LENGTH(*str*)
CHARACTER_LENGTH(*str*)

All of these return the length in characters of *str*. CHAR_LENGTH and CHARACTER_LENGTH, however, take multibyte characters into consideration when performing the count.

BIT_LENGTH(*str*)

This function returns the length (in bits) of *str* (that is, BIT_LENGTH(*str*) = 8 * LENGTH(*str*)).

LOCATE(*substr*, *str*)
POSITION(*substr* IN *str*)

This function returns the position of the first occurrence of *substr* in *str* (1 if it occurs at the beginning, 2 if it starts after one character, and so on). It returns 0 if *substr* doesn't occur in *str*.

LOCATE(*substr*, *str*, *pos*)

This is the same as LOCATE(*substr*, *str*), but it begins searching from character number *pos*.

INSTR(*str*, *substr*)

This function is the same as LOCATE(*substr*, *str*), but with the argument order swapped.

LPAD(*str*, *len*, *padstr*)

This function shortens or lengthens *str* so that it's of length *len*. Lengthening is accomplished by inserting *padstr* to the left of the characters of *str* (for example, LPAD('!', '5', '.') = '....!').

RPAD(*str*, *len*, *padstr*)

This function shortens or lengthens *str* so that it's of length *len*. Lengthening is accomplished by inserting *padstr* to the right of the characters of *str* (for example, RPAD('!','5','.') = '!....').

LEFT(*str*, *len*)

This function returns the left-most *len* characters of *str*. If *str* is shorter than *len* characters, *str* is returned with no extra padding.

RIGHT(*str*, *len*)

This function returns the right-most *len* characters of *str*. If *str* is shorter than *len* characters, *str* is returned with no extra padding.

SUBSTRING(*str*, *pos*, *len*)
SUBSTRING(*str* FROM *pos* FOR *len*)
MID(*str*, *pos*, *len*)

This function returns a string up to *len* characters long taken from *str* beginning at position *pos* (where 1 is the first character). The second form of SUBSTRING is the ANSI standard.

SUBSTRING(*str*, *pos*)
SUBSTRING(*str* FROM *pos*)

This function returns the string beginning from position *pos* in *str* (where 1 is the first character) and going to the end of *str*.

SUBSTRING_INDEX(*str*, *delim*, *count*)

MySQL counts *count* occurrences of *delim* in *str*, then takes the substring from that point. If *count* is positive, MySQL counts to the right from the start of the string, then takes the substring up to but not including that delimiter. If *count* is negative, MySQL counts to the left from the end of the string, then takes the substring that starts right after that delimiter, and runs to the end of *str*.

LTRIM(*str*)

This function returns *str* with any leading whitespace trimmed off.

RTRIM(*str*)

This function returns *str* with any trailing whitespace trimmed off.

TRIM([[BOTH | LEADING | TRAILING] [*remstr*] FROM] *str*)

This function returns *str* with either whitespace (by default) or occurrences of the string *remstr* removed from the start of the string (LEADING), end of the string (TRAILING), or both (BOTH, the default).

SOUNDEX(*str*)

This function produces a string that represents how *str* sounds when read aloud. Words that sound similar should have the same "soundex string."

For example:

```
SOUNDEX("tire") = "T600"
SOUNDEX("tyre") = "T600"
SOUNDEX("terror") = "T600"
SOUNDEX("tyrannosaur") = "T6526"
```

SPACE(*num*)

This function returns a string of *num* space characters.

REPLACE(*str, from_str, to_str*)

This function returns *str* after replacing all occurrences of *from_str* with *to_str*.

REPEAT(*str, count*)

This function returns a string made up of *str* repeated *count* times, an empty string if *count* <= 0, or NULL if either argument is NULL.

REVERSE(*str*)

This function returns *str* spelled backwards.

INSERT(*str, pos, len, newstr*)

This function takes *str*, and removes the substring beginning at *pos* (where 1 is the first character in the string) with length *len*, then inserts *newstr* at that position. If *len* = 0, the function simply inserts *newstr* at position *pos*.

ELT(*N, str1, str2, str3, …*)

This function returns the Nth string argument (*str1* if $N = 1$, *str2* if $N = 2$, and so on), or NULL if there's no argument for the given *N*.

FIELD(*str, str1, str2, str3, …*)

This function returns the position of *str* in the subsequent list of arguments (1 if *str* = *str1*, 2 if *str* = *str2*, and so on).

FIND_IN_SET(*str, strlist*)

When *strlist* is a list of strings of the form '*string1,string2,string3,…*', this function returns the index of *st****r* in that list, or 0 if *str* is not in the list. This function is ideally suited (and optimized) for determining if *str* is selected in a column of type SET (see Appendix D).

MAKE_SET(*bits, str1, str2, …*)

This function returns a list of strings of the form '*string1,string2,string3,…*' using the string parameters (*str1, str2*, and so on) that correspond to the bits that are set in the number *bits*. For example, if *bits* = 10 (binary 1010), bits 2 and 4 are set, so the output of MAKE_SET will be 'str2,str4'.

EXPORT_SET(*bits*, *on_str*, *off_str*[, *separator*[, *number_of_bits*]])

This function returns a string representation of which bits are—and are not—set in *bits*. Set bits are represented by the *on_str* string, while unset bits are represented by the *off_str* string. By default, these bit representations are comma-separated, but the optional *separator* string lets you define your own. By default, up to 64 bits are read; however, *number_of_bits* lets you specify that a smaller number be read.

For example:

```
EXPORT_SET(10, 'Y', 'N', ',', 6) = 'N,Y,N,Y,N,N'
```

LCASE(*str*)
LOWER(*str*)

This function returns *str* with all letters in lowercase.

UCASE(*str*)
UPPER(*str*)

This function returns *str* with all letters in uppercase.

LOAD_FILE(*filename*)

This function returns the contents of the file specified by *filename* (an absolute path to a file readable by MySQL). Your MySQL user should also have file privileges.

QUOTE(*str*)

This function returns *str* surrounded by single quotes, and with any special characters escaped with backslashes. If *str* is NULL, the function returns the string NULL (without surrounding quotes).

Date and Time Functions

DAYOFWEEK(*date*)

This function returns the weekday of *date* in the form of an integer, according to the ODBC standard (1 = Sunday, 2 = Monday, 3 = Tuesday ... 7 = Saturday).

WEEKDAY(*date*)

This function returns the weekday of *date* in the form of an integer (0 = Monday, 1 = Tuesday, 2 = Wednesday … 6 = Sunday).

DAYOFMONTH(*date*)

This function returns the day of the month for *date*, from 1 to 31.

DAYOFYEAR(*date*)

This function returns the day of the year for *date*, from 1 to 366—remember leap years!

MONTH(*date*)

This function returns the month for *date*, from 1 (January) to 12 (December).

DAYNAME(*date*)

This function returns the name of the day of the week for *date* (for example, 'Tuesday').

MONTHNAME(*date*)

This function returns the name of the month for *date* (for example, 'April').

QUARTER(*date*)

This function returns the quarter of the year for *date* (for example, QUARTER('2005-04-12') = 2).

WEEK(*date*[, *mode*])

This function returns the week of the year for *date* by default in the range 0-53 (where week 1 is the first week of the year), assuming that the first day of the week is Sunday.

By specifying one of the *mode* values in Table C.1, you can alter the way this value is calculated.

Table C.1. Modes for week calculations

mode	Week starts on	Return Value Range	Week 1
0	Sunday	0 to 53	first week that starts in this year
1	Monday	0 to 53	first week that has more than 3 days in this year
2	Sunday	1 to 53	first week that starts in this year
3	Monday	1 to 53	first week that has more than 3 days in this year
4	Sunday	0 to 53	first week that has more than 3 days in this year
5	Monday	0 to 53	first week that starts in this year
6	Sunday	1 to 53	first week that has more than 3 days in this year
7	Monday	1 to 53	first week that starts in this year

YEAR(*date*)

This function returns the year for *date*, from 1000 to 9999.

YEARWEEK(*date*)

YEARWEEK(*date, first*)

This function returns the year and week for *date* in the form '*YYYYWW*'. Note that the first or last day or two of the year may often belong to a week of the preceding or following year, respectively.

For example:

```
YEARWEEK("2006-12-31") = 200701
```

HOUR(*time*)

This function returns the hour for *time*, from 0 to 23.

MINUTE(*time*)

This function returns the minute for *time*, from 0 to 59.

SECOND(*time*)

This function returns the second for *time*, from 0 to 59.

PERIOD_ADD(*period*, *num_months*)

This function adds *num_months* months to period (specified as 'YYMM' or 'YYYYMM') and returns the value in the form 'YYYYMM'.

PERIOD_DIFF(*period1*, *period2*)

This function returns the number of months between *period1* and *period2* (each of which should be specified as 'YYMM' or 'YYYYMM').

DATE_ADD(*date*, INTERVAL *expr type*)
DATE_SUB(*date*, INTERVAL *expr type*)
ADDDATE(*date*, INTERVAL *expr type*)
SUBDATE(*date*, INTERVAL *expr type*)

This function returns the result of either adding or subtracting the specified interval of time to or from *date* (a DATE or DATETIME value). DATE_ADD and ADDDATE are identical, as are DATE_SUB and SUBDATE. *expr* specifies the interval to be added or subtracted and may be negative if you wish to specify a negative interval, and *type* specifies the format of *expr*, as shown in Table C.2.

If *date* and *expr* involve only date values, the result will be a DATE value; otherwise, this function will return a DATETIME value.

Here are a few examples to help you see how this family of functions works.

The following both return the date six months from now:

```
ADDDATE(CURDATE(), INTERVAL 6 MONTH)
```

```
DATE_ADD(CURDATE(), INTERVAL '0-6' YEAR_MONTH)
```

The following all return this time tomorrow:

```
ADDDATE(NOW(), INTERVAL 1 DAY)
```

```
SUBDATE(NOW(), INTERVAL -1 DAY)
```

```
DATE_ADD(NOW(), INTERVAL '24:0:0' HOUR_SECOND)
```

```
DATE_ADD(NOW(), INTERVAL '1 0:0' DAY_MINUTE)
```

Table C.2. Interval types for date addition/subtraction functions

type	Format for *expr*
SECOND	number of seconds
MINUTE	number of minutes
HOUR	number of hours
DAY	number of days
MONTH	number of months
YEAR	number of years
MINUTE_SECOND	'*minutes:seconds*'
HOUR_MINUTE	'*hours:minutes*'
DAY_HOUR	'*days hours*'
YEAR_MONTH	'*years-months*'
HOUR_SECOND	'*hours:minutes:seconds*'
DAY_MINUTE	'*days hours:minutes*'
DAY_SECOND	'*days hours:minutes:seconds*'

TO_DAYS(*date*)

This function converts date to a number of days since year 0. It allows you to calculate differences in dates (that is, TO_DAYS(*date1*) - TO_DAYS(*date2*) = days between *date1* and *date2*).

FROM_DAYS(*days*)

Given the number of *days* since year 0 (as produced by TO_DAYS), this function returns a date.

DATE_FORMAT(*date, format*)

This function takes the date or time value *date* and returns it formatted according to the formatting string *format*, which may contain as placeholders any of the symbols shown in Table C.3.

Table C.3. DATE_FORMAT symbols (2004-01-01 01:00:00)

Symbol	Displays	Example
%M	Month name	January
%W	Weekday name	Thursday
%D	Day of the month with English suffix	1st
%Y	Year, numeric, 4 digits	2004
%y	Year, numeric, 2 digits	03
%a	Abbreviated weekday name	Thu
%d	Day of the month	01
%e	Day of the month	1
%m	Month of the year, numeric	01
%c	Month of the year, numeric	1
%b	Abbreviated month name	Jan
%j	Day of the year	001
%H	Hour of the day (24 hour format, 00-23)	01
%k	Hour of the day (24 hour format, 0-23)	1
%h	Hour of the day (12 hour format, 01-12)	01
%I	Hour of the day (12 hour format, 01-12)	01
%l	Hour of the day (12 hour format, 1-12)	1
%i	Minutes	00
%r	Time, 12 hour (hh:mm:ss AM/PM)	01:00:00 AM
%T	Time, 24 hour (hh:mm:ss)	01:00:00
%S	Seconds	00
%s	Seconds	00
%p	AM or PM	AM
%w	Day of the week, numeric (0=Sunday)	4
%U	Week (00-53), Sunday first day of the week	00
%u	Week (00-53), Monday first day of the week	01
%X	Year of the week where Sunday is the first day of the week, 4 digits (use with %V)	2003

Symbol	Displays	Example
%V	Week (01–53), Sunday first day of week (%X)	53
%X	Like %X, Monday first day of week (use with %v)	2004
%v	Week (01–53), Monday first day of week (%x)	01
%%	An actual percent sign	%

TIME_FORMAT(*time, format*)

This function is the same as DATE_FORMAT, except that the *format* string may only contain symbols referring to hours, minutes, and seconds.

CURDATE()

CURRENT_DATE

This function returns the current system date in the SQL date format '*YYYY-MM-DD*' (if used as a date) or as *YYYYMMDD* (if used as a number).

CURTIME()

CURRENT_TIME

CURRENT_TIME()

This function returns the current system time in the SQL time format '*HH:MM:SS*' (if used as a time) or as *HHMMSS* (if used as a number).

NOW()

SYSDATE()

CURRENT_TIMESTAMP

CURRENT_TIMESTAMP()

LOCALTIME

LOCALTIME()

LOCALTIMESTAMP

LOCALTIMESTAMP()

This function returns the current system date and time in SQL date/time format '*YYYY-MM-DD HH:MM:SS*' (if used as a date/time) or as *YYYYMMDDHHMMSS* (if used as a number).

UNIX_TIMESTAMP()

UNIX_TIMESTAMP(*date*)

This function returns either the current system date and time, or the specified date/time as the number of seconds since 1970-01-01 00:00:00 GMT.

FROM_UNIXTIME(*unix_timestamp*)

The opposite of UNIX_TIMESTAMP, this function converts a number of seconds from 1970-01-01 00:00:00 GMT to '*YYYY-MM-DD HH:MM:SS*' (if used as a date/time) or *YYYYMMDDHHMMSS* (if used as a number), local time.

FROM_UNIXTIME(*unix_timestamp*, *format*)

This function formats a UNIX timestamp according to the *format* string, which may contain any of the symbols listed in Table C.3.

SEC_TO_TIME(*seconds*)

This function converts some number of *seconds* to the format '*HH:MM:SS*' (if used as a time) or *HHMMSS* (if used as a number).

TIME_TO_SEC(*time*)

This function converts a *time* in the format '*HH:MM:SS*' to a number of seconds.

Miscellaneous Functions

DATABASE()

This function returns the currently selected database name, or an empty string if no database is currently selected.

USER()
SYSTEM_USER()
SESSION_USER()

This function returns the current MySQL username, including the client host name (for example, 'kevin@localhost'). The SUBSTRING_INDEX function may be used to obtain the username alone:

```
SUBSTRING_INDEX(USER(), "@", 1) = 'kevin'
```

CURRENT_USER()

This function returns the user entry in the MySQL access control system that was used to authenticate the current connection—and which controls its privileges—in the form '*user@host*'. In many cases, this will be the same as the value returned by USER, but when entries in the access control system contain wild cards, this value may be less specific (for example, '@%.mycompany.com').

PASSWORD(*str*)

This is a one-way password encryption function that converts any string (typically a plain-text password) into an encrypted format precisely 16 characters in length. A particular plain-text string always will yield the same encrypted string of 16 characters; thus, values encoded in this way can be used to verify the correctness of a password without actually storing the password in the database.

This function uses a different encryption mechanism to UNIX passwords; use ENCRYPT for that type of encryption.

ENCRYPT(*str*[, *salt*])

This function uses standard UNIX encryption (via the crypt() system call) to encrypt *str*. The *salt* argument is optional, and lets you control the seed that's used for generating the password. If you want the encryption to match a UNIX password file entry, the salt should be the two first characters of the encrypted value you're trying to match. Depending on the implementation of crypt() on your system, the encrypted value may only depend on the first eight characters of the plain-text value.

On systems where crypt() is unavailable, this function returns NULL.

ENCODE(*str*, *pass_str*)

This function encrypts *str* using a two-way password-based encryption algorithm with password *pass_str*. To subsequently decrypt the value, use DECODE.

DECODE(*crypt_str*, *pass_str*)

This function decrypts the encrypted *crypt_str* using two-way password-based encryption with password *pass_str*. If the same password is given that was provided to ENCODE, the original string will be restored.

MD5(*string*)

This function calculates an MD5 hash based on *string*. The resulting value is a 32-digit hexadecimal number. A particular string will always produce the same MD5 hash; however, MD5(NOW()) may be used, for instance, to obtain a semi-random string when one is needed (as a default password, for instance).

LAST_INSERT_ID()

This function returns the last number that was automatically generated for an AUTO_INSERT column in the current connection.

FOUND_ROWS()

When you execute a SELECT query with a LIMIT clause, you may sometimes want to know how many rows would have been returned if you omitted a LIMIT clause. To do this, use the SQL_CALC_FOUND_ROWS option for the SELECT query (see Appendix B), then call this function in a second SELECT query.

Calling this function is considerably quicker than repeating the query without a LIMIT clause, since the full result set doesn't need to be sent to the client.

FORMAT(*expr*, *num*)

This function formats a number *expr* with commas as "thousands separators" and *num* decimal places (rounded to the nearest value and padded with zeros).

VERSION()

This function returns the MySQL server version (for example, '5.1.34').

CONNECTION_ID()

This function returns the thread ID for the current connection.

GET_LOCK(*str*, *timeout*)

If two or more clients must synchronize tasks beyond what table locking can offer, named locks may be used instead. GET_LOCK attempts to obtain a lock with a given name (*str*). If the named lock is already in use by another client, this client will wait up to *timeout* seconds before giving up waiting for the lock to become free.

Once a client has obtained a lock, it can be released either using RELEASE_LOCK or by using GET_LOCK again to obtain a new lock.

GET_LOCK returns 1 if the lock was successfully retrieved, 0 if the time specified by *timeout* elapsed, or NULL if some error occurred.

GET_LOCK is not a MySQL command in and of itself; it must appear as part of another query.

For example:

```
SELECT GET_LOCK("mylock", 10)
```

RELEASE_LOCK(*str*)

> This function releases the named lock that was obtained by GET_LOCK. It returns 1 if the lock was released, 0 if the lock wasn't locked by this thread, or NULL if the lock doesn't exist.

IS_FREE_LOCK(*str*)

> This function checks if the named lock is free to be locked. It returns 1 if the lock was free, 0 if the lock was in use, or NULL if an error occurred.

BENCHMARK(*count*, *expr*)

> This function repeatedly evaluates *expr count* times for the purposes of speed testing. The MySQL command line client allows the operation to be timed.

INET_NTOA(*expr*)

> This function returns the IP address represented by the integer *expr*. See INET_ATON to create such integers.

INET_ATON(*expr*)

> This function converts an IP address *expr* to a single integer representation.
>
> For example:

```
INET_ATON('64.39.28.1') = 64 * 2553 + 39 * 2552 + 28 * 255 + 1
                        = 1063751116
```

Functions for Use with GROUP BY Clauses

Also known as **summary functions**, the following are intended for use with GROUP BY clauses, where they'll produce values based on the set of records making up each row of the final result set.

If used without a GROUP BY clause, these functions will cause the result set to be displayed as a single row, with a value calculated based on all the rows of the complete result set. Without a GROUP BY clause, mixing these functions with columns where there are no summary functions will cause an error, because you're unable to collapse those columns into a single row and gain a sensible value.

COUNT(*expr*)

This function returns a count of the number of times that *expr* had a non-NULL value in the ungrouped result set. If COUNT(*) is used, it will simply provide a count of the number of rows in the group, irrespective of NULL values.

COUNT(DISTINCT *expr*[, *expr* ...])

This function returns a count of the number of different non-NULL values (or sets of values, if multiple expressions are provided).

AVG(*expr*)

This function calculates the arithmetic mean (average) of the values appearing in the rows of the group.

MIN(*expr*)
MAX(*expr*)

This function returns the smallest or largest value of *expr* in the rows of the group.

SUM(*expr*)

This function returns the sum of the values for *expr* in the rows of the group.

STD(*expr*)
STDDEV(*expr*)

This function returns the standard deviation of the values for *expr* in the rows of the group (either of the two function names may be used).

BIT_OR(*expr*)
BIT_AND(*expr*)

This function calculates the bit-wise OR and the bit-wise AND of the values for *expr* in the rows of the group, respectively.

Appendix D: MySQL Column Types

When you create a table in MySQL, you must specify the data type for each column. This appendix documents all the column types that MySQL provides as of version 5.5.22 (current this writing).

In this reference, many column types can accept **optional parameters** to further customize how data for the column is stored or displayed. First, there are the M and D parameters, which are indicated (in square brackets when optional) immediately following the column type name.

The parameter M is used to specify the display size (that is, maximum number of characters) to be used by values in the column. In most cases, this will limit the range of values that may be specified in the column. M may be any integer between 1 and 255. Note that for numerical types (for example, INT), this parameter doesn't actually restrict the range of values that may be stored. Instead, it causes spaces (or zeros in the case of a ZEROFILL column—see further on for details) to be added to the values so that they reach the desired display width when they're displayed. Additionally, storing values longer than the specified display width can cause problems when the values are used in complex joins, and thus should be avoided whenever possible.

The parameter D lets you specify how many decimal places will be stored for a floating-point value. This parameter may be set to a maximum of 30, but M should always allow for these places (that is, D should always be less than or equal to $M - 2$ to allow room for a zero and a decimal point).

The second type of parameter is an optional **column attribute**. The attributes supported by the different column types are listed for each; to enable them, simply type them after the column type, separated by spaces. Here are the available column attributes and their meanings:

ZEROFILL   Values for the column always occupy their maximum display length, as the actual value is padded with zeros. This option automatically sets the UNSIGNED option as well.

UNSIGNED   The column may accept only positive numerical values (or zero). This restriction frees up more storage space for positive numbers, effectively doubling the range of positive values that may be stored in the column, and should always be set if you know that there's no need to store negative values.

BINARY   By default, comparisons of character values in MySQL (including sorting) are case-insensitive. However, comparisons for BINARY columns are case-sensitive.

For a complete, up-to-date reference to supported SQL column types, see the MySQL Reference Manual.[1]

Numerical Types

TINYINT[(*M*)]

Description:
A tiny integer value

Attributes allowed:
UNSIGNED, ZEROFILL

Range:
-128 to 127 (0 to 255 if UNSIGNED)

Storage space:
1 byte (8 bits)

SMALLINT[(*M*)]

Description:
A small integer value

Attributes allowed:
UNSIGNED, ZEROFILL

Range:
-32768 to 32767 (0 to 65535 if UNSIGNED)

---

[1] http://dev.mysql.com/doc/mysql/en/data-types.html

Storage space:
2 bytes (16 bits)

MEDIUMINT[(*M*)]

Description:
A medium integer value

Attributes allowed:
UNSIGNED, ZEROFILL

Range:
-8588608 to 8388607 (0 to 16777215 if UNSIGNED)

Storage space:
3 bytes (24 bits)

INT[(*M*)]

Description:
A regular integer value

Attributes allowed:
UNSIGNED, ZEROFILL

Range:
-2147483648 to 2147483647 (0 to 4294967295 if UNSIGNED)

Storage space:
4 bytes (32 bits)

Alternative syntax:
INTEGER[(*M*)]

BIGINT[(*M*)]

Description:
A large integer value

Attributes allowed:
UNSIGNED, ZEROFILL

Range:

-9223372036854775808 to 9223372036854775807 (0 to 18446744073709551615 if `UNSIGNED`)

Storage space:

8 bytes (64 bits)

Notes:

MySQL performs all integer arithmetic functions in signed `BIGINT` format; thus, `BIGINT UNSIGNED` values over 9223372036854775807 (63 bits) will only work properly with bit functions (for example, bit-wise AND, OR, and NOT). Attempting integer arithmetic with larger values may produce inaccurate results due to rounding errors.

FLOAT[(*M*, *D*)]
FLOAT(*precision*)

Description:

A floating point number

Attributes allowed:

ZEROFILL

Range:

0 and ±1.175494351E-38 to ±3.402823466E+38

Storage space:

4 bytes (32 bits)

Notes:

precision (in bits), if specified, must be less than or equal to 24, or else a `DOUBLE` column will be created instead.

DOUBLE[(*M*, *D*)]
DOUBLE(*precision*)

Description:

A high-precision floating point number

Attributes allowed:

ZEROFILL

Range:

0 and ±2.2250738585072014-308 to ±1.7976931348623157E+308

Storage space:

8 bytes (64 bits)

Notes:

precision (in bits), if specified, must be greater than or equal to 25, or else a FLOAT column will be created instead (see earlier). *precision* may not be greater than 53.

Alternative syntax:

DOUBLE PRECISION[(*M*,*D*)] or REAL[(*M*,*D*)]

DECIMAL[(*M*[, *D*])]

Description:

A floating point number stored as a character string

Attributes allowed:

ZEROFILL

Range:

As for DOUBLE, but constrained by *M* and *D* (see Notes)

Storage space:

Depends on the stored value. For a value with X digits before the decimal point and Y digits after, the storage space used is approximately $(X + Y) \times 4 \div 10$ bytes.

Notes:

If D is unspecified, it defaults to 0 and numbers in this column will have no decimal point or fractional part. If M is unspecified, it defaults to 10.

Alternative syntax:

NUMERIC([*M*[,*D*]])

BIT(*M*)

Description:

An *M*-bit binary value, where *M* can be 1 to 64. In other words, a series of *M* digits, each of which may be 1 or 0.

Range:

As constrained by *M*

Storage space:

M + 2 bytes (8 × *M* + 16 bits)

Notes:

Intended for storing sets of Boolean (`true` or `false`) flags. To write `BIT` values, use the form b'*ddd…*', where each digit *d* can be 1 (to indicate "true") or 0 (to indicate "false"). For example, an 8-bit binary value where all the flags are true is b'11111111'.

Character Types

CHAR(*M*)

Description:

A fixed-length character string

Attributes allowed:

BINARY

Maximum length:

M characters

Storage space:

M bytes (8 × *M* bits)

Notes:

CHAR values are stored as strings of length *M*, even though the assigned value may be shorter. When the string is shorter than the full length of the field, spaces are added to the end of the string to bring it exactly to *M* characters. Trailing spaces are stripped off when the value is retrieved.

CHAR columns are quicker to search than variable-length character column types such as VARCHAR, since their fixed-length nature makes the underlying database file format more regular.

M may take any integer value from 0 to 255, with a CHAR(0) column able to store only two values: NULL and ' ' (the empty string), which occupy a single bit.

Alternative syntax:
CHARACTER(*M*)

VARCHAR(*M*)

Description:
A variable-length character string

Attributes allowed:
BINARY

Maximum length:
M characters

Storage space:
Length of stored value, plus 1 byte to store length (2 bytes if *M* > 255)

Notes:
As VARCHAR values occupy only the space they require, there's usually no point specifying a maximum field length *M* of anything less than 255 (the maximum for MySQL versions before 5.0.3). From 5.0.3 onward, MySQL will let you specify a maximum length up to 65,535 characters; however, 65,535 also happens to be the maximum number of bytes of data that a single table row is allowed to contain, so in practice you'll want to stick to much smaller limits, or consider a more appropriate column type like TEXT.

Strings longer than the specified limit will be chopped to the maximum length when inserted. MySQL versions before 5.0.3 would strip trailing spaces from values before they were stored, but this usually unexpected (and nonstandard) behavior has been removed and values are stored as supplied in MySQL 5.0.3 and later.

Alternative syntax:
```
CHARACTER VARYING(M)
```

BINARY(M)

Description:

A fixed-length binary string

Maximum length:

M characters

Storage space:

M bytes ($8 \times M$ bits)

Notes:

Just like CHAR, except MySQL treats the values stored in this column as non-textual byte strings.

VARBINARY(M)

Description:

A variable-length binary string

Maximum length:

M characters

Storage space:

Length of stored value, plus 1 byte to store length

Notes:

Just like VARCHAR, except MySQL treats the values stored in this column as non-textual byte strings.

TINYBLOB
TINYTEXT

Description:

A short, variable-length character string

Maximum length:

255 characters

Storage space:

Length of stored value, plus 1 byte to store length

Notes:

These types are basically equivalent to VARCHAR(255) BINARY and
VARCHAR(255), respectively. However, these column types do not trim
trailing spaces from inserted values. The only difference between TINYBLOB
and TINYTEXT is that the former performs case-sensitive comparisons and
sorts, while the latter does not.

BLOB
TEXT

Description:

A variable-length character string

Maximum length:

65,535 characters (65KB)

Storage space:

Length of stored value, plus 2 bytes to store length

Notes:

The only difference between BLOB and TEXT is that the former performs case-
sensitive comparisons and sorts, while the latter does not.

MEDIUMBLOB
MEDIUMTEXT

Description:

A medium, variable-length character string

Maximum length:

16,777,215 characters (16.8MB)

Storage space:

Length of stored value, plus 3 bytes to store length

Notes:

The only difference between MEDIUMBLOB and MEDIUMTEXT is that the former performs case-sensitive comparisons and sorts, while the latter does not.

LONGBLOB
LONGTEXT

Description:

A long, variable-length character string

Maximum length:

4,294,967,295 characters (4.3GB)

Storage space:

Length of stored value, plus 4 bytes to store length

Notes:

The only difference between LONGBLOB and LONGTEXT is that the former performs case-sensitive comparisons and sorts, while the latter does not.

ENUM(*value1*, *value2*, ...)

Description:

A set of values from which a single value must be chosen for each row

Maximum Length:

One value chosen from up to 65,535 possibilities

Storage space:

- 1 to 255 values: 1 byte (8 bits)
- 256 to 65,535 values: 2 bytes (16 bits)

Notes:

Values in this type of field are stored as integers that represent the element selected. 1 represents the first element, 2 the second, and so on. The special value 0 represents the empty string ' ', which is stored if a value is assigned that doesn't appear in a column declaration.

NOT NULL columns of this type default to the first value in the column declaration if no particular default is assigned.

SET(*value1*, *value2*, ...)

Description:

A set of values, each of which may be set or not set

Maximum length:

Up to 64 values in a given SET column

Storage space:

- 1 to 8 values: 1 byte (8 bits)
- 9 to 16 values: 2 bytes (16 bits)
- 17 to 24 values: 3 bytes (24 bits)
- 25 to 32 values: 4 bytes (32 bits)
- 33 to 64 values: 8 bytes (64 bits)

Notes:

Values in this type of field are stored as integers representing the pattern of bits for set and unset values. For example, if a set contains eight values, and in a particular row the odd values are set, the binary representation 01010101 becomes the decimal value 85. Values may therefore be assigned either as integers, or as a string of set values, separated by commas (for example, 'value1,value3,value5,value7' = 85). Searches should be performed either with the LIKE operator, or the FIND_IN_SET function.

Date/Time Types

DATE

Description:

A date

Range:

'1000-01-01' to '9999-12-31', and '0000-00-00'

Storage space:

3 bytes (24 bits)

TIME

Description:

A time

Range:

`'-838:59:59'` to `'838:59:59'`

Storage space:

3 bytes (24 bits)

DATETIME

Description:

A date and time

Range:

`'1000-01-01 00:00:00'` to `'9999-12-31 23:59:59'`

Storage space:

8 bytes (64 bits)

YEAR

Description:

A year

Range:

1901 to 2155, and 0000

Storage space:

1 byte (8 bits)

Notes:

You can specify a year value with a four-digit number (1901 to 2155, or 0000), a four-digit string (`'1901'` to `'2155'`, or `'0000'`), a two-digit number (70 to 99 for 1970 to 1999, 1 to 69 for 2001 to 2069, or 0 for 0), or a two-digit string (`'70'` to `'99'` for 1970 to 1999, `'00'` to `'69'` for 2000 to 2069). Note that you cannot specify the year 2000 with a two-digit number, nor the year 0 with a two-digit string. Invalid year values are always converted to 0.

TIMESTAMP[(*M*)]

Description:
A timestamp (date/time), in *YYYYMMDDHHMMSS* format

Range:
19700101000000 to some time in 2037 on current systems

Storage space:
4 bytes (32 bits)

Notes:
An INSERT or UPDATE operation on a row that contains one or more TIMESTAMP columns will automatically update the first TIMESTAMP column in the row with the current date/time. This lets you use such a column as the "last modified date/time" for the row. Assigning a value of NULL to the column will have the same effect, thereby providing a means of "touching" the date/time. You can also assign actual values as you would for any other column.

Allowable values for *M* are 14, 12, 10, 8, 6, 4, and 2, and correspond to the display formats *YYYYMMDDHHMMSS, YYMMDDHHMMSS, YYMMDDHHMM, YYYYMMDD, YYMMDD, YYMM*, and *YY* respectively. Odd values from 1 to 13 automatically will be bumped up to the next even number, while values of 0 or greater than 14 are changed to 14.

Index

Symbols

A

488